Data for AI

Data Infrastructure
for Machine Intelligence

Scott Burk and Kinshuk Dutta

Technics Publications
SEDONA, ARIZONA

TECHNICS PUBLICATIONS

115 Linda Vista, Sedona, AZ 86336 USA
https://www.TechnicsPub.com

Edited by Steve Hoberman

Cover design by Lorena Molinari

First Printing 2025

ISBN, print ed.	9781634627290
ISBN, Kindle ed.	9781634627306
ISBN, PDF ed.	9781634627313

Library of Congress Control Number: 2025935924

Scott's dedication:

To my wife Jackie, thank you for the greatest adventure of my life.

Kinshuk's dedication:

This work is dedicated to my parents, Krishna Dutta and Lal Mohan Dutta, because their enduring values and guidance constituted the foundational training set from which my principles and purpose have been derived. To my wife, Noirita, and my daughter, Rachael— your unwavering support has been a continuous source of positive reinforcement, refining my thinking, broadening my perspective, and anchoring my priorities. In a world increasingly driven by data and models, you remind me that true intelligence is grounded in empathy, love, and human connection.

Contents

Figures

Tables

Foreword

AI is like a mirror—it can only reflect what it's shown. Feed it distorted information, and you'll get distorted results. Give it a clear, accurate view of the world, and it becomes a powerful lens for understanding and decision-making. Having spent decades championing and building cybersecurity tools powered by high-fidelity data, I've watched the profound shift the underlying data makes to the risk of an organization.

From my time in the Air Force, I learned that data integrity can mean the difference between mission success and catastrophic failure, a lesson that becomes even more critical as reliance on AI-powered systems becomes more ubiquitous.

This book illuminates what others miss. While the industry chases the latest models, the authors reveal why major cloud providers invest billions annually in data infrastructure, why security teams spend the majority of their time on data governance, and why every successful AI deployment starts not with code, but with architecture.

But here's what should give you hope: unlike the AI talent shortage, building a robust data infrastructure is achievable for any organization. It doesn't require genius mathematicians or bleeding-edge research. It requires discipline, methodology, and the roadmap these pages provide.

Throughout my career, I've seen how quality data transforms security from reactive to predictive. This book codifies that transformation. It shows how proper data infrastructure turns billions of noisy signals into clear intelligence, how governance creates trust for autonomous decisions, and how the unglamorous work of data pipelines becomes your competitive edge.

The quality of AI's insights is forever limited by the quality of its training data. Garbage in, garbage out—but excellence in, excellence out.

Turn the page. The revolution starts here.

Harman Kaur
AI Executive and Military Officer

Introduction

Artificial Intelligence (AI) is only as powerful as the data that fuels it, and this book is your comprehensive guide to understanding the critical data infrastructure that makes AI work.

AI has become a transformative force across industries, from healthcare and finance to retail and manufacturing. However, while much attention is given to AI models and algorithms, the data that feeds these systems is often overlooked. This book shifts the focus to the foundational elements of AI—data architecture, storage, processing, and governance—so that organizations can effectively harness the potential of AI. Even the most advanced AI models cannot deliver reliable results without high-quality, well-structured data.

Part I lays the groundwork for understanding how AI has developed alongside advances in data technology.

- **Chapter 1: Introduction to Data for AI**: This chapter introduces the book's central theme: the importance of data in AI. It highlights the three major pillars driving AI adoption—computing power, data technology, and novel applications—while emphasizing that data remains the most overlooked yet essential component.
- **Chapter 2: Data Mining for AI**: Explores the origins of data mining and its foundational role in AI, detailing key methodologies like the CRISP-DM process and how data preprocessing, cataloging, and visualizing support AI.
- **Chapter 3: Data Challenges in Machine Learning**: Addresses the technical debt associated with ML systems, outlining common data dependencies, feedback loops, and strategies to overcome these issues in AI development.
- **Chapter 4: Deep Learning and Data Infrastructure**: Examines the rise of deep learning, the impact of Apache Spark, and the shift to data lakes that enabled more advanced AI models, including Convolutional Neural Networks (CNNs).
- **Chapter 5: ChatGPT and Large Language Models**: Discusses the evolution of large language models, the massive data requirements needed for training, and the challenges of fine-tuning and deployment.

- **Chapter 6: Data in Generative AI**: Covers the specific data challenges of generative AI, such as storage, movement, and ethical considerations related to training on vast datasets.

Part II provides practical guidance on managing and optimizing data for AI-driven organizations.

- **Chapter 7: Modern Data Storage and Processing for AI**: Reviews current trends in data storage, including cloud-based solutions, edge computing, and data lake architectures tailored for AI applications.
- **Chapter 8: MDM and Data Quality for AI**: Explores the importance of master data management, the "garbage in, garbage out" principle, and strategies for ensuring high data quality in AI pipelines.
- **Chapter 9: Ethical Data Management and Governance for AI**: Discusses the critical role of governance frameworks, compliance requirements, and the technology needed to enforce ethical AI practices.
- **Chapter 10: How Data Moves in AI-Powered Organizations**: Provides insights into data pipelines, orchestration, and real-time processing in AI-driven enterprises, ensuring data is effectively utilized across systems.
- **Chapter 11: Making AI Operational**: Examines the deployment of AI systems, from model integration to real-world application, with an emphasis on maintaining performance over time.
- **Chapter 12: Avoiding Common Pitfalls and The Future of AI**: Highlights frequent mistakes in AI projects and explores emerging trends in AI data infrastructure, preparing organizations for the next wave of technological advancement.

This book offers a structured and practical approach to understanding data for AI by bridging theoretical concepts with real-world applications. It equips readers with the insights and tools necessary to build robust AI-driven systems that are efficient, ethical, and scalable.

## PART I

AI Evolution and Data Overview

In this part, we explore the evolution of AI and its reliance on data. We begin with an overview of AI's history, including data mining's role in early ML. From there, we examine the challenges of managing ML data, the infrastructure required for deep learning, and the unique data needs of large language models such as ChatGPT. The book also delves into generative AI, which requires vast datasets and specialized storage and processing solutions.

## Chapter 1

Introduction to Data for AI

Welcome to a journey through the world of data, where information becomes the bedrock of innovation in AI. This book explores the often overlooked yet critically important aspect of AI: data. While much has been written about the algorithms and models that drive AI, we will focus on the architecture, types, and technologies that make these advancements possible.

In the pages ahead, we will delve into the diverse data landscape, unveiling the infrastructure that supports it, the methodologies that process it, and the technologies that harness its potential. From data lakes and cloud-based storage to intricate pipelines and feature engineering platforms, we will uncover how these elements coalesce to fuel the powerful AI engine.

This book is not about algorithms or the theoretical underpinnings of AI. Instead, it is about the practical and tangible components that form the foundation upon which AI systems are built. We will examine the tools, platforms, and innovations that allow data to be collected, processed, and utilized effectively, driving the remarkable capabilities of modern AI.

Whether you are a seasoned professional or new to the field, this book aims to provide you with a comprehensive understanding of data's critical role in AI. By focusing on the infrastructure and technologies that make data work for AI, we hope to offer valuable insights and knowledge that will empower you in your AI endeavors.

Join us as we explore the dynamic interplay between data and AI and discover how the right architecture and technologies can transform raw information into intelligent action.

Three Pillars of Accelerated AI Adoption

Recent advancements have significantly accelerated the adoption and value of AI, driven by three key pillars:

- **Computing Power:** The increased use of Graphics Processing Units (GPUs) has provided the necessary computational muscle for training and running complex AI models.

- **Data Technology and Volume:** Improved data handling capabilities have enabled the collection, storage, and processing of massive datasets, which are crucial for training AI systems.

- **Novel Applications:** Popular tools like ChatGPT™, Google Gemini™, and LLaMA™ have demonstrated the potential of AI in various domains, sparking widespread interest and adoption.

While algorithm research, development, and data science training also contribute to AI growth, this book focuses on the data aspect of AI. The aim is to delve deep into the types, architecture, and technologies that make data the lifeblood of AI systems. We will explore how data is gathered, processed, and harnessed to enable AI, rather than discussing the algorithms and models themselves.

Failure to adopt AI, especially for small and medium-sized businesses, can be detrimental. Relying on hope or delaying action is not a viable business strategy.

Focus on Data

Out of the major advances driving AI adoption, this book is dedicated to the pillar of data technology. While numerous books exist on novel AI applications and AI development tools, data remains the least addressed yet most critical driver of AI value and adoption.

This book delves into data structures, architectures, and technologies, acknowledging that data is the foundation of reliable AI and is critical for decision-making and information technology. Without robust data technology, there can be no reliable AI.

Data technology has experienced significant growth, and this book serves as a comprehensive "101 course" in Data for AI. We aim to provide an overview of the most important elements in AI data technology without delving deeply into technical jargon. This is not a manual on using specific data systems but rather an accessible guide to understanding the essential components of data technology for AI.

No other book on the market provides a survey course on this subject. Our goal is to fill this gap by offering an easy-to-read format that equips readers with a solid understanding of data technology in AI.

## CHAPTER 2

Data Mining in AI

A I has evolved significantly since its inception in the 1950s, primarily due to technological advancements. While we do not cover the earliest methods of AI in this book, we focus on methods that have been applied over the last 30 years. These methods remain highly useful and are still employed daily by AI engineers and data scientists. According to the Lindy effect, which implies that the longer something has survived, the longer its remaining life expectancy, these methods will likely be around for many more years.

We begin with data mining, which emerged in the mid-1990s when advancements in data technology enabled the storage of large amounts of digital information. The term "data mining" gained prominence at the "First International Conference on Data Mining and Knowledge Discovery" in 1995. Usama Fayyad, a co-founder of the conference, also launched the journal Data Mining and Knowledge Discovery in 1996.

Data mining (DM) is "the extraction of implicit, previously unknown and potentially useful information from data" (Witten et al., 2016). Another definition describes it as "the analysis of (often large) observational data sets to find unsuspected relationships and to summarize the data in novel ways that are both understandable and useful to the data owner."" (Hand et al., 2001)

Despite being three decades old, data mining is more relevant today than ever. As of early 2025, it is widely used by the Department of Government Efficiency (DoGE) to identify waste, fraud, and abuse of taxpayer dollars. For instance, a recent report states, "Musk employed a tech-first perspective, leveraging software, artificial intelligence, and data mining to make cuts."[1]

In the next chapter, we will cover ML. There is a significant overlap between DM and ML, and no clear demarcation. For our purposes, we will describe DM as discovering useful relationships or patterns in data.

> *DM is often descriptive and diagnostic in nature. ML is commonly the next step after these initial relationships are determined. ML is the development of AI models that can be used to predict an outcome or prescribe an action that should be taken.*

One of the most significant advancements in DM is the CRISP-DM (Cross-Industry Standard Process for Data Mining). This standardized process enhances efficiency, reproducibility, and business alignment by providing a structured approach to data mining. A key benefit of the framework is its emphasis on business understanding, which addresses a common pitfall in AI projects: too much focus on IT and data analysis at the expense of core business knowledge. We delve into CRISP-DM in the next section.

We will then cover the key activities of data mining and supporting data technologies, followed by practical uses and applications of DM and its emergence as a key discipline in AI.

Modeling Paradigms for DM

Standardizing the DM process is invaluable as it provides an efficient, reproducible framework for AI projects. This allows organizations to learn and adapt more quickly than if each project were to take on a life of its own.

While other frameworks are available for data mining projects, CRISP-DM is the most commonly used baseline workflow, often tweaked for specific applications and industries. Developed in 1996

---

[1] https://www.msn.com/en-us/money/companies/elon-musk-s-doge-is-real-now-here-s-what-it-is-and-how-it-actually-works/ar-AA1xIwaA.

by analysts representing Daimler Chrysler, SPSS, and NCR, it offers a nonproprietary and freely available standard process for integrating data mining into the general problem-solving strategies of businesses or research units. References for this process are widely available, such as in Larose (2005).

According to the standard, most data mining projects follow a lifecycle comprising six interrelated phases. The sequence of these phases is adaptive, meaning that the progression to the next phase depends on the results of the previous phase. The process is iterative, requiring revisits to earlier phases based on new knowledge or results from later phases. For example, during the modeling phase, it may become evident that certain variables need transformation, prompting a return to the data preparation phase. A simple diagram of the CRISP-DM appears in Figure 1.

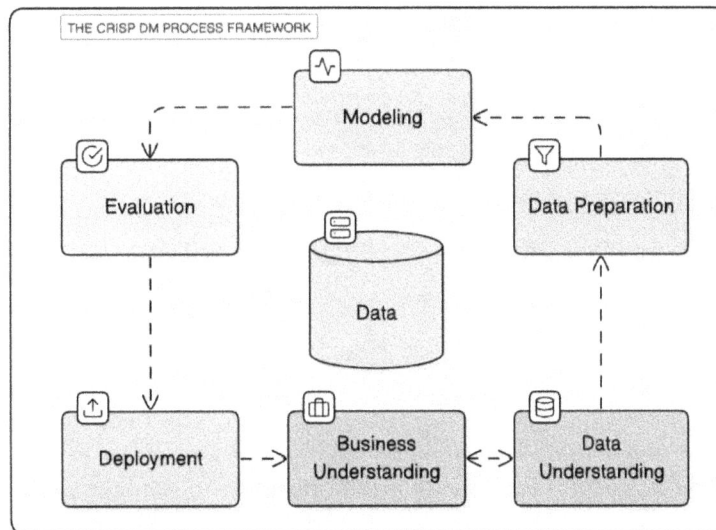

Figure 1: The CRISP-DM Process Framework.

Figure 1 illustrates the major components of the CRISP-DM process. We will cover only a simplified, high-level view of the six steps. There are good references available for the CRISP-DM process. For example, SPSS, one of the original participants, was purchased by IBM and has several documents available online.

NOTE: The models mentioned in this section are descriptive and diagnostic. What has happened? Why do we think it happened? They apply to the discovery of useful relationships and patterns in data. The next chapter on ML will include models for prediction and prescription.

Business Understanding

- Determine business objectives.
- Determine resources available and constraints.
- Create specific goals with specified metrics.
- Create a project plan.

Data Understanding

- Identify data sources and data definitions, and collect relevant data.
- Include subject matter experts and use exploratory data analysis to discover initial insights.
- Evaluate the quality of the data.
- Select interesting subsets that may contain actionable patterns.

Data Preparation

- Select, cleanse, and transform the relevant base data sets.
- Integrate multiple data sets into a single data store logically or physically.
- Perform any additional transformations and combine or extract data from individual variables.

Modeling

- Select and apply appropriate modeling techniques.
- Generate test design. Split the data into training, test, and validation sets, if required.
- Build models and calibrate model settings to optimize results.
- Use several different techniques for the same data mining problem.
- Assess models based upon pre-defined success criteria and the test design.

Evaluation Phase

- Evaluate the DM pipeline model results in the context of the business problem. Do the models meet the business success criteria?
- Review the work accomplished. Was anything overlooked? Were all steps properly executed? Summarize findings and correct anything if needed.
- Determine whether to proceed to deployment, iterate further, or initiate new projects.

Deployment Phase

- Make use of the results and models created.

- Example of a simple deployment is to generate a report.

- Example of a more complex deployment is to implement a parallel data mining process in another department using a completely new dataset.

Data Mining and Supporting Data Technology

We present data mining as a precursor to more powerful analytic techniques. This chapter presents pattern discovery, dimension reduction, and descriptive modeling. Future chapters will cover more advanced modeling that requires more complex data and typically larger data volumes.

Data Preprocessing

Effective data preprocessing is crucial for the success of data mining projects, as it ensures the accuracy and usability of data. Getting data 'right and usable' has been challenging since computers started storing data. In his book, Data Preparation for Data Mining (Pyle 1999), Dorian Pyle estimates that data preparation alone accounts for 60% of the time and effort spent in the entire data mining process. Modern data technology has improved efficiency, and we will cover data quality in Chapter 8 and feature engineering in Chapter 3. A few of the basic operations in data preprocessing technology automate:

- Removing duplicates ('deduping')
- Standardizing formats
- Validating entries
- Handling missing data
- Handling data format errors
- Handling outliers
- Data validation.

Example Providers: Trifacta, OpenRefine, and Integrate.io.

Data Catalog Platforms

Data catalog platforms enable business professionals to access and understand data across departments, leading to more informed decision-making. Originally, organizations had to create their own metadata repositories, a huge undertaking often lacking. Data catalog platforms were created to provide a unified context, control, and collaboration layer of all metadata. It provides technical, governance, operational, collaboration, quality, and usage across the entire data ecosystem. Key elements included in these systems are:

- Data catalogs make data accessible
- Data catalogs provide context
- Data catalogs help visualize the data lifecycle
- Data catalogs enable data governance.

We will touch on related material in Chapter 8, discussing master data management and data quality for AI. However, the basic issue is that professionals in different departments and roles need access to quality data and to understand which data definition and context applies to their purpose.

Example – Product Management. A product manager needs to create a report on the viability of several products. The company has many departmental databases that reference products. However, product identifiers are not the same column/variable across these databases. Engineering R&D uses a product identifier different from manufacturing. Manufacturing uses a different product ID than sales, etc. This causes confusion, but with a Data Cataloging Platform, the product manager can be sure they are accessing and mining the correct data elements for their needs.

Example Providers: Atlan, Talend, Alation, and Collibra.

Data Technology for Visualization, BI, and Exploratory Data Analysis

Recognizing patterns is part of our human DNA, and tools that support data visualization are great these days. We see them as collaboration tools across companies, boardroom presentations, and embedded in smartphone applications.

One of the major contributors to the advances in these tools is modern data technology. For example:

- Automated database connections for static data, in-motion, in-database, and in-memory sources.
- Integration with open-source coding languages and libraries (Python, R, etc.).
- Integration with public and private APIs.
- Data linkage across data sources.
- Custom data functions and data wrangling (in-stream).
- Built-in geoanalytics data and industry-specific data capabilities.

Example –Sales. A sales manager needs to quickly identify members of her sales force who effectively execute a sales campaign across North America. With a visual dashboard, the manager can easily access the information on a dynamic map to filter the data as needed. This is due to the advances in real-time in-memory data sources enhanced with geoanalytics.

Example Providers: Spotfire, Qlik Sense, Tableau, and Microsoft Power BI.

Note: Next generation BI and Exploratory Data Analysis (EDA), the next generation of visualization and EDA, are now occurring. The underlying technology or engine that creates the outputs will be much the same, but the interface between humans and these engines will utilize modern AI technology. We discuss generative AI and the associated data technologies in Chapters 5 and 6.

Example - Imagine the same scenario as the previous example. However, the sales manager does not have to know how to create a dashboard or collaborate with a BI professional. They can merely ask questions, and the AI will interpret the query and then create output to support it. This overcomes many of the reasons dashboards fail. For example, ad hoc requests are often vague or misunderstood and take several iterations to be valuable. Businesses need real-time results. Also, analysis paralysis or complexity often frustrates the business user.

These issues have been overcome with AI-assisted visual discovery. With self-service technology, a business user can access valuable insights quickly and easily, and this technology does not require any technical expertise.

Data Technology for Dimensionality Reduction

Organizations are collecting more data than ever. One of the core benefits of data mining is dimension reduction. The goal is to find useful nuggets of information by discarding irrelevant data. We can apply several data mining techniques, including principal component analysis, factor analysis, multidimensional scaling, and random projections.

Example – Banking. A major issue for banks is financial risk, which includes fraud. Banks handle millions of transactions daily, which may contain hundreds of AI features, resulting in high data dimensionality. Detecting fraudulent transactions is challenging due to the high dimensionality of the data, which can make it difficult to spot patterns and anomalies. With the right data technology and subject matter expertise, dimension reduction techniques can simplify the dataset and improve the performance of fraud detection models.

Example Providers: Encord, Nexocode, and IBM.

Data Technology Supporting Knowledge Graphs

Knowledge graphs represent and manage structured knowledge by capturing entities, relationships, and properties. They are more of a recent analytic methodology. Data mining techniques often involve extracting patterns, relationships, and insights from large datasets, which align well with the objectives of knowledge graphs. Graph databases represent and manage structured knowledge by capturing entities, relationships, and properties. A graph database that uses graph structures for semantic queries with nodes, edges, and properties to represent and store data. Relationship integrity is a key priority of a graph database, so querying relationships is fast and efficient. These relationships can be intuitively visualized using knowledge graphs. This makes them useful for heavily interconnected data, such as any network, including communication and social networks.

Example – Marketing. A marketing company wants to identify key market influencers within a specific social media platform to target for an upcoming product campaign. Influencers can sway the opinions and behaviors of their followers, making them valuable for marketing efforts. The difficulty is with millions of users and interactions, identifying the most influential individuals based on connections and engagement is a complex task. With a network graph, the company can quickly identify key influencers who can effectively promote its product.

Example Providers: Neo4j, FalkorDB, and Amazon Neptune.

Data Virtualization for Data Mining

Data virtualization provides real-time integration and access to data from multiple sources without physically moving the data. It allows for unified access to data from different sources as if in a single location. Integration and transformation of data elements are done in real time for the user without the user knowing the underlying data's relationships. It also provides accurate and consistent data for users, given a business context. Data virtualization vendors often include data cataloging capabilities in their offerings. However, the primary purpose of data catalogs is data discovery and metadata management, while data virtualization focuses on providing unified, real-time access to distributed data.

Example – Retail and Inventory Management. Global retailers have operations and warehouses across several countries. Each country may have its own inventory management system vendor, leading to data silos and difficulties in obtaining a unified view of inventory levels. With data virtualization technology, IT can formulate logical integrations and transformations that make a single global view possible. An analyst does not have to understand any of the complexities in the underlying data. They have optimized access to data with a data virtualization system. They can access the data and then discover important relationships and patterns in the data.

Example Providers: SAP HANA Cloud, Denodo Platform, and IBM Cloud Pak for Data.

Application Case Highlight – Data Mining to Support Accountable Healthcare

Key Data Terms - Data Standards, APIs, Clinical Notes, Data Virtualization, Visual BI platforms, chronic disease, diabetes.

Chronic disease is a huge problem in the US. Ninety percent of the nation's $4.5 trillion in annual health care expenditures are for people with chronic and mental health conditions.[2] Interventions to prevent and manage these diseases can have significant health and economic benefits.

If you were a healthcare payer in the United States in 2024, you would be involved in 'meaningful use' requirements. You would be responsible for implementing the CMS (Centers for Medicare and Medicaid Services) payer mandate. Many payers viewed this as additional work and expense with more government requirements. However, one solution provider created a way to look at this requirement as an opportunity for payers to use as a path to drive innovation and be part of their value-based care initiatives.

CMS has been pushing data interoperability standards for several years. A standard that has broad use and global acceptance is HL7® FHIR® standard (pronounced FIRE, Fast Healthcare Interoperability Resource). This standard enables a common data model that users must adhere to when applying the standard so that data is consistent and coherent with a specified definition.

Thinking of the mandate as an opportunity, a large enterprise solution provider created a solution that would leverage HL7® FHIR® as well as APIs (Application Programming Interfaces, see Chapter 11), Data Virtualization (DV), data science, and visual BI platforms. Bringing all this technology together is extremely powerful.

One application was developed to assist case managers in managing their diabetes patients. As part of the ACO, diabetes patients must receive frequent eye exams, HbA1c tests, foot exams, and nephropathy screening. Due to socioeconomic and other challenges, getting patients in to get these screenings is often difficult. Case managers are assigned lists of patients to manage and assist in getting their prescribed ACO screenings. An innovative DM solution can assist them in getting this done.

It all starts with data. Using HL7® FHIR® APIs embedded within a DV platform, data is accessed from the patient's data within an Electronic Medical Record (EMR). This data includes patient demographics, clinical history, and physician notes. The raw data is abstracted and transformed into a viable data source for the visual BI platform. The transformation process includes some data

---

[2] https://www.cdc.gov/chronic-disease/data-research/facts-stats/index.html; 2/2/2025.

mining techniques. For example, many diagnostic procedures, such as foot exams, have no defined procedure codes. It is beneficial to scour the physician notes for items like this to include in the transformed data for analysis. This is done with text mining or Natural Language Processing (NLP) to overcome the coding deficits. Figure 2 illustrates the system components.

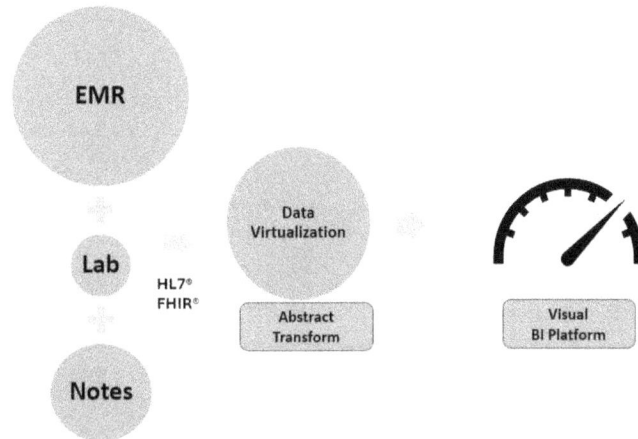

Figure 2: Data Flows for Visual BI using HL7® FHIR® APIs Data Standards.

Once the data is processed and verified, it can be made available to case managers via interactive visual dashboards. They are interactive in the sense that case managers can select the appropriate dashboards and drill into visual elements with a single click. They can rapidly apply queries and filters via click-throughs, and no coding is required. Two visual displays are included here, but there are many more available. The user can also customize these.

Figure 3 represents a high-level visual dashboard of ACO screenings previously mentioned. This dashboard illustrates the rich visual tools available to care managers. It is an "interactive" dashboard, meaning that each element can be further investigated with a single click. The dashboard is "smart," meaning that a case manager's actions or queries drill into the logical next step of inquiry.

This dashboard covers seven panels. We will briefly discuss 2 of them, the upper left and upper right panels. The upper leftmost section of Figure 3 shows four pie charts. Each circle represents a case manager, with the larger areas representing the proportion of patients they manage who had a foot exam. One circle is solid meaning 100% compliance. There is one circle, the uppermost left, where about 15% of patients are non-compliant. This is a useful tool to determine opportunities for improvement by each manager. In the upper right, each pie represents the number of months a patient has been under the care management and prevention program. The metric is neuropathy compliance. Patients should be compliant. The top two pies are patients who have been in the program the longest, and it can be seen that these patients are highly compliant. The two pies at the bottom are patients new to the program or patients who have not yet entered the program. Compliance for these two groups is low. This indicates that the program is positively correlated with more successful neuropathy compliance.

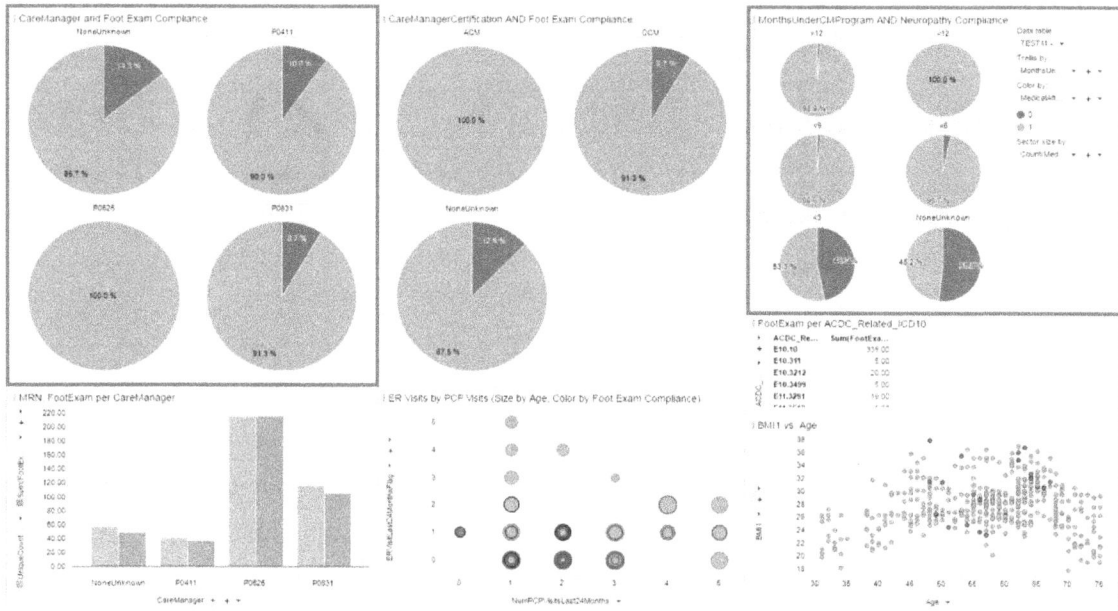

Figure 3: A Care Manager Overview Dashboard for Foot Screenings with Related metrics.

After viewing this top-level dashboard, a care manager can drill down into their panel of patients with a "single click". This "geographic view," showing where these patients are located, is very beneficial. Figure 4 is an example of a geoanalytics dashboard. It is Austin, Texas, but the underlying data is contrived. Some metrics and categories can be viewed on the left, such as age, BMI, BPControl (blood pressure), ZIP code, diagnosis codes, and much more. The care manager can modify their dashboard by selecting different elements. In the visual, each circle represents a zone around a clinic and the proportion of patients who are compliant in that zone. A care manager can quickly see differences in compliance across the zones. When a user clicks on a circle, the table underlying patients in this zone appears, including contact information so that the care team can get the person into the clinic for the required exams. This improves their CMS standing and national preventative care scores.

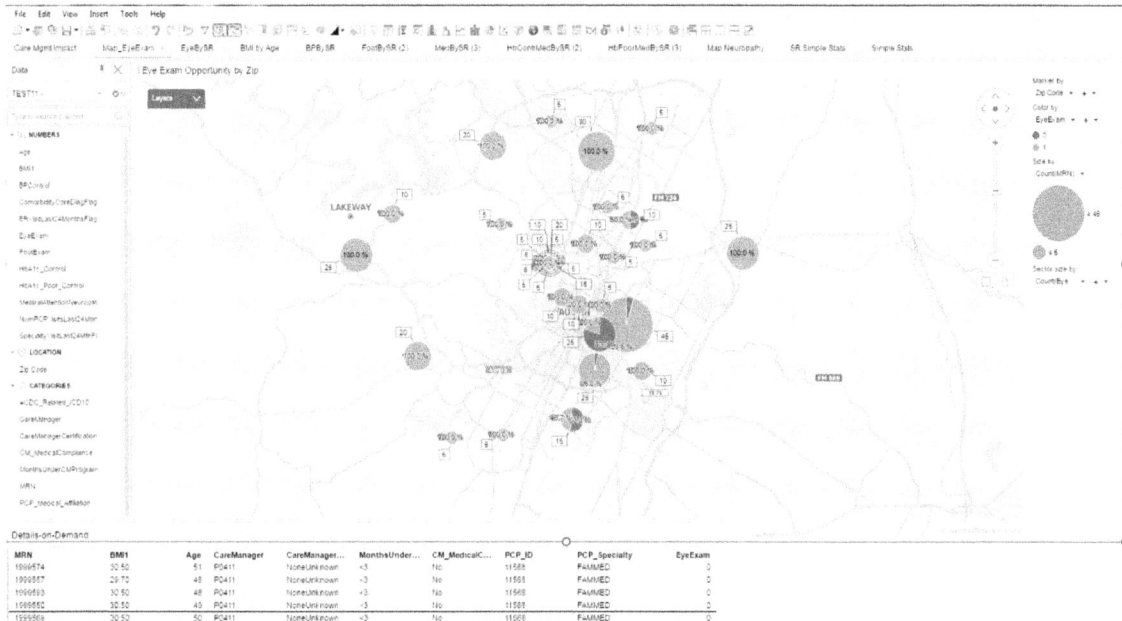

Figure 4: Geoanalytics Enabled Diabetes Care Manager Dashboard for Foot Screenings with Related Metrics.

Summary

This chapter covered the basics of data mining and the CRISP-DM framework. We explored data preprocessing, data catalog platforms, visualization tools, dimension reduction techniques, knowledge graphs, and data virtualization. These technologies support the data mining process, a precursor to more advanced AI techniques covered in subsequent chapters.

References

Hand, D., Mannila, H. and Smyth, P., *Principles of Data Mining*, MIT press, Cambridge, MA, 2001.

Larose, Daniel T; (2005), *Discovering Knowledge in Data: An Introduction to Data Mining*, John Wiley and Sons.

Pyle, Dorian, Data Preparation for Data Mining, Morgan Kaufman, San Francisco, CA, 1999.

Witten, I., Frank, E. and Hall, M.A; (January 2016), *Data Mining: Practical Machine Learning Tools and Techniques (The Morgan Kaufmann Series in Data Management Systems) 4th Edition*. Morgan Kaufmann.

CHAPTER 3

Data Challenges in Machine Learning

Advancements in computing power and data technology have made AI practical and transformative for businesses. The first wave of modern AI, known as data mining, laid the groundwork. The second wave, Machine Learning (ML), leverages increased computing power and larger, more diverse datasets to enable computers to learn and make decisions without explicit programming.

ML is at the heart of AI. When most people think of AI, they think of ML. But ML has evolved over time and grown in complexity. This evolution required the development of new and innovative data technologies. In this and the following three chapters, we discuss the evolution of data technologies that support each ML iteration.

This chapter focuses on data technology for the first iteration of practical ML. We define this first iteration as ML before developing the first practical application of a Convolutional Neural Network (CNN) called AlexNet. AlexNet won the ImageNet 2012 challenge (A. Krizhevsky et al). AlexNet didn't just win; it dominated the contest and represented a major shift in AI. So, in this chapter, we discuss ML before Alexnet.

In the next chapters, we will explore Deep Learning (DL), CNNs, and the advancements in AI up to the practical adoption of large language models like ChatGPT. We conclude by discussing Generative AI for non-text-based applications, highlighting the continuous evolution of data technology.

25

Our previous discussion covered the overlap between data mining and ML, focusing on descriptive analytics and discovery. Now, we shift to developing AI models for predictive and prescriptive analytics, driving actionable business insights.

Getting Machine Learning Infrastructure Right

Successfully developing and deploying ML systems requires navigating a myriad of challenges, particularly those related to data and data technology. One critical concept to understand in this context is *technical debt.* In systems development, technical debt refers to the cost of additional rework caused by choosing an easy (limited) solution now instead of using a better approach that would take longer. This concept is highly relevant to ML infrastructures, where data dependencies and management play a significant role.

Technical Debt in Machine Learning

D. Sculley and colleagues at Google have highlighted several components of technical debt specific to ML (Sculley et al.). Their research reveals that actual ML code is only a small part of the overall system architecture. In Figure 5, the size of the block for each system component is meant to represent the burden of technical debt. The ML code itself represents a very small component—a small white block. System architects should consider the following components when planning their infrastructure. The following components represent significant burdens of technical debt .

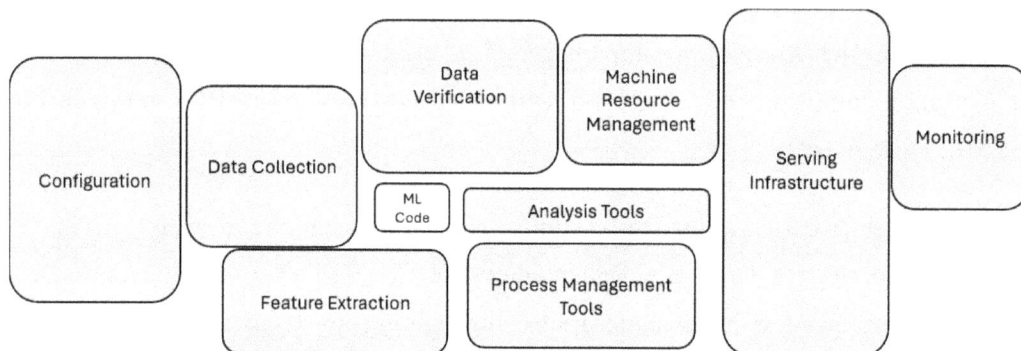

Figure 5: Machine Learning System Components.

Model Dependencies

There are three model dependencies to consider. The first is **entangled abstraction layers**. ML systems often intermingle signals. Changes to an ML feature in one system can inadvertently affect features in other systems due to these tangled layers. The second is **cascading correlations.** When using a model tailored for a specific problem to address a related but slightly different issue, improvements in one area can cause unforeseen issues in the other. This dependency complicates model enhancement efforts.

Finally, we have **unknown model consumers**. The outputs of a model, such as predictions, logs, and metadata, can be consumed by other systems without the primary system owner's knowledge. This hidden consumption introduces a higher risk of system breakage due to unforeseen linkages.

Data Dependencies

There are also three data dependencies to consider. The first is **changing data inputs**. When one model's input is derived from another model's output, any changes in the original or raw input data can significantly impact the model's performance. Monitoring these changes is crucial. For instance, shifts in data distribution, known as data drift, can lead to model degradation if not addressed promptly.

The second data dependency is **unneeded data**. Incorporating variables with little to no effect on model output increases data-related technical debt. Redundant inputs add complexity without offering significant predictive power. It is essential to regularly assess and prune unnecessary features to maintain model efficiency.

Finally, there is a **static data dependency analysis**. Traditional coding practices include compiler tools to generate dependency graphs, but such tools for data-related issues are less common. Comprehensive error checking and data management tools are essential for maintaining and updating data consumers. Effective data lineage tracking and data quality monitoring can help mitigate issues arising from static data dependencies.

Feedback

There are two types of feedback to consider. The first is **direct feedback**. This occurs when a model influences the selection of its future training data. The model's predictions can shape the data it subsequently learns from, creating a feedback loop. Ensuring that feedback loops are well-monitored and managed is vital to prevent biases and maintain model accuracy.

The second is when two different systems interact in the real world, they may inadvertently influence each other. This type of feedback is less apparent but equally significant. Understanding and mitigating hidden feedback loops can help maintain system stability and reliability.

By addressing these data-centric challenges, businesses can develop robust ML systems that minimize technical debt and ensure long-term success.

> *Carefully planning and managing the data infrastructure is crucial to harnessing the full potential of ML.*

Major Types of Machine Learning and Data to Support Them

We will look at various AI methods, the data requirements to support them, and the associated data systems. For ML, we will discuss five major ML paradigms to solve various problems organizations face.

Supervised Learning

Supervised learning is one of the most common and foundational forms of ML. It involves predicting an outcome based on historical data. Examples include predicting whether a patient has a disease, whether a customer will make a purchase, whether a machine will require maintenance next week, and whether a customer will be able to pay off their loan.

The data required for this type of problem includes a historical set of predictors and the outcome you want to predict, known as the target. The task of ML is to learn patterns from this historical set and create a model for predicting future outcomes.

The key difference between supervised learning and other methods we will discuss in this section is the necessity of a target. This means that the correct output is known for each input. Therefore, you must explicitly capture this in your data system. Otherwise, you have to create a label for each occurrence post hoc. We will see how this is done in the following section on semi-supervised learning.

Predicting Loan Default

To illustrate a business case and the associated data requirements, consider a simple case of predicting loan default. Banks and lending companies provide loans to generate revenue. Most loans are paid off and are profitable for the bank. However, banks know that a subset of loans will go into default, costing them money. It is crucial for banks to judiciously select the right circumstances in which to approve loans.

Banks collect operational data that provides a wealth of information on customers they approve for loans. They store this data across time and capture which loans default. This historical customer data signals a potential loan default.

A predictive model can be developed with ML training on the right data, which includes predictive parameters and the target outcome. For example, the K-nearest neighbors method is a simple and popular ML algorithm that classifies new data points by finding the most similar labeled data points.

Once the K-nearest neighbors model is trained and evaluated, it can be used to score new customers on the likelihood they will be able to repay the loan, aiding the bank's loan decision. Note that the data here includes a label or variable that guides the ML process in learning the differences between successful and unsuccessful loans.

Unsupervised Learning

Unlike supervised learning, where a label or outcome variable guides the ML training process, an unsupervised learning process determines which cases tend to group or "cluster" together. Instead of predicting an outcome, unsupervised learning aims to find hidden patterns or intrinsic structures in the input data.

The data required for this type of problem includes only a historical set of variables of interest that may provide inherent patterns or relationships among themselves. It does not require an outcome or target variable.

There are numerous application areas in science and business for unsupervised learning. Broadly speaking, there are two goals:

- Develop an ML model to determine if a new event looks odd and flag it for further scrutiny (e.g., anomaly detection in network security, detecting unusual patterns in network traffic that may indicate security breaches).
- Develop an ML model to determine the category new items should be assigned (e.g., claim clustering in insurance).

Claim Clustering for Property and Casualty Insurance

One of the biggest financial risks to property and casualty insurance providers is fraud and abuse. These insurers hire actuaries and data scientists to predict the total amounts of claims anticipated in a future period. The firms then use these amounts to estimate their risk pools, the monies set aside to pay future claims. If the predicted amounts are too low, the firm will lose money. If the predicted amounts are too high, they will have higher premiums and may lose potential business.

The profit margin for these firms is low, and saving every dollar is worthwhile. Fraud and abuse are major expenses, so the more judiciously and efficiently the firm can cut these expenses, the better. Companies have dedicated special investigative units (SIUs) that review claims for fraud. Historically, a subset of claims was sampled from the total population and sent to the SIU for review. Agents in this group manually investigate and follow up on these claims. This manual process is expensive and often misses fraudulent claims.

Data availability and ML methods have greatly improved the efficacy and efficiency of the SIUs. The goal is to employ methods that properly identify fraudulent claims with high accuracy. This means that "true" fraudulent claims get sent to the SIU to avoid the payment expense, while "false" fraudulent claims do not, reducing operational expenses.

Using an unsupervised ML clustering technique is beneficial for achieving these objectives. Why not use a supervised method? There is no label or target variable since the firm has not historically captured it in its data systems. Denoting an accurate label is more difficult than it seems. This may be captured in the future, but most firms use unsupervised methods to begin their AI journey. This is done using an ML clustering technique. Dozens of variables, including free text, are fed into the clustering pipeline. The ML algorithm performs two key functions in the process. The first is to use text mining to create principal components from the text, reducing a high-dimensional space into a lower-core space. The second function is to use these principal components and other variables to mathematically separate claims so that similar claims cluster together and dissimilar claims are maximally separated. These models may have dozens of inputs, but Figure 6 shows a simple illustration with two components that form three clusters. The non-overlapping cluster on the left is highly suspicious. The claims in this cluster are great candidates for investigation by a SIU.

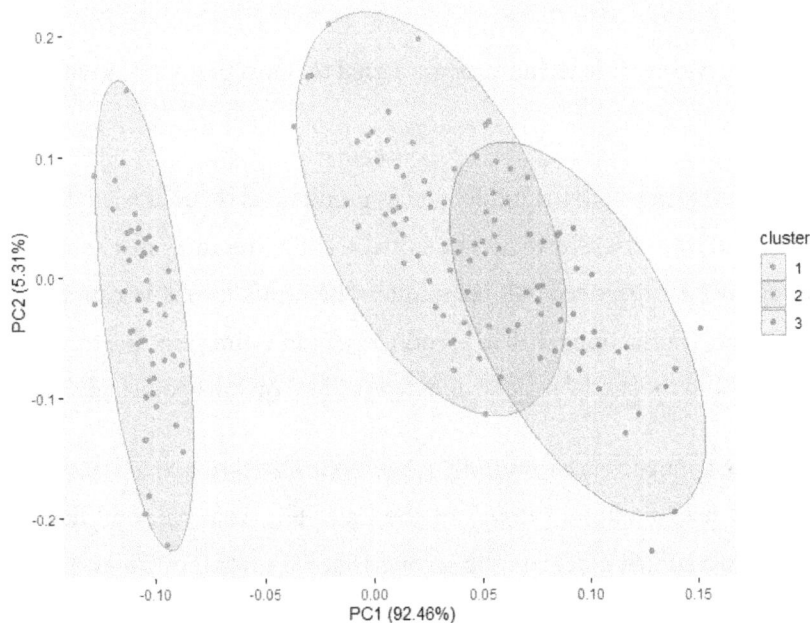

Figure 6: A simple illustration of how two principal components can form three separate clusters.

The figure shows how the claims may be mathematically separated into clusters. Different data will produce different separations, and there may be an overlap across clusters. However, the separation of data points demonstrates differences in claim characteristics. Sending anomalous claims to an SIU supports the goal of saving time and improving accuracy. For additional information, see Frees et al, 2014.

Semi-Supervised Learning

The data available determines the potential AI methods available to the organization. When outcomes or targets are labeled and available in the dataset, supervised ML methods are more powerful and preferred for predictive modeling. Unsupervised methods are more readily available when these data requirements are unmet; they are less restrictive.

A bridge method is semi-supervised learning. Around the early 2000s, it started gaining significant attention and wider adoption. This was driven by the realization that labeled data can be expensive and time-consuming, while unlabeled data is often abundant and easier to collect. Semi-supervised learning methods can improve learning accuracy with fewer labeled examples by combining labeled and unlabeled data.

During this era of ML, two specific techniques were used to boost predictions with a limited amount of labeled data.

The first was *self-training,* in which the model makes predictions on unlabeled data and treats those predictions as labels to train itself further. The initial training requires just some of the data to be labeled and run against a supervised ML technique. Then, this model is run against some of the unlabeled data to create transactions with a 'pseudo label' (an estimate of the true label). The results can then be analyzed, and the model may be updated (tuned) or run against additional transactions.

The second technique applied was *co-training.* A method related to active learning. In co-training, the predictive model uses multiple "views" of the data. For example, one data set is based on demographic and transactional data, and the second is based on text or notes. Each data set can be used to create a predictive model. The method is not fully unsupervised and works best when you have a rich set of predictor data and a small set of labeled outcomes. If no labels exist, the technique requires a human to review a sample of data to investigate and label cases.

Once you have two sets, a predictive model can be trained for each with the transactional data set. A second predictive model can be trained on textual data. You now have two models that can be run against unlabeled cases. After running them, the most confident predictions are selected and used as pseudo-labels.

In the co-training process, the pseudo-labeled cases (confident predictions) from one predictive model are added to the training set of the other predictive model and vice versa. Both models are then retrained with these new pseudo-labeled cases. The process is iterated to improve the performance of the models until they converge in performance. This is a form of self-supervised learning. Final model evaluations are performed, and when satisfied, these AI models may be deployed into a production process.

NOTE: This method assumes that the data sets are conditionally independent and sufficient. See Krogel and Scheffer, 2004.

Property and Casualty Insurance Example with Self-Training

How would self-training work with our previous example of predicting fraudulent claims? One of the metrics available after creating the clusters is distance measures. An AI practitioner can assess how far individual claims are from a universal center (centroid) or individual cluster centroids. For example, suppose they take five percent of the overall claims with the farthest distance from the overall population centroid. They label these claims as "anomalous" and the remaining 95% as "nonanomalous." Then they take a simple random sample of this anomalous pool and a simple random sample from the pool that was nonanomalous. They combine these data sets, creating a labeled dataset for supervised training. Several candidate models are trained using different ML techniques to detect anomalous claims. The best-performing model(s) are selected and run against a larger set. The results are then sent to an SIU, which captures results across the data and identifies the performance of accurately predicting true fraudulent claims versus false positive predictions. The process continuously improves by updating the data as it moves forward, gathering richer data for AI and ML modeling.

Property and Casualty Insurance Example with Co-Training

How would we approach our suspected insurance fraud problem with co-training? The SIUs in our insurance company have likely been investigating cases of fraud for years. This data may be kept in a separate system but could be merged with existing historical data. Remember, this method works best when you have a rich set of predictors and a small set of labeled outcomes. Insurance companies keep vast amounts of data, including demographic and transactional data stored in a data warehouse (structured information) and textual information stored in non-structured or semi-structured data stores. We cover these systems in Chapter 7, Modern Data Storage and Processing for AI.

Since some insurance cases have been noted as fraudulent, we can use them to build co-training models. We also have two data "views" that we can use to build prediction models for fraud.

We label the dataset from the data warehouse with the historical SIU data and the investigative outcome. This is binary based on the final determination: the case was "fraudulent" or "non-fraudulent." We do the same for the text-based data repository. Now, we have two datasets to build two predictive models. We also have a large number of unlabeled cases.

First, we build two independent predictive models with the labeled cases in the two datasets. We then take a simple random sample of the available unlabeled cases, splitting this sample into two sets. We run one set against the demographic and transactional data model and the second set against the text-based predictive model. After running these models, we have a predictive probability for the likelihood of fraud for each case. We create a pseudo-label and designate a label of "fraudulent" for cases deemed most likely to be fraudulent and "non-fraudulent" for cases deemed least likely to be fraudulent.

We now perform co-training. The pseudo-labeled cases from the demographic and transactional predictive model are added to the training set of the text-based predictive model, and vice-versa. Both models are then retrained with these new pseudo-labeled cases. We iterate the process to improve the performance of the models until their performance does not substantially improve. Finally, we perform final evaluations and are ready to deploy these AI models into a production process.

Reinforcement Learning

Reinforcement Learning (RL) is not a new concept. It precedes AI but has been increasing in importance in AI research and application over the last couple of decades. In the latest AI iteration, it holds a more prominent role. In the next three chapters, we will examine its key use in some of the most novel and powerful applications that employ RL.

In reinforcement learning, an agent learns by interacting with its environment and receiving rewards or penalties (training). Human learning is reinforcement learning. We navigate and interact with our environment. When attempting to accomplish a task, we learn what gets us closer to or further from the objective. AI researchers have developed algorithms to build AI based on mimicking human thought and behavior. Again, we will cover RL for deep learning and forms of Generative AI in the next three chapters. But many applications precede these methods. Some examples are inventory management, pricing, scheduling, resource allocation, and making purchase recommendations for shoppers.

Inventory Management Example

The goal of inventory management is to determine the optimal inventory levels for a product to maximize profit while minimizing costs. An RL algorithm would train an AI model by trial and error, interacting with a simulated or real inventory environment. It would try different scenarios and capture the results. It would learn the results of various inventory states and then mathematically infer results between them. This process helps determine optimal decisions that management should make given the situation. Note that these are crude beginnings with limited data. Today, with vast quantities of data, RL can do much more, especially in Generative AI.

Ensemble Learning

As the name implies, ensemble learning involves mixing or combining multiple ML models together to improve performance. These improvements can be made by a serial combination of models, meaning the output of one model becomes the input for the next model. Alternatively, they can be combined simultaneously.

One of the simplest forms of ensemble modeling is model averaging. It was used in many of the original applications of neural networks (NNs). In training the AI, the algorithm generates several NN models and then uses these models to intelligently make average model predictions.

Bagging (Bootstrap Aggregating)

This technique involves training multiple instances of the same model on different subsets of the training data and then averaging their predictions. A popular bagging method is the random forest algorithm.

Boosting Methods

Finally, boosting methods—for example, AdaBoost and gradient boosting—are a class of popular serial ensemble ML training algorithms that have been used for decades and are still very popular. These methods train models sequentially, with each new model focusing on correcting the errors made by the previous ones.

For more information, see Kuhn and Johnson (2013).

Property and Casualty Insurance Example with Boosting

In the previous Supervised Learning section, we illustrated applying a supervised learning method to predict bank loan default with a K-nearest Neighbor (KNN) training algorithm. Suppose we have an adequate KNN model in operation. However, we can improve fraud detection with an ensemble ML method. How would an AdaBoost model be useful?

We could use our labeled dataset to train this model. This model works by iteratively building weak classifiers and combining them to create a strong classifier. The algorithm assigns higher weights to the misclassified instances in each iteration, focusing more on difficult cases. This helps the model become more accurate in identifying fraudulent transactions.

We could evaluate and test this model. We could run this AdaBoost model simultaneously against our product KNN model and compare performance. We could then choose a champion model and deploy it to operations.

Section Summary

The data available in the organization determines what ML techniques are viable. As organizations mature in their AI journey, they gain knowledge and begin collecting higher-value data along the way. They improve the volume of this data and the performance of the systems that store it. They increase the variety and predictive power of the data they capture. They improve the quality of the data and access available to it. They do all these things simultaneously. And as they improve their data, they improve their ability to benefit from AI.

The Rise of Big Data and a Technology Paradigm Shift

Over the last few decades, much has been rightfully said—and even more hyped—about "Big Data." But what does big data even mean? Is it simply a lot of data, or is there more to it? The definition often depends on who you ask, and the answer can be influenced by how someone stands to gain from their response. Typically, big data is described either conceptually or by the data technology developed to support it.

Big data conceptually may include the 5 V's (characteristics) of big data:

1) Data Volume – the sheer amount of data
2) Data Variety – diverse data types, different structures, and formats of data
3) Data Velocity – how fast data is being added to systems, refreshed
4) Value – What is the usefulness or return on investment for sourcing this data?
5) Veracity – What is the quality, reliability, and trustworthiness of the data?

These characteristics created new data challenges and therefore have greatly influenced the development of big data technology. The true value of big data was realized only after a paradigm shift in technology. ML platforms and data stores have been kept in separate enterprise systems for decades. The ML systems resided in their unique environments, while vast volumes of data were housed in data warehouses. When data scientists wanted to build AI models, they had to move the appropriate data from the data warehouse to the ML environment, where the AI models were trained. Once trained, these models typically continued to live in this same environment and were "productionized" or placed in operations. See Figure 7.

Challenges of Traditional ML Architecture

This traditional ML architecture posed several significant challenges:

- **Data Duplication**: Large capacities of data were duplicated across data warehouses and ML platforms, leading to inefficiencies and increased storage costs.
- **Data Quality Issues**: Maintaining two sets of data introduced potential data quality issues, as data is dynamic and constantly changing.
- **Data Transfer Time**: Moving large volumes of data over the network was time-consuming and could delay the ML model development process.
- **Security Risks**: Transferring data over a network increases the risk of security breaches and potential data loss.

These challenges underscore the need for a new approach to managing and utilizing big data. Figure 7 illustrates this architecture.

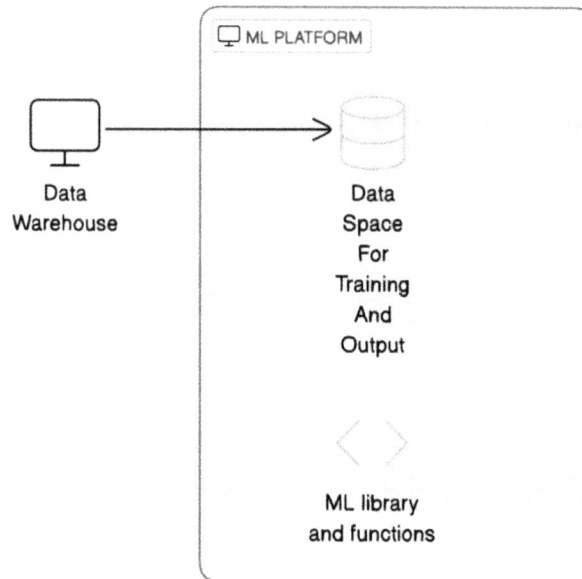

Figure 7: Traditional ML Systems Architecture.

This figure shows that the data used for training ML models lives in a data warehouse. When it is time to train ML models, the data is transferred over a network. The ML platform must make disk space available for all this data. The size of the ML platform consists mostly of data space, and the ML library and tools are small by comparison.

The technology paradigm shifted when it occurred to technologists that the larger the data, the more time-consuming and expensive it is to move the data to the algorithms. Data volumes were huge and getting bigger. ML algorithm libraries were small. What if instead of moving the data to where the ML algorithms live, we move the ML algorithms to where the data lives instead? This is known as the problem of data locality. At the same time, there was an explosion of data technologies to support big data and AI. Most notable was Apache Hadoop.[3] Then Apache Spark® was introduced, which we will discuss in the next chapter.

Hadoop® enabled distributed data storage and processing, making moving computations close to the data easier. Hadoop surpassed traditional data processing systems that struggled to manage the volume, variety, and velocity of data generated in the early 2000s and 2010s. It was designed to handle massive datasets efficiently. It was also scalable and allowed for more cost-effective computation hardware. This enabled it to process larger datasets without a significant drop in performance. Additionally, it was fault-tolerant, flexible, and open source. Combining Apache Hadoop with Apache Mahout®[4], a library for scalable ML, allowed AI technologists and data scientists to overcome many traditional ML training constraints.

An example of a Hadoop data store with associated ML systems appears in Figure 8. This figure shows that data used for training ML models and the Mahout® libraries and functions coexist in the same Hadoop environment. Contrasting Figure 7 and Figure 8, you can see the inherent advantages of this architecture. These include the lack of data duplication, elimination of time to move data, data fidelity, and security.

---

[3] https://hadoop.apache.org/.

[4] https://mahout.apache.org/.

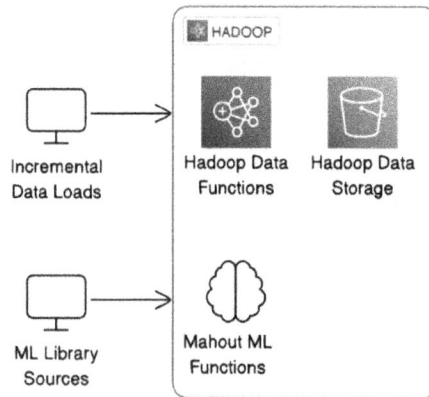

Figure 8: ML Big Data Paradigm Shift, Hadoop + ML training.

Application Case Highlight – The Next Generation of Medicine - Predicting Asthma

Key Terms – Asthma, Predictive Modeling, EMR, DaaS, iPaaS, Case Management, ACOs

Asthma is scary. It is dangerous, and it triggers primal fear in its victims as they struggle for air. It affects over 25 million Americans and costs an estimated $82 billion per year.[5] There are no tests to signal an oncoming asthma attack, and many factors that cause these events are not stored in electronic medical records. This case highlights the impact of asthma and presents ML methods to more effectively and efficiently predict a severe asthma attack. Everyone in the US knows of a family member or friend affected by asthma. They may not know that it accounts for one-quarter of the emergency room visits in the U.S. each year and one-half million hospitalizations with an annual cost of $18 billion.[6] Medical evidence points to the determinants of asthma-related events, especially severe asthma attacks. The difficulty lies in combining all the important data, using it methodically, and acting upon it. We define a severe asthma attack (SAA) as an asthma-related event that results in an emergency room visit or hospitalization. With AI ML predictive modeling, we can predict an

---

[5] https://www.ajmc.com/view/cdc-study-puts-economic-burden-of-asthma-at-more-than-80-billion-per-year [Accessed 02 Feb. 2025].

[6] https://www.cdc.gov/asthma-data/about/index.html?CDC_AA_refVal=https%3A%2F%2Fwww.cdc.gov%2Fasthma%2Fasthmadata.htm.

SAA and notify the patient at risk before it happens. Additionally, we can aggregate geolocations and estimate the number of patients that might come into an ER, allowing administrators to prepare accordingly.

Data Technology was the Barrier for Years

Medical research had identified a number of contributors to asthma-related events well before a practical solution was available to predict SAAs. Why did it take so long to build an effective prediction system? The acquisition of the requisite data for predicting many diseases is **not** readily available in the EMR. Historical clinical data is there, but many factors that substantially contribute to asthma attacks are not. Many of these predictive factors, which are causal or associative in nature, exist outside the EMR. Clinical data is only one of several dimensions crucial to determining the likelihood of an SAA. Research shows that at least four data dimensions affect SAAs: physical, behavioral, psychological, and environmental factors. Cross-correlating all these factors is very difficult!

With modern data technology, we can source all that disparate data across those four dimensions, transform, and integrate that data meaningfully. We can deliver results so stakeholders are informed and can take action.

Medical Science and Acquiring the Right Data

The four dimensions identified by the American College of Allergy, Asthma, and Immunology[7] are population-based factors. Researchers have studied what factors contribute to the population as a whole. These are general and not patient-specific. Individual patients may react to these factors uniquely. This distinction is between population health and personalized medicine. AI promises to provide very focused, targeted individual health guidelines and therapies.

The first module of the SAA solution involved gathering all the disparate data across the four domains that impact asthma-related events into a centralized Data-as-a-Service (DaaS) platform.

---

[7] https://acaai.org/.

DaaS provides on-demand access to data and allows users to access, manage, and analyze data without worrying about the underlying infrastructure, storage, or maintenance.

Data included twelve physical characteristics, such as diagnoses, family history of asthma and allergy, recent respiratory infections, BMI, and more. Also included were four behavioral metrics: inhaler and other medication compliance, time since the last Primary Care Provider (PCP) visit, tobacco use, and activity level. Twenty-seven environmental factors were included, including weather-related metrics, pollen counts, and air quality metrics. Finally, three metrics were included to gauge psychological stress, a known asthma trigger.

Figure 9 demonstrates the data pipeline for the first system module. In the upper left corner of Figure 9, we see the sourcing of data from the EMR using an iPaaS (integration Platform as a Service) solution.

Module 1 Asthma (SAA) System

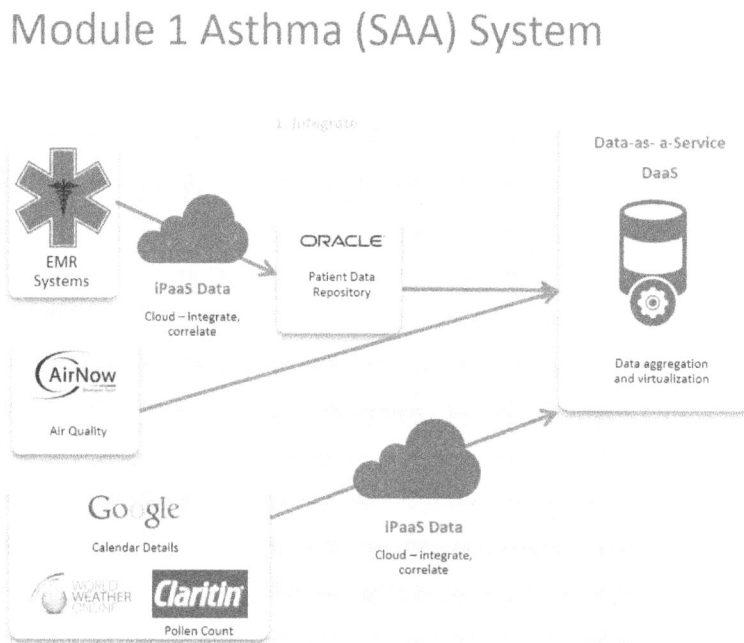

Figure 9: The flow of data from multiple sources into a centralized data storage (DaaS).

This data is stored in an Oracle® repository. In the middle left, data is sourced through a public API from AirNow,[8] which delivers important air quality information using the ZIP Code. The bottom

---

[8] https://www.airnow.gov.

left corner illustrates the integration of weather information from World Weather Online,[9] social and self-reported information via the internet, and allergy and pollen information from Claritin.[10] This diverse data is aggregated and pulled into the DaaS platform using iPaaS.

Machine Learning for AI Asthma Models

With the information now available in a centralized location, users can access, manage, and analyze the data. Data scientists utilize this data to train AI models with ML. Figure 10 illustrates the second module of the system. In the upper corner of Figure 10, data is pulled from the DaaS platform into the ML environment. Using ML techniques, multiple AI models are created. Advanced predictive analytics techniques capture the likelihood of SAA events by ZIP Code based on individual patient clinical data, individual patient determinants of health (such as socio-economic and self-reported information), weather, air quality, and allergen information.

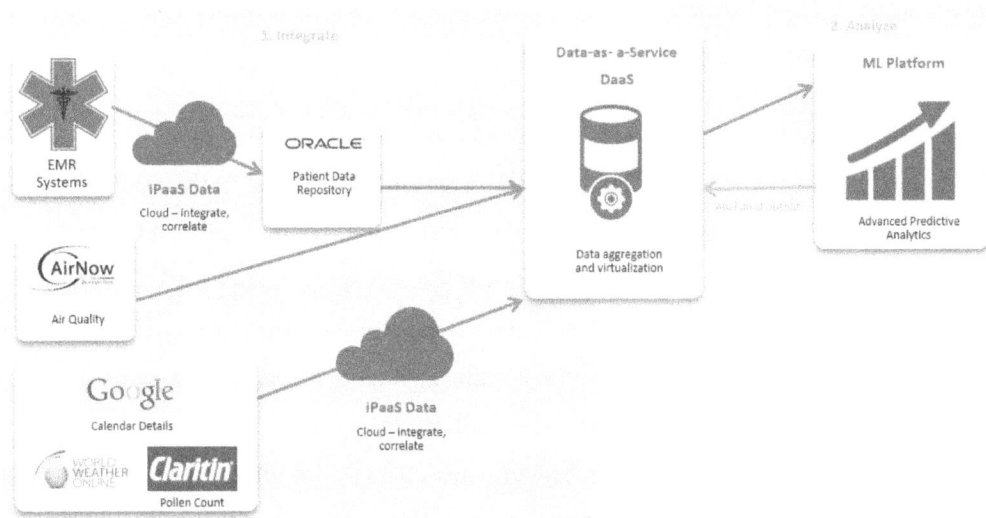

Figure 10: Data Flows and AI Model Creation with an ML Platform.

---

[9] https://www.worldweatheronline.com/.

[10] https://www.claritin.com/.

Developing these models requires a vast amount of data as the training algorithms perform millions of complex associations to mine both linear and nonlinear patterns within the data. These models determine which factors have a meaningful relationship to an SAA and which are insignificant or transitory. Moreover, they assess how different factors interrelate to have a combinatory effect on a severe asthma attack for a specific patient within a given week. Lastly, they estimate the confidence in the model's performance, i.e., how well it will perform on new data. There are dozens of candidate models trained, including combinations or ensembles of models that compete for selection. Once developed, the models can be stored in the DaaS platform, where they are run on a production schedule. These intelligent AI models provide daily predictions of an SAA for a specific patient for the upcoming week.

Model Results and Applications

Once the AI models are developed, they are stored back in the DaaS environment for easy access. These models are operationalized and set to function on a systematic schedule, ensuring timely predictions and alerts. This is the final component of our SAA system, as illustrated in Figure 11. In this figure, we see the complete flow of the system:

- **Data Integration**: Data is sourced from various channels (EMR, AirNow, World Weather Online, social and self-reported data, and Claritin) and centralized in the DaaS platform.
- **Model Training**: Data scientists use this integrated data to train multiple AI models within the ML environment, identifying critical factors that influence SAAs.
- **Model Storage and Scheduling**: Trained models are stored in the DaaS environment and operationalized to run on a production schedule. Using the latest data, these models provide daily predictions of SAAs for individual patients.
- **Real-Time Alerts**: The system generates real-time alerts and notifications for patients at risk, enabling proactive management and intervention.
- **Administrative Insights**: Aggregated data and predictions offer insights into potential ER visits by geolocation, allowing administrators to prepare for influxes of patients.

This system enhances the ability to predict and manage severe asthma attacks effectively by leveraging advanced data technology and ML.

Final Solution – Asthma (SAA) System

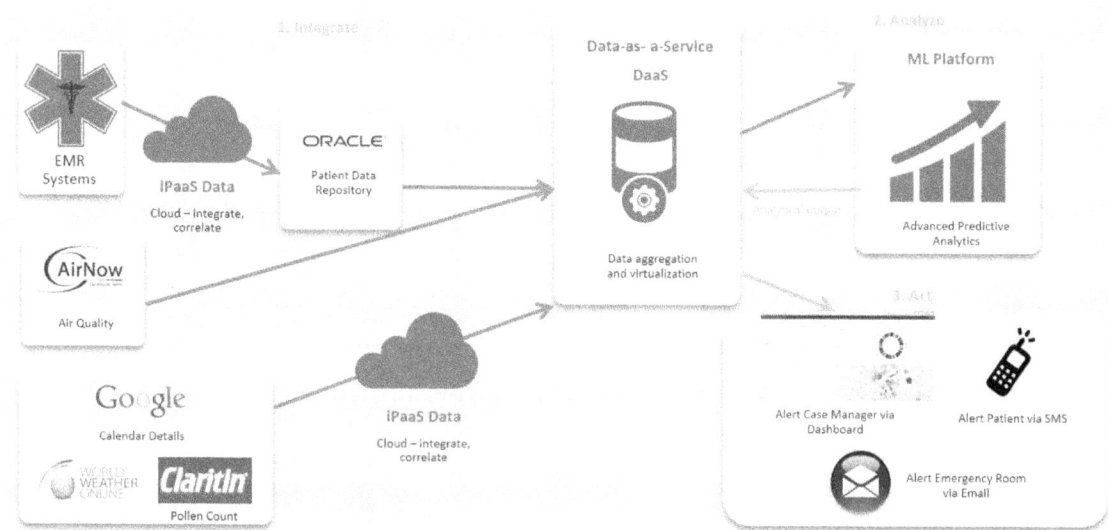

Figure 11: Operationalization and Application of AI Models for SAA Prediction.

Multiple Applications

In the upper right corner of Figure 11, the optimal AI models are shown being sent back to the DaaS environment where they can become operational. Once operational, a number of results and activities are generated, as represented in the lower right corner of the figure. We will dive deeper into three of these.

Case Management Application

The first action is for the case management application within the solution. At the end of the last chapter, we illustrated the importance of case management for Accountable Care Organizations (ACOs) in managing diabetes care. Similarly, there are case managers for asthma and other chronic diseases. These asthma care managers need to track and manage their panel of patients effectively. This solution allows them to interact with the data for their patients.

The dashboard provides asthma care managers with real-time insights into their patients' health status, enabling them to take proactive measures to prevent severe asthma attacks. It includes key metrics such as medication adherence, recent healthcare visits, and environmental factors affecting individual patients. By leveraging this integrated data and AI models, care managers can provide personalized care and improve outcomes for asthma patients.

In Figure 12, the case manager can filter patients by various demographic and clinical data elements, including whether the patient is at risk. This dashboard allows users to view ZIP Codes and geolocations, enabling them to drill down into a specific ZIP code or bubble. Each row of the associated table represents a patient and the data the case manager is interested in viewing, displaying at-risk patients. The user can select a row, triggering an EMR query to pull contact information, which allows the case manager to connect with the patient.

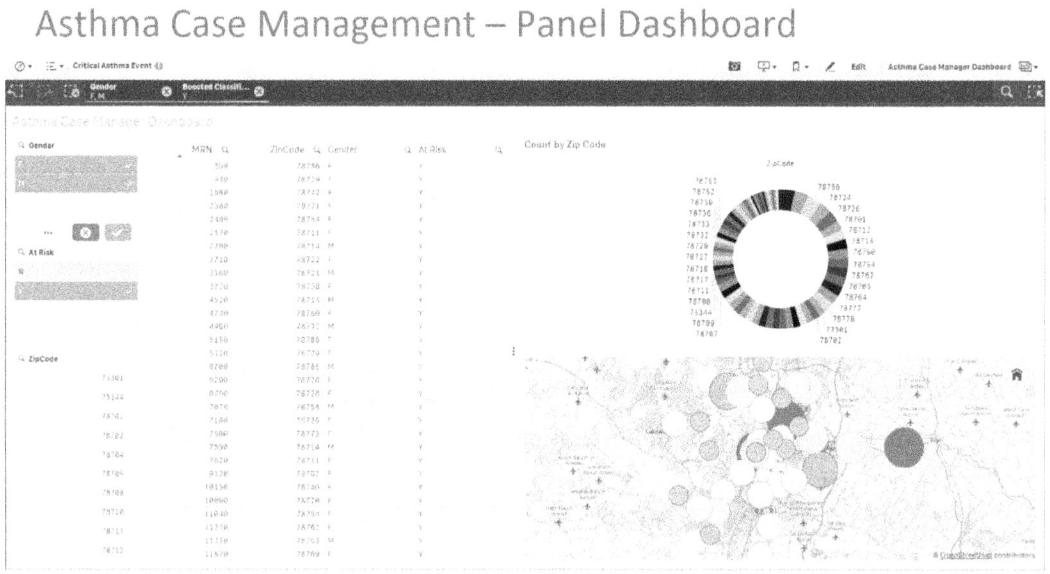

Figure 12: Example of a Case Management Dashboard.

SMS Text Alerts

The second action involves sending an SMS text message directly to the patient, provided they have opted to receive these messages. The text states that based on their medical profile and current conditions, they are at risk of having an asthma-related event this week. Figure 13 illustrates this process. Patients can use this information to take precautions and appropriate actions, such as avoiding outdoor activities, ensuring they have their emergency inhalers with them, using their home peak flow meter, or scheduling an appointment with their care provider.

Emergency Management Reports

The final action is triggering an emailed emergency management report to the associated Emergency Rooms (ERs). This report provides patient listings for those who have opted into the system and are at risk, specifically indicating whether the patient is likely or highly likely to have an SAA. It includes other statistics, such as the expected number of SAA-related ER visits over the next week. This information is valuable to ER directors and EMS staff for planning anticipated staffing levels and managing the ER effectively. All three action steps appear in Figure 13.

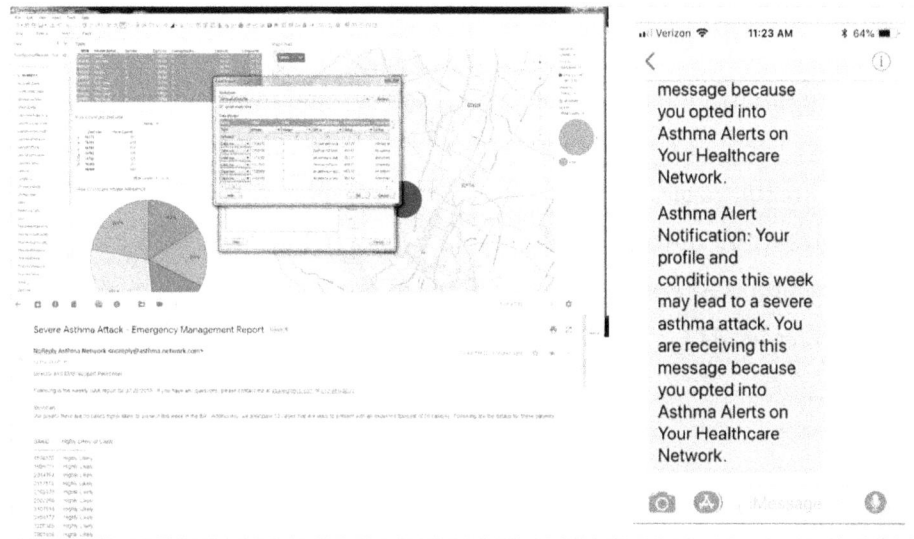

Figure 13: Summary of the Three Actions Made by the SAA System.

Figure 13 provides a summary of the three actions enabled by the system:

- **Top Center**: A display of the case management dashboard with geoanalytics and interactive data capability. This dashboard allows case managers to filter patients by demographic and clinical data elements, including at-risk status. It enables drill-down into specific ZIP codes or geolocations, displaying patient data and facilitating EMR queries and patient contact.
- **Right Side**: An example SMS text message sent to a patient who has opted to receive these notifications. The message informs the patient of their risk for an asthma-related event based on their medical profile and current conditions, encouraging them to take precautions and appropriate actions.

- **Bottom**: The Emergency Management Report, which is emailed to associated Emergency Rooms (ERs). This report includes patient listings for those at risk of severe asthma attacks, indicating the likelihood of an SAA. It also provides statistics on expected SAA-related ER visits over the next week, helping ER directors and EMS staff prepare for anticipated staffing levels and ER management.

Summary

We are progressing through the evolution of AI technology and the associated data requirements and data technology needed to support those AI methods. We have covered data mining and ML version 1.0, which are still viable and used daily. The next chapter will explore Deep Learning (DL), which began in 2012 with Convolutional Neural Networks (CNNs) and their cousins. The theory and methodologies for this AI existed for decades. What caused them to become practical? Yes, new data technology. *Data for AI.*

References

A. Krizhevsky, I. Sutskever, G. Hinton, ImageNet Classification with Deep Convolutional Neural Networks (2012), NeurIPS.

Frees, E. W., Derrig, R. A., and Meyers, G. (2014). Predictive Modeling applications in Actuarial Science. Cambridge University Press.

Kuhn, M., and Johnson, K. (2013). *Applied Predictive Modeling*. Springer Science and Business Media.

Krogel, MA., Scheffer, T. Multi-Relational Learning, Text Mining, and Semi-Supervised Learning for Functional Genomics. *Machine Learning* **57**, 61–81 (2004). https://doi.org/10.1023/B:MACH.0000035472.73496.0c.

Sculley, D., Holt, G., Golovin, D., Davydov, E., Phillips, T., Ebner, D., Chaudhary, V., and Young, M. (2014). *SE4ML: Software Engineering for Machine Learning (NIPS 2014 Workshop)*.

## CHAPTER 4

Deep Learning and Data Infrastructure

We continue our journey across the ever-evolving landscape of AI innovation. Our story began with data mining, a foundational AI discipline that remains highly relevant today. Data mining is particularly accessible for two reasons. First, it requires only a basic level of education and experience—anyone with a basic understanding of analytics can become a data miner. Second, unlike the more advanced realms of AI we've encountered, such as ML, it doesn't demand specific data types, large volumes of data, or specialized data technologies.

As discussed in the previous chapter, ML typically requires large datasets for training. Certain AI methods demand massive amounts of data, which only became feasible with the advent of "Big Data" technologies like Apache Hadoop.

This chapter delves into the next evolution, Machine Learning 2.0, known as Deep Learning (DL). Before the rise of ChatGPT® and Large Language Models, DL began to gain wide acceptance around 2013. As noted earlier, Convolutional Neural Networks (CNNs) were a primary method utilized in DL. Recurrent Neural Networks (RNNs) also played a significant role during this period. However, transformer models have since surpassed RNNs in popularity, with ChatGPT® serving as a prominent example of AI based on transformer methods.

This chapter will explore DL and the data technologies that made it practical. We will trace its development up to adopting ChatGPT and large language models around 2017, which we will delve into further in Chapter 5.

The Role of Apache Spark in Enabling Deep Learning

As we transitioned from ML 1.0 to the era of DL, one significant advancement was the introduction of Apache Spark. While Apache Hadoop was pivotal in making effective ML 1.0 possible by enabling large-scale data storage and processing, Spark brought about transformative changes that paved the way for DL.

Apache Spark, introduced in 2014, provided a more efficient and user-friendly platform for big data processing. Its in-memory computing capabilities significantly improved the speed and performance of data processing tasks, which was essential for the complex computations required in DL. Unlike Hadoop's batch processing, Spark's ability to handle real-time data streams allowed for more responsive and interactive data analysis.

In-Memory Computing and Distributed Computing

One of the most notable features of Spark is its in-memory computing capability. By keeping data in memory rather than writing it to disk between operations, Spark significantly reduces the time required for data processing tasks. This is particularly important for DL, where training deep neural networks often involves numerous iterative computations.

Another notable feature was Spark's support for distributed computing, making it possible to process and analyze large-scale datasets efficiently. By distributing data and computations across multiple nodes in a cluster, Spark enables faster processing and training of DL models. This was particularly crucial for training deep neural networks, which often require substantial computational resources and time.

Integration with DL Libraries and Real-Time Data Processing

Spark's flexibility and ease of integration with various data sources and formats made it an ideal choice for handling the diverse and large-scale datasets needed for DL. Spark's MLlib library provided scalable and efficient ML algorithm implementations, facilitating DL experimentation and development. Spark's integration with DL frameworks like TensorFlow and Keras also allowed data scientists and engineers to leverage Spark's processing power while using familiar DL tools.

Spark's ability to handle real-time data streams was a significant advantage for DL applications that required immediate insights. For example, in fields like fraud detection, recommendation systems, and real-time analytics, Spark's real-time processing capabilities enabled the deployment of DL models that could make instant decisions based on streaming data.

Ease of Use and Community

Spark's high-level APIs in Java, Scala, Python, and R made it accessible to a broad audience of developers and data scientists. Its user-friendly interface and robust documentation facilitated the rapid development and deployment of DL models. Spark's ecosystem also included a wide range of libraries and tools for tasks such as graph processing (GraphX), ML (MLlib), and SQL querying (Spark SQL), making it a versatile platform for various data processing needs.

The vibrant community and ecosystem around Apache Spark contributed to its rapid adoption and continuous improvement. Regular updates, contributions from industry leaders, and comprehensive documentation ensured that Spark remained at the forefront of big data processing technologies. The strong community support also facilitated sharing best practices, case studies, and innovative solutions, further enhancing Spark's capabilities.

In summary, the introduction of Apache Spark revolutionized data processing and analysis, making it possible to efficiently handle the large-scale and complex datasets required for DL. Spark's in-memory computing, real-time processing, distributed computing capabilities, and ease of integration with DL libraries provided the foundation for the practical implementation and widespread adoption of DL techniques.

The Role of Data Lakes in Enabling Deep Learning (2013-2017)

The rapid advancements in Deep Learning (DL) between 2013 and 2017 required the ability to store and process vast amounts of diverse and unstructured data. Data lakes emerged as a critical infrastructure component, providing the scalability and flexibility needed to support DL workflows.

Introduction and Importance of Data Lakes: A data lake is a centralized repository that allows organizations to store all their structured and unstructured data at any scale. Unlike traditional data warehouses, which store data in predefined schemas, data lakes store raw data in its native format until it is needed for analysis. This flexibility makes data lakes ideal for handling the diverse and large-scale datasets required for DL.

Key Benefits of Data Lakes

The four key benefits of data lakes are scalability, flexibility, cost-effectiveness, and data integration.

Data lakes can scale horizontally, allowing organizations to store and manage petabytes of data without the need for complex and costly infrastructure. This scalability is essential for DL projects, which often involve processing and analyzing massive datasets.

Data lakes also support a wide variety of data types, including structured, semi-structured, and unstructured data. This flexibility enables organizations to store raw data from multiple sources, such as text, images, videos, sensor data, and more, which are often used in DL applications.

Data lakes are cost-effective. By using inexpensive storage solutions, such as cloud-based object storage, data lakes offer a cost-effective way to store large volumes of data. Organizations can save on storage costs while maintaining the ability to access and analyze their data as needed.

Finally, data lakes facilitate the integration of data from disparate sources, providing a unified view of an organization's data assets. This integration is crucial for DL, allowing data scientists to combine and analyze diverse datasets to train more accurate and robust models.

Key Data Lake Technologies

As we have discussed, Hadoop was one of the pioneers in big data storage. It remains a vital technology for big data and data lake technologies. Hadoop's distributed file system (HDFS) laid the groundwork for modern data lakes. HDFS allowed organizations to store and manage large datasets across distributed clusters, providing the scalability and reliability needed for DL.

Amazon Web Services (AWS) is a leading provider of infrastructure and tools for enabling AI and ML applications. We will cover AWS in a few sections, as these technologies often interconnect, making it challenging to distinctly categorize them. Amazon S3 became a popular choice for cloud-based data lakes. Its durability, scalability, and cost-effectiveness made it an ideal solution for storing large volumes of raw data. Amazon S3's integration with other AWS services facilitated seamless data processing and analysis for DL workflows.

Microsoft Azure Data Lake Storage offered a scalable and secure cloud-based storage solution for big data analytics. Its ability to handle large-scale data processing and integration with other Azure services made it a valuable component of DL workflows. Google Cloud Storage provides a highly durable and available object storage solution, making it suitable for building data lakes. Its seamless integration with Google Cloud's big data and ML services enabled efficient data processing and analysis for DL.

Data lakes played a pivotal role in enabling the practical adoption of DL by providing the necessary infrastructure to store and manage vast amounts of diverse data. Their scalability, flexibility, and cost-effectiveness allowed organizations to capture and analyze the data needed to train complex DL models. By supporting data integration from multiple sources, data lakes facilitated the development of more accurate and comprehensive DL models.

In summary, data lakes were a crucial enabler of DL between 2013 and 2017. Their ability to store, manage, and integrate diverse and large-scale datasets provided the foundation for building, training, and deploying sophisticated DL models. The adoption of data lake technologies significantly contributed to the advancement and practical application of DL techniques during this period.

Additional Cloud-Based Data Platforms (2013-2017)

From 2013 to 2017, significant advancements in cloud-based data platforms occurred, which played a pivotal role in enabling the practical adoption of Deep Learning (DL). These platforms provided scalable, flexible, and cost-effective data storage, processing, and analysis solutions, making them essential for DL workflows.

Cloud-based data platforms offer infrastructure, tools, and services to manage large-scale data processing tasks without needing on-premises hardware. These platforms provide the elasticity to scale resources up or down based on demand, making them ideal for handling the fluctuating requirements of DL projects. Additionally, cloud platforms offer various services and integrations that streamline the development and deployment of DL models.

Key Cloud-Based Data Platforms

We mentioned AWS in the previous section. During this period, AWS emerged as a leading cloud platform, offering a comprehensive suite of services for data storage, processing, and analysis. Services like Amazon S3 for scalable storage, Amazon EC2 for flexible computing power, and AWS Lambda for serverless computing made building and scaling DL applications easier. AWS also introduced Amazon SageMaker, a fully managed service for building, training, and deploying ML models, further simplifying the DL workflow.

Google Cloud Platform (GCP) offers robust tools and services for DL practitioners. Google Cloud Storage provides scalable and durable storage, while Google Compute Engine offers customizable virtual machines for compute-intensive tasks. GCP's BigQuery enables fast and scalable analysis of large datasets, and its integration with TensorFlow, Google's open-source DL framework, provides seamless workflows for building and deploying DL models. Additionally, Google introduced Cloud Machine Learning Engine (now known as AI Platform), a managed service for training and deploying ML models at scale.

Microsoft Azure provides a wide array of services to support DL projects. Azure Blob Storage and Azure Data Lake Store offer scalable storage solutions, while Azure Virtual Machines and Azure

Batch provide computing power for training DL models. Azure Machine Learning, a suite of services for building, training, and deploying ML models, facilitates the entire DL lifecycle. Azure's integration with popular DL frameworks like TensorFlow and PyTorch allows for seamless development and deployment of DL applications.

IBM Cloud offers a range of services to support DL and AI projects. IBM Watson Studio provides a collaborative environment for data scientists, developers, and analysts to work on DL models. IBM Cloud Object Storage offers scalable and secure storage, while IBM Cloud Functions provides serverless computing capabilities. IBM also integrates its cloud services with popular DL frameworks, making building, training, and deploying DL models easier on the IBM Cloud platform.

Advantages of cloud-based data platforms include:

- **Scalability**: Cloud platforms offer the ability to scale resources up or down based on demand, making it possible to handle large-scale DL projects without significant upfront investment in hardware.

- **Flexibility**: Cloud platforms provide a wide range of services and tools that can be tailored to specific DL workflows, enabling organizations to choose the best solutions for their needs.

- **Cost-Effectiveness**: Cloud platforms, with pay-as-you-go pricing models, allow organizations to manage costs efficiently by paying only for the resources they use.

- **Accessibility**: Cloud platforms provide access to powerful computing resources and tools from anywhere, enabling collaboration among distributed teams and facilitating remote work.

- **Integration**: Cloud platforms offer seamless integration with popular DL frameworks and tools, making it easier to build, train, and deploy DL models.

The availability of cloud-based data platforms significantly lowered the barriers to entry for DL, enabling organizations of all sizes to leverage advanced DL techniques. By providing scalable, flexible, and cost-effective data storage, processing, and analysis solutions, these platforms empowered data scientists and engineers to focus on developing innovative DL models and applications without worrying about infrastructure limitations.

The rise of cloud-based data platforms from 2013 to 2017 played a crucial role in the advancement and practical adoption of DL.

These platforms provided the necessary infrastructure and services to handle the demands of DL workflows, making it possible to build, train, and deploy complex DL models at scale.

Data Pipelines (2013-2017)

The rapid advancements in DL between 2013 and 2017 necessitated the development of robust data pipelines to handle the increasingly complex and large-scale datasets required for training sophisticated models. Data pipelines enabled efficient data ingestion, processing, and transformation, laying the foundation for effective DL workflows.

A data pipeline is a series of data processing steps that transform raw data into a format suitable for analysis and model training. These pipelines automate data flow from its source to its final destination, ensuring that data is cleaned, transformed, and enriched at each stage. Effective data pipelines are essential for maintaining data quality, consistency, and scalability, which are critical for DL applications.

Key components of data pipelines include:

- **Data Ingestion**: Data ingestion is the process of collecting raw data from various sources, such as databases, APIs, and data streams. During this period, frameworks like Apache Kafka gained popularity for real-time data ingestion, allowing organizations to capture and process data as it arrives. Using tools like Apache Sqoop, batch ingestion methods were also common for extracting data from traditional databases.

- **Data Processing**: Once ingested, data needs to be processed and transformed into a suitable format for analysis and model training. With its in-memory computing capabilities, Apache Spark became popular for distributed data processing. Spark allowed for efficient data cleaning, aggregation, and feature engineering, significantly speeding up the preparation of large datasets for DL.

- **Data Storage**: Storing processed data in a scalable and accessible manner was crucial for DL workflows. Distributed file systems like Apache Hadoop's HDFS and cloud storage solutions like Amazon S3 were widely used to store vast amounts of data. These storage systems provided the necessary infrastructure to handle the scale and variety of data required for DL.

- **Data Transformation**: Data transformation involves converting data into a format suitable for analysis and model training. Tools like Apache Spark and Apache Flink were used for this purpose, enabling complex transformations and feature engineering tasks. These transformations ensured that the data was in the right shape and format for DL models to learn effectively.

- **Data Orchestration**: Orchestrating the various stages of a data pipeline requires tools that can manage dependencies and automate workflows. Apache Airflow emerged as a popular choice for workflow orchestration, allowing data scientists and engineers to define, schedule, and monitor complex data pipelines. Airflow's extensibility and integration with various data processing tools make it an essential component of modern data pipelines.

Data pipelines were designed to seamlessly integrate with DL frameworks like TensorFlow, PyTorch, and Keras. By automating the flow of data from raw sources to DL models, these pipelines ensured that data was consistently prepared and delivered for training and evaluation. This integration facilitated efficient experimentation and iteration, enabling rapid development and deployment of DL models.

Scalability was a key consideration for data pipelines during this period. As DL models grew in complexity and size, the ability to process and analyze large-scale datasets became increasingly important. Real-time processing capabilities, enabled by tools like Apache Kafka and Spark

Streaming, allowed organizations to build responsive and adaptive DL applications that could react to incoming data in real time.

The vibrant open-source community and ecosystem greatly supported the development and adoption of data pipelines. Contributions from industry leaders and collaborative efforts ensured that data pipeline tools remained at the cutting edge of technology. Regular updates, comprehensive documentation, and community-driven best practices further enhanced the capabilities and usability of these tools.

The development of robust data pipelines between 2013 and 2017 played a pivotal role in enabling the practical adoption and advancement of DL. These pipelines provided the necessary infrastructure to handle large-scale and complex datasets, ensuring efficient data ingestion, processing, and transformation for DL workflows.

Data Processing Frameworks (2013-2017)

In addition to Apache-based solutions, several other data processing frameworks emerged from 2013 to 2017, significantly advancing the field of DL. These frameworks provided the necessary tools and libraries to build, train, and deploy complex DL models, revolutionizing the field. These include:

- **TensorFlow**: Introduced by Google in 2015, TensorFlow quickly became one of the most popular frameworks for DL. Its flexibility, scalability, and comprehensive ecosystem made it a go-to choice for researchers and practitioners. TensorFlow's ability to run on multiple platforms, including CPUs, GPUs, and TPUs, allowed for efficient model training and deployment. Its extensive support for various neural network architectures and a rich set of pre-trained models and APIs enabled developers to tackle a wide range of DL tasks. TensorFlow's vibrant community and robust documentation further contributed to its widespread adoption, making it a cornerstone in the DL landscape.

- **PyTorch**: Developed by Facebook's AI Research lab (FAIR) and released in 2016, PyTorch gained popularity for its dynamic computation graph, which made model building and debugging more intuitive. PyTorch's user-friendly interface and strong community support contributed to its rapid adoption in both academia and industry. Researchers and developers appreciated PyTorch's flexibility in experimentation, as its eager execution mode allowed for immediate feedback during model development. Additionally, PyTorch's interoperability with other libraries, such as NumPy and SciPy, facilitated seamless integration into existing data processing pipelines.

- **Keras**: Initially released in 2015, Keras is a high-level neural networks API that provides a simple and consistent interface for building and training DL models. Keras can run on top of other DL frameworks, such as TensorFlow and Theano, offering flexibility and ease of use. Its simplicity and readability made it an excellent choice for beginners and prototyping. Keras abstracted away the complexities of lower-level frameworks, allowing users to focus on designing and experimenting with neural network architectures. Keras significantly accelerated the development process by providing a wide array of pre-built layers and functions, enabling rapid prototyping and iteration.

- **Theano**: While Theano was first released in 2007, it remained a foundational DL library during this period. Developed by the Montreal Institute for Learning Algorithms (MILA) at the University of Montreal, Theano provided efficient numerical computation and symbolic differentiation, making it a valuable tool for researchers. Theano's ability to optimize and compile mathematical expressions for efficient execution on CPUs and GPUs paved the way for developing more sophisticated DL models. Despite its eventual deprecation, Theano's influence persisted by integrating with other frameworks like Keras.

These frameworks collectively contributed to the practical adoption and advancement of DL by providing powerful tools and libraries for building, training, and deploying complex neural networks.

Their contributions laid the groundwork for developing sophisticated DL models and applications, enabling breakthroughs in various domains such as computer vision, natural language processing, and reinforcement learning.

Interoperability in Data Processing and Deep Learning (2013-2017)

Interoperability is the ability of different systems, tools, and platforms to work together and exchange information seamlessly. From 2013 to 2017, the growing complexity of DL projects necessitated robust interoperability between various data processing tools, frameworks, and cloud platforms. Ensuring interoperability enables data scientists and engineers to build, train, and deploy DL models more efficiently and effectively.

Key aspects of interoperability include:

- **Seamless Integration of Tools**: Data processing tools like Pandas, NumPy, and Scikit-learn were designed to work well together, providing a cohesive ecosystem for data manipulation, numerical computation, and ML. Using these tools in combination allowed for streamlined workflows and efficient data processing. For example, data scientists could use Pandas for data cleaning and transformation, NumPy for numerical operations, and Scikit-learn for ML tasks, all within the same environment.

- **Interoperability with Deep Learning Frameworks**: DL frameworks like TensorFlow, PyTorch, and Keras were built to be compatible with existing data processing tools. This compatibility allowed data scientists to leverage each tool's strengths without switching between different environments. For instance, TensorFlow and Keras could directly accept NumPy arrays as input data, making it easy to transition from data preprocessing to model training.

- **Cross-Platform Compatibility**: The ability to run DL models on different platforms, including CPUs, GPUs, and TPUs, was essential for maximizing performance and efficiency. DL frameworks like TensorFlow and PyTorch support various hardware accelerators, enabling faster training and inference. Cloud platforms like AWS, GCP, and Azure offered scalable infrastructure that could be easily configured to run DL models on the most suitable hardware.

- **Data Storage and Access**: Interoperability also extended to data storage solutions. Cloud-based storage services like Amazon S3, Google Cloud Storage, and Azure Blob Storage provided APIs and connectors that allowed seamless integration with DL frameworks and data processing tools. This ensured data could be easily accessed, processed, and analyzed across different platforms and environments.

- **Standardized Data Formats**: Using standardized data formats, such as CSV, JSON, Parquet, and HDF5, facilitated interoperability between different tools and frameworks. These formats allowed data to be easily exchanged and shared, ensuring compatibility across various stages of the DL workflow. Standardized data formats also made collaborating and sharing data with others in the community easier.

- **Open-Source Collaboration**: The open-source nature of many data processing tools and DL frameworks fostered collaboration and innovation. Open-source projects often provided extensive documentation, tutorials, and community support, enabling users to integrate different tools and frameworks effectively. Contributions from the community also led to the development of libraries and extensions that enhanced interoperability.

- **APIs and Data Exchange Protocols**: Application Programming Interfaces (APIs) and integration tools enable different systems to interact and share data. APIs provide a standardized way for applications to access data and services, making building and deploying deep learning models easier across various platforms. Protocols like REST (Representational State Transfer) and gRPC (gRPC Remote Procedure Call) facilitate data exchange between different systems. These protocols ensure that data can be transferred efficiently and securely between disparate systems.

Benefits of Interoperability

Interoperability's benefits include efficiency, flexibility, scalability, and collaboration. It improves efficiency with seamless integration of tools and frameworks and reduces the time and effort required to preprocess data, train models, and deploy applications. It also provides flexibility by allowing data scientists to choose the best tools for each task, leading to more effective and customized workflows.

Interoperability offers cross-platform compatibility and cloud integration, enabling scalable and efficient processing, storage, and computation, essential for large-scale DL projects.

It also allows for collaboration with standardized data formats and open-source collaboration, facilitating sharing and collaboration among researchers, practitioners, and organizations.

Impact on Deep Learning

Interoperability played a crucial role in advancing the field of DL by enabling efficient and flexible workflows. Seamlessly integrating various tools, frameworks, and platforms allowed data scientists and engineers to focus on developing innovative DL models and applications without compatibility issues. This, in turn, contributed to the rapid development and practical adoption of DL techniques during this period.

In summary, interoperability was a key factor in the success of DL from 2013 to 2017. Data scientists and engineers could build, train, and deploy complex DL models more efficiently and effectively by ensuring that different tools, frameworks, and platforms could work together seamlessly.

Feature Engineering Platforms (2013-2017)

From 2013 to 2017, the rise of DL necessitated the development of robust feature engineering platforms. These platforms provided the tools and capabilities to create, transform, and manage features essential for training effective DL models. Feature engineering platforms played a critical role in enhancing the performance and accuracy of DL models by enabling the extraction of meaningful and relevant features from raw data.

Feature engineering is the process of creating and transforming features from raw data to improve the performance of ML models. In the context of DL, feature engineering involves identifying and extracting the most relevant features that contribute to model training and prediction. Effective feature engineering can significantly enhance the accuracy and efficiency of DL models.

Key Feature Engineering Platforms

Featuretools is an open-source library Alteryx (formerly Feature Labs) developed for automated feature engineering. Introduced in 2017, Featuretools allows data scientists to create meaningful features from raw data through automated processes. By leveraging deep feature synthesis, Featuretools can generate hundreds of features from multiple data tables, facilitating the discovery of valuable patterns and relationships in the data.

Turi, formerly known as GraphLab, offered a suite of tools for scalable ML and feature engineering. Turi's platform provided data exploration, feature transformation, and model building capabilities. Integrating Turi's tools with distributed computing frameworks enabled efficient processing of large datasets, making it a valuable resource for DL projects.

H2O.ai is an open-source platform for ML and feature engineering. H2O's automatic ML (AutoML) capabilities include automated feature engineering, simplifying the process of creating and selecting features. H2O's platform supports a wide range of ML algorithms and provides scalability for handling large datasets, making it suitable for DL applications.

DataRobot is a ML platform that offers automated feature engineering as part of its AutoML capabilities. DataRobot's platform provides tools for data preprocessing, feature creation, and model training. By automating the feature engineering process, DataRobot enables data scientists to focus on higher-level tasks and improve the efficiency of their DL workflows.

The advantages of feature engineering platforms include:

- **Automation:** Automated feature engineering platforms reduce the time and effort required to create and transform features, allowing data scientists to focus on higher-level tasks.

- **Scalability:** These platforms support processing large-scale datasets, making them suitable for DL applications that require extensive data manipulation and transformation.

- **Efficiency:** These platforms enhance the efficiency and accuracy of DL models by automating the feature engineering process, leading to better performance and predictive capabilities.

- **Integration:** Feature engineering platforms often integrate with popular DL frameworks and data processing tools, enabling seamless workflows and data management.

Impact on Deep Learning

The development of feature engineering platforms during this period played a crucial role in advancing the field of DL. By providing the tools and capabilities to create and transform meaningful features, these platforms enhanced the performance and accuracy of DL models. Automated feature engineering streamlined the data preparation process, enabling data scientists to build more effective DL models more efficiently.

In summary, feature engineering platforms were essential in the advancement of DL from 2013 to 2017. These platforms provided the necessary tools and capabilities to create and transform features, improving the performance and accuracy of DL models. The automation and scalability offered by these platforms significantly contributed to the practical adoption and development of DL techniques during this period.

ML Lifecycle Platforms (2013-2017)

From 2013 to 2017, the growing complexity of DL projects necessitated the development of comprehensive ML lifecycle platforms. These platforms provided end-to-end solutions for managing the various stages of the ML lifecycle, from data preparation to model deployment, ensuring efficiency, scalability, and reproducibility.

ML lifecycle platforms are integrated environments that support the entire ML workflow, including data ingestion, preprocessing, model training, evaluation, deployment, and monitoring. These platforms aim to streamline the ML process, reduce time-to-market, and ensure the reproducibility and scalability of ML projects.

Key ML Lifecycle Platforms

Sagemaker was Introduced by AWS in 2017. Amazon SageMaker is a fully managed service that covers the entire ML lifecycle. SageMaker provides tools for data labeling, data preprocessing, model training, hyperparameter tuning, model evaluation, and deployment. Its built-in algorithms and support for popular DL frameworks like TensorFlow, PyTorch, and MXNet enable seamless integration and efficient model development. SageMaker's modular architecture allows data scientists to pick and choose services based on their needs, making it a versatile platform for DL projects.

Google AI Platform (formerly Google Cloud Machine Learning Engine) offers a comprehensive suite of tools for developing, training, and deploying ML models. The platform integrates with Google Cloud's data storage and processing services, such as BigQuery, Cloud Storage, and Dataproc, enabling seamless data management. Google AI Platform supports TensorFlow and other popular ML frameworks, providing scalable infrastructure for training and serving DL models. The platform's managed services simplify the deployment and monitoring of models in production.

Microsoft Azure Machine Learning (Azure ML) is a cloud-based platform that provides end-to-end support for the ML lifecycle. Azure ML offers tools for data preparation, experimentation, model training, and deployment. The platform's integration with other Azure services, such as Azure Blob Storage and Azure Databricks, facilitates seamless data processing and management. Azure ML's support for popular DL frameworks, such as TensorFlow, PyTorch, and Keras, enables efficient model development and deployment.

IBM Watson Studio is an integrated environment for data scientists, developers, and analysts to collaboratively build and deploy ML models. Watson Studio offers tools for data preparation, model training, and deployment, along with support for popular ML and DL frameworks. The platform's integration with IBM Cloud services provides scalable infrastructure for managing and processing large datasets. Watson Studio's collaborative features, such as notebooks and dashboards, enhance teamwork and productivity in DL projects.

H2O.ai Driverless AI is an automated ML platform that simplifies the ML lifecycle through automated feature engineering, model training, and hyperparameter tuning. The platform provides tools for data preprocessing, model evaluation, and deployment, enabling efficient development of

DL models. Driverless AI's support for various ML algorithms and integration with popular DL frameworks make it a valuable resource for data scientists working on DL projects.

The advantages of ML lifecycle platforms include:

- **End-to-End Support:** These platforms provide comprehensive tools for managing the entire ML lifecycle, from data preparation to model deployment and monitoring.
- **Scalability:** Cloud-based infrastructure ensures that ML projects can scale to handle large datasets and complex models, which is essential for DL applications.
- **Reproducibility:** Integrated environments and version control features ensure that ML experiments can be reproduced and tracked, enhancing the reliability of DL projects.
- **Efficiency:** Automated tools for data preprocessing, feature engineering, model training, and hyperparameter tuning reduce the time and effort required for DL model development.
- **Integration:** Seamless integration with data storage, processing, and analytics services enables efficient data management and workflow orchestration.

Impact on Deep Learning

ML lifecycle platforms were crucial in advancing DL by providing end-to-end solutions for managing complex DL projects. These platforms streamlined the ML process, reduced time-to-market, and ensured the scalability and reproducibility of DL models. By offering comprehensive tools and scalable infrastructure, ML lifecycle platforms empowered data scientists and engineers to focus on developing innovative DL applications without being hindered by operational complexities.

In summary, the period from 2013 to 2017 saw the rise of ML lifecycle platforms that significantly contributed to the practical adoption and advancement of DL. These platforms provided end-to-end support for the ML lifecycle, enabling efficient, scalable, and reproducible DL workflows. The next chapter will cover exciting new AI technologies that are revolutionizing how everyday people interact with AI, ChatGPT, and Large Language Models.

## CHAPTER 5

ChatGPT and Large Language Models

The evolution of Large Language Models (LLMs) has transformed AI, enabling highly sophisticated and human-like interactions. While AI research and deep learning have been evolving for decades, the real breakthrough in conversational AI emerged post-2017 with the advent of transformer-based models like BERT, GPT-2, and GPT-3. Among these, OpenAI's ChatGPT has significantly reshaped how businesses and individuals interact with AI. This chapter explores the development of LLMs, their real-world applications, technical underpinnings, customization techniques, and their competitive landscape while addressing the challenges and future trends in conversational AI. The next chapter covers data as the lifeblood of Generative AI and the text data and technology needed to support LLMs.

The Evolution of Large Language Models (Post-2017)

The Transition from DL to NLP Breakthroughs

Deep learning advancements in **2017** set the stage for NLP dominance. The introduction of Transformer **architecture** (Vaswani et al., 2017) revolutionized AI by allowing models to process entire sentences in parallel, leading to a series of groundbreaking LLMs.

In this section, we run through timelines for foundational models and advancements in LLMs. This is visually represented in Figure 14.

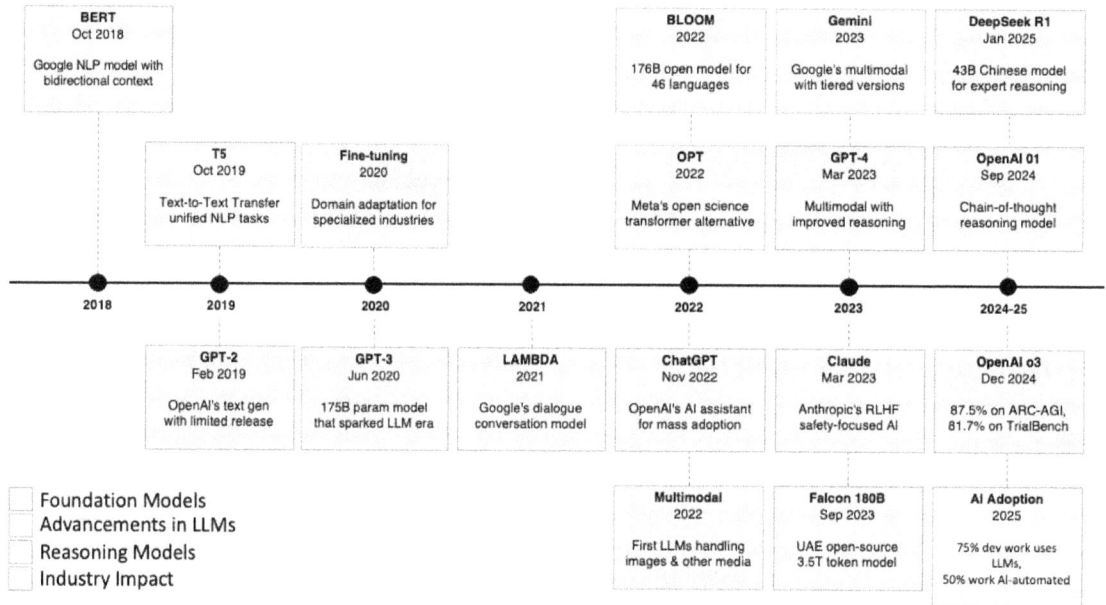

BERT
Oct 2018

Google NLP model with bidirectional context

BLOOM
2022

176B open model for 46 languages

Gemini
2023

Google's multimodal with tiered versions

DeepSeek R1
Jan 2025

43B Chinese model for expert reasoning

T5
Oct 2019

Text-to-Text Transfer unified NLP tasks

Fine-tuning
2020

Domain adaptation for specialized industries

OPT
2022

Meta's open science transformer alternative

GPT-4
Mar 2023

Multimodal with improved reasoning

OpenAI o1
Sep 2024

Chain-of-thought reasoning model

2018 2019 2020 2021 2022 2023 2024-25

GPT-2
Feb 2019

OpenAI's text gen with limited release

GPT-3
Jun 2020

175B param model that sparked LLM era

LAMBDA
2021

Google's dialogue conversation model

ChatGPT
Nov 2022

OpenAI's AI assistant for mass adoption

Claude
Mar 2023

Anthropic's RLHF safety-focused AI

OpenAI o3
Dec 2024

87.5% on ARC-AGI, 81.7% on TrialBench

Foundation Models
Advancements in LLMs
Reasoning Models
Industry Impact

Multimodal
2022

First LLMs handling images & other media

Falcon 180B
Sep 2023

UAE open-source 3.5T token model

AI Adoption
2025

75% dev work uses LLMs, 50% work AI-automated

Figure 14: Timelines for Foundational Models and Advancements in LLMs.

The first major breakthrough in this new era came with **BERT (2018)**, developed by Google. BERT (Bidirectional Encoder Representations from Transformers) introduced a fundamentally different way for AI to understand language. Unlike previous models that processed text sequentially or unidirectionally, BERT enabled bidirectional learning, meaning it could consider both preceding and succeeding words in a sentence simultaneously. This made BERT significantly more adept at comprehending contextual relationships within text, leading to substantial improvements in search engines, sentiment analysis, and other NLP applications. Its deep contextual understanding made it an essential tool for enterprises looking to enhance their AI-driven customer interactions and search functionalities. [11]

---

[11] Google AI Blog, "BERT: Pre-training of Deep Bidirectional Transformers for Language Understanding," 2018. [Online]. Available: https://ai.googleblog.com/2018/11/open-sourcing-bert-state-of-art-pre.html.

Following BERT, **GPT-2 (2019)** marked a new milestone in generative AI. Developed by OpenAI, GPT-2 showcased the power of unsupervised learning and generative capabilities. Unlike earlier models that relied heavily on labeled datasets, GPT-2 demonstrated that a model trained on vast amounts of unstructured internet text could generate remarkably coherent and contextually relevant responses. It could compose human-like text, write stories, and even mimic different writing styles with minimal prompting. However, its release was controversial, as OpenAI initially withheld the full model due to concerns over potential misuse, highlighting the growing ethical concerns around powerful LLMs.

In **2020**, OpenAI unveiled **GPT-3**, a model that set a new gold standard in AI-powered text generation. With an astounding 175 billion parameters, GPT-3 was exponentially larger and more powerful than its predecessors. This model was not just an improvement in scale—it brought a qualitative leap in AI's ability to engage in free-flowing, near-human conversations. It enabled ChatGPT's first practical applications, providing businesses, developers, and content creators with an unprecedented tool for automating text-based tasks. GPT-3's versatility extended beyond chatbot functionalities, being used for content creation, programming assistance, tutoring, and even creative writing, marking the beginning of mainstream adoption of AI-driven conversational agents.

By **2022**, OpenAI released ChatGPT, a fine-tuned version of GPT-3 designed explicitly for conversational AI. ChatGPT became the first widely adopted LLM chatbot, setting off the AI boom and making generative AI accessible to everyday users. Unlike previous models, ChatGPT could maintain context over extended interactions, adapt to different conversational styles, and provide highly personalized responses. Businesses rapidly integrated it into customer service, virtual assistants, and workflow automation, drastically reducing response times and improving user engagement.

The same year, **Anthropic** released **Claude**, an AI assistant developed using a novel technique called Constitutional AI. Released in March 2023, Claude demonstrated proficiency in tasks like summarization, search, creative writing, and coding. What set Claude apart was its focus on being helpful, harmless, and honest, with users reporting it was less likely to produce harmful outputs and easier to converse with than other AI models. Claude showed particular strength in understanding user intentions and requests but had some limitations in coding, math, and reasoning capabilities.[12]

Google entered the advanced LLM space with the release of **Gemini (December 2023)**, their most capable and general AI model. Gemini was designed to be natively multimodal, processing text, images, audio, video, and code simultaneously. The model was released in three sizes: Ultra for highly complex tasks, Pro for a wide range of tasks, and Nano for on-device applications. Gemini Ultra made headlines by becoming the first model to outperform human experts on the MMLU benchmark, which tests knowledge across 57 subjects, including math, physics, history, law, medicine, and ethics.[13]

2023 also saw the Technology Innovation Institute (TII) release **Falcon 180B,** a significant advancement in open-source LLMs. With 180 billion parameters trained on 3.5 trillion tokens, Falcon 180B quickly rose to the top of the Hugging Face leaderboard for pre-trained open-access models. It demonstrated state-of-the-art results across various natural language tasks, outperforming Meta's Llama 2 and OpenAI's GPT-3.5, while rivaling Google's PaLM-2. Unlike many proprietary models, Falcon 180B was made available for both research and commercial use, though under specific licensing conditions.[14]

GPT-4 (2023) has pushed the boundaries even further. Unlike its predecessors, GPT-4 incorporates **multimodal capabilities**, meaning it can process not just text but also images and other data types. It exhibits improved reasoning abilities, enhanced factual accuracy, and a broader understanding of complex queries. Additionally, GPT-4 has been optimized for efficiency, reducing computational costs while improving performance.

Beyond GPT-4, OpenAI introduced several enhancements that extend the capabilities of AI. One such innovation is **DALLE-3**, an advanced AI-powered image generation model that enables users to create high-resolution, detailed images based on text prompts. This represents a significant leap in generative AI, making it easier than ever to generate visually compelling artwork, concept

---

[12] https://en.wikipedia.org/wiki/Claude_(language_model).

[13] https://en.wikipedia.org/wiki/Gemini_(language_model).

[14] https://mlarchive.com/deep-learning/falcon-180b/.

illustrations, and photorealistic imagery. Furthermore, OpenAI has expanded its suite of tools with video-generation models, allowing users to create short AI-generated video sequences by providing simple descriptions, bridging the gap between text-to-image and full multimedia generation.

Alongside these improvements, OpenAI introduced **GPT-4-turbo**, a more cost-effective, faster, and optimized version of GPT-4, providing users with reduced latency and improved processing efficiency. Additionally, OpenAI released **GPT-01, GPT-01-Mini**, and other scaled-down models, making LLMs more accessible for lightweight applications. These models are designed to balance computational efficiency with accuracy, allowing developers and businesses to integrate AI into embedded systems, mobile applications, and real-time decision-making environments.

Each of these advancements had various impacts and repercussions. These advancements collectively push AI beyond simple text-based interactions into a new era of multimodal, autonomous AI ecosystems, where users can generate not just text, but also graphs, pictures, videos, and interactive visual content. These tools open up immense possibilities in education, content creation, digital marketing, and personalized AI-driven experiences, paving the way for the next generation of AI-integrated platforms and services.

Real-world applications of ChatGPT and LLMs include:

- **Customer Support and Virtual Assistants**: The advent of LLMs has revolutionized customer support, enabling businesses to provide instant, efficient, and scalable virtual assistance. ChatGPT-powered chatbots are now integrated into help desks, handling customer inquiries, complaint resolution, and troubleshooting with near-human accuracy. Unlike traditional scripted chatbots that follow rigid workflows, ChatGPT-based assistants can adapt dynamically to user queries, understand nuanced language, identify sentiment, and personalize responses based on previous interactions. Companies like Microsoft, Salesforce, and Zendesk leverage LLMs to automate and enhance customer experiences, reducing response times and ensuring 24/7 availability.

- **Content Generation and Marketing Automation**: LLMs are transforming content creation by producing high-quality, contextually relevant, and audience-specific materials at an unprecedented scale. Businesses now use AI-powered tools to generate blog articles, marketing copy, social media content, and product descriptions, significantly reducing the time and effort required for manual content development. ChatGPT and other LLMs can analyze brand tone, adjust writing style, and even optimize content for SEO, making them invaluable for marketing teams. AI-driven personalization engines can dynamically tailor email campaigns and ad copy based on customer behavior, enhancing engagement and conversion rates.

- **Code Assistance and Software Development**: In the domain of software engineering, LLMs serve as intelligent coding assistants, improving development efficiency, reducing errors, and accelerating debugging processes. Tools like **GitHub Copilot and Tabnine**, powered by OpenAI's GPT models, suggest code snippets, complete functions, and even provide inline documentation,[15] making them indispensable for developers. These models can analyze vast repositories of open-source and proprietary code, enabling automated code reviews, security vulnerability detection, and real-time error correction. By integrating AI-assisted programming tools, enterprises can significantly enhance software development lifecycles while mitigating common coding inefficiencies.

- **Healthcare and Legal Research**: LLMs are proving to be powerful tools in the fields of medicine and law, where the ability to process large volumes of text-based information is critical. In healthcare, AI models assist in summarizing research papers, analyzing patient data, and generating diagnostic insights. Hospitals and pharmaceutical companies leverage LLMs for clinical documentation automation, drug discovery, and personalized treatment recommendations. Meanwhile, in the legal sector, ChatGPT-driven platforms help attorneys and researchers sift through legal documents, extract precedents, and automate contract analysis, reducing manual workload and improving decision-making accuracy. These applications are particularly valuable for professionals handling time-sensitive and complex information retrieval tasks.

---

[15] OpenAI, "GPT-3 and GPT-4 Documentation," 2023. [Online]. Available: https://openai.com/research.

Data Flow in Conversational AI: A Deep Dive

The following diagram represents the sequential flow of how conversational AI models process inputs, tokenize text, generate responses, and improve through feedback loops. It illustrates the stages from user input to AI model processing and response generation.

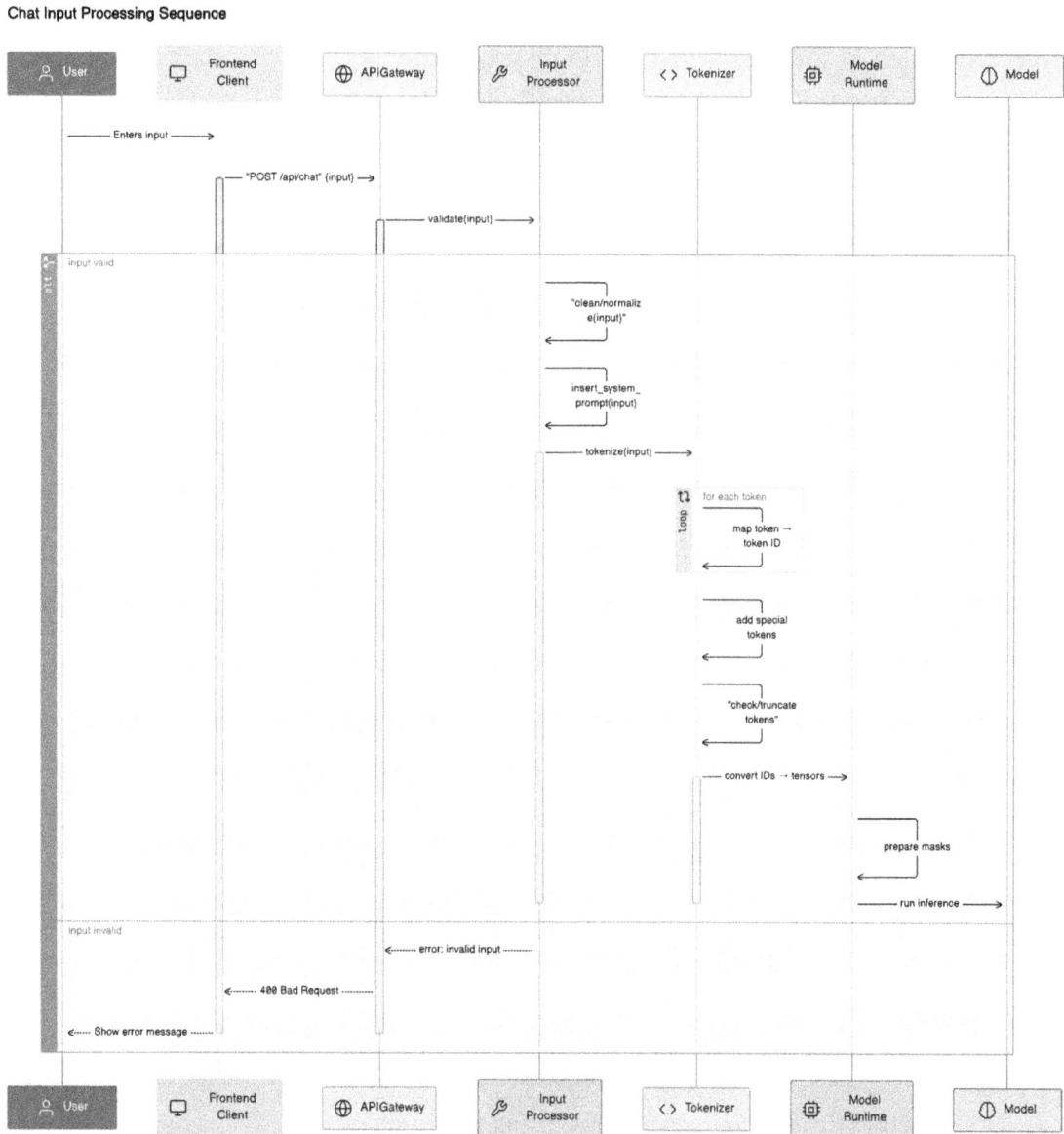

Figure 15: Data Flow in Conversational AI: A Deep Dive.

Figure 15 illustrates the data flow for a conversational AI system, detailing the sequence of steps involved in processing a user's query. It begins with the API Request, where the input is received, followed by Preprocessing and Tokenization, which prepare and structure the data for processing. Next, key stages like Embedding and Model Inference transform the input into meaningful representations, enabling the system to generate a response. Beam Search and Sampling help create coherent and relevant outputs, which are then polished in post-processing before the user receives the API Response. Elements such as Cloud Orchestration and Deployment ensure the system operates efficiently and reliably, supporting the entire workflow. This pipeline reflects the interplay of multiple sophisticated processes working seamlessly to deliver conversational intelligence.

How ChatGPT Processes and Generates Text

The conversational AI pipeline follows a structured sequence to transform user input into coherent, context-aware responses. This journey begins when a user submits a query and continues through tokenization, processing, generation, and feedback integration. Understanding this process in detail provides insights into the inner workings of ChatGPT and similar language models.

- **User Input**: Users interact with ChatGPT through various input methods, including text, voice, and multimodal inputs. When a voice query is received, it is first converted into text using Automatic Speech Recognition (ASR). Similarly, multimodal interactions, such as images paired with text, require specialized processing before being passed into the model. Before the text is fed into the AI, it undergoes preprocessing to ensure uniformity and coherence. This involves removing special characters, correcting typos, and expanding abbreviations, making it easier for the model to interpret the content. ChatGPT retains contextual memory for multi-turn conversations, allowing the model to reference previous messages and provide responses that maintain continuity and logical flow.

- **Tokenization**: Tokenization breaks down user input into manageable subunits that the AI can process efficiently. Two common methods include **Byte-Pair Encoding (BPE)**, which decomposes words into frequently occurring subword units (e.g., "unhappiness" becomes "un" and "happiness"), and **WordPiece**, which prioritizes the most frequent subword combinations, optimizing efficiency. Each token corresponds to a unique identifier in a predefined vocabulary, with special tokens designed to handle punctuation, emojis, or language-specific characters. Despite its advantages, tokenization presents challenges, such as ambiguity in splitting phrases (e.g., "New York" versus "newyork") and managing rare or complex words, particularly in multilingual inputs.

- **Processing**: The backbone of ChatGPT lies in its **Transformer Architecture**, which leverages self-attention mechanisms to analyze the relationships between words in a sentence. This enables the model to understand contextual meaning dynamically. Through **positional encoding**, the system preserves the order of words, ensuring coherent sentence structure. The model consists of multiple layers—GPT-4, for instance, utilizes over 120 layers—each refining the representation of text. When processing a query, the model assigns probability distributions to possible next words, iterating through layers until an optimal output is determined. This inference process continues until a stopping condition, such as a maximum token limit or an end-of-sequence token, is met.

- **Generation**: Several techniques govern how ChatGPT selects words during response generation. **Greedy Search** picks the most probable token at each step, leading to rapid but sometimes repetitive responses. **Beam Search**, on the other hand, maintains multiple candidate sequences, enhancing response quality and diversity. **Top-k Sampling** introduces randomness by selecting from the top-k most likely tokens, fostering creative outputs. Meanwhile, **Temperature Control** dictates response variation, where lower values yield more deterministic results, while higher values introduce greater diversity. Once generated, responses undergo post-processing to filter inappropriate content, improve readability, and, when relevant, incorporate additional formatting such as bullet points or links.

- **User Feedback**: ChatGPT continually refines its performance through **Feedback Loops**. Implicit signals, such as dwell time and user engagement, inform ongoing improvements, while explicit ratings and corrections provide structured insights into response quality. OpenAI utilizes **Reinforcement Learning from Human Feedback (RLHF)** to further align AI-generated content with human expectations. Annotators rank model outputs, helping to fine-tune the reward system guiding the AI's responses. These refinements are incorporated into periodic retraining cycles, ensuring the model remains adaptive and responsive to evolving user needs.

APIs and Real-Time Processing in AI Chatbots

Integration via APIs: ChatGPT is seamlessly integrated into various applications through APIs, which facilitate communication between the model and external systems. OpenAI's API utilizes **RESTful endpoints**, transmitting requests in JSON format over HTTPS. For instance, a Python-based query can be executed using OpenAI's SDK:

```
import openai
response = openai.ChatCompletion.create(
model="gpt-4",
messages=[{"role": "user", "content": "Explain quantum computing."}]
)
```

These APIs come with built-in rate limits to prevent overuse and maintain server stability, typically restricting requests per minute based on user tier. Figure 16 illustrates a cloud-based chatbot infrastructure, showcasing components like API requests, data processing layers, and real-time interaction elements, such as AWS Lambda, Apache Kafka, or Edge AI capabilities.

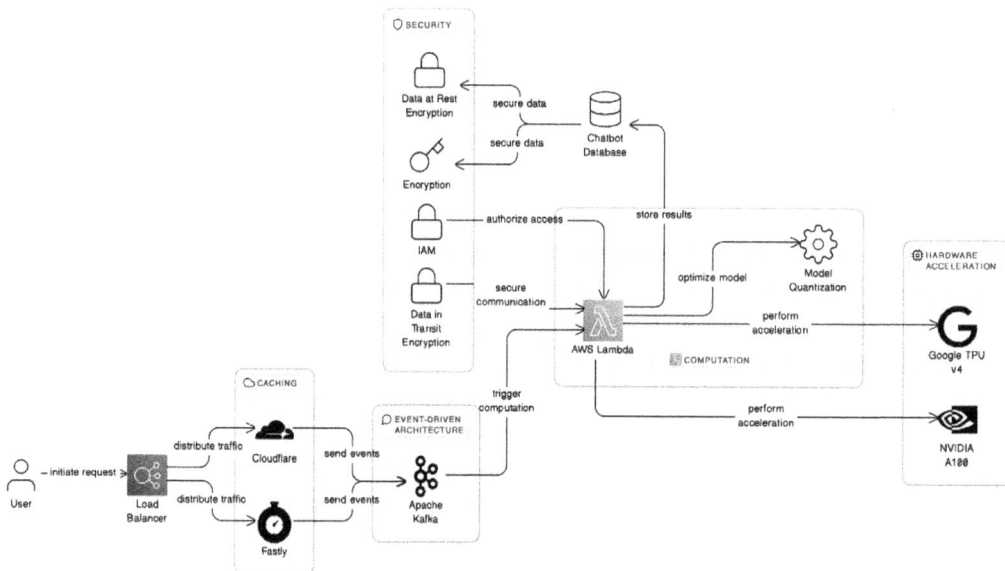

Figure 16: Real-Time AWS Chatbot Architecture.

Real-Time Infrastructure: Modern chatbots require robust infrastructure to support real-time interactions. This is achieved through event-driven architectures such as **Apache Kafka®**, which facilitates message queueing for large-scale deployments, and **AWS Lambda®**, which triggers on-demand computations without maintaining persistent server instances. To optimize response times, frequently requested queries like FAQs are cached at edge locations via networks like **Cloudflare** or **Fastly**, significantly reducing latency. Additional optimizations include **model quantization**, which compresses neural networks for faster processing, and **hardware acceleration**, leveraging **GPUs (e.g., NVIDIA A100)** and **TPUs (e.g., Google v4)** to enhance parallel computing performance. This architecture is illustrated in Figure 17.

The Role of Cloud Computing in Scaling LLMs

Training Infrastructure: Training large-scale models like ChatGPT requires immense computational power, facilitated by distributed training frameworks. **TensorFlow** and **PyTorch** orchestrate workloads across thousands of GPUs, implementing **data parallelism**, where multiple copies of a model process different subsets of data in parallel, and **model parallelism**, which distributes segments of a single model across multiple devices for enhanced efficiency. Cloud providers like AWS and Google Cloud offer spot instances and preemptible VMs to mitigate costs, reducing expenses by leveraging excess compute capacity.

Figure 17 illustrates how cloud computing enables the large-scale training and deployment of LLMs. It shows distributed GPU clusters, TensorFlow/PyTorch frameworks, and data pipelines that support AI scalability.

- **Deployment at Scale**: Once trained, models must be efficiently deployed to handle user interactions. Cloud services such as **AWS SageMaker** and **Google Vertex AI** facilitate scalable hosting and version management. Meanwhile, **Kubernetes** orchestrates containerized deployments, ensuring load balancing and automatic failover. By leveraging **autoscaling mechanisms**, inference workloads dynamically adjust based on demand, minimizing operational costs while ensuring high availability.

- **Hybrid Architectures**: For industries requiring stringent data controls, hybrid architectures integrate on-premises GPU clusters with cloud-based inference pipelines. This ensures compliance with regulations governing data residency, such as GDPR in Europe or HIPAA in healthcare. Furthermore, Edge AI solutions deploy lighter versions of models, such as GPT-4-Turbo, on local devices, enabling low-latency processing without persistent internet connectivity.

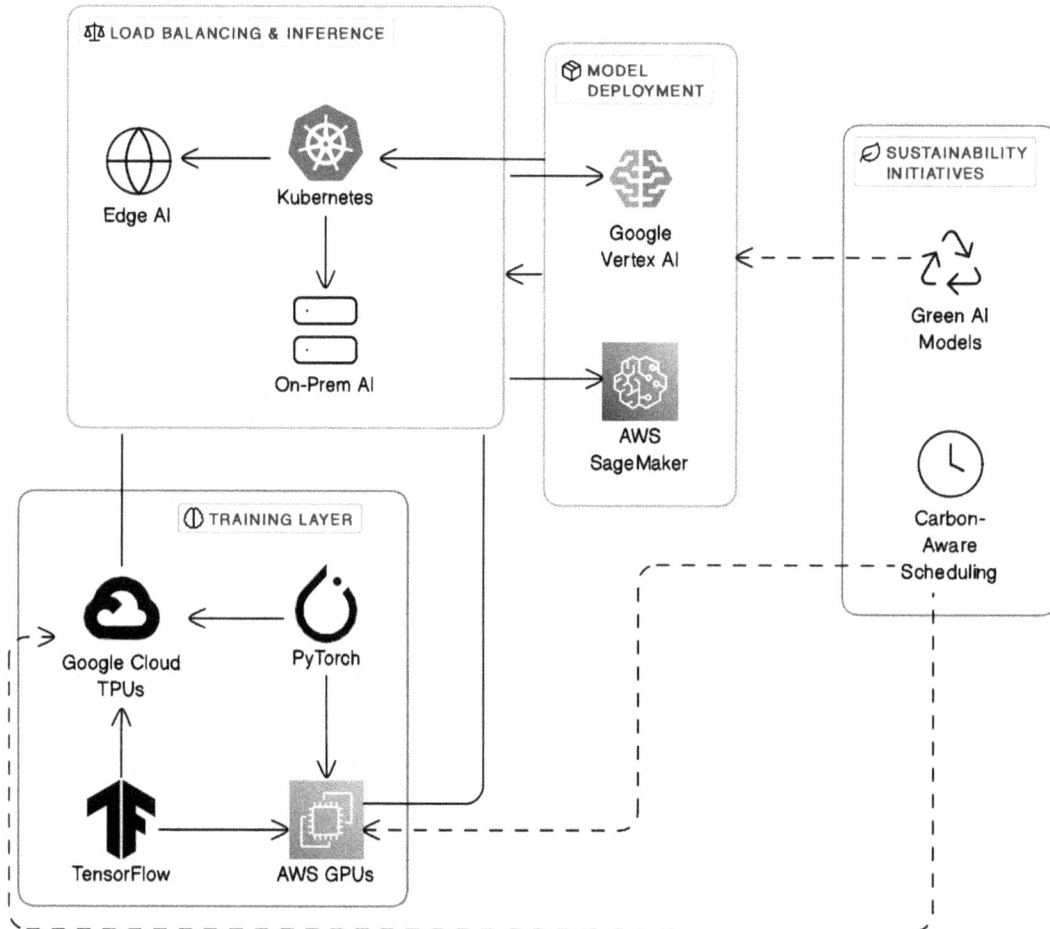

Figure 17: Cloud-Based Infrastructure for Scaling Large Language Models (LLMs).

The following diagram illustrates a hybrid AI deployment model, where AI workloads are distributed across on-premises hardware and cloud-based inference pipelines. It highlights data residency compliance (e.g., GDPR, HIPAA), Edge AI capabilities, and hybrid cloud infrastructure.

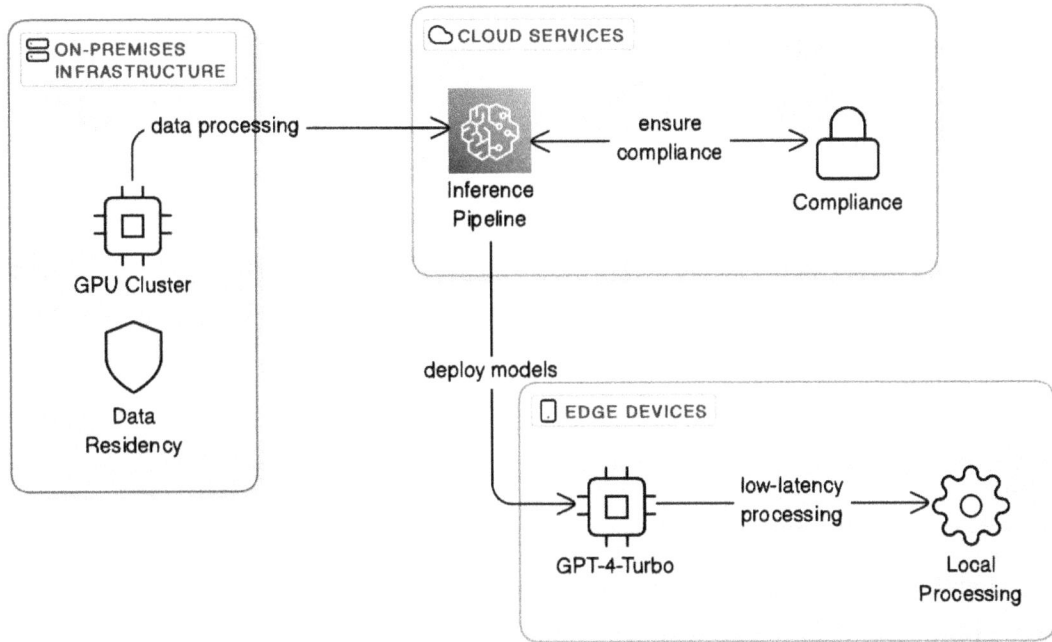

Figure 18: Hybrid AI Architecture for On-Premises and Cloud-Based Model Deployment.

Sustainability Challenges: Given the escalating energy demands of AI, cloud providers are increasingly investing in sustainable solutions. **Google's TPU v5e** is engineered for higher energy efficiency, consuming half the power of its predecessors while maintaining peak performance. Additionally, **carbon-aware scheduling** dynamically allocates training workloads to regions with surplus renewable energy, reducing the environmental impact of large-scale AI training operations.

Section Summary

ChatGPT's data processing pipeline harmonizes efficiency with contextual awareness, ensuring responsive and accurate AI-generated interactions. APIs and cloud infrastructure play a pivotal role in enabling enterprise-grade scalability, while feedback loops guarantee continuous refinement. As AI continues to evolve, future enhancements will focus on optimizing computational efficiency, integrating multimodal capabilities, and expanding real-time interactive functionalities, paving the way for a new generation of AI-driven applications.

Fine-Tuning and Customization of LLMs

General-purpose LLMs are powerful but often require fine-tuning to meet the specific needs of various industries such as **healthcare, finance,** and **legal** sectors. Customization ensures that models not only understand domain-specific terminology, but also align with compliance regulations, ethical considerations, and business objectives. For example, in healthcare, an AI model needs to comprehend medical jargon, while in finance, it must interpret regulatory frameworks and market trends. Custom AI solutions enable businesses to optimize performance while maintaining the highest standards of accuracy and relevance. Figure 19 presents various fine-tuning approaches, such as:

- **Supervised Fine-Tuning** (training on labeled datasets)
- **Reinforcement Learning from Human Feedback** (RLHF)
- **LoRA** (Low-Rank Adaptation) for parameter-efficient fine-tuning
- **Prompt Engineering** and **Few-Shot Learning.**

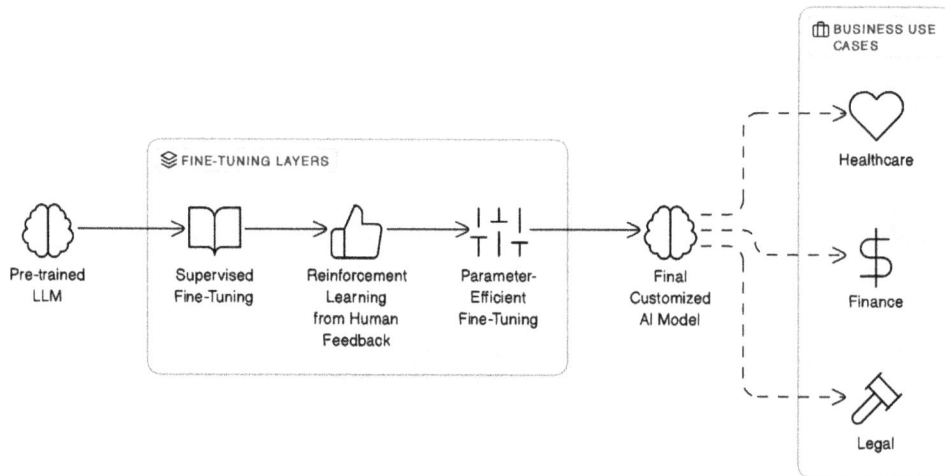

Figure 19: Techniques for Fine-Tuning Large Language Models (LLMs).

- **Supervised Fine-Tuning:** Supervised fine-tuning involves training a pre-trained model on a labeled dataset, ensuring it aligns with specific use cases. This process involves curating domain-specific datasets and feeding them into the model, allowing it to learn **contextual accuracy, industry terminology,** and **business rules.** For instance, a legal AI model can be fine-tuned with contract documents and case law to improve legal reasoning.

- **Reinforcement Learning from Human Feedback (RLHF)**: Reinforcement Learning from Human Feedback (RLHF) enhances model performance by incorporating human preferences. The process involves human annotators ranking different AI responses, helping the model refine its decision-making process. By leveraging human-in-the-loop methodologies, RLHF ensures that AI-generated content aligns with ethical standards, reduces bias, and enhances user satisfaction.

- **Parameter-Efficient Fine-Tuning**: Parameter-efficient fine-tuning techniques, such as LoRA (Low-Rank Adaptation), allow businesses to customize AI models without requiring extensive computational resources. LoRA works by freezing most of the model's weights while introducing trainable layers that adapt pre-trained models to new tasks with minimal resource consumption. This technique is particularly useful for organizations that require frequent updates but aim to reduce computational costs and optimize energy efficiency.

Infrastructure Required for Customization

- **Distributed Computing Frameworks**: Fine-tuning large-scale AI models requires robust infrastructure, including TensorFlow and PyTorch, which support distributed training across multiple GPUs and TPUs. These frameworks facilitate parallel processing, reducing training time and improving scalability. Additionally, tools like Kubeflow and MLflow provide automated workflows for managing ML pipelines, ensuring seamless integration with cloud-based and on-premises environments.

- **Hybrid and On-Premises Deployments**: Certain industries, particularly those handling **sensitive** or **confidential data**, require AI deployments that prioritize security and compliance. Hybrid architectures enable companies to combine **cloud scalability** with **on-premises data control**, ensuring regulatory adherence while benefiting from cloud-powered AI acceleration. This approach is particularly prevalent in **finance, government, and healthcare sectors**, where stringent data protection laws require AI solutions to operate within secure environments.

Fine-tuning and customizing LLMs are critical steps in developing **domain-specific, high-performance AI models**. Businesses can ensure that AI solutions meet their unique needs by leveraging techniques like supervised fine-tuning, RLHF, and parameter-efficient customization. Furthermore, **the right infrastructure, including distributed computing frameworks and hybrid deployments, plays a vital role in optimizing AI performance while maintaining data security and compliance**. As AI adoption continues to expand, fine-tuning will remain a key enabler of **industry-specific, reliable, and ethical AI solutions**.

Competitors of ChatGPT and their LLMs include:

- **Google Bard (LaMDA and Gemini)**: Google has developed two powerful language models: **LaMDA** and **Gemini**.
- **LaMDA (Language Model for Dialogue Applications)**: LaMDA is optimized specifically for **conversational AI** and designed to improve contextual retention and generate more natural, engaging responses. Unlike traditional models that struggle with prolonged dialogues, LaMDA leverages advanced neural architectures to maintain context, ensuring better conversational continuity. It enhances Google's AI-driven products, such as Google Assistant and AI-powered search features. **Availability:** Free for basic use, premium features available via subscription.
- **Gemini**: Gemini is Google's next-generation multimodal AI, integrating capabilities in text, image, and video understanding. Unlike text-only models, Gemini processes and generates content across different media formats, making it ideal for dynamic AI applications. This positions Gemini as a direct competitor to OpenAI's **GPT-4 Turbo**, enabling businesses and developers to create immersive AI-driven experiences beyond just textual interactions. **Availability:** Free-tier version available; advanced versions require a Google subscription.
- **OpenAI's GPT-4 Turbo: GPT-4 Turbo**: OpenAI's latest iteration offers a more efficient and cost-effective alternative to GPT-4. It powers **ChatGPT Plus** and features faster response times and lower computational costs than previous models. **Availability:** Free for limited use, with a ChatGPT Plus subscription ($20/month) required for enhanced performance and premium features.

CHATGPT AND LARGE LANGUAGE MODELS • 83

- **Anthropic's Claude AI (Claude 1, 2, and 3)**: Claude AI, developed by **Anthropic**, strongly emphasizes AI alignment and safety. Claude models prioritize user-friendly conversational abilities while minimizing harmful outputs. The latest iteration, **Claude 3**, improves contextual reasoning and long-form understanding. **Availability:** Free tier available, with premium options for enterprise users.

- **Alibaba's Tongyi Qianwen**: Alibaba's **Tongyi Qianwen** is a China-focused LLM specializing in business intelligence, e-commerce automation, and multilingual NLP. Unlike Western-developed models, Tongyi Qianwen is deeply integrated with **Alibaba Cloud services**, allowing enterprises to leverage cloud-powered AI solutions seamlessly. Its ability to process vast amounts of business data, optimize supply chain operations, and enhance customer interactions gives it a strategic edge in the rapidly growing e-commerce sector. **Availability:** Subscription-based via Alibaba Cloud.

- **DeepSync's Neural Conversational Models**: DeepSync has emerged as a leader in next-generation **memory-augmented learning**, a field that goes beyond standard LLM capabilities. Unlike traditional models that generate responses based solely on immediate context, DeepSync incorporates long-term memory retention, making it highly effective for customer relationship management (CRM), healthcare assistance, and personalized AI interactions. This approach enables AI to remember user preferences, past conversations, and dynamic behavioral patterns, resulting in a much more tailored and human-like interaction experience. **Availability:** Enterprise licensing required.

- **Meta's LLaMA (Large Language Model Meta AI)**: Meta's **LLaMA** is an open-source LLM that prioritizes efficiency, accessibility, and decentralized AI applications. Unlike other models that rely heavily on cloud-based processing, LLaMA is designed to be deployable on edge devices, such as smartphones, IoT devices, and local servers. This makes it an attractive option for developers and organizations looking for privacy-centric AI solutions, reducing reliance on centralized cloud infrastructure. By offering an open-source ecosystem, Meta enables research communities and businesses to fine-tune LLaMA for specific use cases without the constraints of proprietary licensing. **Availability:** Free and open-source for developers.

- **Mistral AI**: Mistral AI focuses on lightweight and efficient open-source models, optimized for both enterprise and developer communities. It offers models that rival GPT-level performance with fewer computational requirements, making it ideal for low-latency AI applications. **Availability:** Open-source with commercial licenses for enterprise users.

- **Cohere's Command R+ Model**: Cohere has built a specialized **Retrieval-Augmented Generation (RAG)** model designed for knowledge-based enterprise applications. Command R+ enhances information retrieval and knowledge synthesis, making it ideal for use in research-intensive industries and documentation automation. **Availability:** Requires subscription or enterprise licensing.

Feature	Google Bard (LaMDA/Gemini)	OpenAI GPT-4 Turbo	Anthropic Claude 3	Alibaba Tongyi Qianwen	DeepSync Neural Conversational Models	Meta LLaMA	Mistral AI	Cohere Command R+
Developer	Google	OpenAI	Anthropic	Alibaba Cloud	DeepSync	Meta	Mistral AI	Cohere
Model Type	Large Language Model	Large Language Model	Large Language Model	Business-Focused LLM	Memory-Augmented Conversational Model	Open-Source LLM	Lightweight Open-Source LLM	Retrieval-Augmented Generation (RAG) Model
Release Date	2023 (LaMDA), 2024 (Gemini)	2023	2024	2024	2024	2023	2024	2024
Performance	Strong contextual retention, multimodal	Versatile, strong multi-domain capabilities	Emphasizes safety, long-form under-standing	Excels in business automation and e-commerce	Long-term memory retention, personalized AI	Efficient, deployable on edge devices	Optimized for lightweight AI applications	Strong in research and knowledge retrieval
Efficiency	High, optimized for Google ecosystem	Requires significant computational power	Designed for AI alignment and safety	Cloud-based optimization	Memory-efficient for dynamic conversations	Edge deploy ability enhances efficiency	Low-latency model execution	Retrieval-enhanced for rapid document search
Cost	Free-tier; premium versions available	Free basic use; ChatGPT Plus ($20/month)	Free-tier; premium options for enterprise	Subscription-based via Alibaba Cloud	Enterprise licensing required	Free and open-source	Open-source with commercial licenses	Subscription or enterprise licensing required
Deployment	Integrated into Google Search, Assistant, and AI services	Used across multiple industries	Safety-focused AI applications	Business intelligence, finance, e-commerce	CRM, healthcare, and long-term personalized AI	Research, edge AI, and decentralized applications	Low-cost AI deployment	Enterprise-level research automation
Governance and Transpar-ency	Proprietary, closed-source	Proprietary, limited transparency	AI-alignment focused, safety measures	Regulatory compliance for Chinese market	Focus on ethical AI with memory persistence	Fully open-source	Open-source, community-driven	Proprietary, optimized for enterprise

Table 1: Comparison of Major LLMs.

The competition in the LLM space is rapidly evolving, with each model offering unique strengths tailored to different applications. **Google Bard's LaMDA and Gemini** focus on conversational retention and multimodal capabilities, while **OpenAI's GPT-4 Turbo** leads in general-purpose AI. **Anthropic's Claude AI** emphasizes AI alignment and safety, whereas **Alibaba's Tongyi Qianwen** dominates business intelligence and e-commerce applications. **DeepSync's memory-augmented models** revolutionize long-term AI interactions, and **Meta's LLaMA** provides a decentralized, open-source alternative. **Mistral AI** and **Cohere's Command R+** further expand the competitive landscape, offering unique features tailored for specialized applications. As AI advances, the diversity of LLMs ensures that businesses and developers have access to the right tools for their unique requirements.

Challenges in Implementing LLMs

Figure 20 shows a Venn diagram illustrating key challenges in implementing Large Language Models (LLMs). These challenges are complicated and not independent of each other. Each challenge affects the other two challenges.

The figure consists of three main overlapping categories:

1. **Ethical Bias and Fairness** (e.g., biased datasets, cultural stereotypes)
2. **Computational and Energy Costs** (e.g., high power usage, sustainability concerns)
3. **Security and Privacy Risks** (e.g., prompt injection, adversarial attacks)

The intersections highlight overlapping concerns such as:

1. Bias amplified by high compute requirements,
2. Security risks due to energy constraints, and
3. The balancing act of AI ethics, efficiency, and security.

Challenges in Implementing Large Language Models (LLMs)

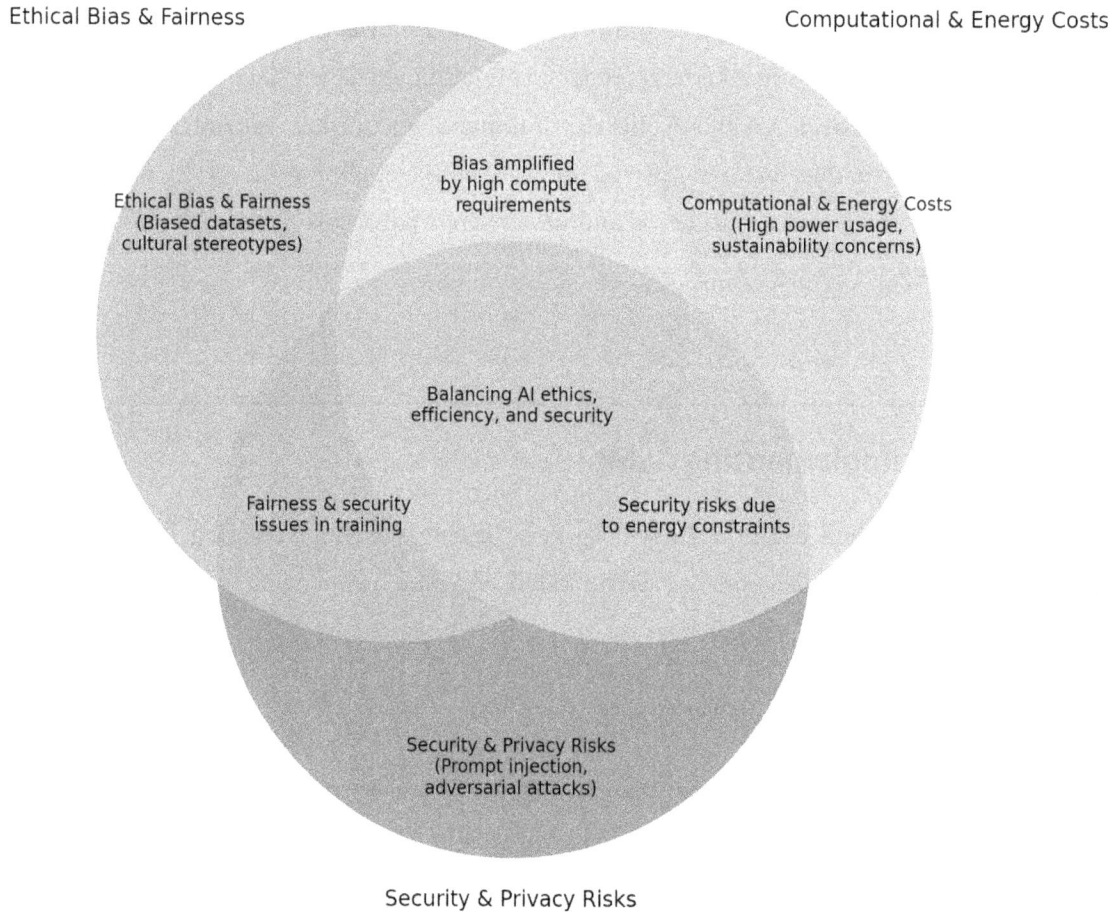

Ethical Bias & Fairness   Computational & Energy Costs

Bias amplified
by high compute
requirements

Ethical Bias & Fairness   Computational & Energy Costs
(Biased datasets,   (High power usage,
cultural stereotypes)   sustainability concerns)

Balancing AI ethics,
efficiency, and security

Fairness & security   Security risks due
issues in training   to energy constraints

Security & Privacy Risks
(Prompt injection,
adversarial attacks)

Security & Privacy Risks

Figure 20: Challenges in Implementing LLMs.

Ethical Concerns and AI Bias

Large Language Models are trained on massive datasets sourced from diverse platforms, including books, articles, and user-generated content across the internet. However, these datasets inherently contain human biases, cultural stereotypes, and societal prejudices, which can manifest in AI-generated responses. This raises significant ethical concerns in areas such as hiring, lending, law enforcement, healthcare, and political discourse, where biased AI decisions can lead to real-world consequences.

Bias in AI can be overt or subtle, impacting how models generate responses. Historical biases, linguistic inequalities, and cultural dominance in training data can lead to unfair representation of minority groups or the propagation of misinformation. Additionally, bias amplification occurs when AI disproportionately reinforces commonly occurring patterns, often at the expense of nuanced perspectives.

Researchers are developing fairness-aware algorithms, employing adversarial training techniques, and using bias-detection frameworks to mitigate bias. Ethical AI development also involves human-in-the-loop moderation, where diverse annotator teams help assess AI outputs for fairness, inclusivity, and ethical alignment. However, achieving completely unbiased AI remains an ongoing challenge that necessitates continuous monitoring, regulatory frameworks, and transparency in AI model development and deployment.

Computational Costs and Energy Consumption

Developing, training, and deploying cutting-edge LLMs demand extraordinary computational power, often necessitating **thousands of GPUs and TPUs** running in parallel for weeks or months. The computational requirements for training LLMs like GPT-4, Gemini, and Claude are very high, with energy consumption equivalent to powering small cities for an extended period.

The carbon footprint associated with AI development has become a pressing environmental concern, leading researchers to explore energy-efficient AI models. Strategies such as model pruning, quantization, and distillation are being developed to reduce unnecessary parameters and optimize performance without compromising accuracy. Additionally, AI hardware advancements, such as **Google's TPU v5e and NVIDIA's H100 GPUs**, aim to reduce power consumption while maintaining computational efficiency.

Cloud providers like **AWS, Google Cloud, and Microsoft Azure** also invest in green AI initiatives, integrating carbon-aware scheduling, which dynamically shifts workloads to regions powered by renewable energy. Furthermore, the rise of low-power AI inference models enables AI-driven applications to run efficiently on mobile devices, edge computing platforms, and embedded systems, reducing overall energy costs while enhancing accessibility.

Security and Data Privacy in LLM Applications

LLMs present significant security challenges as they process, store, and generate vast amounts of data, including sensitive, confidential, or personally identifiable information (PII). Threats such as data leaks, adversarial attacks, prompt injection vulnerabilities, and AI-generated misinformation pose risks to enterprises and individuals alike. A major concern in AI security is model inversion attacks, where adversaries attempt to reconstruct training data from the model's outputs. This can **expose** sensitive corporate data, proprietary research, or personal user information. Another emerging risk is prompt injection attacks, where maliciously crafted queries manipulate AI responses, leading to misinformation, bias reinforcement, or even exposure of system vulnerabilities. Therefore, those implementing AI must adopt **robust security measures**, including:

- **Zero-trust AI architectures**, ensuring strict access controls.
- **Differential privacy techniques**, which add controlled noise to training data to prevent data reconstruction.
- **Real-time content moderation systems**, which monitor for hallucinated, biased, or harmful responses.
- **Regulatory compliance frameworks**, such as **GDPR, CCPA, and AI-specific governance policies**, ensuring responsible AI deployment.

Additionally, enterprises deploying LLMs should consider on-premise AI models **or** private cloud deployments to safeguard sensitive business data while maintaining control over AI governance and ethical compliance.

Future Trends in Conversational AI

More Efficient, Smaller LLMs

As AI adoption grows, the demand for smaller, faster, and more efficient models continues to rise. The future of conversational AI will involve compact, fine-tuned models that deliver high performance with significantly reduced computational overhead. Models such as **GPT-4-Turbo** and

Mistral-7B showcase the potential for distilled architectures, which preserve the strengths of large-scale models while eliminating redundant parameters. These advancements are crucial for expanding AI accessibility, particularly in resource-constrained environments, mobile devices, and edge computing platforms. Lightweight AI models will power smart assistants, embedded IoT devices, and AI-driven applications, enhancing user experience with minimal energy consumption.

AI-Powered Search Engines and Hybrid AI Assistants

The future of AI will witness deep integration between conversational models and search engines, revolutionizing how users interact with information retrieval systems. AI-powered search engines will transition from keyword-based querying to full-context understanding, enabling:

- **Conversational search experiences**, where users receive natural, dynamically generated responses instead of static search results.
- **Hybrid AI models**, combining symbolic AI with deep learning, enhancing logical reasoning and structured data processing.
- **Autonomous AI agents**, capable of executing multi-step reasoning tasks, conducting research, summarizing findings, and even providing proactive recommendations based on user intent.

Expansion into Multimodal AI (Text + Image + Video)

The next frontier in AI involves multimodal models that seamlessly integrate text, speech, images, and videos, enabling richer, more dynamic interactions. Advancements in **DALL·E** 3 (image generation), **Sora** (AI-generated video), and **Whisper** (speech recognition) highlight the growing convergence of AI modalities. Integrating multimodal AI unlocks transformative use cases, such as:

- **AI-generated video summaries**, where AI models convert lengthy content into digestible visual storytelling.
- **Interactive storytelling AI**, capable of creating rich, adaptive narratives blending text, sound, and visuals.
- **Real-time media synthesis**, enabling businesses to generate AI-assisted marketing videos, presentations, and training content.

Summary

The rapid advancement of **ChatGPT and LLMs** signifies a **transformative shift in artificial intelligence**, reshaping how humans interact with machines. These AI models have demonstrated immense potential in revolutionizing industries, automating workflows, and providing seamless human-like interactions. However, challenges related to **bias mitigation, computational sustainability, and AI security** must be addressed to ensure their ethical and responsible deployment. Organizations and researchers must prioritize transparency, regulatory compliance, and infrastructure optimization to develop more ethical and reliable AI systems as AI progresses toward multimodal capabilities and autonomous agents. The future of AI lies in **fine-tuning advancements, optimizing computational efficiency, and integrating AI seamlessly into real-world business applications**, ensuring that AI remains an **accessible, intelligent, and transformative tool for global progress**.

In this chapter, we've delved into the intricacies of LLMs, exploring their architecture, functionality, and real-world applications. By understanding LLMs, we lay the groundwork for the emerging field of generative AI, which leverages these powerful models to create innovative solutions. Stay tuned for Chapter 6, where we'll dive deeper into the exciting world of Generative AI, building upon the knowledge we've established with LLMs, and explore how AI revolutionizes content creation, digital artistry, and synthetic media production.

References

A. Vaswani, N. Shazeer, N. Parmar, J. Uszkoreit, L. Jones, A. N. Gomez, Ł. Kaiser, and I. Polosukhin, "Attention is all you need," Advances in Neural Information Processing Systems, vol. 30, 2017. [Online]. Available: https://arxiv.org/abs/1706.03762.

OpenAI, "GPT-3 and GPT-4 Documentation," 2023. [Online]. Available: https://openai.com/research.

Google AI Blog, "BERT: Pre-training of Deep Bidirectional Transformers for Language Understanding," 2018. [Online]. Available: https://ai.googleblog.com/2018/11/open-sourcing-bert-state-of-art-pre.html.

## CHAPTER 6

Data in Generative AI

Generative AI has changed the game on AI by allowing for human-like text, images, audio, and even video. These abilities, once only available in science fiction, creating vibrant imaginary landscapes, composing music, or writing books, are now widely available. One thing that is foundational to this transformation is data. The training, refinement, and deployment of Generative AI models depend on quality, diverse, and well-processed data. This is evident in systems like OpenAI's GPT-4 and DALL·E—GPT-4, which are great at sounding like a person because they have been trained on massive curated text datasets. Meanwhile, DALL·E transmutes text prompts into visual marvels through rich image datasets.

In this chapter, we uncover Generative AI's critical interrelation with data in its training, infrastructure complications, and ethical dilemmas surrounding this technology.

Generative AI: A Brief Overview

Generative AI algorithms generate new output by extracting patterns from prior datasets. Generative AI, unlike traditional or classification prediction-based AI, generates novel outputs that replicate the patterns or structures of its input. Large Language Models (LLMs), such as GPT and LaMDA, output coherent text; image generators, like DALL·E, create visual content; and systems like Jukebox, compose music or synthesize speech.

These models have been made possible thanks to cutting-edge architectures like the Generative Adversarial Networks (GANs), useful for image generation; Variational Autoencoders (VAEs), allowing data compression to enhance creativity; and Transformers, the basis of language models like GPT and BERT. Figure 21 illustrates the phases of the data lifecycle.

Data: The Lifeblood of Generative AI

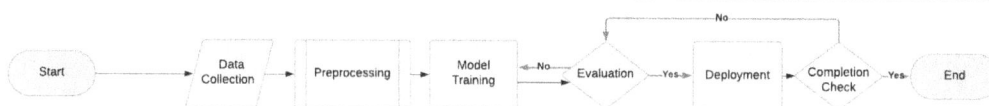

Figure 21: Phases in Data Lifecycle.

The quality and diversity of training data dictate the scope and depth of what a Generative AI model can accomplish. These datasets must be large and representative of the contexts in which the AI will be used. Text data is vital because it holds sentiment, context, and various types of information. Additionally, text exists in so many varied forms and locations. Figure 22 demonstrates the variety of data sources from social media to corporate knowledge bases to emails and chat spaces.

Figure 22: Diverse Text Sources.

The predictive power of Large Language Models (LLMs) such as GPT-3 and GPT-4 to generate increasingly coherent, contextually relevant, and novel text derives from their training on large and diverse datasets. From books, articles, and dialogues to websites, social media, and more, these datasets provide diverse language exposure, allowing the model to learn from various contexts and styles.

Books, for example, contain a wide array of structured language types across genres, from fiction to non-fiction to technical writing. They serve models of complex sentence structures, narrative forms, and thematic depth. Models can learn poetic turns through classic literature; technical manuals improve domain-specific query handling. Those academic papers add extra precision and depth, exposing models to formal, rigorous language grounded in specific knowledge domains. Research repositories like arXiv and PubMed offer invaluable material, particularly for models developing scientific or technical capabilities, like summarizing research papers or writing lengthy reports.

Online articles and blogs help to diversify tone, style, and subject matter. Articles from news platforms expose models to current events and factual reporting, whereas blogs showcase informal, conversational writing. All of this works together to allow the model to respond appropriately to different user requests. Conversational logs—transcripts from customer service calls and exchanges from online forums—provide vital richness to the training data by exposing the model to how people talk naturally, including colloquialisms, idioms, and slang. This is crucial for the model to be able to communicate like a human.

Web pages scraped with Common Crawl[16] and similar tools also introduce a tremendous scope of unstructured data that spans numerous topics, from general knowledge to very specific interests. The beauty of this data is in its variety, but it carries a lot of spam, misinformation, and irrelevant content that needs to be filtered. The diversity of the sources provides the model access to a wide variety of linguistic configurations, contextual adaptations, and domain-specific understanding, enabling it to carry out a multitude of tasks with versatility and precision.

---

[16] Common Crawl, "Web Data Used in Large Language Model Training," 2023. [Online]. Available: https://commoncrawl.org.

Enhancing Large Language Models with Taxonomies and AI-Generated Labels

One of the key challenges in training Large Language Models (LLMs) is ensuring data quality, structure, and relevance. While LLMs are highly effective at processing vast amounts of unstructured text, they often suffer from noise, inconsistencies, and lack of contextual precision. Taxonomies and AI-generated labels offer structured methodologies that significantly enhance LLM training datasets, improving both retrieval efficiency and content accuracy.

How Taxonomies Improve LLM Training

A taxonomy provides a hierarchical classification system that organizes data into structured categories. Unlike unstructured text, taxonomies create logical groupings that improve how LLMs understand relationships between concepts. This approach eliminates redundant or irrelevant data, helping models focus on high-signal content:

- **Reducing Data Noise**: Without structure, LLMs often process excessive or misleading information. Taxonomies filter out irrelevant data points, ensuring cleaner inputs for training.
- **Enhancing Contextual Understanding**: By categorizing similar concepts under a defined hierarchy, LLMs gain a more granular and domain-specific understanding.
- **Optimizing Retrieval-Augmented Generation (RAG)**: Taxonomies play a crucial role in retrieval-based AI systems, ensuring that models fetch relevant information instead of generating speculative or incorrect outputs.

A practical example of taxonomy-driven LLM training is seen in **WAND, Inc.**, a company specializing in domain-specific taxonomies. Their structured datasets help enterprises organize and tag unstructured content, making it more accessible for AI-driven retrieval and generation.

AI-Generated Labels for Adaptive Learning

In addition to taxonomies, AI-generated labels dynamically classify and annotate data, providing models with context-aware learning signals. These labels can be:

- **Rule-based** (derived from predefined taxonomies)
- **Machine-learned** (generated via clustering algorithms)
- **Human-AI hybrid** (reviewed for quality and bias correction).

By leveraging AI-generated labels, LLMs can:

- Learn from structured feedback loops, improving accuracy over time
- Reduce human annotation efforts while maintaining high-quality training data
- Adapt to new concepts dynamically, ensuring continuous knowledge expansion.

The Future of Structured AI Training

As Generative AI evolves, taxonomies and AI-generated labels will become standard practice for ensuring scalable, explainable, and efficient model training. Companies investing in structured taxonomies, such as **WAND, Inc.,** are at the forefront of optimizing LLMs for industry-specific applications.

By integrating taxonomy-driven classification and AI-generated labels, organizations can eliminate data ambiguity, reduce computational overhead, and improve model interpretability—critical components for the next generation of Generative AI systems.

Continuing with Text Datasets in Generative AI

A well-known example of utilizing such datasets is OpenAI's GPT-3, which has been trained on around 570GB of clean text—hundreds of billions of tokens. This data was obtained from Common Crawl, BookCorpus, Wikipedia, and other curated datasets. Common Crawl offered a treasure trove of web-sourced data but needed substantial filtering to be considered relevant and of good enough quality.

While there are benefits to these datasets, their curation has a number of challenges.

More data means more linguistic diversity, but it also means low-quality or biased data. Filtering and curation help avoid leaks into model outputs. Bias detection algorithms, adversarial training, and data augmentation help mitigate these issues, ensuring responsible AI development.

The success of LLMs relies on the design and curation of text datasets. As researchers create innovative publicly available datasets, focusing on data quality ensures AI models evolve responsibly while holding to ethical standards.

Image Datasets: The Backbone of Visual Generative AI

Picture a world where creative and imaginative visual content bursts forth, all thanks to Generative AI models like DALL·E and Stable Diffusion, which rely on the foundation of image datasets! These datasets are carefully curated collections of millions of annotated images across different objects, environments, styles, and angles. Exposed to these vibrant datasets, the models can generate realistic renditions of real-world events and artistic expressions inspired by textual descriptions.

Image datasets are characterized by their diversity, volume, and granularity of annotations. ImageNet and COCO (Common Objects in Context) are two notable examples that highlight these qualities.

ImageNet is a large dataset with over 14 million images in thousands of categories. Every image is accompanied by comprehensive metadata information, such as object class and hierarchical relationships, which enables the models to learn with a deep insight into visual concepts. ImageNet's diversity allows models to apply their learning to a variety of visual challenges, ranging from object detection to scene composition.

In contrast, COCO aims to enable context-aware processing of images. It contains more than 330,000 images, with more than 200,000 having (inferred) bounding boxes and segmentation masks that can be used to find and locate objects within an image. Besides, COCO contains annotations in natural language describing the images, making it a great base dataset for developing multimodal AI models across both image and text domains.

Generative AI models are trained on other specialized datasets for specific activities. For more information, see the Open Images Dataset, which offers even richer annotations that extend beyond just what the objects are, including object relationships and visual properties like color and texture. Another example is datasets of facial images, such as Celebi, which enable AI systems to create realistic portraits or adjust facial features according to user instructions. Figure 23 shows the relative proportions of images by category for COCO versus ImageNet.

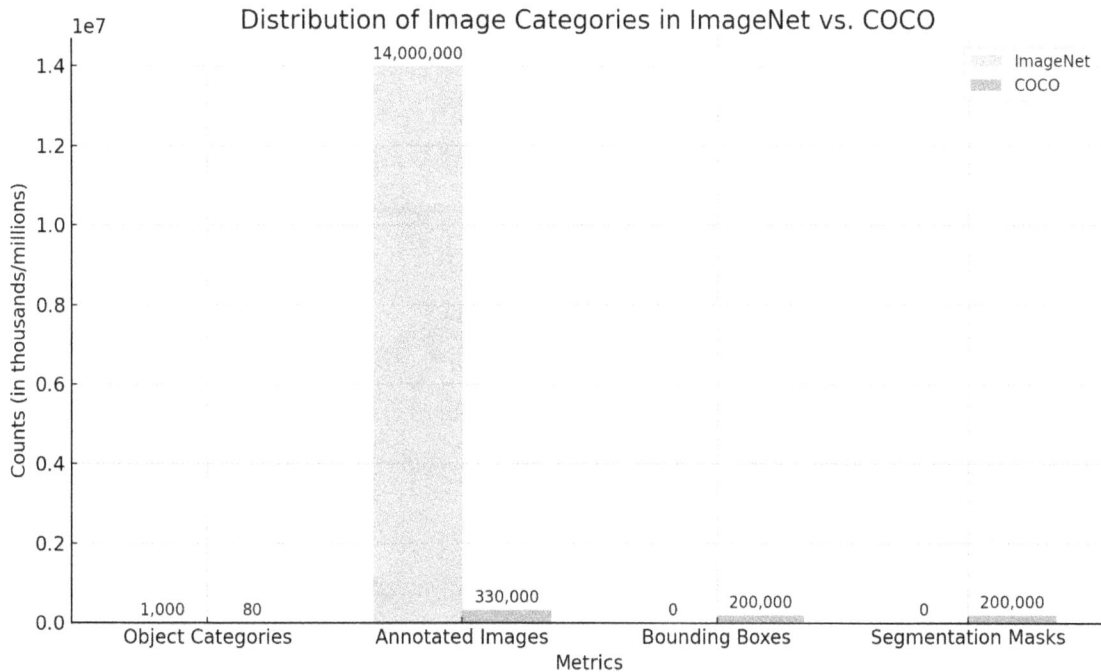

Figure 23: Distribution of Image Categories in ImageNet vs COCO.

Figure 24 shows that while both datasets contain a high frequency of annotated images across categories, COCO has a greater emphasis on contextual annotations and object localization compared to ImageNet.

Annotations: The Key to Image Dataset Utility

The richer the image datasets are, the more images there are, and the deeper the annotations. Annotations give key context that enables models to learn and reproduce complex visual characteristics. Some main types of annotations are:

- **Class Labels:** These indicate the object within an image that is most prominent for the model to learn regarding object classification (e.g., dog, tree, etc.).
- **Bounding Boxes:** Rectangular boxes mark an object's location in an image. It helps models localize multiple objects in a scene.
- **Image Segmentation Masks:** Pixel-level annotations that contain the exact shape and bounds of an object, allowing models to have finer visual understanding.
- **Captions:** As descriptive texts attached to an image bridging visual and linguistic data required for multimodal models such as DALL·E.

For example, an image of a park labeled "dog" together with a bounding box around it, a segmentation mask around the animal fur, and the caption "A dog playing fetch in a park" contains rich information that models can use to generate similar images.

Curating and Preprocessing Image Datasets

Data Cleaning and Preprocessing Raw image datasets can be very noisy, leading to redundancy and irrelevant data that cannot help enhance model performance. Such datasets need to be curated and preprocessed to make them usable:

- **Cleaning and Filtering**: Cleaning includes eliminating duplicate, low-quality, or irrelevant images. Common Objects in Context data sets can introduce incorrect patterns, such as irrelevant or mislabeled images.
- **Resizing and Normalization**: Other data pre-processing steps: Resizing images to the same dimension and use the same color profile before feeding the data into your reconstruction model to keep the shapes uniform for easier training. Earlier, we mentioned that exposing both the subject and the scene of the image to a deep learning model will yield a robust model. Generative AIs such as Stable Diffusion usually depend on fixed input sizes, so resizing is a must preprocessing step.
- **Balancing Dataset Composition**: A comprehensive dataset will consist of a variety of categories and styles so that it does not bias the model toward specific images. For example, a balance of natural scenes and urban environments in the dataset can lead to strong performance regardless of context.

Challenges in Image Dataset Design

There are several challenges involved in curating image datasets. Diversity is important to ensure the model does not overfit specific styles or subjects. For example, where the dataset is biased significantly towards urban landscapes, it will likely underperform in generating rural or natural scenes. Annotation also presents another challenge in terms of accuracy. Unreliable or wrong labels confuse the model, resulting in mistakes during training and inference. Solving these problems often calls for human inspection and cognitive refinement.

That raises a major concern about bias. Datasets may unintentionally mirror societal biases regarding demographic representation and cultural artifacts. For example, a dataset heavily biased toward Western architecture may fail to create realistic images of Asian architectural forms. These limitations create challenges to using only data augmentation, synthetic data creation, and analyzing bias.

Applications of Image Datasets in Generative AI

Figure 24: Generative AI image.

Image datasets are not only used to train models, but they are also applied in the real world. Such models trained on datasets, including COCO and ImageNet, are so good they can produce beautiful art, mimic real images, or manifest entirely new visuals from a written phrase. For example, make something that DALL· E can visualize, e.g., "*a cat riding a bicycle in a futuristic city,*" heavily depends on the diversity of its training data. These models have practical applications in advertising for generating product mockups, architecture for visualizing design ideas, and education for creating interactive learning materials. The strength of such applications highlights the need for well-curated image datasets.

Multimodal Datasets: Bridging Modalities for Cross-Functional AI

By combining multiple data types—text, images, audio, and occasionally video—multimodal datasets drive the evolution of Generative AI, enabling models that perform cross-functional tasks.

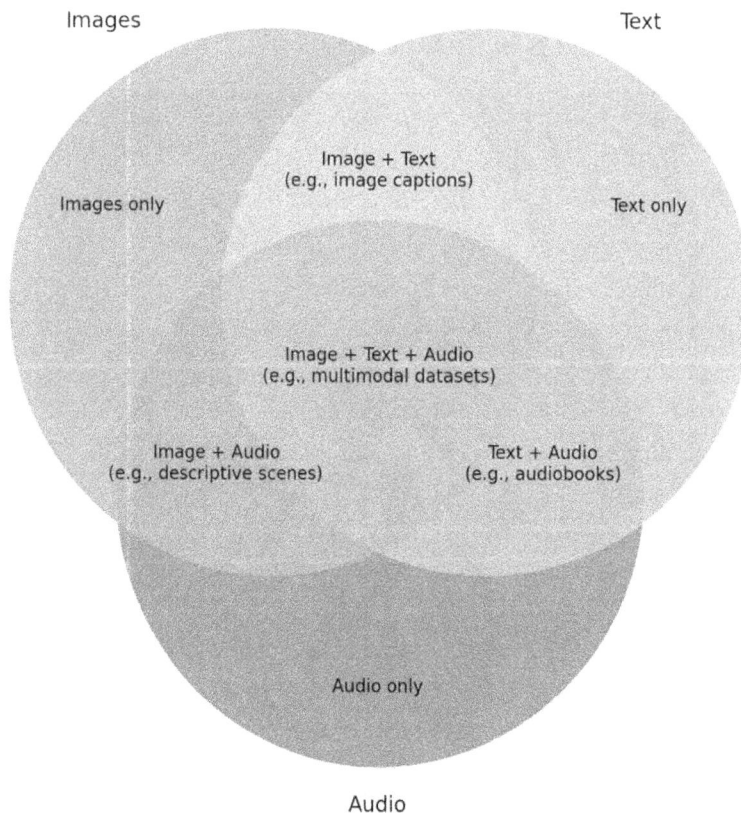

Figure 25: Multimodal Dataset Alignment: Images, Text, Audio.

These datasets empower AI systems to access and generate across modalities, paving the way for tasks such as captioning images, designing imagery from textual descriptions, and emphasizing context in audiovisual experiences. An exemplary system that takes advantage of multimodal datasets is OpenAI's CLIP, which can comprehend and produce results that correlate with the text and visual domains.

What Are Multimodal Datasets?

Some examples of multimodal datasets are carefully organized collections that align data from various sources or types to define significant correlations. While unimodal datasets focus on a single data type, multimodal datasets combine different information streams to accommodate how humans perceive and interact with the world. For example, an image in a multimodal dataset can have a textual caption, audio narration, and even metadata related to the image.

These datasets contribute massively to training AI models to work across modalities. For example, the multimodal datasets enable a system such as OpenAI's CLIP, which connects text and visual data, to harness explicit similarities between labels and images in a way that allows it to produce meaningfully contextually-relevant outputs. DALL·E models, for instance, rely on multimodal data to generate rich, creative images from text.

Components of Multimodal Datasets

Multimodal datasets usually comprise different types of data, aligned with great care to create a semantic relationship:

- **Text and Image Alignment**: One typical multimodal dataset pairs textual descriptions with corresponding images. One example is the MS-COCO dataset, which contains over 330,000 images and several captions describing each image's scene, objects, and context. This aligns the models to correlate textual input with visual inputs, which is beneficial for caption generation and creating images from textual descriptions.
- **Text, Image, and Audio**: Some datasets incorporate audio with text and images, allowing models to learn relationships between all three modalities. For example, AVA-Speech contains datasets that integrate visual media with audio and textual annotations, leading to

video-level systems capable of audio-visual understanding, such as identifying the spoken word in a clip.

- **Video and Metadata:** Most video datasets are multimodal, where they pair video clips with respective text metadata (like instructions or subtitles), such as HowTo100M. This kind of dataset can serve activities like video summarization or making step-by-step tutorials.

- **Temporal Multimodal Datasets:** Datasets that align data streams in time—for instance, when a video is combined with its corresponding audio and subtitles—are especially well-suited for tasks such as real-time translation, lip-reading, or recognition of the action taking place in the video.

Curating and Preprocessing Multimodal Datasets

The complexity of multimodal datasets makes their curation and preprocessing a multifaceted challenge. To ensure their utility, several key steps are essential:

- **Data Collection:** The first step is gathering data from diverse sources. For example, text-image datasets might be compiled from photo-sharing websites where users provide captions, while audio-visual datasets could draw from publicly available videos with subtitles.

- **Alignment Across Modalities:** The value of multimodal datasets lies in their alignment. Techniques like embedding alignment or manual tagging help ensure that corresponding text, images, and audio are correctly paired. For example, in an image-captioning dataset, the text "A dog playing fetch in a park" must be precisely linked to the relevant image.

- **Cleaning and Filtering:** As with unimodal datasets, clean multimodal datasets to remove noise, irrelevant content, or mismatched alignments. For instance, an inaccurate caption describing an image could confuse the model during training. Automated validation tools and manual inspection are employed to improve data quality.

- **Balancing Modalities:** Balancing representation across modalities is crucial. For example, a dataset skewed heavily toward one type of text-image pair (e.g., urban scenes) might limit the model's ability to generalize to other contexts, such as rural or natural environments.

Applications of Multimodal Datasets

Because multimodal datasets can be used in numerous ways, the resulting data opens up new avenues for AI use cases:

- **Text-to-Image Generation:** DALL·E and similar models are trained on datasets that link textual prompts to images and enable the generation of visuals from descriptive input. For example, a simple prompt like "a cat sitting on a beach at sunset" becomes rendered as an imaginative, vibrant image.
- **Image Captioning:** Datasets such as MS-COCO can help train systems that describe natural language with images. These systems have applications in accessibility tools, e.g., screen readers, which generate real-time text descriptions of visual content for users suffering from vision impairment.
- **Audio-Visual Synthesis:** Applications such as speech synthesis and dubbing are powered by multimodal datasets consisting of both audio and visual data. For example, aligning video scenes with speech enables the AI to create matching voice-overs.
- **Interactive Systems:** Multimodal datasets can be used to develop AI systems that enable interactive experiences — think virtual assistants — that understand spoken commands, analyze visual input, and offer contextually relevant responses.

Challenges in Multimodal Dataset Development

Creating and managing multimodal datasets involves unique challenges. It is particularly challenging to ensure that the modalities are aligned; even small mismatches can severely affect the model's performance. Another challenge involves data diversity; datasets should include a range of possible contexts, styles, and cultures to eliminate bias. Moreover, the overwhelming diversity of multimodal data poses challenges to data storage and processing systems, requiring scalable infrastructure. Ethical concerns such as copyright compliance and privacy issues must also be covered, especially when the content is sourced from the Internet.

Case Study – GPT3's Training Data

GPT-3 is a prime example of the significance of training data. It was trained on datasets from a variety of domains, ranging from informal language in blogs to more formal prose in encyclopedias. These sources were also carefully filtered to exclude anything destructive or prejudicial so that the model's output was ethical and useful.

Data Preprocessing: Preparing Data for AI

Raw data, in the form in which it was obtained, is usually unprocessed, messy, and polluted with repetitive or insignificant info. The first step in effectively training Generative AI models is transforming this raw input into structured formats that fit the model's training requirements. Data preprocessing plays a fundamental role in this process as it ensures that the data input to the model is clean, precise, and context-relevant. In this section, we discuss the essential steps of data preprocessing, emphasizing the significance and influence of each step on the performance of AI.

Deduplication: Data Uniqueness and Diversity

Remove duplicate or near-duplicate records from datasets. Deduplication is an important preprocessing step. That repetition can skew the learning activity towards redundancy, where the model will begin to acquire the same knowledge about things, causing it to get overfitted, over and over again. In overfitting, the model learns to recognize patterns in the repetitive data too well and fails to generalize to unseen or new examples.

For example, if a text dataset contained repeated parts of sentences or paragraphs, e.g., boilerplate from webpages, it could negatively impact the model's ability to generate original outputs. Likewise, in image datasets, many near-duplicate images (e.g., the same photo with a different slight resize or crop) can limit the diversity of visual forms the model will learn. Well-applied deduplication will eliminate these, keeping the dataset covered in real-world terms. We often use similarity detection algorithms to detect near-duplicates that can go unnoticed with simple matching for better deduplication.

Normalization: Achieving Standardization among Different Data Formats

Diversity measures the extent of various differences between categories or groups and allows models to learn from all kinds of input. In text datasets, for example, normalization includes changing everything to the same case (lower, for example), removing special characters, standardizing encoding format, etc. This normalization step mitigates training inconsistencies by ensuring that minor format variations do not introduce spurious distinctions or noise into the model's learned representations.

For instance, normalize the images in the image dataset size to the same dimension, color profile (RGB), and brightness and contrast level to the same range. Take DALL·E as an example.

Aside from keeping formats standard, normalization also controls the scale of input values. For instance, in numerical datasets, normalization can consist of scaling the values to a specific range (like 0 to 1), so that one or more values do not disproportionately influence the model training.

Annotation — Adding Contextual Metadata to Data

Annotation represents meaning and context for data by attaching labels, tags, or metadata. For example, in image datasets, the annotations might consist of object labels like "dog" or "car", spatial tags such as bounding boxes indicating the location of the objects, or segmentation masks delineating specific regions of interest. By learning from the accompanying annotations, the model becomes better equipped to comprehend the association between objects and their properties, a fundamental aspect of object detection and scene construction activities.

In text datasets, annotation might mean tagging sentences with extra context like sentiment (positive, neutral, negative), intent (question, request, command) , or named entities (person, location, organization). And more semantically accurate outputs.

A customer support chatbot dataset will often include annotations of the intents, such as whether the user is asking for a "billing inquiry" or "technical support," which are examples of labels. For example, in a multimodal dataset, annotations may provide the association of captioned images, which helps the model learn to associate visual information with textual information.

Preprocessing Steps for GPT Models: A Detailed Overview

Preprocessing consists of a series of specialized steps specifically tuned to process massive amounts of text data efficiently:

- **Text Cleaning**: The raw text data for LLMs needs cleaning to remove unnecessary data, advertisements, broken sentences, offensive language, etc. Text cleaning filters out such content to ensure that the data is relevant, coherent, and safe. This step also removes extraneous whitespace, punctuation errors, formatting errors, etc.

- **Tokenization:** Tokenization is the process of dividing the text into smaller units (tokens), like words, sub words, or characters the model can work with. For example, the sentence "The sky is blue" can be tokenized into ["The," "sky", "is", "blue"] or even further into sub words depending on the tokenizer design. The capability of the model to respond to multiple languages, different sentence formations, and vocabulary ensures effective storage.

- **Filtering:** Removing biased/harmful/sensitive information from the dataset. Because LLMs can retain biases from their training data, filtration is paramount to align the outputs of the model with the benchmarks of ethical AI. The first step of this process is to identify and filter out content that could contribute to stereotypes, misinformation, or unethical behaviors. For instance, OpenAI implements strict filtering mechanisms to prevent GPT models from exhibiting harmful biases or generating offensive material.

Data Preprocessing Challenges

Preprocessing can enhance the quality of training data, but it can also lead to issues. Clean and filter carefully because overregularization can lead to loss of context or subtlety so that the dataset will be rich in terms but lack broadness or flavor. Over-applying Python's pre-processing functions, like removing informal language or colloquialisms, could hurt your model's capacity to read conversational text. This is especially true for multimodal datasets, requiring a trade-off between standardization and retaining original data properties.

The other challenge is scaling preprocessing processes for very large datasets. Manual annotation and validation are often time-consuming and costly, particularly for datasets containing millions of entries. Automated tools can offer great efficiencies, but if they are not monitored and fine-tuned, they risk introducing errors.

Data Augmentation: Expand and Enhance Datasets

Generative AI relies on data augmentation, the process of adding controlled randomization to the existing data to artificially expand the amount and diversity of training datasets. It gives the model more variations of the input patterns, thereby making it less prone to overfitting (memorizing the training examples instead of learning the patterns). Simulating variability from the real world through augmentation assists models in generalizing well on unseen cases.

Image Data Augmentation: Increasing Visual Variability

Data augmentation techniques are particularly useful for enhancing the robustness of visual models in image datasets. One common augmentation technique is modifying images to simulate different perspectives, lighting conditions, or perspective distortions in real-world habits. Some of the commonly used image augmentation techniques are:

- **Rotation**: This approach simulates different perspectives by rotating the picture at a random angle. For example, an image of a car, rotated 15 degrees clockwise or counterclockwise, will teach the model that the vehicle is still a "car," irrespective of how it looks. This enhances the model's ability to identify objects even if shown at unusual angles.
- **Scaling**: Scaling resizes the image, either enlarging or reducing it without changing its aspect ratio. Scaling allows the model to capture objects across a large number of variations of different sizes and distances by zooming in or out. For example, a small image of a tree lets the model recognize the tree as "small", yet still something pertinent to the scene.
- **Adjusting the Brightness and Contrast**: Changing an image's brightness or contrast levels mimics different artificial light sources: dawn, midday, or evening. This allows the model to recognize objects in different levels of lighting so they perform well under both high- and low-lighting situations.

- **Flipping and Mirroring**: Vertical and horizontal flipping produce mirror images of the original input. This is especially valuable in training models to identify symmetrical objects or view scenes from mirrored perspectives.
- **Color Jittering**: Altering the color distribution in an image, say by varying the hue or saturation or adjusting the RGB channels slightly, can enable models to generalize across sources or settings of the image so that it produces good results on images captured through different camera filters or under different lighting environments.

Such augmentation strategies lead to impressive generalization of a visual model across varied environments and enable many applications such as object detection, scene segmentation, and image synthesis.

Text Data Augmentation: Diversifying Linguistic Patterns

Data augmentation of text datasets, in contrast to vision datasets, often has augmentation methods that allow you to change them semantically and syntactically to generate a broader dataset without altering the content of which the dataset is formed. This is how language models, like GPT, learn different language patterns and sentence structures:

- **Synonym Replacement:** Synonym replacement replaces words in a sentence with their synonyms. Consider, for example, the sentence, "The boy quickly ran to the store." It can be augmented to "The boy sprinted to the store." This variation in phrasing enables the model to associate multiple lexical choices with the same semantic meaning, improving its adaptability and robustness across diverse natural language processing tasks.
- **Paraphrasing**: Paraphrase to slightly rewrite whole sentences but still convey the same meaning. For example, the sentence, "She loves reading science fiction novels," can be rephrased as "She enjoys reading books that belong to the science fiction genre." By paraphrasing, we make structural changes to the text so the model learns to represent the same idea in different batches of phrasings.
- **Sentence Shuffling**: Some datasets shuffle the order of the sentences in a paragraph to help the model learn to grasp the narrative, even if the facts are presented in a different

order than expected. This is especially beneficial for training summarization and reordering models.

- **Insertion and Deletion**: It might add a descriptive detail, remove extra phrases, etc. For instance, adding the words "in the afternoon" to the phrase "He walked to the park" gives us a richer, context-augmented version of it.

Benefits of Data Augmentation

Augmenting datasets helps in many ways when the original dataset is small or has some bias. Thus, augmentation allows models to be exposed to diverse scenarios and linguistic variations by synthetically expanding the dataset:

- **Improved Generalization:** Augmented data aids in building a better generalizing model because it feeds the model with mimicked variations in data that are not present in the real data set. For example, an image model trained with brightness-adjusted images will be more robust against changes in brightness in the real world, like autonomous driving in various weather conditions.
- **Reduction of Overfitting:** This is also known as overfitting in the model, i.e., when a model learns well on the training data but works poorly when we try the same model on the unseen data. Having variability introduced through augmentation allows the model to focus more on the relevant pattern rather than memorizing the exact input-output correspondences for given samples, reducing overfitting.
- **Bias Mitigation:** If the dataset is imbalanced. For example, it has more images of urban than rural areas, apply augmentation so that both the urban and rural images are evenly represented. By adding synthetic variations of rural photos, the dataset becomes more balanced, reducing the model's bias toward the overrepresented category and improving fairness across all classes.
- **Cost-Effective Dataset Expansion:** Acquiring and labeling fresh training data is costly and time-consuming, particularly for image and audio datasets. Data augmentation allows for increasing the dataset size and diversity without cumbersome manual collection in a very cost-effective way.

How Data Augmentation is Used in the Real World

In the realm of Generative AI, data augmentation proves to be a well-established method with diversified applications.

In medicine, augmented medical imaging (MRI or CT scans, etc.) mimics tissue density and angles. This enables models to become more versatile in diagnosing diseases across patient demographics.

For example, augmented datasets that mimic various weather conditions, including rain and fog, for self-driving vehicles allow visual recognition systems to train with data that reflect real-life driving conditions.

Augmented datasets for sentiment analysis or machine translation in NLP applications allow the models to understand varied expressions of the same language and differences in language used across different demographics.

While this extract provides only one part of the transformation, data augmentation has thus the benefits of reward. There must also be a careful hand still to prevent unintentional distortions. Over-augmentation can add noise, making a dataset less representative of real-world data. Deep augmentation, such as extreme image rotation or unrealistic text paraphrasing, can make the model learn how to fit a non-appeared use case. Also, certain types of augmentation might change the semantic value of data. In text augmentation, replacing with synonyms needs to be context-aware, as it can create nonsense sentences.

If augmentation is not properly tuned, it can lead to irrelevant or incoherent data generation. These forms of augmented datasets can be timidly speculated by monitoring for quality and ensuring that the augmentations do not introduce biases or factual errors.

Technologies that Make Generative AI Possible

Modern generative AI models are powerful achievements, blending breakthroughs in discovery and engineering. Behind their success lies a robust ecosystem of technologies that support them, ranging from scalable infrastructure and efficient data pipelines to high-performance computing hardware. This section explores the core technologies that power generative AI, including storage systems, data processing frameworks, and computational resources that enable their capabilities.

Scalable Data Infrastructure: Storing Large and Very Large Datasets

Storing the training data, which can be terabytes or petabytes, is a bedrock upon which any Generative AI model is built. Massive data sets need to be stored using scalable, high-performance storage solutions that enable accessibility and flexibility:

- **Cloud-Based Storage Systems:** Amazon S3 (Simple Storage Service), Google Cloud Storage, Azure Blob Storage. Cloud platforms have virtually unlimited capacity, and organizations can store and access data from distributed locations. For example, cloud-based storage is particularly advantageous in that organizations can scale up their storage as needed, minimizing the expenditure on physical infrastructure. Another benefit of cloud services is built-in redundancy and disaster recovery, allowing data to survive system failures.

- **On-Premises Solutions:** Hadoop Distributed File System (HDFS), for example, is designed for organizations requiring data privacy, regulatory compliance, or low-latency access. Hosting data locally enables organizations to have closer control over sensitive information. On-premises infrastructure, on the other hand, can be expensive and labor-intensive to scale, requiring the addition of physical hardware and the maintenance of that equipment.

- **Hybrid Solutions:** Many organizations take a hybrid approach, using cloud and on-premises storage to balance the benefits of flexibility, security, and performance. For example, sensitive data might be stored on-premises, while less-critical data is hosted in the cloud for cost-effective scaling. This method allows organizations to consume cloud-native capabilities such as automated backup and AI integration.

Data Pipelines: Ensuring Seamless Data Flow

Efficient data pipelines are essential for ingesting, transforming, and serving data to Generative AI models. These pipelines orchestrate the data flow from its source to its final destination, ensuring that the model has continuous access to high-quality input during training and inference:

- **Apache Kafka**: Apache Kafka is widely known for real-time data streaming and messaging queuing. Using it, data streams can be continuously ingested and processed in real time, which is necessary for some applications that depend on up-to-the-minute data. For example, a Generative AI model that ingests streams of user data to return personalized recommendations can use Kafka to process live user interactions and update its outputs in real time.

- **Kubeflow**: Kubeflow is an open-source toolkit for end-to-end ML on Kubernetes. It facilitates automating data preprocessing, model training, and model versioning. Alongside the tooling, Kubeflow provides continuous integration in containerized environments, thus making data pipelines scalable, reproducible, and easier to monitor.

- **Apache Airflow**: Apache Airflow orchestrates multi-step data workflows. The framework allows developers to declare and orchestrate data pipeline tasks as directed acyclic graphs (DAGs). This feature is particularly useful in building large-scale Generative AI projects, where many preprocessing, training, and validation stages need to be executed in a chain.

Computing Needs and Stress on High-Performance Hardware

The architectural complexity of these models and the size of datasets they are subject to means that training Generative AI models requires a lot of compute power. Meeting these demands requires the use of specialized hardware accelerators like GPUs (Graphics Processing Units) and TPUs (Tensor Processing Units).

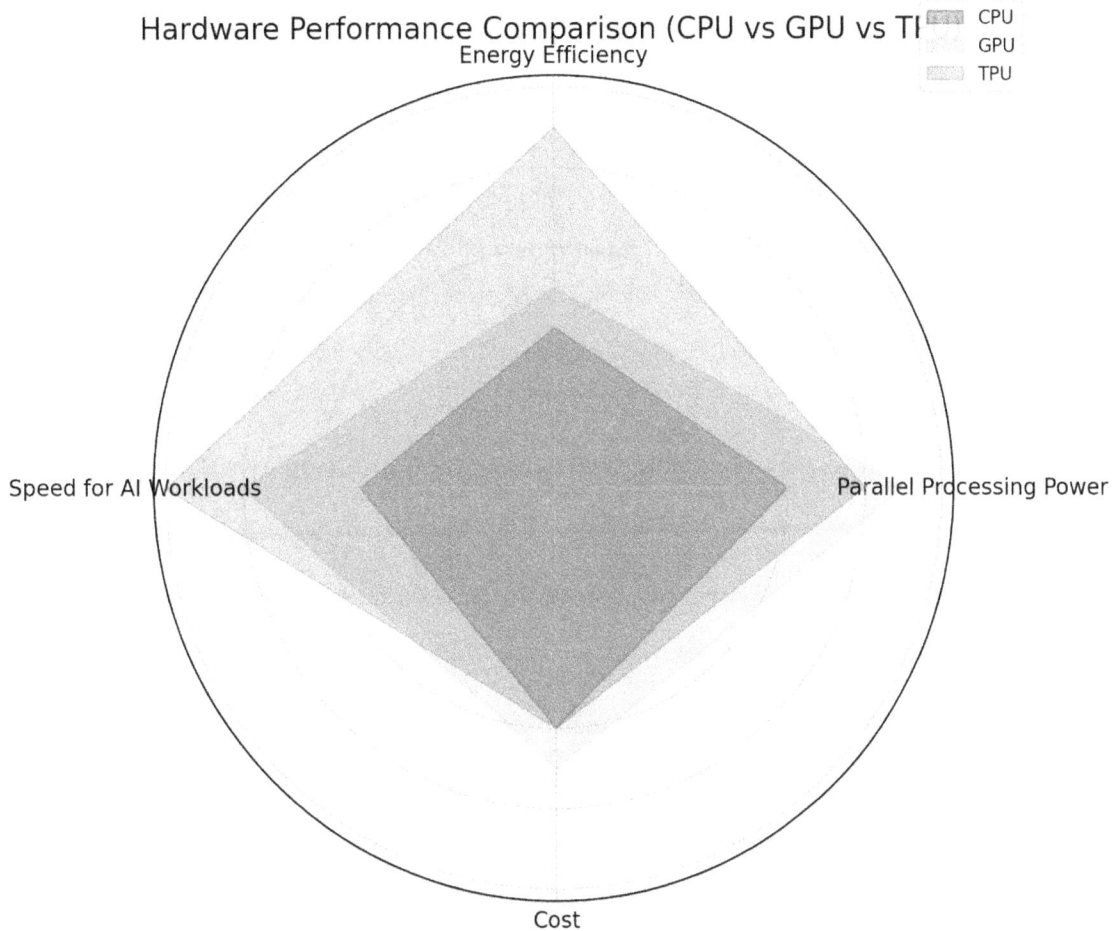

Figure 26: Hardware Performance Comparison (CPU vs GPU vs TPU).

- **Graphics Processing Units (GPUs):** The A100 and H100 Nvidia Deep Learning GPUs are the industry standard. GPUs are designed for high-throughput parallel processing, which makes them suitable for training large neural networks, as multiple operations must be performed simultaneously on millions of parameters. For example, the Nvidia A100 provides outstanding performance for such work as matrix multiplications, which lie at the heart of neural network operations.

- **TPUs (tensor processing units):** TPUs are application-specific integrated circuits (ASICs) designed by Google specifically for ML workloads. TPUs, on the other hand, are custom hardware specifically designed to accelerate tensor calculations—the main operation involved in most deep learning models—unlike general-purpose GPUs. TPUs are optimized for per-accelerator, large-scale matrix computations, which are also well aligned with tasks like training LLMs such as GPT.

- **Central Processing Units (CPUs):** GPUS and TPUS (graphic processing units and tensor processing units) are two relevant hardware-level components. While GPUs and TPUs are primarily used to train AI models, CPUs still play a critical role in data preprocessing, input-output operations, and orchestrating workflows. Within parallel processes, low latencies are achieved in non-parallel tasks; high-performance CPUs such as Intel and AMD accomplish this.

Parallel Data Processing and Model Training with Distributed Frameworks

For Generative AI projects that use large datasets and complex models, distributed frameworks facilitate distributed processing over many nodes to increase the speed and scale of model training:

- **Apache Spark:** Apache Spark is one of the most popular distributed computing frameworks for processing large and massive data in parallel. The most sensitive tool to stream the big data in parallel on multiple machines is very helpful in processing the data during the preprocessing stage, such as deduplication, normalization, or aggregation. Spark reduces the latency of data transformations by using in-memory computations instead of accessing data frequently stored on disks.
- **Horovod:** Uber created Horovod, a framework for optimizing distributed deep learning model training across multiple GPUs or TPUs. Based on popular frameworks like TensorFlow and PyTorch, it facilitates the implementation of parallelized training workflows. Horovod is an efficient framework for collective learning based on Ring AllReduce, a parallel algorithm that efficiently distributes data.
- **Ray:** Ray is a distributed computing framework that allows the parallelization of ML workloads, such as hyperparameter tuning and reinforcement learning. Its configurable nature suits training and inference workloads, particularly for large-scale Generative AI systems requiring substantial resource management.

AI as a Managed Service: Build on Top of Cloud AI Solutions

Also, with cloud-based generative AI services, they offer managed hardware and software frameworks, which make it easier to create and deploy generative AI models—plugging these into AWS SageMaker, Google Vertex AI, and Azure Machine Learning, respectively, as they also provide pre-configured environments for Machine Learning, scalable compute, storage, and data pipeline integrations. These tools abstract away the complexity of the infrastructure, enabling data scientists to concentrate on the design and experimentation of the model.

Now, let's look at some real-life examples using this tech:

- **OpenAI's GPT-4:** OpenAI utilizes a combination of high-performance Nvidia GPUs with custom-built data pipelines to train its models on massive text datasets. Their infrastructure consists of optimized data loading and distributed training frameworks to support the scale of their large language models.
- **DALL·E 2 Visual Processing:** For generating images, OpenAI utilizes cloud storage systems and distributed frameworks designed for multimodal datasets with images and their textual descriptions. Cloud-native tools allow data to be effortlessly accessed and scaled.
- **Self-Driving Cars**: Tesla and Waymo use distributed data pipelines to ingest millions of hours' worth of driving footage. These pipelines connect to high-performance compute clusters powered by GPUs and TPUs that can process real-time image and sensor data.

Challenges in Data Management

Because of this, Generative AI systems are very dependent on data. However, managing this data poses serious volume, quality, and privacy challenges. To counter these challenges, they need advanced infrastructures, validation tools, and compliance with regulatory frameworks. This section will discuss the major data management challenges in Generative AI and how to face them.

Volume and Storage:

This segment examines additional methods to manage the enormous datasets. Data is a critical component for training any machine learning system and represents one of the biggest challenges in generative AI. These models require petabytes of diverse data, including text, images, audio, and video formats, to support applications such as large language models (LLMs) and image generation.

The large data size puts a lot of pressure on storage systems and data-processing pipelines. However, traditional storage solutions often cannot manage large datasets, leading to the need for distributed systems such as Hadoop Distributed File System (HDFS), Amazon S3, or Google Cloud Storage. With this infrastructure, multiple nodes are used in large distributed systems to store the data, which allows scalability and redundancy. Yet the challenges of data volume go beyond storage. It becomes a bottleneck, especially when loading data for training a model. Slow data pipelines can slow down training, use more resources, and cost money while causing delays. This, however, sometimes leads to bottlenecks in data processing. Organizations use high-speed data access, such as caching, and in-memory processing frameworks like Apache Spark to speed up data transfer and preprocessing.

A further challenge is the storage and transference of the immense datasets, particularly present in the cloud, where charges are associated with egress and scaling up. Organizations adopt hybrid storage architectures to balance the scalability of cloud storage with the economy of on-premises storage.

Data Quality and Biases

Data quality plays a crucial role in the effectiveness and dependability of Generative AI models. Low-quality data can result in biased, inaccurate, or nonsensical outputs. Data quality issues can occur for a number of reasons. For example, Facebook posted a large-scale dataset from Common Crawl, a web corpus of noise and irrelevant content.

- **Bias**: The training data frequently mirrors the societal biases ingrained in its source materials. For instance, textual datasets can include gender-specific language, biases, and cultural imbalances.

- **Discrepancies**: Differences in format or naming conventions can create confusion during training, as incorrectly annotated images in an image dataset could decrease the model's object detection accuracy.

Organizations utilize frameworks such as TensorFlow Data Validation (TFDV)and Great Expectations to identify anomalies, inconsistencies, and biases in the dataset to ensure data quality. These tools examine data distribution, count missing values, and identify outliers.

Deduplication, normalization, annotation, and other data preprocessing techniques ensure your data is as clean as possible and in a standard format. However, after extensive scrubbing, bias still remains. Mitigating bias often involves augmenting the dataset with more samples from underrepresented categories or bias correction techniques during the model training process.

Privacy and Security

Generative AI brings certain implications for data privacy, especially when training models on data sets that potentially include sensitive or personally identifiable information (PII). Privacy laws like the General Data Protection Regulation (GDPR)in Europe and the California Consumer Privacy Act (CCPA) in the United States impose tight constraints on data collection, storage, or usage. Failure to comply can lead to heavy financial penalties and reputational harm.

There are several key privacy challenges. Sensitive data is difficult to locate and extract PII from large and unstructured datasets. Also, although anonymization techniques (e.g., masking, pseudonymization, etc.) can mitigate the risks of privacy disclosure when using sensitive data, they also risk diminishing the usefulness of the data for model training. Finally, datasets can come from external sources with limited usage or require user consent.

In response to privacy concerns, organizations are moving towards strategies such as:

- **Synthetic Data Generation:** These datasets are artificially generated to mimic real-world data but do not contain any real PII. Synthetic customer interaction logs, for example, can simulate authentic speech without revealing actual identities.

- **Federated Learning:** With federated learning, the model is trained on-device and only aggregate updates are sent to a central server. It enables the NH to learn from data sources rather than transferring sensitive information to a single facility.
- **Differential Privacy:** Differential privacy injects noise into the dataset or model outputs so that specific data points cannot be easily identified, preventing the identification of individual user contributions.

Data security refers to the method of protecting training data from unauthorized access, theft, and tampering. The training datasets in Generative AI projects are usually stored and migrated across distributed environments, which exposes them to various types of cyberattacks and breaches.

What are the most acute security challenges?

- **Privacy**: Risks of privacy of the personal data used for training (and stored) in the AI Model.
- **Data Integrity**: Ensuring that data has not been tampered with during collection, storage, or transfer is essential to maintaining trustworthy datasets.
- **Fair Access Control**: Granting the right to access to huge teams of data scientists and engineers can be challenging, especially in collaborative settings.

Organizations apply data security measures, including encryption of data at rest and in transit, to secure sensitive information. Role-based access control (RBAC) restricts access to certain datasets only to authorized personnel. Enhanced Security: Audit Logs and Monitoring Tools.

Legal and Ethical Considerations: Why Responsible Data Use Is Necessary

Generative AI projects also have to navigate legal and ethical concerns about data use. The practice raises questions about intellectual property rights, such as training models on copyrighted material. Similarly, collecting data from social media platforms or user-generated content requires explicit consent from the data owners. Also, with these challenges in mind, organizations follow practices like:

- **Explainability and Documentation**: Keeping detailed records of included data sources, preprocessing steps, and usage rights helps verification and compliance.
- **Copyright**: Organizations issue copyright notices on web pages and legal disclaimers to ensure their datasets are used according to legal agreements.
- **Ethical Assessments:** Numerous organizations have ethics review boards specifically to evaluate the ethical implications of employing specific datasets, especially those tied to sensitive content or contentious subjects.
- **Practical Example:** Privacy and bias challenges with GPT models.

OpenAI's GPT-3 and GPT-4 models are under serious multidisciplinary scrutiny relating to data privacy and bias. They run a check against the entire internet, meaning the models can pick up on biased language or stereotypes found in the training data. Persistent challenges for large language models: Furthermore, these debates on transparency and ethical data usage were prompted by concerns surrounding the potential for using copyrighted materials, user-generated content, and ethical considerations about machine-generated media.

OpenAI has introduced more aggressive filtering, bias detection, and anonymization processes in response to these challenges.[17]

The Future of Data in Generative AI

Synthetic Data Generation

Synthetic data generation is a process that generates an artificial dataset that retains the statistical properties of a real-world dataset without containing any real personally identifiable information (PII). This technique is crucial for tackling data privacy issues and addressing cases where real data is limited or nonexistent. Synthetic data can be generated at a high level using generative techniques such as Generative Adversarial Networks (GANs), Variational Autoencoders (VAEs), and diffusion

---

[17] OpenAI, "Research on Data Anonymization and Differential Privacy," 2023. [Online]. Available: https://openai.com/research.

models. Synthetic data is the computer-generated representation of real-world scenarios. For example, healthcare organizations can generate synthetic patient records that capture realistic variances without compromising individual privacy. Companies like NVIDIA also use synthetic datasets to improve the training of their self-driving cars to run simulations in complex driving conditions that would otherwise be hard to capture in real life.

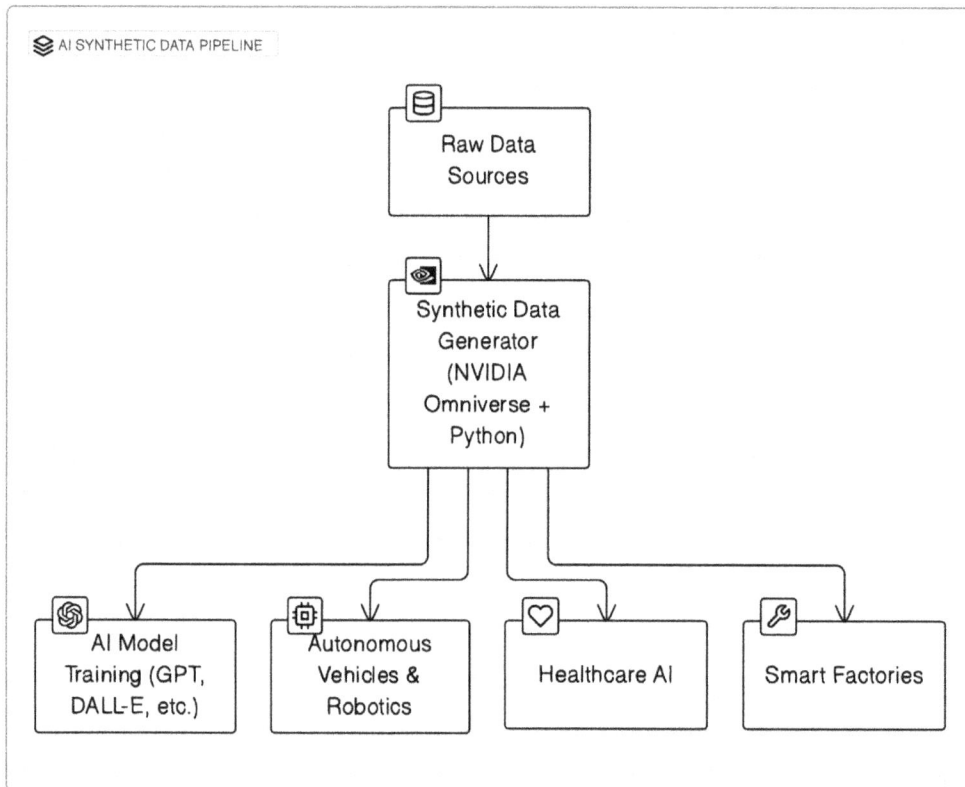

Figure 27: Generating Data at Scale.

Multimodal Data Fusion

Unlike earlier AI models, which primarily focused on a single domain of data, such as text writing or image generation, multimodal data fusion combines this data from multiple modalities: text, images, audio, and video, making AI systems more contextual and complex. Haven't heard about it yet. Models such as OpenAI's CLIP showcase multimodal data fusion's potential by combining images and text to create correlations. For instance, CLIP recognizes that the caption "a majestic mountain landscape" relates to a certain graphic scene. Multimodal models will incorporate audio and even sensory inputs as the technology progresses, allowing use cases, including virtual assistants that understand visual prompts, spoken input, and response outputs. Furthermore, a multimodal fusion also enables cross-domain applications in the area of AR/VR. For example, users can manipulate real-time interactive environments, realistic visuals, sound, and narratives.

Edge Computing

Edge computing involves processing data near the sources of the data—on local devices or right at the point of data generation, rather than on centralized cloud-based servers. This transition is essential for Generative AI applications that require instantaneous responses as seen in AR/VR systems, autonomous vehicles (see Chapter 7), and Internet-of-Things (IoT) devices. Edge computing reduces the amount of data transmitted to and processed in remote servers by processing data locally, thereby minimizing latency and improving responsiveness. In this case, an edge-based AI model can up-res video in real time for virtual meetings, making it possible to apply a background filter on the device of the user rather than up inside the cloud. Edge computing also improves privacy due to reduced transmission of sensitive data, which is especially valuable in privacy-sensitive applications such as smart home devices, wearable health monitors, and security cameras. Edge computing improves the utilization of resources and energy efficiency by distributing computation between local and cloud environments, thus making it possible to compute AI on mobile and embedded devices.

Self-Supervised Learning

This paradigm shift, known as self-supervised learning (SSL), allows AI systems to learn from massive amounts of unlabeled data by identifying and capturing relevant patterns and relationships from the data itself. Doing so greatly reduces the need to annotate data manually, saving a lot on annotation costs and speeding up the generation of large training datasets. This approach is especially relevant for tasks with large datasets of unlabeled data, such as predicting missing holes in the input (e.g., next token in a sequence, masked part of an image, etc.) Leading architectures such as GPT-4 and BERT leverage SSL to learn contextual relationships that can be fine-tuned for tasks. Exploring beyond textual data, SSL also encompasses multimodal datasets, allowing models to establish relationships among text, images, and audio, all without explicit paired data. This feature accelerates the production of cross-modal results, including generating descriptive captions for images or producing matching soundtracks for video information.

The following graphic illustrates the breakdown of SSL vs Traditional Learning:

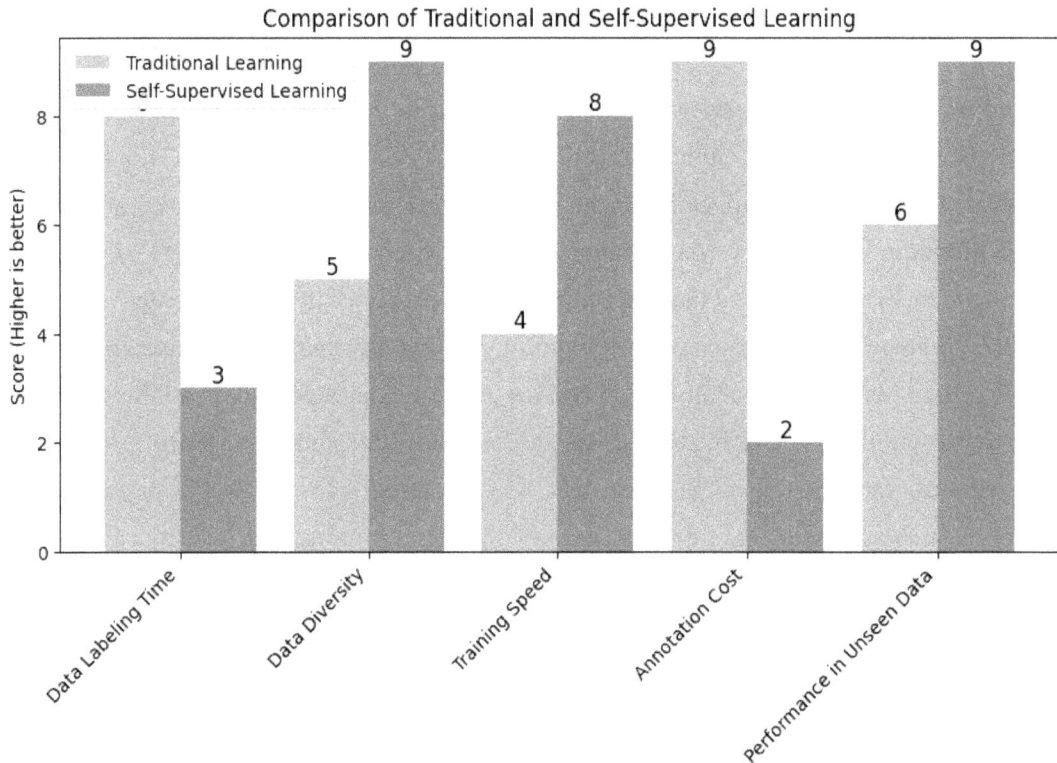

Figure 28: Breakdown of Self-Supervised Learning vs Traditional Learning.

Federated Learning

Federated learning is a specialized training method for AI models that can work across scattered, heterogeneous datasets while ensuring that data never leaves the premise of devices or institutions retaining raw information. This method overcomes privacy issues and allows for collaborative model training across organizations without sharing sensitive data. Federated learning allows the use of the information the model learns without actually sharing the data, unlike traditional shared learning, where raw data must be shared. This approach is especially useful in industries like healthcare and finance, bound by regulations that prevent sharing sensitive data. For example, hospitals can work together to train diagnostic AI models with local datasets without compromising patient privacy. Federated learning promotes global collaboration by allowing institutions worldwide to participate in model development while maintaining data privacy, thereby driving AI research in a privacy-preserving way. The following diagram shows an example of the federated learning process.

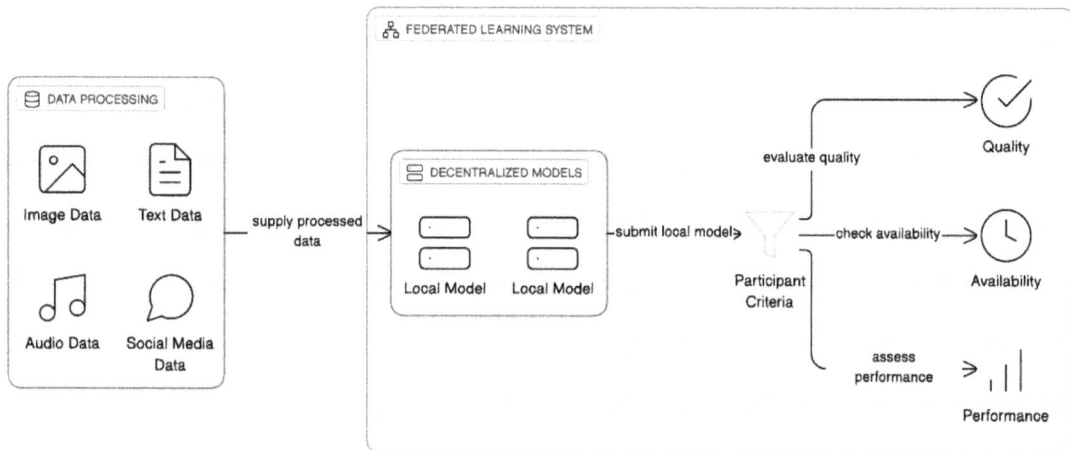

Figure 29: Example of a Federated Learning Process.

Summary

The use cases for Generative AI are endless, but as is true for all AI, without *data*, the power of models' strengths and weaknesses wouldn't mean much to transform or disrupt markets or find a new paradigm for how man and machine work together. As a discipline matures, multimodal fusion, edge computing, and synthetic data will enable previously uncharted realms of capability. This data-enabled framework, along with ethical AI guardrails, will pave a collaborative future, not just where machines create in lockstep with humans but also where they amplify creativity, solve complex problems, and seamlessly enhance our everyday human experiences.

References

Common Crawl, "Web Data Used in Large Language Model Training," 2023. [Online]. Available: https://commoncrawl.org.

TensorFlow, "TensorFlow Data Validation (TFDV) for AI Data Quality," 2023. [Online]. Available: https://www.tensorflow.org/tfx/data_validation/get_started.

OpenAI, "Research on Data Anonymization and Differential Privacy," 2023. [Online]. Available: https://openai.com/research.

## PART II

Operationalizing Data for AI

This part moves from theory to practice, detailing how organizations can operationalize data for AI. This includes modern storage solutions, master data management (MDM), data quality, governance, and the ethical considerations surrounding AI-driven decision-making. We explore real-time data pipelines, how data moves within AI-powered organizations, and the technical and business processes required to make AI truly operational. Additionally, we discuss common pitfalls and provide insights into the future of AI data infrastructure.

CHAPTER 7

Modern Data Storage and Processing for AI

Data is the lifeblood of AI, and the ability to store, process, and retrieve massive datasets efficiently is critical for building advanced AI systems. Over the past decade, the evolution of storage and processing technologies has transformed how organizations manage data for AI, enabling breakthroughs in real-time analytics, generative models, and decision intelligence.

In this chapter, we'll explore the modern landscape of data storage and processing for AI, examining the tools, techniques, and strategies that drive today's most successful AI systems. From distributed computing frameworks to the rise of data lakehouses, this chapter will provide actionable insights for organizations navigating the complexities of data architecture for AI.

Big Data Platforms for AI

AI's reliance on vast datasets makes big data platforms essential for managing and processing data at scale. These platforms enable the ingestion, transformation, and analysis of structured and unstructured data, supporting both training and inference workflows.

AI's reliance on vast datasets makes big data platforms essential for managing and processing data at scale. These platforms enable the ingestion, transformation, and analysis of structured and unstructured data, supporting both training and inference workflows.

- **Apache Hadoop:** We have seen Hadoop as a foundational framework that revolutionized how organizations approach big data storage and processing. By breaking down large datasets into smaller blocks and distributing them across multiple nodes, Hadoop ensures both reliability and scalability. The cornerstone of Hadoop's architecture is the Hadoop Distributed File System (HDFS),[18] which guarantees fault tolerance by replicating data across clusters. This redundancy allows data to remain accessible even if a node fails. HDFS also supports high-throughput access to large datasets, making it an ideal choice for batch processing at scale. Another key component, MapReduce, provides a programming model for parallel processing of large datasets. The Hadoop ecosystem also includes complementary tools such as Hive for SQL-like querying, Pig for scripting MapReduce jobs, and YARN for resource management. See Figure 30. These components make Hadoop a pivotal tool for preprocessing massive amounts of data, such as text corpora for training natural language models.

- **Apache Spark:** Apache Spark[19] builds upon Hadoop's foundation but improves upon it by providing in-memory data processing capabilities. Spark is designed to handle complex and iterative workflows, such as those required for ML tasks. Unlike Hadoop's disk-based MapReduce, Spark processes data in memory, dramatically increasing the speed of data transformations and computations. This makes Spark particularly effective for tasks like iterative model training, where data needs to be processed repeatedly. Spark's ecosystem includes Spark SQL for querying structured data, MLlib for distributed ML, Spark Streaming for real-time data streams, and GraphX for graph computations. A common AI use case for Spark is training recommendation systems based on user interaction datasets, where quick access to large volumes of data is crucial. This appears in Figure 31.

- **Apache Flink:** Apache Flink is a high-performance, stream-processing framework designed for real-time data analysis. Unlike traditional batch processing systems, Flink processes data continuously as it arrives, ensuring low-latency responses. This capability is

---

[18] Apache Software Foundation, "Hadoop Distributed File System (HDFS) Overview," 2023. [Online]. Available: https://hadoop.apache.org/docs/stable/hadoop-project-dist/hadoop-hdfs/HdfsUserGuide.html.

[19] Apache Software Foundation, "Apache Spark Documentation," 2023. [Online]. Available: https://spark.apache.org/docs/latest/

critical for use cases that demand real-time insights, such as fraud detection in financial transactions or monitoring IoT sensor data. Flink's event-driven architecture supports stateful computations and exactly-once processing guarantees, ensuring that no data points are missed or processed multiple times, even in distributed environments. Flink integrates seamlessly with message brokers like Apache Kafka and object storage systems, making it highly adaptable for unified data pipelines.

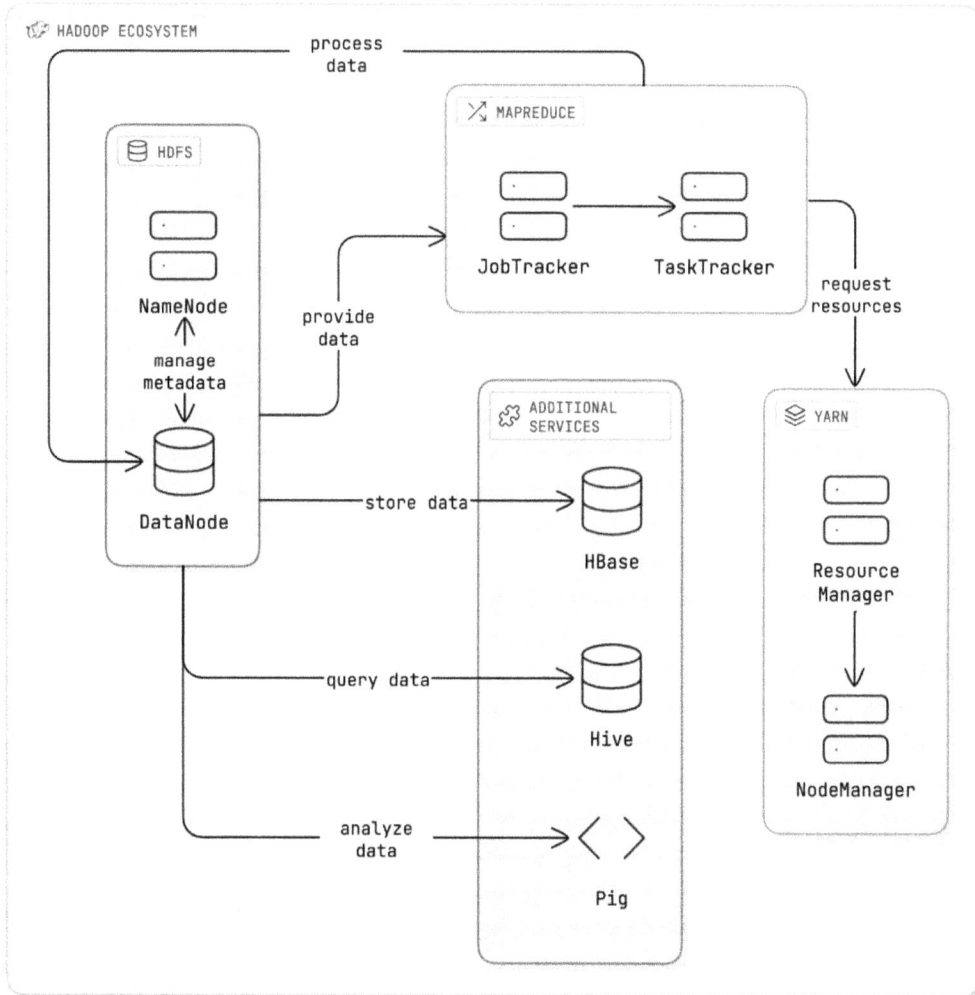

Figure 30: Hadoop Ecosystem.[20]

---

[20] https://www.geeksforgeeks.org/hadoop-ecosystem/?utm_source=chatgpt.com

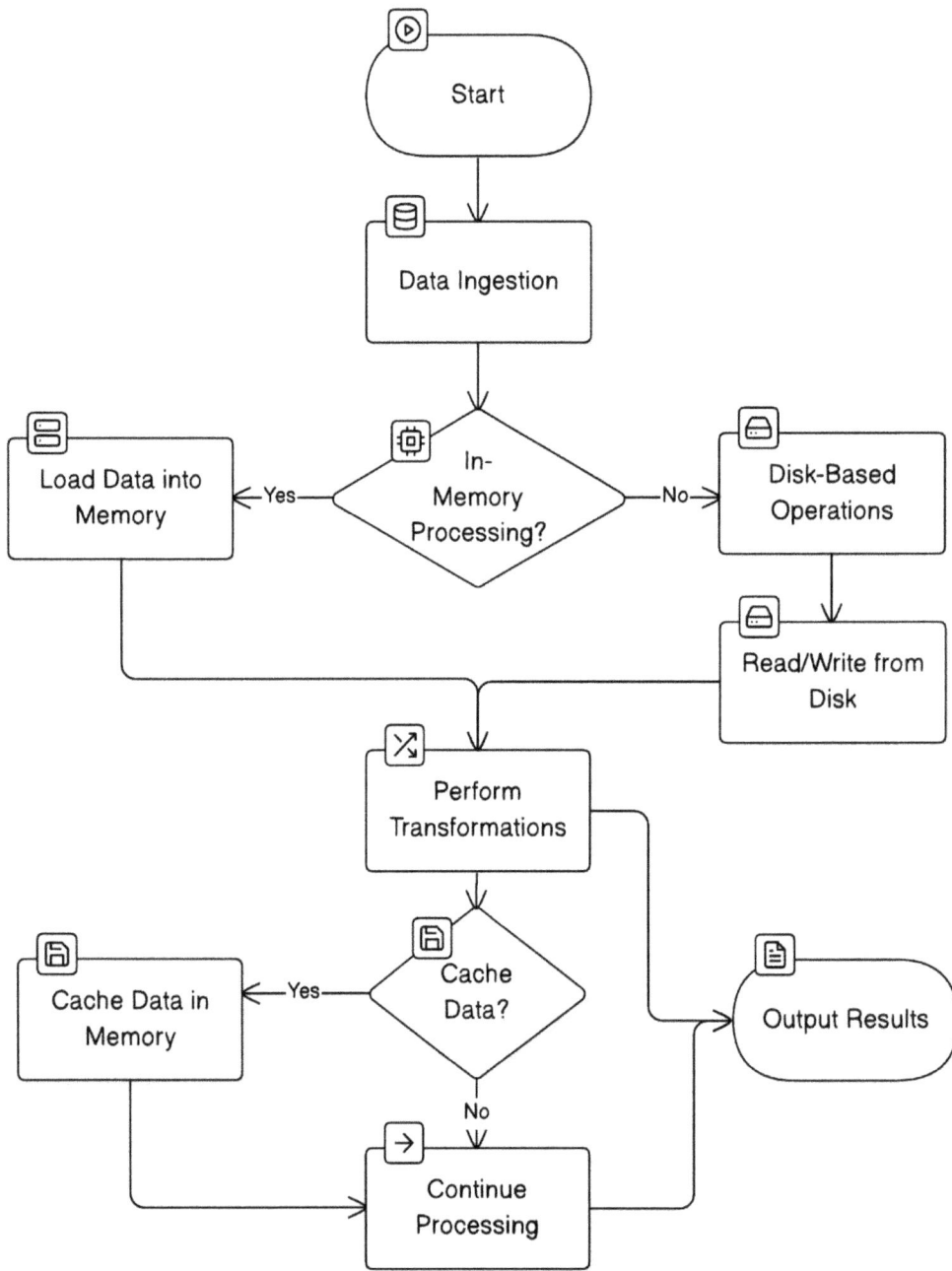

Figure 31: Spark Processing Flow. [21]

---

[21] https://www.chaosgenius.io/blog/apache-spark-architecture/?utm_source=chatgpt.com

Flink Stream Processing

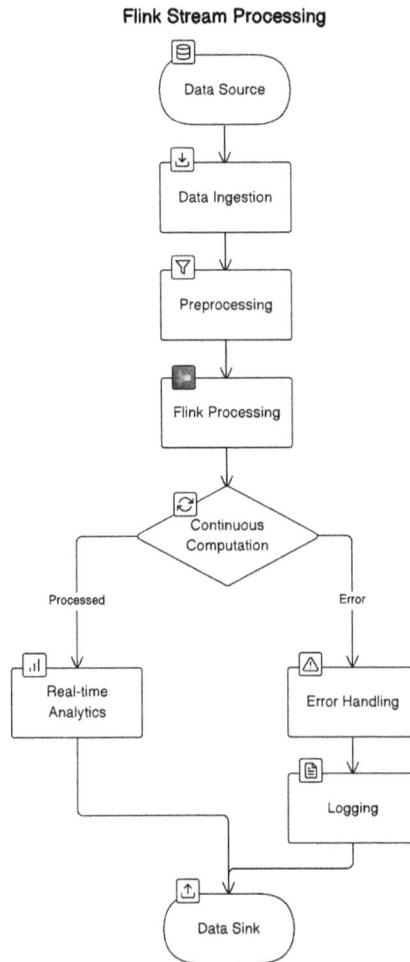

Figure 32: Flink Stream Processing.[22]

- **Apache Kafka:** Apache Kafka is a distributed event streaming platform that enables real-time data ingestion and processing. It acts as a message broker that streams data to downstream consumers such as Apache Spark and Flink. Kafka supports high-throughput, fault-tolerant streaming with partitioning and replication to ensure resilience. Kafka Streams, a lightweight library, allows applications to process data directly within the platform. A typical AI use case involves real-time anomaly detection in transactional systems or clickstream analysis.

---

[22] https://www.interviewbit.com/blog/apache-spark-architecture/?utm_source=chatgpt.com.

- **Dask:** Dask is a parallel computing library that extends Python data science workflows to distributed systems. It scales DataFrame and array operations across multiple nodes, allowing users to process large datasets without rewriting their code. Dask's dynamic task scheduler enables parallel computations for ML, ETL (extract, transform, load) operations, and numerical simulations, making it a preferred choice for Python-based AI workflows.

- **Presto/Trino:** Presto,[23] now known as Trino, is a distributed SQL query engine designed for running ad-hoc, low-latency queries on large datasets. It supports querying data from various storage systems, including HDFS, S3, and relational databases, enabling federated queries across different data sources. Presto is commonly used in data lake architectures to perform interactive data exploration.

- **Apache Storm:** Apache Storm is a distributed real-time computation system that processes streams of data in continuous pipelines called topologies. Storm is ideal for use cases such as IoT sensor monitoring and alerting. Its ability to process millions of tuples per second with low latency makes it a valuable tool for real-time AI inference and dashboarding.

- **Delta Lake:** Delta Lake is an open-source storage layer that brings ACID (atomicity, consistency, isolation, durability) transactions to data lakes. It ensures data consistency and supports time travel queries through data versioning. This makes it a crucial component for maintaining reliable feature stores in ML pipelines, where tracking changes in historical data is important.

Additional Tools and Integrations

- **Ceph:** A distributed storage system that provides object, block, and file interfaces, enabling massive scalability.
- **Google Cloud Filestore:** A managed file storage solution that supports applications requiring a shared file system.

---

[23] PrestoDB, "Presto/Trino Query Engine Documentation," 2023. [Online]. Available: https://prestodb.io/docs/current/.

- **Kubernetes and Kubeflow:** Container orchestration tools for deploying scalable ML workflows.
- **NVIDIA DGX and Horovod:** Hardware and frameworks optimized for multi-GPU distributed training.
- **Ray Distributed Framework:** A Python-based framework for scaling AI workloads across clusters.

These tools, alongside Hadoop, Spark, and Flink, form a comprehensive ecosystem for big data processing and AI workloads. Organizations can choose the appropriate combination of technologies based on their specific needs, such as real-time stream processing, batch computation, or federated querying, to create robust, efficient, and scalable data pipelines.

Distributed Systems and Their Role in Scaling AI

The rise of large-scale AI applications has placed unprecedented demands on computational infrastructure. Traditional single-machine setups are no longer sufficient for the data processing and model training requirements of advanced AI systems. Distributed systems, whether built using on-premises clusters or cloud platforms, provide the scalability and flexibility needed to support these workloads by distributing tasks across multiple machines. This section delves into the core principles of distributed systems and explains how they contribute to scaling AI operations effectively.

Core Principles of Distributed Systems

Horizontal Scaling

Horizontal scaling involves adding more machines (nodes) to a system to handle increased workloads rather than upgrading the resources of a single machine (vertical scaling). This approach offers greater flexibility and cost-efficiency, as organizations can incrementally increase capacity using commodity hardware rather than investing in high-performance, expensive machines.

- **Key Advantages**:
  - o **Incremental Growth**: Organizations can add nodes as demand increases, avoiding the need for large upfront investments.
  - o **Fault Isolation**: Distributing workloads across multiple nodes ensures that the failure of one node does not impact the entire system.

- **In AI Workloads**: Horizontal scaling is particularly important for handling massive datasets during training and inference. For example, training a large language model requires splitting data into smaller chunks and distributing computation across a cluster of GPUs or TPUs. This parallelism significantly reduces training time and allows for processing datasets that would otherwise exceed the memory and computational limits of a single machine.

Figure 33 shows the overall structure of a distributed system, with nodes grouped into clusters, handling distributed queries, and returning results efficiently.

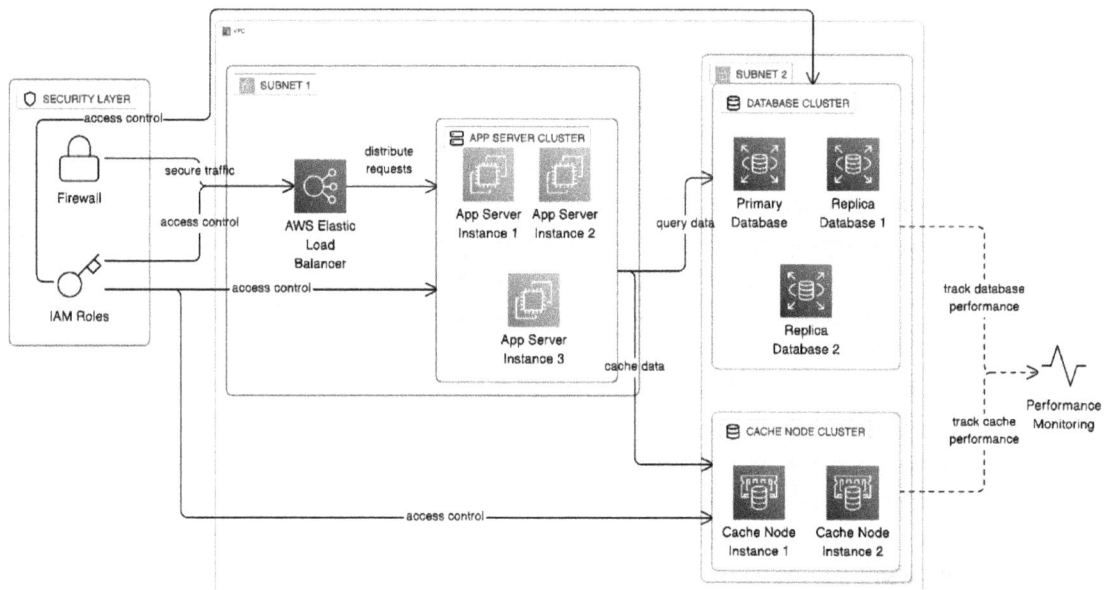

Figure 33: Distributed System Architecture. [24]

---

[24] https://phoenixnap.com/kb/apache-hadoop-architecture-explained?utm_source=chatgpt.com.

Fault Tolerance

Fault tolerance is the ability of a distributed system to remain operational despite the failure of one or more components. Distributed systems achieve fault tolerance by replicating data across multiple nodes and implementing recovery mechanisms to restore the system after a failure.

- **Key Techniques**:

  o **Data Replication**: Data is duplicated across several nodes so that if one node fails, another can take over without data loss.

  o **Checkpointing**: In AI training, checkpointing saves the intermediate states of the model at regular intervals. In the event of a node failure, the training process can resume from the last checkpoint rather than starting from scratch.

  o **Consensus Algorithms**: Systems often use consensus protocols (e.g., Paxos, Raft) to ensure that all nodes agree on a single source of truth, even in the face of partial failures.

- **Example**: Distributed training systems for neural networks often rely on fault tolerance to prevent massive disruptions. When a training node crashes due to hardware failure, checkpointing allows the system to reload the model's state and continue training without wasting hours or days of computation.

Figure 34 visualizes the recovery steps after a node failure, showing how replication and checkpoints ensure continuity.

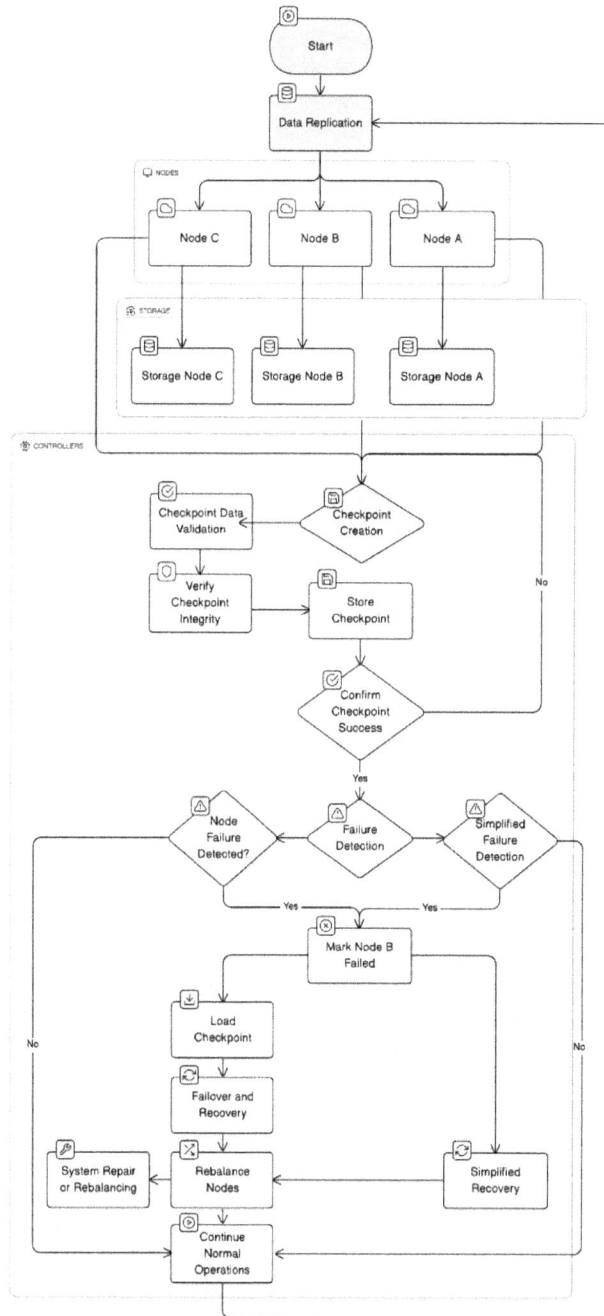

Figure 34: Fault Tolerance Process.[25]

[25] https://www.interviewbit.com/blog/apache-spark-architecture/?utm_source=chatgpt.com.

Data Localization

Data localization minimizes the movement of data across the network by processing data close to where it is stored. In distributed systems, this principle is crucial for reducing latency, conserving bandwidth, and improving overall efficiency in large-scale AI operations.

- **Key Benefits**:

    o **Reduced Latency**: By processing data locally, systems avoid the delays associated with transmitting large datasets over long distances.

    o **Bandwidth Conservation**: Data-intensive operations, such as video or image preprocessing, can be performed near the data source, minimizing the amount of data sent across the network.

    o **Optimized Compute Resources**: Geographically dispersed data centers can handle local data requests, ensuring that nearby nodes share the workload efficiently.

- **Use Case**: Consider an AI system analyzing satellite imagery for real-time weather predictions. By using local edge nodes located near data sources, the system can preprocess and analyze massive image files without uploading the entire dataset to a central server, significantly speeding up the analysis.

Figure 35 shows geographically distributed data centers, each processing local datasets and contributing aggregated insights to the global model.

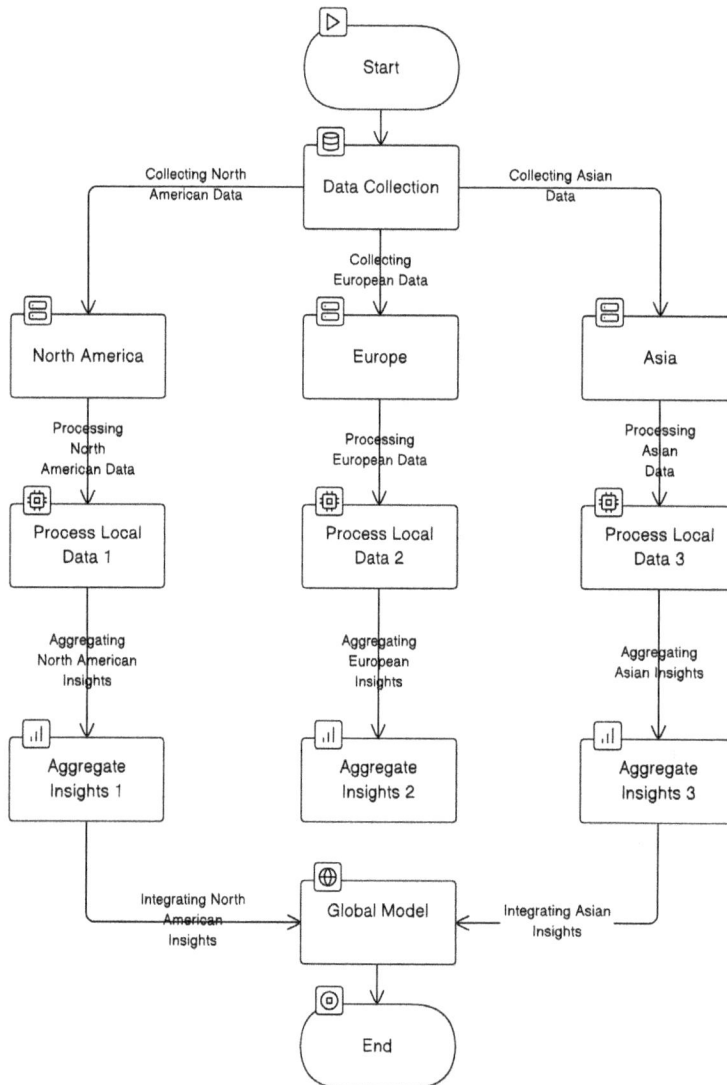

Figure 35: Data Localization Flow. [26]

Key Technologies

The successful implementation of distributed systems for AI workloads depends on various cloud-based platforms, distributed databases, stream processing tools, and orchestration frameworks. This

---

[26] https://www.geeksforgeeks.org/hadoop-architecture/?utm_source=chatgpt.com.

section provides a comprehensive overview of the key technologies that enable scalable, efficient, and fault-tolerant distributed AI systems.

Cloud-Based Platforms: Cloud service providers offer managed services that simplify the setup and scaling of distributed systems for AI workloads:

- **AWS Dataproc** and **Google Dataproc** provide Hadoop and Spark clusters as managed services, enabling large-scale distributed data processing without the need to manage infrastructure.
- **BigQuery** (Google) and **Azure Synapse Analytics** offer serverless data warehouses optimized for large-scale analytics.
- **Vertex AI** (Google) and **AWS SageMaker** provide environments for training and deploying ML models on distributed hardware, such as GPUs and TPUs.
- **IBM Cloud and Watson AI** offer specialized services for NLP, predictive analytics, and data lakes.
- **Oracle Cloud Infrastructure (OCI)** provides high-performance compute instances and specialized databases for AI workflows.
- **Alibaba Cloud** offers Elastic GPU services and AI tools for organizations in the Asia-Pacific region.
- **Red Hat OpenShift** is a Kubernetes-based platform for managing distributed applications in hybrid and multi-cloud environments.

Distributed Databases: Distributed databases provide scalable, highly available storage solutions that can handle both structured and unstructured data:

- **Cassandra:** A NoSQL database designed for high availability and scalability, commonly used for real-time analytics and IoT data storage.
- **DynamoDB:** Amazon's fully managed NoSQL database that supports single-digit millisecond response times at any scale:
- **CockroachDB:** A distributed SQL database known for strong consistency and fault tolerance, ideal for transaction-heavy AI applications.
- **Neo4j:** A graph database for relationship-heavy data such as recommendation systems and fraud detection.

- **TiDB:** A hybrid transactional and analytical processing (HTAP) database designed for large-scale distributed SQL workloads.
- **FaunaDB:** A globally distributed, serverless database known for strong consistency and developer-friendly APIs.
- **ArangoDB:** A multi-model NoSQL database that supports document, key-value, and graph storage.

Stream Processing Platforms: These platforms handle real-time data streams for AI systems that require continuous data ingestion and processing:

- **Apache Kafka:** A robust messaging system that supports high-throughput, fault-tolerant streaming for real-time AI applications.
- **Apache Pulsar:** Known for multi-tenancy and geo-replication, Pulsar is often used in complex distributed streaming architectures.
- **Amazon Kinesis:** AWS's managed streaming service for building real-time data pipelines, suitable for real-time anomaly detection and event-based processing.

Specialized Distributed File Systems: Distributed file systems store massive amounts of unstructured data and enable parallel access for AI workloads:

- **Ceph:** A distributed storage system providing object, block, and file interfaces with massive scalability.
- **Google Cloud Filestore:** A managed file storage solution optimized for AI applications requiring shared file systems.

Container and Orchestration Tools: Containers and orchestration frameworks are essential for deploying and managing distributed AI workloads:

- **Kubernetes:** A widely used platform for orchestrating containerized applications, enabling horizontal scaling across distributed nodes.
- **Docker Swarm:** A native clustering tool for managing Docker containers, useful for smaller-scale distributed systems.
- **Kubeflow:** A ML toolkit built on Kubernetes, designed for scalable AI workflows and seamless model deployment.

AI Model Distribution and Optimization: These tools and systems help optimize and distribute AI workloads across nodes and GPUs:

- **NVIDIA DGX Systems:** Hardware-optimized distributed systems designed for large-scale AI model training and inference.
- **Horovod:** A distributed training framework that supports TensorFlow, PyTorch, and Keras for multi-node, multi-GPU training.
- **Ray Distributed Framework:** A framework for scaling Python-based AI and data science workloads across clusters.

Serverless Compute and Edge Platforms: Serverless and edge solutions provide event-driven compute environments that enhance real-time AI inference and edge processing:

- **AWS Lambda:** A serverless compute service that runs AI inference tasks without provisioning infrastructure.
- **Azure Functions:** A serverless compute service for event-driven AI workloads.
- **Google Cloud Functions:** Supports real-time actions based on incoming data events.
- **NVIDIA Jetson** and **AWS IoT Greengrass:** Platforms for running distributed AI workloads on edge devices, ideal for IoT and autonomous systems.

Real-World Example: OpenAI's GPT-4 is a prime example of how distributed systems enable large-scale AI innovation. To train a model with trillions of parameters, OpenAI leveraged distributed clusters of GPUs and TPUs across multiple data centers. This approach allowed the system to process terabytes of data simultaneously, ensuring timely model convergence and reducing training time. By distributing tasks across nodes, OpenAI overcame limitations in memory and computational capacity, demonstrating the power of distributed systems in advancing the field of generative AI.

Data Warehouses, Data Lakes, Data Lakehouses, and Cloud Storage

Data Warehouses

Data warehouses are purpose-built solutions designed to store structured data and support complex analytical queries. These systems organize data into schemas, such as star or snowflake schemas that optimize query performance for reporting and business intelligence. By centralizing historical data from various sources, data warehouses make it easy to perform trend analysis, generate reports, and create dashboards. Modern cloud-based data warehouses, such as **Snowflake** and **Amazon Redshift**, have enhanced scalability and can process large datasets while providing on-demand compute resources. These solutions also integrate seamlessly with AI tools, enabling organizations to apply ML to their analytical workflows. For instance, analyzing customer purchase histories to provide personalized product recommendations requires the structured and high-performance query capabilities that data warehouses offer.

Data Lakes

Data lakes provide a storage architecture that accommodates raw, unstructured, and semi-structured data in its native format. Unlike data warehouses, data lakes do not enforce rigid schemas, making them highly flexible for storing diverse data types, such as text documents, images, and audio files. **AWS S3** and **Azure Data Lake** are widely used cloud-based data lake platforms that offer virtually limitless scalability and cost-effective storage. Data lakes are particularly useful for AI workloads that require access to large volumes of heterogeneous data. For example, a multimodal AI system might aggregate text, visual, and audio data from various sources to train models capable of generating rich, context-aware outputs. However, data lakes can become inefficient without proper management, as unstructured data may lead to "data swamps" if metadata and governance practices are not implemented.

Data Lakehouses

Data lakehouses combine the flexibility of data lakes with the performance and governance features of data warehouses. This hybrid architecture addresses the limitations of traditional data lakes by adding support for ACID (atomicity, consistency, isolation, durability) transactions, data versioning, and optimized query engines. **Databricks' Lakehouse Platform** and **Apache Iceberg** are prominent examples of this approach, providing a unified platform for data engineers and analysts to run both analytical and ML workloads. By enabling real-time analytics and supporting ML pipelines, data lakehouses simplify workflows requiring raw data and refined insights access. An AI use case for data lakehouses includes building end-to-end pipelines that train large language models while simultaneously running business analytics, all within the same infrastructure. This reduces data duplication and operational complexity, making lakehouses a cost-effective solution for organizations handling massive datasets.

Cloud Storage

Cloud storage solutions are general-purpose platforms that offer scalable, redundant, and highly available data storage integrated with compute services. Popular providers such as **AWS S3**, **Google Cloud Storage**, and **Azure Blob Storage** allow organizations to store vast amounts of data and access it from anywhere with minimal latency. These platforms support data encryption, replication, and disaster recovery features, ensuring robust data security and resilience. In AI use cases, cloud storage serves as a foundational component for hosting training datasets and serving data during inference in real-time applications. For instance, a recommendation system may rely on cloud storage to provide quick access to customer interaction data during inference, ensuring fast and personalized responses. Additionally, cloud storage integrates seamlessly with data processing tools, enabling organizations to build scalable AI pipelines without investing in expensive on-premises infrastructure. Figure 36 illustrates a hybrid data flow.

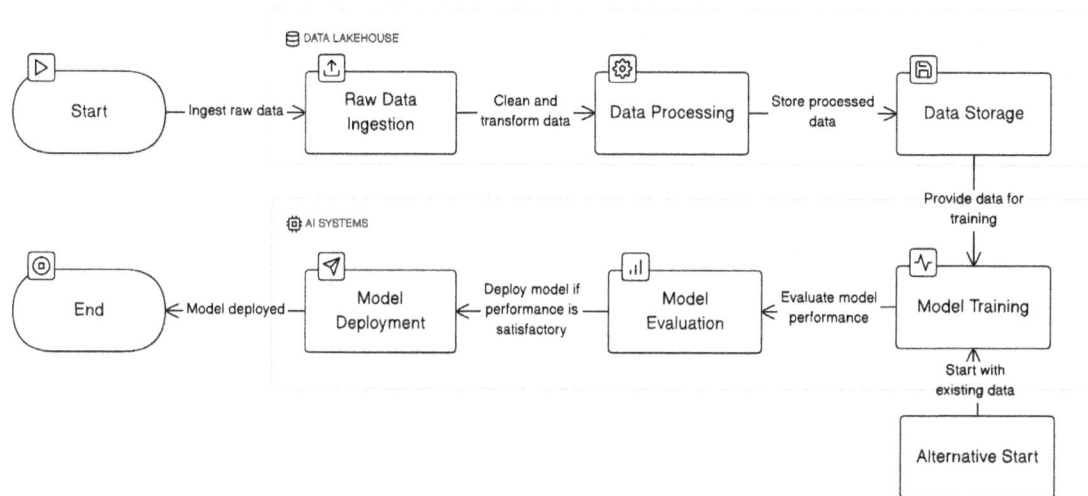

Figure 36: Hybrid Data Flow.[27]

Table 2 compares different storage types and provides examples.

Storage Type	Primary Use	Examples
Data Warehouses	Storing and analyzing structured data with optimized query performance and support for business intelligence workflows.	Snowflake, Amazon Redshift
Data Lakes	Storing raw, unstructured, and semi-structured data for flexibility and large-scale aggregation across various data types.	AWS S3, Azure Data Lake
Data Lakehouses	Providing a hybrid solution that combines the flexibility of data lakes with the performance and governance of data warehouses.	Databricks Lakehouse Platform, Apache Iceberg
Cloud Storage	Offering general-purpose, scalable storage solutions with integration into compute services and data processing pipelines.	AWS S3, Google Cloud Storage, Azure Blob Storage

Table 2: Comparison and examples of storage types.[28]

---

[27] https://medium.com/nerd-for-tech/apache-spark-visual-intro-9eb3fd2709f9?utm_source=chatgpt.com.

[28] https://www.turing.com/kb/hadoop-ecosystem-and-hadoop-components-for-big-data-problems?utm_source=chatgpt.com.

The Evolution of Data Storage Technologies

As storage technologies have evolved, competing reasons exist for employing one type of storage over another.

Relational Database Management Systems (RDBMS) are some of the oldest database technologies and are sometimes referred to as traditional storage systems. They are designed to manage structured data with fixed schema and relationships between the data points. RDBMS stores data in tables consisting of rows and columns, where each row represents a unique record, and each column represents a specific attribute. This structure allows for the use of SQL (Structured Query Language) to perform complex queries, updates, and management of the data:

- **MySQL**: MySQL is a widely-used open-source RDBMS known for its robustness and performance. It is particularly suited for web applications and online transaction processing (OLTP). MySQL uses a client-server model and supports ACID (Atomicity, Consistency, Isolation, Durability) properties to ensure data integrity. Common use cases include e-commerce platforms, where reliable and fast transaction handling is critical.

- **PostgreSQL**: PostgreSQL is an advanced open-source RDBMS emphasizing extensibility and SQL compliance. Known for its strong support for advanced data types, such as JSON and XML, PostgreSQL is ideal for complex applications requiring sophisticated data manipulation and analysis. It supports a variety of indexing methods and has built-in support for procedural languages like PL/pgSQL. Common use cases include financial systems and scientific applications requiring complex queries and data integrity.

NoSQL Databases

NoSQL databases are designed to handle the scalability and flexibility needs of modern applications. Unlike traditional relational databases, NoSQL databases support dynamic schema design, allowing unstructured and semi-structured data to be stored and queried efficiently:

- **MongoDB**: MongoDB is a popular NoSQL database known for its document-oriented design, which stores data in JSON-like BSON format. This flexible schema design is ideal for managing unstructured data, such as image metadata or customer profiles. MongoDB also supports horizontal scaling with built-in sharding, making it well-suited for large-scale applications that require fast read and write operations. Common use cases include powering content management systems and storing data for recommendation engines.

- **Cassandra**: Apache Cassandra is a distributed NoSQL database designed for high availability and fault tolerance, making it an excellent choice for real-time analytics and IoT data. It uses a peer-to-peer architecture where each node in the cluster holds equal importance, ensuring no single point of failure exists. Cassandra excels at handling massive datasets across multiple geographical locations. An example use case is maintaining an always-available recommendation system that processes millions of daily user interactions.

The following table illustrates some tradeoffs between traditional RDBMS and NoSQL databases.

Traditional RDBMS versus Modern Solutions

Feature	Traditional RDBMS (e.g., MySQL)	Modern Solutions (e.g., NoSQL, Cloud Databases)
Data Type Support	Structured	Structured, Semi-Structured, Unstructured
Scalability	Vertical	Horizontal
Query Flexibility	SQL	SQL + NoSQL (e.g., JSON, graph queries)
AI Suitability	Limited	Designed for large-scale AI and big data

Table 3: Comparison of traditional RDBMS vs NoSQL databases.[29]

Cloud Databases

Cloud databases provide scalable, fully managed database solutions that eliminate the need for on-premises infrastructure. These databases can handle large-scale analytical and transactional workloads with minimal administrative overhead:

- **BigQuery (Google)**: Google BigQuery is a serverless, highly scalable data warehouse designed to quickly query petabyte-scale datasets. Its columnar storage and parallel query

[29] https://www.turing.com/kb/hadoop-ecosystem-and-hadoop-components-for-big-data-problems?utm_source=chatgpt.com.

execution enable rapid processing of large datasets, making it an essential tool for real-time data analytics. BigQuery integrates seamlessly with AI and ML services, allowing organizations to run predictive analyses directly within the database.

- **Amazon Aurora**: Amazon Aurora is a managed relational database service compatible with MySQL and PostgreSQL. It offers high performance and scalability while maintaining compatibility with existing applications. Aurora is optimized for AI workloads that require complex queries, such as real-time data enrichment and feature extraction for ML models. Its fault-tolerant and self-healing storage system ensures data resilience and consistency.

Choosing the Right Database for AI

Choosing the right database for AI applications is a critical decision that depends on various factors, including the nature of the data, performance requirements, integration with existing workflows, and budget constraints. Below, we expand on each selection criterion and provide practical guidance for practitioners.

Data Type

The types of data an organization needs to store and process significantly impact the database choice. Databases can store structured data, like tables with predefined fields, or unstructured data, like free-form text, images, and videos. Many modern AI systems require support for mixed data types to ensure comprehensive data processing and analysis:

- **Consideration:** What types of data are being handled—structured, unstructured, or mixed?
- **Expansion:** For example, an AI system designed for financial modeling may require structured transaction data, while an AI-based sentiment analysis tool may rely on unstructured customer feedback data.
- **Example:** "Our AI system must handle structured financial data and unstructured customer feedback to perform predictive analysis and trend identification."

Performance Needs

Databases differ in their ability to handle real-time versus batch operations. Some workloads require low-latency access for real-time decision-making, while others may prioritize high-throughput batch processing for periodic analysis:

- **Consideration:** Does your workload prioritize low-latency queries, batch processing, or both?
- **Expansion:** Low-latency systems are critical for AI-powered applications such as fraud detection that require immediate alerts, while batch processing is commonly used for generating periodic reports from historical data.
- **Example:** "Our fraud detection model requires real-time data access for instant alerts, but we also need batch capabilities for daily reporting."

Integration

Seamless compatibility with AI and ML tools is essential for building efficient data pipelines. The database should easily integrate with data processing tools, AI frameworks, and cloud services:

- **Consideration:** Does the database integrate with tools like Apache Spark, TensorFlow, and cloud-based services?
- **Expansion:** Integration with tools like Apache Spark enables distributed data processing, while frameworks like TensorFlow require fast data access for model training and inference.
- **Example:** "We need our database to work with Apache Spark for distributed processing and TensorFlow for model training workflows."

Cost

Balancing scalability and cost-effectiveness is crucial for long-term success. Database solutions should align with budget constraints while offering the flexibility to scale as data volumes grow:

- **Consideration:** What are the budget constraints and scalability requirements?

- **Expansion:** Some databases offer pay-as-you-go pricing, suitable for fluctuating workloads, while others may have a fixed-cost model ideal for consistent data usage.
- **Example:** "We seek a cost-effective solution for current data needs but can scale to petabytes without significant cost increases."

The following checklist is useful to determine their database selection.

Criteria	Guiding Questions	Sample Answer	Score (1-5)
Data Type	What types of data does the system need to support?	"Our use case involves structured customer data and unstructured reviews."	
Performance Needs	Does the workload prioritize low latency or batch processing?	"We need real-time updates for fraud detection and batch processing for reports."	
Integration	Is the database compatible with existing AI tools and pipelines?	"Integration with Apache Spark and TensorFlow is essential."	
Cost	What are the budget constraints and scalability requirements?	"We need a cost-effective solution that scales from gigabytes to petabytes."	

Table 4: Comparison of traditional RDBMS vs NoSQL DBs.

Using Table 4, practitioners can assign scores to each criterion based on importance (1 = low, 5 = critical) and use the totals to inform their final database selection. This structured approach ensures the chosen database aligns with organizational goals and operational demands.

Optimizing Data Access for AI Applications

Real-Time Streaming

Real-time streaming enables continuous data ingestion and processing as events occur, which is crucial for AI applications requiring instant decision-making. Platforms like **Apache Kafka** and **Apache Pulsar** serve as robust messaging systems that stream data directly to AI models, facilitating real-time processing of event data:

- **Key Features**: Kafka and Pulsar support high-throughput, fault-tolerant streaming and offer flexible configurations for partitioning and replication, ensuring resilience and scalability.
- **AI Use Case**: An example of real-time streaming is fraud detection systems that process live transaction data to identify anomalies and flag suspicious activities within milliseconds. This approach reduces false positives and improves the speed of alerting, enhancing the overall security of financial operations.
- **Best Practices**: Implement checkpointing to ensure data consistency and use schema registries to maintain data format compatibility across services.

Caching Layers

Caching layers accelerate the retrieval of frequently accessed data, reducing the need for repeated queries to primary databases or storage systems. Tools like **Redis** and **Memcached** provide in-memory data caching, drastically improving read performance during AI model inference:

- **Key Features**: Redis supports advanced data structures like sorted sets, lists, and hash maps, making it highly adaptable for AI workloads. On the other hand, Memcached is optimized for simple key-value pair caching with minimal overhead.
- **AI Use Case**: Caching is essential for recommendation engines that serve personalized content based on user preferences in near real-time. By caching precomputed model outputs, these systems can handle high request volumes without performance degradation.
- **Best Practices**: Use Time-To-Live (TTL
) settings to expire outdated cache entries and implement cache invalidation strategies to ensure data accuracy.

Organizations can optimize data access patterns by combining real-time streaming and caching layers, ensuring that AI applications remain responsive and efficient despite heavy workloads.

Future Trends and Emerging Concepts

Edge Storage and Processing

Edge storage and processing refer to the practice of processing data near its source, such as on local devices or edge servers, rather than sending it to centralized cloud servers. This approach significantly reduces latency and enhances response times, making it ideal for applications like autonomous vehicles, smart home devices, and industrial IoT systems. By processing data locally, edge systems can quickly respond to critical events, such as an obstacle appearing in front of a self-driving car:

- **Key Benefits**: Lower latency, reduced data transmission costs, and enhanced privacy since sensitive data can be processed locally without needing to be sent over the network.
- **Use Case**: In autonomous vehicles, edge storage and processing enable real-time decision-making by analyzing data from sensors, cameras, and radars directly on the vehicle's onboard system.

A schematic of an edge computing system appears in Figure 37. Raw data is generated from cameras and sensors and pushed to edge computing devices. The devices are AI-capable, meaning they transform the raw data into processed data that can be pushed to the vehicle control systems.

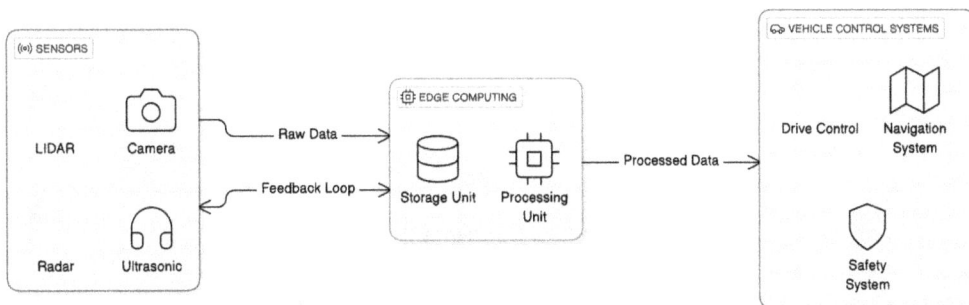

Figure 37: Edge Computing System in an Autonomous Vehicle.[30]

---

[30] https://www.linkedin.com/posts/rocky-bhatia-a4801010_one-diagram-to-refer-for-spark-application-activity-7142841174196740097-pU7h?utm_source=chatgpt.com.

AI-Optimized Storage Systems

AI-optimized storage systems are platforms specifically designed to handle the unique demands of AI workloads, such as massive data throughput, parallel read/write operations, and low latency. These systems are built with features like GPU-direct access and hierarchical data caching to speed up training and inference processes:

- **Key Features**: Support for large file formats (e.g., Parquet, ORC), efficient data retrieval for iterative model training, and compatibility with distributed storage systems.
- **Use Case**: A deep learning research team training large language models may use AI-optimized storage solutions to ensure smooth access to datasets spanning petabytes without performance bottlenecks.

A schematic of hierarchical storage is illustrated in Figure 38.

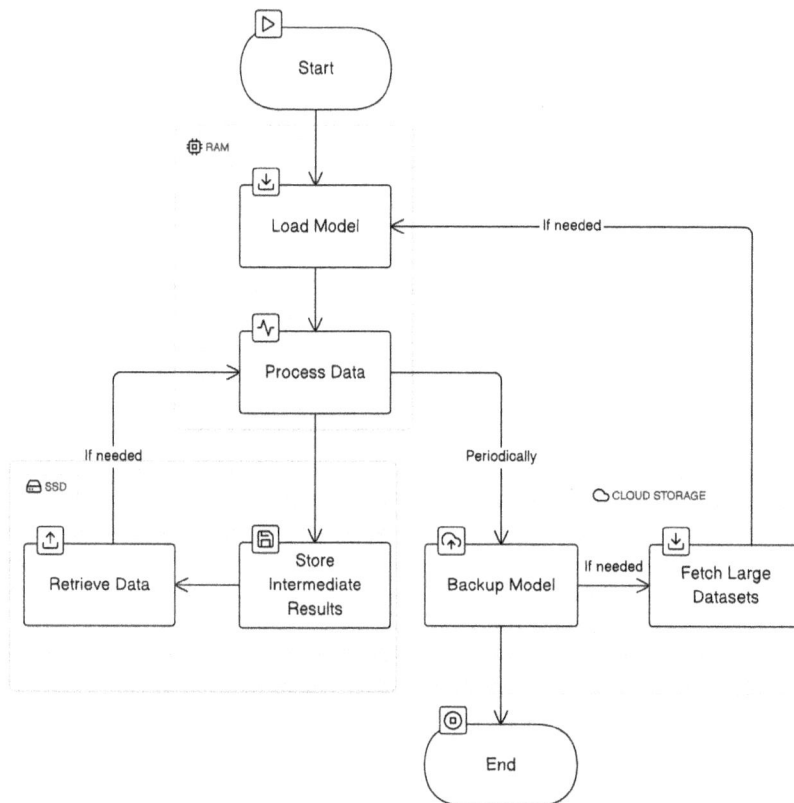

Figure 38: AI-Optimized Storage Layers.

Data Governance

Data governance involves establishing policies, processes, and frameworks to ensure that data is accurate, secure, and used responsibly. Effective data governance is crucial for AI projects to maintain data integrity, ensure reproducibility, and comply with regulations like GDPR and CCPA:

- **Key Components**: Access controls, audit trails, and standardized data documentation.

- **Use Case**: A healthcare organization implementing predictive analytics must enforce strict data governance to manage patient data securely, ensuring that all actions are logged and that sensitive information is accessible only to authorized personnel.

A schematic of a modern AI data pipeline is illustrated in Figure 39.

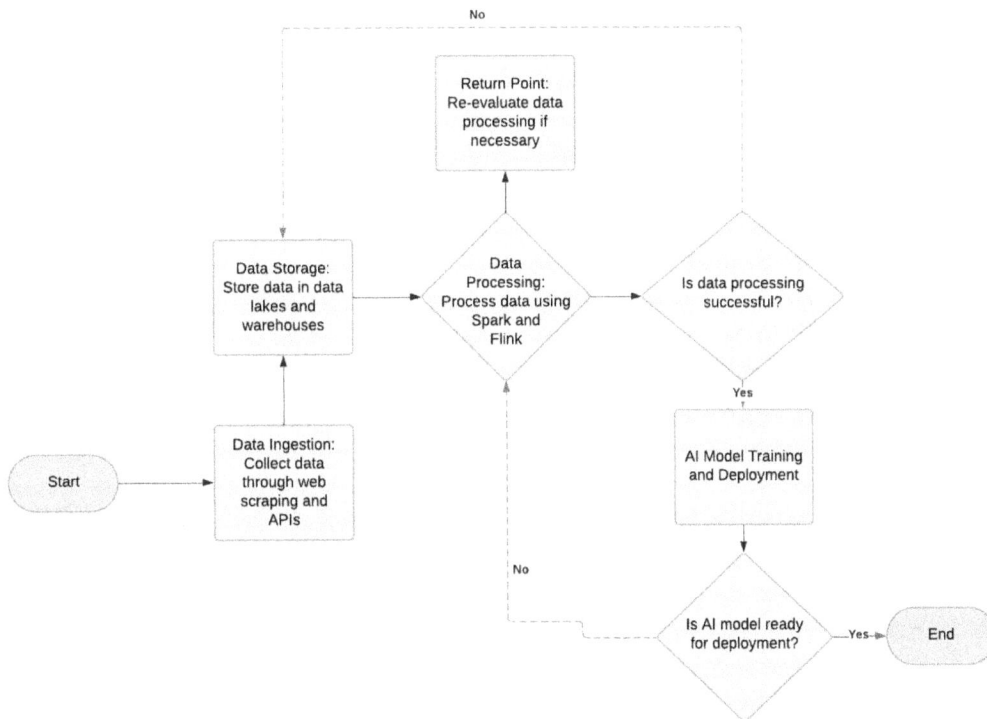

Figure 39: Modern AI Data Pipeline.

Summary

The success of AI hinges on efficient data storage and processing. Modern technologies like distributed systems, data lakehouses, and real-time streaming platforms are critical enablers for managing the vast datasets required for AI innovation. Organizations can design scalable, cost-effective architectures tailored to their AI needs by selecting the right technologies and optimizing data access.

However, beyond storage and processing, managing the quality, consistency, and governance of core business data is equally vital for AI. In the next chapter, we'll dive into the world of **Master Data Management (MDM) Technologies for AI**, exploring how MDM systems ensure clean, consistent, and reliable data for AI models. We'll examine strategies for integrating MDM into AI workflows, highlight tools and platforms, and discuss how MDM supports AI applications in industries like healthcare, finance, and retail. By mastering MDM, organizations can unlock the full potential of their AI initiatives.

References

Apache Software Foundation, "Hadoop Distributed File System (HDFS) Overview," 2023. [Online]. Available: https://hadoop.apache.org/docs/stable/hadoop-project-dist/hadoop-hdfs/HdfsUserGuide.html.

Apache Software Foundation, "Apache Spark Documentation," 2023. [Online]. Available: https://spark.apache.org/docs/latest/.

PrestoDB, "Presto/Trino Query Engine Documentation," 2023. [Online]. Available: https://prestodb.io/docs/current/.

## CHAPTER 8

Master Data Management (MDM)
and Data Quality for AI

A I systems rely on good, consistent, and reliable data. While cutting-edge algorithms are important, they are only as good as the data pipeline on which they are built. Organizations often struggle with broken-down systems, outdated records, and inconsistent data sources, all of which can derail AI initiatives.

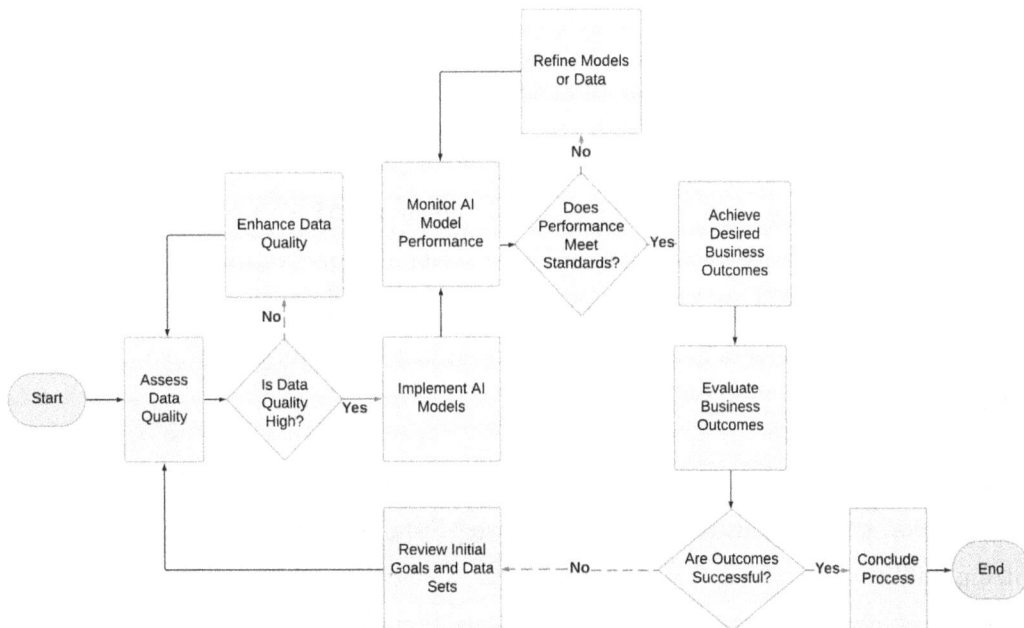

Figure 40: The Role of Data Quality: Understanding its Impact on AI Accuracy and Business Outcomes.

Core Types of Data

To fully understand the importance of data consistency in AI, it is essential to consider the different types of data based on their nature of change and their role in AI workflows:

- **Master Data:** Core business entities such as customers, products, suppliers, and employees that form the foundation of an organization's data landscape. Master data remains relatively stable, supporting consistent analytics and decision-making. It provides the **"truth"** to organizational data, ensuring a single, reliable source of foundational information.

- **Reference Data:** Reference data provides **context** by classifying information such as industry codes, geographies, organizational structures, currencies, and standards. It complements master data by offering classifications and hierarchies critical for AI workflows, ensuring alignment and consistency across data systems.

- **Metadata:** Descriptive information that provides **meaning** and context to other data types, such as data formats, creation timestamps, lineage, and critical data elements. Metadata enhances transparency and traceability, making data more accessible and understandable.

- **Transactional Data:** Real-time operational data like purchases, payments, and interactions that feed AI decision-making. This dynamic data type drives day-to-day operations while enabling AI systems to react to real-time scenarios.

The interplay among these data types in Figure 41 enhances AI workflows. Metadata enriches Master Data with descriptive context, while Master Data anchors real-time Transactional Data. Reference Data complements Master Data by offering hierarchical structures like geographies for suppliers. Together, these types form a comprehensive framework for contextual and operational AI systems.

In AI, Transactional Data takes precedence due to its dynamic nature, driving use cases like recommendation systems and fraud detection. Master Data, while less voluminous, is pivotal for organizing and contextualizing Transactional Data. Metadata plays a smaller but critical role, ensuring traceability and transparency. Reference Data, though static, provides vital classifications that underpin data consistency across workflows.

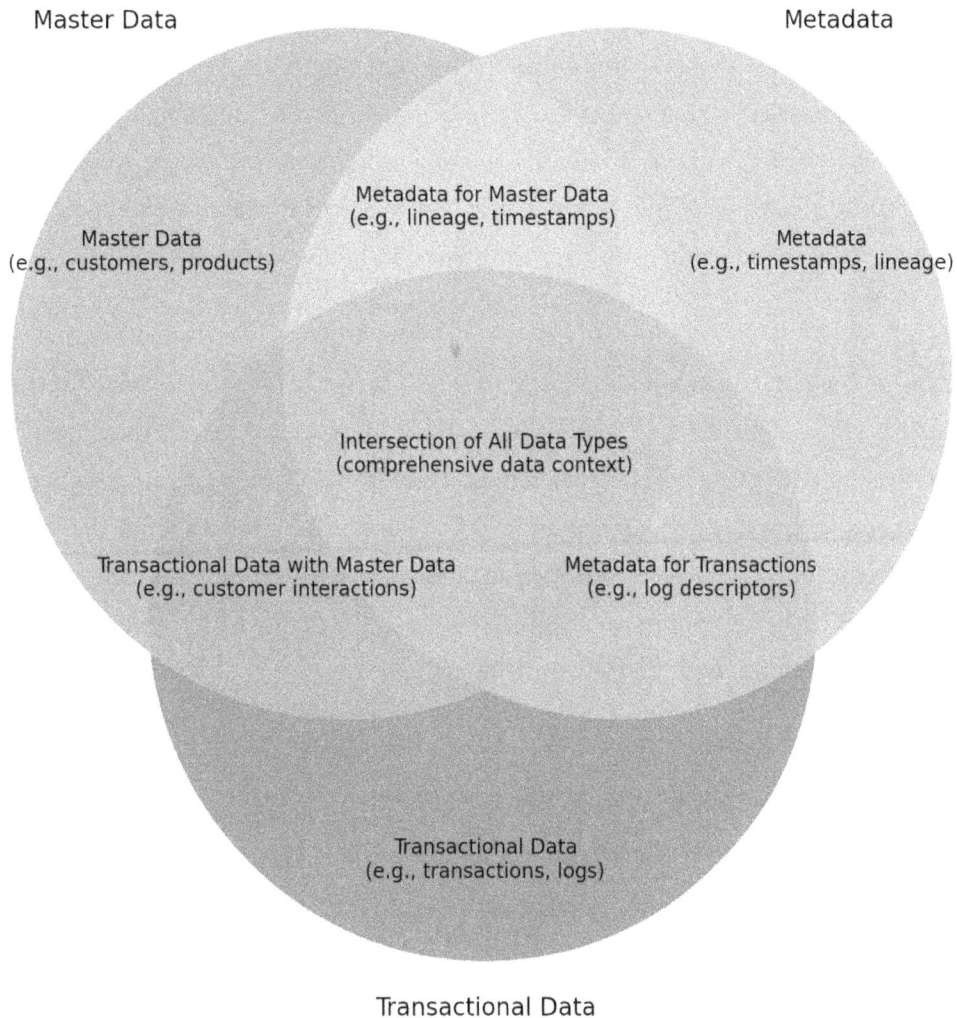

Figure 41: Relationship Between Core Types of Data in AI Workflows.

The Role of Data Quality and Master Data Management (MDM) in AI

Data quality and Master Data Management (MDM) are critical pillars for ensuring the reliability and accuracy of AI systems. Both processes address fundamental challenges in managing and maintaining high-quality data, which is essential for AI models to produce reliable and insightful predictions:

- **Data Quality and Profiling:** Data quality ensures that datasets are accurate, complete, consistent, timely, and valid. Poor data quality can undermine AI model performance, leading to unreliable predictions and flawed insights. As a foundational step, data profiling assesses datasets to uncover anomalies, missing values, inconsistencies, and outliers. This diagnostic process helps tailor data quality improvement efforts to the unique requirements of AI workflows, fostering the creation of robust datasets that AI systems can rely on.

- **Master Data Management (MDM):** Master data serves as the "single source of truth" for organizations, consolidating core business entities such as customer, product, and supplier information. Fragmented or outdated master data can lead AI models to produce erroneous outputs. MDM systems address this issue by unifying disparate data sources into a centralized framework, ensuring data is consistent, accurate, and contextually relevant. This unified approach enables AI systems to operate with a reliable foundation, enhancing their accuracy and trustworthiness.

By integrating robust data quality processes with effective MDM systems, organizations can establish a comprehensive data management framework that supports the development of AI models capable of delivering accurate, actionable insights.

Advanced Data Quality (DQ) Techniques

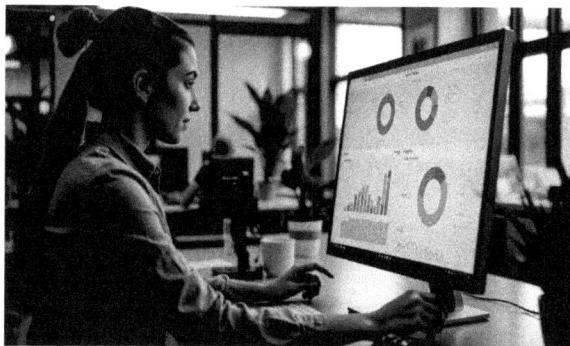

Figure 42: A data analyst leveraging advanced analytics tools to visualize and interpret key performance metrics, ensuring data-driven decision-making in a collaborative workspace.

Data quality enhancement is fundamental for ensuring consistent, accurate data flows that support AI applications. This section elaborates on key techniques with detailed descriptions.

Data Profiling: Analyzing Data for Insights

Data profiling involves comprehensively examining data sources to uncover patterns, anomalies, inconsistencies, and outliers. This foundational step not only informs the development of data quality processes but also aids in building data confidence within the organization by enabling a clear understanding of data characteristics.

Traditionally, legacy systems required data analysts to manually write SQL queries and compile static reports to detect data inconsistencies and discrepancies. This manual approach was both labor-intensive and prone to human error, especially in large and complex datasets. Analysts would spend significant time validating findings, often missing subtle patterns or relationships within the data.

Modern platforms, such as Informatica Data Quality (see Informatica 2023), Ataccama ONE, and Talend Profiling Engine (see Talend 2023), have transformed this process by utilizing ML algorithms to automate the detection of anomalies and inconsistencies. These tools go beyond simple checks by evaluating data distributions, identifying missing values, and highlighting unusual data points in real time. Their ML capabilities allow for adaptive profiling to identify evolving trends or sudden data shifts.

Additionally, these platforms provide intuitive and interactive dashboards that allow data professionals to visualize trends, compare datasets, and drill down into specific records for deeper inspection. This visualization capability enhances collaboration by presenting data insights in accessible formats to both technical teams and business stakeholders. Users can interact with the profiling results to identify root causes of issues, prioritize data remediation efforts, and track improvements over time.

Moreover, advanced data profiling tools often integrate seamlessly with data governance frameworks, enabling organizations to document metadata, monitor data quality KPIs, and maintain transparency in data operations. They support real-time data ingestion and continuous monitoring, making them invaluable for data ecosystems that rely on real-time decision-making processes.

By incorporating advanced analytics and automated workflows, modern data profiling solutions streamline the quality assurance process and contribute to creating robust, AI-ready datasets that foster innovation and support informed decision-making. Organizations that implement these tools benefit from faster time-to-insight, improved operational efficiency, and enhanced data governance, positioning themselves for sustained success in the era of AI.

Data Cleansing and Standardization: Ensuring Uniformity

Data cleansing is a comprehensive process that identifies, corrects, and removes inaccurate or incomplete data to ensure datasets are accurate and reliable. This step is vital for preparing data that can support robust AI models. On the other hand, standardization ensures that data adheres to a consistent format and structure, regardless of the source. Together, cleansing and standardization improve data interoperability across systems and workflows.

Historically, legacy data management relied on rule-based scripts written in SQL or Python. These scripts applied pre-defined logic to consistently detect errors, correct data, and format values. However, such approaches required constant maintenance and updates, as they lacked flexibility and were prone to errors when encountering unexpected data changes.

In contrast, modern platforms such as Talend, Trifacta, and OpenRefine apply context-aware rules that adapt to the nature of the data, allowing for more intelligent handling of inconsistencies. These tools use ML to recognize patterns and detect anomalies, enabling automatic error correction, intelligent field matching, and the automated removal of duplicates. By integrating real-time data correction workflows, these tools ensure that data is standardized as soon as it enters the system, reducing latency and preventing downstream disruptions.

Additionally, these platforms provide user-friendly interfaces and visual tools that support collaboration between data engineers and business users. Interactive dashboards allow teams to monitor the progress of cleansing operations, track changes in data quality metrics, and refine rules based on feedback. For instance, users can create custom templates for recurring data issues, automate workflows for commonly encountered problems, and receive alerts for unexpected data discrepancies.

Moreover, modern data cleansing and standardization tools often integrate seamlessly with master data management (MDM) and data governance frameworks, ensuring that cleansed data aligns with organizational policies and regulatory requirements. They support schema validation, enforce naming conventions, and enhance metadata documentation, further supporting transparency and traceability.

By adopting advanced cleansing and standardization solutions, organizations can build a foundation of high-quality data that drives reliable, accurate AI insights, minimizes operational risks, and enhances decision-making across departments.

Data Deduplication: Removing Redundancies

Data deduplication is crucial in maintaining dataset integrity by identifying and eliminating duplicate records that can skew AI models, inflate data storage costs, and undermine decision-making processes. In traditional data management, deduplication often relied on static rules and manual fuzzy string matching to identify duplicates. Analysts created pre-defined patterns and compared records based on simple attributes, such as names and IDs, which made it difficult to detect subtle or complex duplications across large datasets.

Modern data deduplication platforms, such as Informatica, Talend, and Reltio, employ sophisticated AI-based entity resolution techniques to identify near-duplicates with greater accuracy. These tools use advanced algorithms, including graph-based matching and probabilistic models, to understand complex relationships within data. By mapping connections across multiple attributes and datasets, they detect duplicates that traditional methods often miss, such as entries with minor typos, variations in formatting, or differences in data representation across systems.

For example, Informatica's entity resolution engine utilizes ML to refine matching criteria over time, adapting to changing data patterns. Talend's deduplication features integrate real-time data pipelines to cleanse records dynamically during data ingestion, ensuring that duplicate records do not propagate downstream. Reltio's graph database capabilities provide a comprehensive view of entity relationships, making it easier to detect and resolve duplication across interconnected datasets, such as customer profiles spread across CRM, sales, and support systems.

The latest deduplication tools also support user-defined rules for conflict resolution, enabling organizations to prioritize trusted data sources and define how conflicting data points are merged. This ensures the creation of a reliable 'golden record'—a single, authoritative representation of an entity. Additionally, interactive dashboards provide transparency by displaying matching scores, data discrepancies, and resolution history, empowering data stewards to review and adjust rules as needed.

Organizations can enhance data quality, reduce redundancy, and build a strong foundation for ML models that rely on consistent and accurate data by adopting AI-powered deduplication processes. Effective deduplication not only optimizes storage and improves query performance but also strengthens compliance efforts by eliminating outdated and conflicting records that could result in regulatory issues.

Data Lineage and Provenance: Tracing Data Journeys

Data lineage involves tracking the complete lifecycle of data, from its origin and transformations to its final destination, ensuring transparency and traceability across the entire data pipeline. This process is crucial for understanding how data changes over time, verifying its accuracy, and identifying potential sources of errors.

In traditional systems, data lineage was managed manually through static flowcharts and spreadsheets, which required significant effort to update and often became outdated quickly. These manual processes made it challenging to identify how data fields were altered across different stages or to pinpoint discrepancies in a timely manner.

Modern platforms like Collibra, Alation, and Apache Atlas have revolutionized data lineage by automating data flow and transformation visualization. These tools create interactive maps that display each step of the data journey, highlighting key processes, dependencies, and transformation points. This comprehensive view allows data stewards and engineers to trace errors back to their source, enabling faster root-cause analysis and correction.

Beyond visualization, these platforms often integrate with data governance frameworks to provide detailed metadata, ensuring that every data entry is documented with context, such as timestamps, user edits, and system modifications. This level of detail supports compliance with regulations like GDPR and CCPA by making data access and changes auditable.

Additionally, data lineage tools help organizations manage schema evolution, track changes in data structures, and detect schema drift that could disrupt downstream applications. Advanced features, such as automated alerts, notify teams of unexpected modifications, reduce operational risks, and prevent data integrity issues.

Lineage tools enhance data trust and foster collaboration between data teams and business stakeholders by providing clear, real-time insights into data transformations. They are critical in maintaining robust data pipelines, ensuring organizations can confidently build and deploy AI models based on accurate and transparent data.

Data Imputation: Addressing Missing Data

Data imputation is a vital process in data quality management aimed at addressing the challenges posed by missing values, which can compromise the completeness and accuracy of datasets used in AI and ML models. This process ensures that incomplete records do not lead to skewed analyses or degraded model performance. Historically, data imputation involved simple statistical methods, such as replacing missing values with the mean, median, or mode of a dataset. While straightforward, these approaches often fail to capture the underlying patterns in the data, leading to oversimplified assumptions that could introduce bias or dilute predictive accuracy.

Modern data imputation techniques have significantly evolved and leverage advanced algorithms to provide more context-aware and accurate estimates. Methods such as K-Nearest Neighbors (KNN) imputation use similarities between data points to estimate missing values based on the most comparable records. Multiple Imputation by Chained Equations (MICE) performs iterative imputations by creating multiple plausible datasets and averaging their results, offering robust estimates in cases where multiple variables have missing values. Deep learning-based autoencoders have also emerged as a powerful imputation method, capable of learning complex representations of the data to reconstruct missing values with remarkable precision.

These modern techniques are implemented in tools like Python's Scikit-learn library, which offers built-in imputation functions, and specialized platforms like DataRobot, which automate and optimize imputation workflows. Additionally, data profiling tools such as Talend and Informatica Data Quality integrate imputation capabilities, enabling real-time handling of missing data during data ingestion and preprocessing.

Furthermore, organizations can enhance imputation strategies by combining domain expertise with algorithmic insights. For example, healthcare providers can use clinical knowledge to guide imputation for patient records, ensuring medically relevant estimations. Financial institutions can refine their imputation processes based on historical transaction patterns to avoid introducing errors in risk assessments.

By adopting sophisticated imputation techniques, organizations can maintain dataset completeness, improve data reliability, and support more accurate and unbiased AI models. Effective imputation not only addresses data gaps but also strengthens the overall integrity of data ecosystems, ensuring that comprehensive and high-quality data inform decision-making processes.

Data Consistency Validation

Data consistency validation ensures that related fields within and across datasets maintain logical relationships and conform to established rules. This process verifies that data points representing the same entity, such as customer names and addresses across different systems, are harmonized and consistent.

Historically, validation was performed manually or enforced through static, hardcoded rules embedded in scripts and database triggers. These methods were labor-intensive and prone to errors, especially when dealing with large, evolving datasets. Discrepancies between related fields often went unnoticed until they caused downstream issues in reporting or model outputs.

Modern platforms like Informatica, Talend, and Ataccama ONE have transformed consistency validation by integrating ML to automatically learn validation rules from historical patterns and detect inconsistencies across datasets in real time. These platforms apply cross-field checks, comparing fields such as billing and shipping addresses or product prices across multiple sources to ensure alignment.

Advanced validation systems also incorporate context-aware rules that adapt to unique business processes. For example, financial institutions can enforce consistency rules to ensure transaction amounts match balance updates, while healthcare providers validate those medical codes align with patient records.

Furthermore, these platforms offer visual dashboards displaying validation progress, highlighting detected inconsistencies, and providing actionable insights. Teams can configure alerts to detect sudden deviations from expected data trends and adjust validation parameters based on feedback.

By implementing advanced data consistency validation tools, organizations enhance the integrity of their datasets, prevent cascading data issues, and build a reliable foundation for AI applications and operational analytics.

Data Enrichment: Adding Context

Data enrichment supplements existing datasets by adding contextually relevant information to enhance their meaning, accuracy, and usability in decision-making and AI workflows. This process allows organizations to transform isolated data points into comprehensive insights by integrating supplementary information such as demographic, geographic, behavioral, and business intelligence attributes. Enriched data is essential for improving the accuracy and depth of AI-driven insights, enabling more precise predictions, comprehensive customer segmentation, and effective recommendation models.

Legacy approaches to data enrichment relied heavily on static lookup tables and manual data augmentation efforts. These methods were time-consuming and prone to inconsistencies, especially when handling large and dynamic datasets. Static lookups often failed to capture real-time changes, leading to outdated or incomplete context for critical data fields.

Modern platforms, including Clearbit, EnrichIQ, and other API-driven solutions, have revolutionized data enrichment by enabling real-time integration of external datasets. These platforms use APIs to append relevant details—such as income brackets, regional classifications, company size, or social media activity—to existing records dynamically. Some advanced systems also leverage AI-powered inferencing to fill in missing values with predictive insights based on historical data patterns.

For instance, enrichment tools for customer data can provide detailed profiles by adding attributes such as age, occupation, and preferences, enhancing marketing personalization and segmentation. Similarly, geographic enrichment with latitude, longitude, and routing information can optimize supply chain operations by improving delivery predictions. Behavioral enrichment incorporates user interactions such as clickstream events or purchase histories to predict behavior and detect trends, refining AI-driven recommendation systems.

Common enrichment techniques include:

- **Geographic Enrichment:** Adds location-based data such as postal codes, latitude/longitude, and region classifications to improve routing optimizations and demographic insights. Tools like Experian Data Enrichment, Trifacta, and Google Cloud Datasets offer seamless integration for geographic data enhancement.
- **Demographic Enrichment:** Appends customer-specific data like age, gender, income level, and occupation to enhance customer profiling and targeted AI recommendations. Tools like Clearbit, Experian, and Synthesis AI excel at providing diverse and accurate demographic insights.
- **Business Intelligence Enrichment:** Incorporates competitive analysis data, market segmentation, and customer sentiment insights. Platforms like InsideView and Dun and Bradstreet support holistic views of market trends and customer feedback.
- **Behavioral Enrichment:** Integrates user interactions, including app usage data, clickstream events, and purchase histories, to enrich customer journeys and improve predictive AI models. Popular tools include Adobe Experience Cloud, Mixpanel, and Google Analytics.

Additionally, enriched data can help organizations address gaps in AI model training datasets by diversifying input data. This is particularly useful in industries such as healthcare and finance, where enriched datasets contribute to more balanced, unbiased model training. For example, geographic enrichment can address regional disparities in datasets, while synthetic demographic enrichment can improve diversity in underrepresented categories.

Modern data enrichment platforms improve data consistency, boost operational efficiency, and enable deeper, data-driven insights by automating the enrichment process and ensuring seamless integration with master data management (MDM) systems and governance frameworks.

Anomaly Detection: Identifying Irregularities

Anomaly detection is a critical aspect of data quality management that identifies data points or patterns that deviate from expected norms, signaling potential errors, unusual events, or fraud. The purpose of anomaly detection extends beyond simple validation—it ensures data reliability, prevents operational disruptions, and supports fraud prevention and monitoring efforts in real-time AI workflows.

Legacy approaches to anomaly detection often relied on static thresholds—fixed numerical limits set manually based on historical data trends. While effective for basic use cases, these methods lacked adaptability and were prone to false positives or negatives in dynamic environments where data distributions frequently change. For instance, detecting sales spikes due to promotions requires constant threshold adjustments, making manual approaches impractical for real-time systems.

Modern anomaly detection solutions leverage sophisticated algorithms and ML models to identify outliers dynamically. Techniques such as isolation forests detect anomalies by isolating data points with fewer splits, making it easier to recognize rare events. DBSCAN (Density-Based Spatial Clustering of Applications with Noise) excels at detecting clusters and identifying noise points outside normal distributions, making it useful for both time-series data and spatial datasets. Recurrent Neural Networks (RNNs) are often used for sequential anomaly detection, particularly in IoT sensor data and financial transaction monitoring.

Tools like Anodot and BigEye automate anomaly detection across multi-dimensional data streams, providing comprehensive dashboards with trend visualizations, anomaly timelines, and root cause analysis. These platforms also support customizable alerts that notify teams of irregularities based on user-defined thresholds, ML insights, or business-specific rules. This flexibility ensures that data teams can prioritize anomalies that are most impactful, minimizing alert fatigue.

Additionally, advanced anomaly detection systems integrate seamlessly with data governance frameworks, allowing organizations to document incidents, track corrective actions, and ensure regulatory compliance. These systems can also leverage synthetic data to enhance model training and improve anomaly classification accuracy.

By adopting modern anomaly detection methodologies, organizations gain the ability to detect and address data inconsistencies and suspicious patterns before they propagate through downstream systems. This capability not only strengthens AI model performance, but also enhances operational resilience by safeguarding against errors, fraud, and unexpected data shifts.

Schema Drift Detection

Schema drift detection monitors and addresses changes in data structures over time to ensure that data pipelines and models remain stable and functional. Schema drift occurs when the format, structure, or schema definitions of incoming data deviate from expected configurations, disrupting downstream workflows and leading to model inaccuracies or system errors.

Historically, schema drift was tracked manually through static spreadsheets and monitoring logs. This process was slow and often missed subtle changes, such as renamed fields, new columns, or altered data types until they caused failures. Manual methods also struggled to handle frequent updates in dynamic environments, making it difficult to maintain schema consistency.

Modern schema drift detection tools, such as Great Expectations and Datafold, automate the validation process and provide real-time alerts when unexpected schema changes occur. These platforms compare incoming data structures against predefined schema blueprints and flag discrepancies, enabling immediate responses to potential issues. They also support automated testing and validation workflows that prevent schema mismatches from propagating through production systems.

Advanced systems can also handle schema evolution by recognizing legitimate changes—such as adding optional fields or naming conventions—and updating schemas without causing disruptions. Some platforms integrate with version control systems to document schema changes over time, providing traceability and audit logs for regulatory compliance.

Organizations can safeguard data integrity, ensure model reliability, and support seamless integration across evolving ecosystems by implementing comprehensive schema drift detection processes. This approach minimizes downtime, enhances data trust, and strengthens the overall resilience of data-driven operations.

Data Governance and Access Controls

Data governance is a crucial framework for enforcing compliance, maintaining data integrity, and controlling access to sensitive data. It involves defining policies, procedures, and accountability mechanisms to ensure data is managed responsibly throughout its lifecycle.

In legacy systems, access control was often managed using static spreadsheets and rigid permission groups, which posed challenges in environments with frequent role changes or growing datasets. These outdated approaches were prone to human error, lacked scalability, and offered limited visibility into data usage patterns.

Modern governance platforms, such as Collibra, Immuta, and Privacera, have transformed how organizations enforce data permissions by implementing dynamic, Role-Based Access Controls (RBAC). These tools allow administrators to assign permissions based on user roles, ensuring that individuals can only access the data necessary for their tasks. In addition to RBAC, these platforms support Policy-Based Access Controls (PBAC), which can adapt permissions based on contextual information, such as location or time.

One key feature of modern governance tools is data masking, which obscures sensitive fields in datasets to prevent unauthorized exposure while retaining the utility of the data for analysis. Advanced systems can apply dynamic masking rules that adapt in real time based on user credentials or compliance requirements. This ensures that sensitive information, such as Personally Identifiable Information (PII), remains secure even during collaborative workflows.

Furthermore, governance tools offer detailed audit trails and logging features that track data access and modification activities, supporting compliance with regulations like GDPR, CCPA, and HIPAA. These logs provide insights into who accessed what data, when, and for what purpose, enabling organizations to demonstrate accountability and transparency during audits.

By implementing comprehensive data governance frameworks with robust access control mechanisms, organizations can enhance data security, foster trust, and support scalable, compliant data practices that empower data-driven innovation.

Data Masking and Synthetic Data Generation

Data masking is a technique designed to protect sensitive information while retaining the utility of the data for analysis and testing. This process ensures that critical data, such as personally identifiable information (PII), remains obscured to unauthorized users without compromising the value of the dataset.

Legacy methods for data masking involve static placeholders or simple obfuscation techniques, such as replacing Social Security numbers or account numbers with generic sequences. While these approaches provided a basic layer of protection, they lacked flexibility and were prone to reverse-engineering attacks.

Modern platforms, such as Informatica Data Privacy Management and Delphix, have introduced dynamic masking techniques that apply masking rules in real time, adapting based on user credentials, compliance requirements, and data usage context. This approach ensures that sensitive data remains protected during collaborative workflows and across different environments, such as development, testing, and production.

In addition to masking, synthetic data generation has emerged as a powerful solution for preserving data privacy while maintaining statistical accuracy. Platforms like Synthesis AI and Mostly AI use generative algorithms to create realistic yet entirely artificial datasets that mimic the characteristics of real data without exposing actual records. Synthetic data is particularly valuable in domains such as healthcare and finance, where stringent regulations often limit access to original datasets.

Organizations can enhance model training by generating diverse and representative synthetic datasets while mitigating privacy risks.

Moreover, synthetic data can help address data imbalance issues by generating additional records for underrepresented categories, improving fairness in AI models. These tools also support compliance efforts by providing auditable logs and configuration settings to demonstrate adherence to data protection regulations such as GDPR and CCPA.

By combining advanced data masking with synthetic data generation, organizations can enhance their data privacy frameworks, support secure data sharing, and safeguard sensitive information while maintaining the analytical power of their datasets.

Bias Detection and Mitigation

Bias detection and mitigation are essential for ensuring that AI models produce fair and unbiased results, particularly in systems that impact critical areas such as hiring, lending, healthcare, and law enforcement. Bias in data can arise from historical inequalities, underrepresentation of demographic groups, or flawed collection methods, leading to AI models that perpetuate or amplify these biases.

In traditional practices, bias detection involves manual sampling and demographic comparisons to identify disparities across different data groups. This approach is labor-intensive, subjective, and prone to oversight, especially in large, complex datasets. Manual efforts often fail to account for intersectional biases, instances where overlapping demographic attributes create unique vulnerabilities.

Modern tools such as Fairlearn and Aequitas provide statistical frameworks to detect and quantify biases at multiple levels. These tools offer metrics such as disparate impact, equalized odds, and demographic parity to measure how outcomes differ across demographic groups. Fairlearn integrates seamlessly with ML pipelines, providing actionable insights and visualizations highlighting disparities. Aequitas, an open-source bias audit toolkit, provides fairness reports that guide data teams in understanding where and how biases exist.

Beyond detection, mitigation strategies include reweighting datasets to give more representation to underrepresented groups, applying data augmentation to fill gaps, and using adversarial debiasing algorithms that adjust model training to minimize bias. Techniques such as counterfactual fairness testing are also employed to evaluate how model predictions change when specific demographic variables are altered.

Furthermore, effective bias mitigation requires cross-functional collaboration between data scientists, ethicists, and domain experts to ensure that the chosen metrics and interventions align with ethical standards and organizational goals. Transparency in documentation—detailing data sources, preprocessing steps, and applied fairness metrics—is crucial for maintaining stakeholder trust and supporting compliance with regulations like GDPR, CCPA, and emerging AI governance policies.

By implementing robust bias detection and mitigation practices, organizations can reduce the risk of discriminatory outcomes, improve model accountability, and ensure their AI systems promote fairness, transparency, and inclusivity.

Data Integrity Verification

Data integrity verification ensures that data remains unaltered, accurate, and secure throughout its lifecycle, safeguarding it from unauthorized changes, corruption, or tampering. This process is critical in establishing trust in data-driven operations and ensuring that AI models rely on authentic, untampered datasets.

Legacy systems commonly relied on basic checksums—numerical values derived from data files that verified consistency by comparing recalculated sums against the original. However, these checksums were limited in their ability to detect sophisticated tampering or changes in large-scale datasets.

Modern solutions have advanced significantly, incorporating cryptographic hashing algorithms such as SHA-256 and SHA-3. Cryptographic hashes generate unique, fixed-length values for each data input, ensuring that even minor changes in the data result in entirely different hash values. This makes it virtually impossible for unauthorized users to alter data without detection.

In addition to cryptographic hashes, blockchain-based data integrity solutions have emerged, leveraging decentralized ledgers to store tamper-proof logs of data changes. Each transaction or modification is recorded as a block within the chain, creating an immutable audit trail that enhances transparency and traceability. This approach is especially valuable in sectors like finance, healthcare, and supply chain management, where data authenticity is paramount.

Data integrity platforms also provide automated validation processes, generating alerts when anomalies in data patterns or unauthorized modifications occur. They integrate with data governance frameworks to support regulatory compliance and provide detailed logging for audit purposes.

By adopting modern data integrity verification methods, organizations can fortify their data ecosystems against tampering, enhance stakeholder confidence, and build resilient workflows that support trustworthy AI-driven decision-making.

Golden Record Creation

Golden record creation is an essential process in master data management and is illustrated in the following diagram:

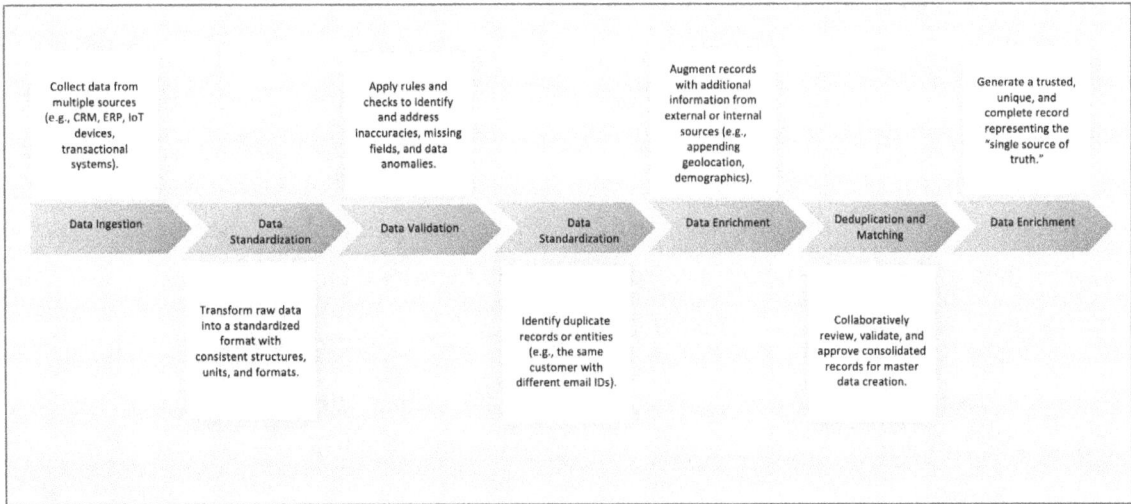

Figure 43: Golden Record Creation Process: A Step-by-Step Workflow from Data Ingestion to the Generation of a Trusted Single Source of Truth.

Golden records are consolidated, authoritative representations of data entities that unify disparate records into a single trusted source. This process involves merging multiple conflicting data records from different systems, ensuring that the resulting data is accurate, consistent, and contextually relevant.

In traditional approaches, golden record creation was a manual, time-consuming process that required data analysts to reconcile discrepancies across records using spreadsheets and manual reviews. These methods were prone to errors and inconsistencies and lacked scalability, making them ineffective for large datasets or organizations with complex data infrastructures.

Modern Master Data Management (MDM) platforms, such as Reltio Connected Data Platform, Informatica MDM, and Semarchy xDM, leverage out-of-the-box ML and artificial intelligence to automate the golden record creation process. These platforms apply data quality scoring algorithms to assess the accuracy, reliability, and completeness of incoming records, prioritizing trusted data sources and resolving conflicts intelligently. ML models refine matching criteria over time, improving their ability to identify duplicates, detect inconsistencies, and resolve anomalies across diverse data points.

In addition to automated data merging, these platforms offer rule-based configurations that allow organizations to customize how records are consolidated. For example, businesses can set rules to prioritize recent updates from specific systems or enforce specific hierarchies for data sources. Real-time dashboards provide transparency by displaying matching scores, discrepancy reports, and lineage details, enabling data stewards to monitor the consolidation process and adjust as needed.

Golden record creation is essential for maintaining high-quality data that supports critical business operations and AI-driven insights. By implementing advanced MDM platforms, organizations can reduce data duplication, streamline data governance, and ensure their data ecosystems align with regulatory requirements and performance goals.

These advanced DQ techniques illustrate the shift from manual, time-consuming processes to automated, AI-driven workflows that enhance data quality for reliable AI applications.

Business Scenarios for Data Quality Tools

Organizations across various industries implement data quality tools to address domain-specific challenges and improve data integrity. Below are descriptions of how these scenarios unfold in different sectors and the role data quality tools play in resolving them:

Fraud Detection in Financial Institutions

Fraud detection requires financial institutions to handle vast amounts of transaction data daily. Even minor inconsistencies or duplicate entries can lead to missed fraud events or, conversely, false positives that burden fraud analysts and disrupt customer trust. Clean and validated data is essential for building accurate fraud detection models that pinpoint genuine anomalies.

A bank attempting to build an AI-driven fraud detection system faced issues with noisy transaction data, duplicate entries, and incomplete records. By deploying Talend Data Quality, the institution was able to cleanse and standardize its financial data, removing duplicates, correcting errors, and detecting data inconsistencies. This not only reduced false positives, but also improved fraud prediction accuracy, enabling fraud analysts to focus on genuine threats and expedite their investigation processes.

Predictive Maintenance in Energy Companies

Energy providers rely heavily on real-time IoT sensor data to predict equipment failures and schedule proactive maintenance. However, sensor data from distributed assets often arrives in inconsistent formats, leading to unreliable predictions.

One energy company faced unreliable maintenance models due to discrepancies in sensor readings collected from various geographic locations. Informatica Data Quality was implemented to standardize and validate incoming data streams, ensuring uniformity across all data sources. This improved the predictive maintenance models, significantly reducing unplanned downtimes and optimizing maintenance schedules to save time and costs.

Customer sentiment analysis in telecommunications understanding requires telecom companies to gather feedback from surveys, social media, and service logs. However, disparate data sources often result in fragmented feedback that undermines accurate sentiment analysis.

A telecom provider encountered difficulties due to fragmented customer feedback data collected from multiple sources. The data, filled with formatting discrepancies and incomplete entries, resulted in poor insights. By using Ataccama ONE, the company was able to consolidate, cleanse, and normalize text-based feedback data. This enhanced sentiment analysis accuracy, allowing the company to predict customer churn patterns and design targeted retention strategies that improved overall customer satisfaction.

Healthcare Data Validation for Diagnostics

Accurate and comprehensive patient records are vital for AI-assisted diagnostics and personalized treatment plans in healthcare. Missing or outdated information can lead to diagnostic errors and delayed treatment.

A hospital system relied on an AI diagnostic tool that struggled with inconsistent and incomplete patient data. By implementing Trifacta, the hospital was able to validate and enrich patient records in real time by integrating data from EHR systems, lab databases, and clinical reports. The result was more precise diagnoses and timely clinical decisions that enhanced patient care and streamlined internal workflows.

These enriched case studies demonstrate how advanced data quality tools address industry-specific challenges, enabling organizations to improve decision-making, operational efficiency, and regulatory compliance.

The bar graph presented above compares the effectiveness of four widely recognized data quality (DQ) tools—Talend Data Quality, Informatica Data Quality, Ataccama ONE, and Trifacta—across four significant AI use cases: fraud detection, predictive maintenance, customer sentiment analysis, and healthcare data validation. The effectiveness scores, which range from 1 to 10, represent how well each tool performs, with higher scores indicating stronger capabilities in each context.

Effectiveness of Data Quality Tools in AI Use Cases

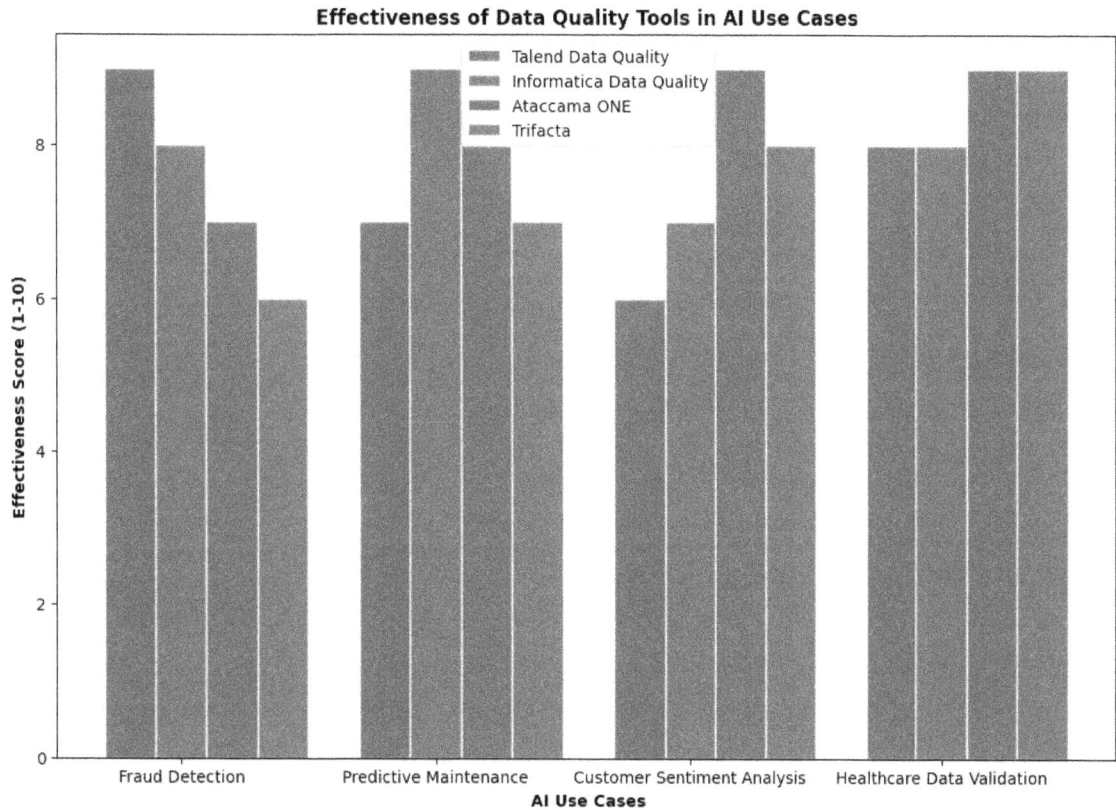

Figure 44: Effectiveness of Data Quality Tools Across AI Use Cases.

In the case of fraud detection, Talend Data Quality achieves an impressive score of 9 out of 10 due to its robust ETL (Extract, Transform, Load) capabilities, which enable real-time cleansing and validation of transactional data. This makes Talend highly effective for financial institutions aiming to detect fraudulent activities quickly and accurately. Informatica Data Quality also performs well, scoring 8 out of 10, owing to its strong anomaly detection features and rule-based validation capabilities. However, the need for more configuration in event-based anomaly detection scenarios can slightly impact its performance. Ataccama ONE, scoring 7 out of 10, excels in AI-powered data validation but is more optimized for handling unstructured data, making it slightly less suited for structured transactional data. Trifacta, scoring 6 out of 10, is primarily known for its visual data preparation and wrangling capabilities. While useful for cleaning structured data, it is less effective for real-time anomaly detection than Talend and Informatica.

Talend Data Quality earns a score of 7 out of 10 for predictive maintenance due to its ability to standardize IoT sensor data. However, it may require additional configurations for continuous data ingestion from distributed assets. Informatica Data Quality stands out in this category with a 9 out of 10 score, thanks to its real-time data processing capabilities and ML integration, which make it ideal for managing and standardizing sensor readings. Ataccama ONE scores 8 out of 10 for its AI-based profiling and standardization features, though its performance can be resource-intensive for large-scale operations. Trifacta scores 7 out of 10 for its batch IoT data cleaning capabilities, enhanced by an intuitive interface, although it lacks some of the automation features needed for streaming data.

Talend Data Quality scores 6 out of 10 in the customer sentiment analysis category, as it handles structured text data well but lacks specialized capabilities for sentiment analysis pipelines. Informatica Data Quality scores 7 out of 10 for its NLP-based text-cleaning features but is generally more effective for structured data. Ataccama ONE scores 9 out of 10, thanks to its advanced AI capabilities for consolidating and enriching unstructured text data, making it highly effective for multi-source sentiment datasets. Trifacta follows closely with a score of 8 out of 10, benefiting from user-friendly workflows for text data wrangling, which supports sentiment analysis tasks across various data sources.

Talend Data Quality earns a strong score of 8 out of 10 in healthcare data validation for its versatility in handling structured healthcare records and its support for compliance frameworks such as HIPAA. Informatica Data Quality also scores 8 out of 10 due to its comprehensive validation capabilities and pre-built data health dashboards that simplify the validation process for healthcare data. Ataccama ONE excels in this use case with a 9 out of 10 score, offering AI-driven validation and deduplication capabilities that make it highly effective in consolidating fragmented patient records. Trifacta matches this score with its visual interface and automation features, which make real-time validation and cleansing of healthcare data efficient and intuitive, particularly when handling missing or outdated records.

The comparison highlights that Talend Data Quality stands out for fraud detection due to its robust ETL and anomaly detection capabilities. At the same time, Informatica Data Quality works best for predictive maintenance thanks to its strong IoT data integration features. Ataccama ONE shines in sentiment analysis with its AI-driven text enrichment capabilities. In contrast, both Trifacta and

Ataccama ONE are exceptional for healthcare data validation, thanks to their real-time data validation features and user-friendly interfaces.

The effectiveness scores were derived from multiple sources, including industry reports such as Gartner's Magic Quadrant and Forrester Wave, which evaluate data quality tools based on their market performance, customer satisfaction, and feature sets. User feedback from platforms such as G2 and TrustRadius provided insights into the practical strengths and limitations of these tools. Additionally, published case studies from tool providers offered real-world examples of how these data quality tools have been implemented across various industries, demonstrating their impact on AI workflows.

Data Governance for AI: Framework, Layers, and Benefits

Framework for Data Governance

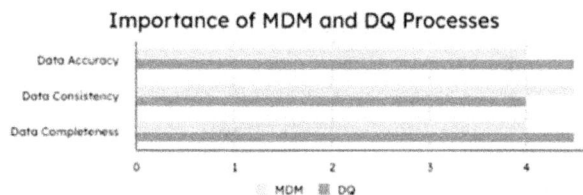

Importance of MDM and DQ Processes

Data Accuracy

Data Consistency

Data Completeness

0   1   2   3   4

MDM   DQ

Strong Data Foundation

Master Data Management (MDM) and Data Quality (DQ)
are foundational for a robust data governance framework.

Figure 45: Data Governance Framework.

A strong data governance framework serves as the backbone for managing and organizing data in AI workflows. At its core, it addresses three pillars: data accuracy, consistency, and completeness. Master Data Management (MDM) ensures that the foundational data, such as customer profiles, product information, and transactional records, is unified and reliable. Simultaneously, Data Quality (DQ) processes validate, cleanse, and standardize this data across systems.

The interplay between MDM and DQ is vital for AI systems to function effectively. For example, ML models risk generating flawed outputs without accurate and consistent data, eroding trust in AI applications. By embedding governance principles into the data lifecycle, organizations can mitigate these risks and lay the groundwork for scalable, high-quality AI systems.

Key Layers in Data Governance

A comprehensive data governance model consists of multiple interconnected layers, each addressing specific aspects of data management. These layers include:

- **Data Foundation Layer:** This layer ensures data accuracy, completeness, and consistency using MDM and DQ processes. It focuses on creating a unified "single source of truth" for all core business data.
- **Data Processing Layer:** During data processing, governance ensures data integrity through lineage tracking, schema drift detection, and bias monitoring. These practices prevent errors and ensure that data transformations remain transparent and traceable.
- **Ethical Governance Layer:** This layer enforces compliance with data privacy regulations, such as GDPR and CCPA, and establishes accountability mechanisms. Organizations can align AI operations with societal expectations by defining ethical policies and enforcing data privacy measures.

Each layer plays a critical role in ensuring that data remains accurate, secure, and compliant across its lifecycle. By understanding these layers, organizations can implement governance practices that support the complex requirements of AI-driven systems.

Benefits of Effective Data Governance

The adoption of a robust data governance framework offers significant benefits, particularly in the context of AI development and deployment. These include:

- **Enhanced AI Model Performance:** With high-quality, consistent data, AI models are better equipped to generate accurate and reliable predictions. This reduces the risk of errors and ensures that AI systems perform as intended.

- **Improved Transparency and Accountability:** A well-implemented governance framework clearly documents data sources, transformations, and usage. This transparency fosters trust among stakeholders and enables organizations to demonstrate accountability in AI outcomes.

- **Ethical and Responsible AI Deployment:** Data governance frameworks establish guardrails for ethical data use, minimizing risks such as bias, discrimination, and privacy violations. This ensures that AI systems align with organizational values and societal expectations.

- **Operational Efficiency:** Governance frameworks enhance operational efficiency by streamlining data processes and reducing redundancies. Organizations can spend less time resolving data quality issues and more time leveraging AI for strategic goals.

In the age of AI, data governance is not just a technical necessity but a strategic enabler. It empowers organizations to harness the full potential of their data assets while upholding ethical standards and fostering trust.

Master Data Management (MDM) Technologies for AI

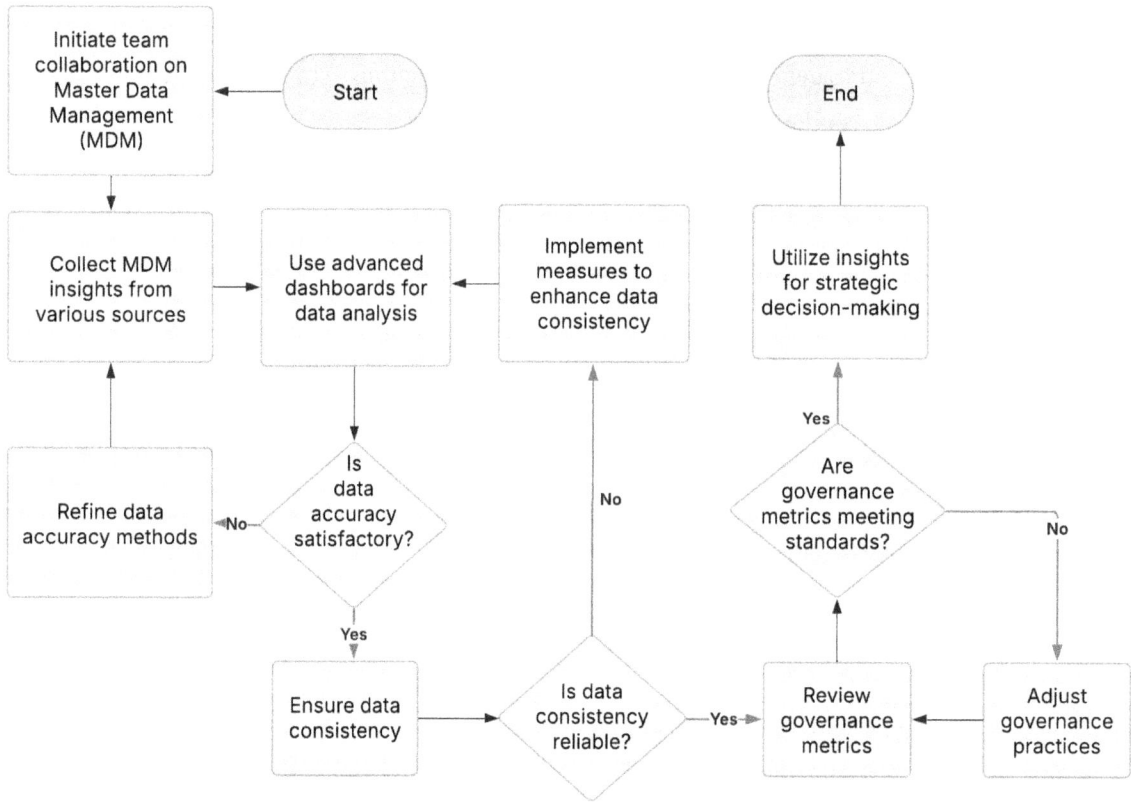

Figure 46: Team collaboration on Master Data Management (MDM) insights, using advanced dashboards to analyze data accuracy, consistency, and governance metrics for strategic decision-making.

MDM plays a critical role in the AI lifecycle by consolidating and governing core business data, such as customer, product, supplier, and employee information, into a single source of truth. This ensures data consistency, resolves duplications, and eliminates inaccuracies, making MDM indispensable for AI models that rely on data from diverse sources. By maintaining data accuracy and unification, MDM tools lay the groundwork for trustworthy, high-performing AI systems, as illustrated in Figure 47.

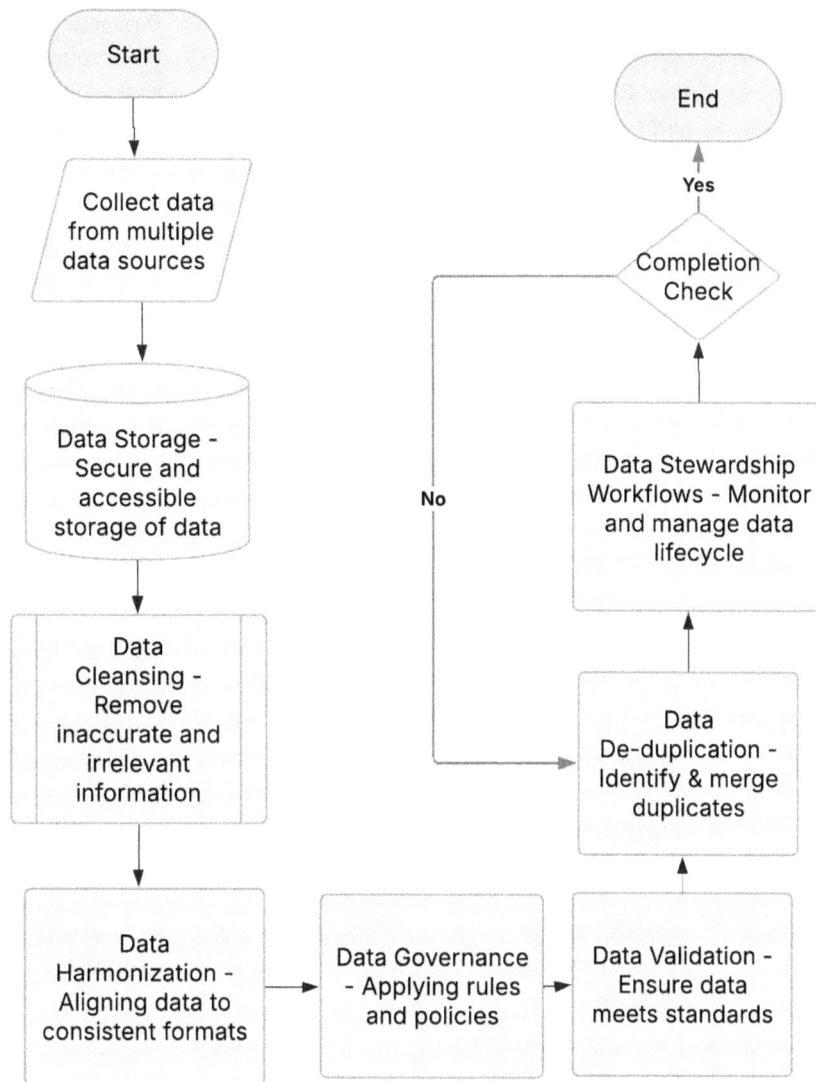

Figure 47: Master Data Management (MDM) Workflow: Ensuring Data Accuracy, Consistency, and Accessibility for AI Systems.

Key Business Scenarios for MDM in AI

There are dozens of challenges businesses face every day. Any organization wanting to compete with AI must take inventory of the business scenarios it faces with related data challenges and determine candidate solutions and anticipated outcomes. Table 5 summarizes many examples.

Scenario	Challenge	MDM Solution	Outcome
Customer 360 for AI Personalization	Fragmented customer data across CRM, marketing, and order systems	Reltio, TIBCO EBX	Unified customer profile, hyper-personalized product recommendations
AI-Powered Supply Chain Optimization	Inconsistent product data across procurement, inventory, and ERP	SAP Master Data Governance	Harmonized supplier data, optimized demand predictions, reduced delays
Financial Risk Management and Compliance	Data silos preventing holistic financial risk analysis	Oracle MDM Suite	Synchronized financial data, accurate default predictions, fraud detection
Healthcare AI for Improved Patient Outcomes	Incomplete patient records across EHR, billing, and clinics	TIBCO EBX	Comprehensive patient data, accurate health risk predictions, personalized care
Product Innovation and Cross-Selling Strategies	Inconsistent product data hindering marketing and cross-sell efforts	Various MDM platforms	Unified product data, targeted product recommendations, increased sales
Regulatory Compliance and Reporting	Disparate regulatory data across departments	MDM platforms supporting regulatory submissions	Consistent regulatory reports, streamlined compliance workflows
Customer Support and Case Resolution	Incomplete support records for resolving customer inquiries	MDM-enhanced customer records	Faster issue resolution, context-aware AI responses
Human Resources and Workforce Planning	Scattered employee data across HR and payroll systems	MDM solutions integrated with HR systems	Improved workforce planning, personalized training programs
Real-Time Data Synchronization for Retail Operations	Unsynchronized POS and online inventory data	MDM with real-time synchronization tools	Accurate demand forecasting, efficient inventory management
Supplier Relationship Management (SRM)	Inconsistent supplier information impacting procurement	MDM for supplier profiles and performance data	Improved vendor negotiations, predictive supplier risk insights

Table 5: MDM Business Scenarios by Challenges, Solutions and Expectations.

Table 5 summarizes key MDM business scenarios by outlining the challenges, MDM solutions, and their respective outcomes for quick reference and enhanced readability:

- **Customer 360 for AI Personalization:** Organizations strive to deliver hyper-personalized customer experiences in an increasingly digital world. Consider a global e-commerce company facing challenges with fragmented customer data scattered across CRM systems, marketing automation platforms, and order management tools. This disjointed view makes it difficult for AI-driven recommendation engines to accurately profile and predict customer preferences. By implementing MDM solutions such as Reltio or TIBCO EBX, the company can consolidate disparate customer data into a unified profile that provides a 360-degree view of customer interactions. The enriched data feeds AI models, enabling hyper-personalized product recommendations that drive customer engagement and retention.

- **AI-Powered Supply Chain Optimization:** Supply chain inefficiencies often arise from inconsistent product data spread across procurement, inventory, and ERP systems. A manufacturing company facing delays due to misaligned supplier and product data can benefit from SAP Master Data Governance to centralize and standardize this information. AI systems can then use clean and harmonized product and supplier data to predict demand trends, optimize inventory levels, and reduce delivery times. This creates a resilient supply chain capable of adapting to changing market conditions.

- **Financial Risk Management and Compliance:** In the financial sector, risk mitigation depends on consistent, accurate, and up-to-date records of customer transactions, credit histories, and financial data. Banks often struggle with data silos across departments, leading to incomplete insights into customer risk profiles. Deploying Oracle MDM Suite allows financial institutions to synchronize financial and customer data across divisions, creating a holistic view of credit risk analysis. By feeding clean, accurate data into AI models, banks can develop sophisticated algorithms to predict loan defaults, detect fraud, and ensure regulatory compliance with frameworks such as Basel III.

- **Healthcare AI for Improved Patient Outcomes:** Healthcare organizations often face challenges with incomplete patient records spread across clinics, billing systems, and electronic health records (EHRs). These fragmented datasets hinder AI models used for predictive diagnostics and personalized treatments. Implementing a robust MDM platform like TIBCO EBX can help consolidate patient data into a unified master record, improving data accessibility and quality. AI models trained on comprehensive patient histories can better predict health risks, recommend personalized care plans, and support clinical decision-making. For example, AI-assisted models can identify early signs of chronic illnesses, enabling timely interventions and improving patient outcomes.

- **Product Innovation and Cross-Selling Strategies:** Retail and consumer goods companies rely on accurate master data to drive product development and cross-selling efforts. By leveraging MDM tools, these organizations can align product data from multiple sources, enabling AI models to identify purchase trends and recommend complementary products.

This unified data also supports AI-driven marketing strategies, ensuring product recommendations are tailored to customer preferences and purchasing histories.

- **Regulatory Compliance and Reporting:** Industries such as pharmaceuticals and finance must adhere to strict regulatory requirements for data accuracy and transparency. MDM platforms enable organizations to centralize regulatory data and ensure consistency across compliance reports. For example, in the pharmaceutical industry, MDM tools can consolidate clinical trial data to support regulatory submissions and pharmacovigilance activities. AI models trained on harmonized data sets can streamline compliance workflows, flag anomalies, and generate real-time reports for regulatory audits.

- **Customer Support and Case Resolution:** MDM enhances AI-driven support systems in customer service by providing accurate and complete customer records. When a customer contacts support, an MDM-powered system can retrieve a consolidated view of their purchase history, previous interactions, and support cases. AI chatbots and virtual assistants can use this data to provide contextually relevant responses and resolve issues faster. This reduces case resolution times and improves overall customer satisfaction.

- **Human Resources and Workforce Planning:** MDM systems can also support AI applications in workforce management by consolidating employee data across HR systems, payroll, and performance management tools. This unified data enables AI-driven insights into employee engagement, turnover prediction, and skill gap analysis. For instance, organizations can use MDM-enhanced AI models to optimize hiring strategies, design personalized training programs, and predict workforce needs based on business growth.

- **Real-Time Data Synchronization for Retail Operations:** In retail environments, maintaining accurate and synchronized master data across point-of-sale systems, inventory management, and online platforms is critical. By integrating MDM with real-time data synchronization tools, retailers can ensure that AI-driven demand forecasting and inventory management systems can access up-to-date data. This enables more accurate stock replenishment, pricing strategies, and promotional offers.

- **Supplier Relationship Management (SRM):** Accurate supplier data is essential for optimizing procurement processes and supplier relationships. MDM platforms help organizations manage supplier profiles, performance data, and contract information. AI models trained on this enriched data can predict supply chain disruptions, recommend alternative suppliers, and optimize vendor negotiations.

These scenarios highlight the transformative role of MDM technologies in enhancing the performance of AI models across industries. By establishing a single source of truth for core business data, organizations can unlock the full potential of their AI investments, driving innovation, operational efficiency, and superior decision-making.

MDM Platforms: Legacy to Cutting-Edge

Master data management is not new, but the related technology improves every year. The following table contrasts legacy system features with cutting-edge features available in new systems.

Platform	Legacy Features	Cutting-Edge Features
Informatica MDM	Data deduplication, real-time synchronization	AI-driven insights, cloud-native architecture
SAP Master Data Governance	Enterprise-grade compliance, static workflows	Predictive data governance, advanced hierarchy modeling
TIBCO EBX	Multi-domain data modeling	Embedded AI for rule creation, workflow automation
Oracle MDM Suite	On-premises integration	Cloud hybrid model, real-time updates
Reltio Connected Data Platform	Customer profile enrichment	Graph database integration, ML-ready unified views
IBM InfoSphere MDM	Entity resolution, data cleansing	AI-based matching, microservices-enabled framework
Profisee MDM	Hierarchical data modeling	Cloud-native deployment, integrated governance
Semarchy xDM	Centralized governance, data hub integration	Self-service data enrichment, visual data lineage
Stibo Systems MDM	Supply chain data integration	360-degree product and supplier views, real-time updates
Ataccama ONE	Integrated data quality and MDM	ML-based anomaly detection, collaborative workflows
Microsoft Master Data Services	Data mastering within SQL Server	Cloud-enabled integration with Azure data services
AWS Glue Data Catalog	Metadata management and ETL	Serverless MDM features, schema versioning
Talend Data Fabric	Data synchronization across sources	Real-time data pipelines, embedded MDM with quality checks
Collibra Data Intelligence Cloud	Governance-driven MDM	AI-powered data stewardship, advanced data lineage
Boomi Master Data Hub	Data integration across applications	Low-code MDM interface, event-driven updates

Table 6: Legacy System Features to Cutting Edge Features Available in New Systems.

The optimal MDM system depends on the features and goals of an organization. There is no "one size fits all" optimal solution. A useful analytic tool is a spider diagram that compares tools across functional dimensions. The following spider diagram is a useful example of candidate platforms across four dimensions.

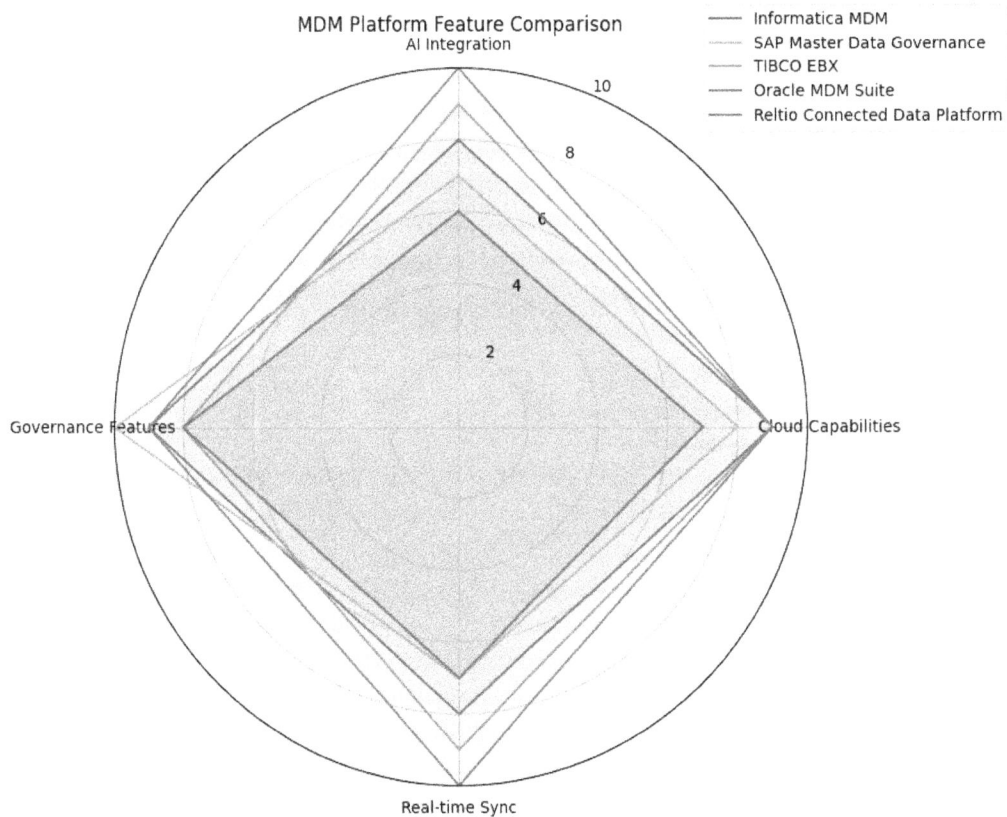

Figure 48: MDM Platform Feature Comparison.

While the information provided above, including the feature comparisons and insights, is designed to guide decision-makers in selecting the right Master Data Management (MDM) tool, it is important to recognize that every enterprise has unique requirements. Tool selection should be a thoughtful process that aligns with the organization's specific goals, data architecture, and operational needs. Additionally, it is good practice to leverage market research and reports from established analysts like Gartner (see Gartner 2023), Forrester, and others to gain deeper insights into the strengths and weaknesses of available MDM solutions. A well-informed choice ensures seamless integration, enhances data quality, and supports the enterprise's long-term data strategy.

Connecting MDM and DQ to Ethical Data Management

As organizations harness the power of Master Data Management (MDM) and Data Quality (DQ) tools to fuel AI systems, addressing broader concerns surrounding data ethics, governance, and compliance becomes imperative. Ensuring that data is accurate and consistent is a foundational step, but it is not the endpoint. Businesses must also prioritize transparency, accountability, and fairness in collecting, processing, and utilizing data. Integrating robust ethical principles with MDM and DQ practices ensures that AI systems operate in a manner that respects societal values and mitigates harm. Ethical Data Management and Governance for AI is the focus of our next chapter.

Summary

Preventing bias in AI systems requires more than just effective data management; it necessitates a governance framework that actively addresses systemic inequities. While MDM and DQ tools can help identify and reduce biases in datasets, ethical oversight ensures that models do not inadvertently amplify existing societal disparities. Data privacy is another cornerstone of ethical data management. Organizations must comply with regulations like GDPR and CCPA, ensuring user consent is respected at every data lifecycle stage. Furthermore, accountability in AI outcomes hinges on clear ownership of data quality and governance processes, ensuring that organizations remain answerable for how data influences AI decision-making.

The absence of robust ethical frameworks has led to significant failures in AI deployment. For instance, in predictive policing, historical crime data has reinforced systemic racism by producing biased AI predictions, perpetuating inequitable law enforcement practices. In the healthcare sector, incomplete or poor-quality patient records used in AI-assisted treatments have resulted in misdiagnoses, endangering lives and eroding trust in AI systems. These failures underscore the necessity of integrating ethical oversight into MDM and DQ processes, ensuring that AI systems deliver fair, accurate, and socially responsible outcomes.

References

Gartner, "Market Guide for Master Data Management Solutions," 2023. [Online]. Available: https://www.gartner.com/en/documents.

Informatica, "Data Quality and Governance Solutions," 2023. [Online]. Available: https://www.informatica.com/data-quality.html.

Talend, "Talend Data Preparation and Governance Strategies," 2023. [Online]. Available: https://www.talend.com/products/data-preparation/.

## CHAPTER 9

Ethical Data Management and Governance for AI

The rapid evolution of AI has brought unparalleled opportunities and challenges. Reports from **Stanford University's Human-Centered Artificial Intelligence Institute** and **Our World in Data** reveal a stark increase in AI-related incidents, from 3 reported cases in 2012 to 78 in 2023, marking a 26-fold escalation. This underscores the urgent need for robust ethical frameworks as AI adoption continues to grow (see Stanford 2023).

Notable incidents, such as deepfake misuse and AI-driven monitoring in sensitive environments, highlight vulnerabilities that demand attention. Additionally, according to the **IBM Institute for Business Value**, executive prioritization of AI ethics surged from under 50% in 2018 to nearly 75% by 2021, reflecting a global shift toward addressing these critical concerns (see IBM 2023). Figure 49 illustrates the number of reported AI incidents and controversies.

This sharp rise underscores the growing challenges and ethical considerations associated with the widespread adoption of AI technologies. Notable incidents include creating deepfake videos and using AI to monitor U.S. prisons, highlighting the need for robust governance and accountability frameworks in AI deployment.

Global annual number of reported artificial intelligence incidents and controversies

Our World in Data

Notable incidents include a "deepfake" video of Ukrainian President Volodymyr Zelenskyy surrendering, and U.S. prisons using AI to monitor their inmates' calls.

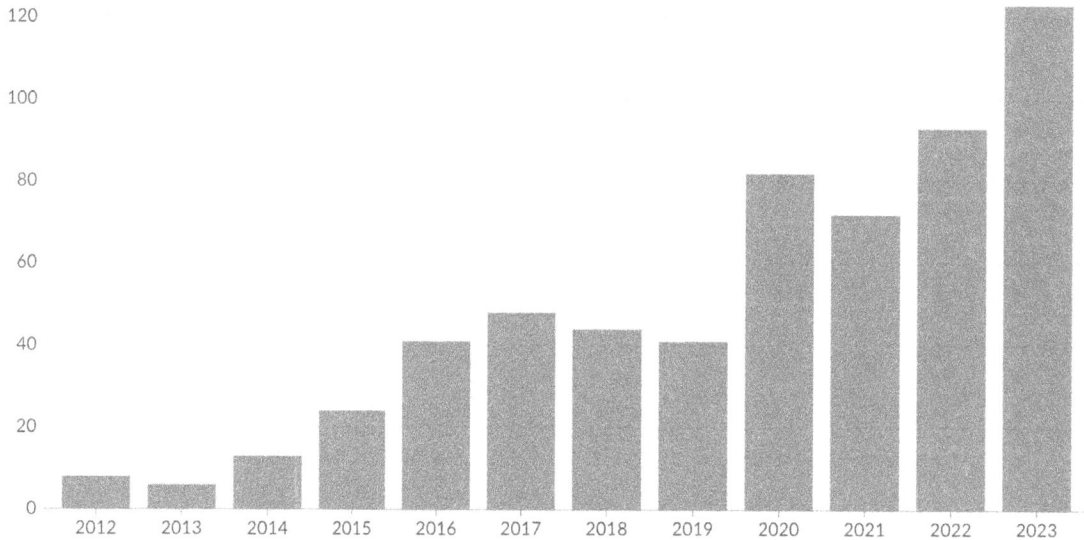

Data source: AI Incident Database via AI Index (2024)   OurWorldinData.org/artificial-intelligence | CC BY

Note: Does not yet include incidents reported in 2022, as incidents must first undergo a vetting process. Reported incidents likely undercount actual incidents, especially in the earliest years of tracking.

Figure 49: Number of reported AI incidents and controversies.

Key takeaways:

- **Ethical AI Governance is Essential:** Structured governance fosters public trust and ensures compliance, enabling responsible AI adoption across industries.

- **Address Core Ethical Challenges:** Issues like privacy, bias, and accountability require targeted, actionable strategies to preserve AI's transformative potential while respecting societal values.

- **Proactive Approaches Yield Results:** Regular audits, ethical AI policies, and transparent governance help prevent reputational harm and costly penalties.

- **Continuous Education:** Ongoing training ensures teams stay vigilant about emerging ethical risks, fostering a culture of accountability and innovation.

By addressing these issues head-on, organizations can avoid the societal and financial risks associated with unethical AI practices while contributing to long-term technological resilience.

These challenges and examples outlined in the Preface lead to the fundamental question: how can we manage AI ethically at its foundation? As established early on, data is the DNA of AI, forming the bedrock upon which ethical practices are built. Hence, we will now discuss how to use data effectively and responsibly to drive the ethical development and deployment of AI systems.

The Responsibility of Data in AI

As AI systems shape decisions that impact society, ensuring these systems are built on ethical and well-governed data has become a critical priority. Poorly managed data can lead to biased models, privacy violations, and a loss of trust among users and stakeholders. Ethical Data Management and Governance for AI focuses on building systems that are fair, transparent, accountable, and compliant with evolving regulations like GDPR and CCPA.

Inadequate ethical frameworks can lead to severe financial and reputational damage. For example:

- **British Airways (2019):** Fined $26 million under GDPR for failing to protect customer data during a breach.

- **Facebook (2019):** Paid $5 billion in fines to the FTC for mishandling user data.

This chapter provides a comprehensive guide to mastering ethical data management and governance. From tools and techniques for ensuring data privacy and compliance to strategies for managing bias, fairness, and transparency, we'll cover every facet of this important topic. By the end of this chapter, you'll be equipped to implement robust governance frameworks and become a champion of ethical AI.

Technologies for Data Privacy and Compliance

Ensuring data privacy and compliance is foundational to ethical AI. With increasing regulations like GDPR (General Data Protection Regulation) in the EU and CCPA (California Consumer Privacy Act) in the US, organizations must implement tools and practices to protect user data and ensure lawful usage.

Data Minimization

Definition: Data minimization is the principle of collecting, processing, and retaining only the data that is strictly necessary for specific, well-defined purposes. It seeks to reduce the risk of data misuse, enhance privacy protections, and ensure compliance with regulations such as GDPR and CCPA.

Why Data Minimization Matters: Minimizing data collection safeguards user privacy, reduces storage costs, and mitigates the risk of non-compliance with privacy laws. Excessive or unnecessary data increases organizational liability and can create inefficiencies in data management systems, complicating audits and security measures.

Figure 50 illustrates the data minimization process.[31]

---

[31] https://www.piiano.com/blog/data-minimization?utm_source=chatgpt.com.

Tools: Apache KAFKA,
Dynamic forms for input
validations

Tools: Snowflake, Erwin
Data Modeler

Implementation &
Controls\nConfigure systems
and enforce controls to
ensure data minimization
during collection and
processing.

Schema Design\nCreate
database schema that
stores only required data
while enforcing field limits.

End

Feedback to Schema Design

Completion
Check\nConfirm compliance with
minimization principles.

Regular Audit &
Monitoring\nConduct
periodic reviews of data
handling practices.

Completeion check
confirms alignment with
minimization principals

Feedback to Requirement Analysis

Tools: Collibra, Tableu for
visualization

Requirement
Analysis\nUnderstand and
define the data points
necessary to achieve
business objectives.

**Output: Identified,
minimal data
requirements**

Data
Mapping\nClassify,
map, and document
data flow across all
systems.

Tools: BigID, Varonis,
Talend

Start

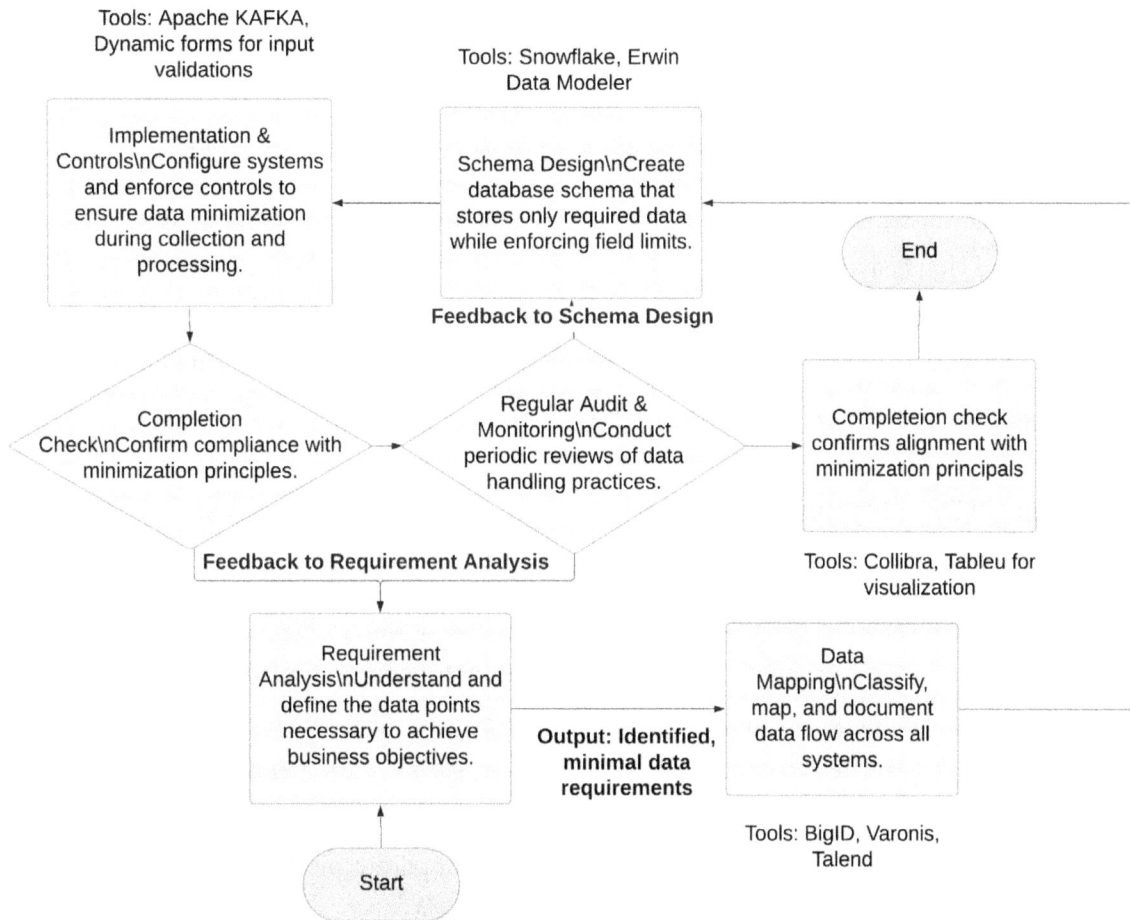

Figure 50: Data Minimization Process.

Requirement Analysis

Conduct a detailed assessment of your AI system's functional and operational needs. Determine the exact data points necessary for achieving your objectives. For example, a retail recommendation engine may need browsing and purchase history to personalize suggestions, but does not require detailed demographic data such as a customer's age or location.

- *Example Tool:* Requirement analysis frameworks like Lucidchart can map business goals to data requirements.

Data Mapping

Data mapping is the process of identifying, classifying, and documenting all data flows within an organization. It serves as the foundation for effective data governance, ensuring that data is utilized responsibly and aligns with business objectives while meeting regulatory requirements.

Organizations must first inventory their data across all systems—structured, unstructured, on-premises, and cloud environments to implement robust data mapping. We can employ specialized tools such as BigID, Varonis, or Talend to automate the discovery of sensitive data (e.g., PII, financial records) and map it against specific business purposes. By understanding how data flows between systems, stakeholders can identify areas of inefficiency, redundancy, and potential security risks.

Key Steps in Data Mapping

1. **Data Discovery:** Use automated tools to locate and classify data based on sensitivity and usage. For example, BigID can scan large-scale datasets and tag PII, while Talend supports integration with various databases and applications for seamless mapping.
2. **Purpose Mapping:** Document the intended purpose for each data flow. Ensure all data is tied to a legitimate and defined business objective, such as customer service optimization or fraud detection.
3. **Elimination of Redundancy:** Identify and remove duplicate, outdated, or unused data attributes. This streamlines operations, reduces storage costs, and minimizes risk exposure.

Benefits

1. Enhances transparency across the organization by clearly documenting where and why data is collected and stored.
2. Supports compliance with regulations like GDPR and CCPA, which require detailed records of data processing activities.
3. Improves data quality and operational efficiency by eliminating unnecessary attributes and standardizing data flows.

Tools and Technologies

1. *BigID:* Facilitates sensitive data discovery and automated policy enforcement.
2. *Varonis:* Offers real-time data classification and security insights.
3. *Talend:* Provides comprehensive ETL (Extract, Transform, Load) capabilities for large-scale data environments.

Best Practice

Maintain an updated data inventory and ensure all stakeholders have visibility into its structure and purpose. Conduct regular audits to validate the accuracy of data mappings and to identify emerging gaps or risks. Use visualization tools like Tableau or Power BI to present data maps in an accessible format for decision-makers.

By adopting a systematic approach to data mapping, organizations can establish a clear and actionable framework for managing their data assets, reducing risks, and enabling ethical AI practices.

Schema Design

Redesigning database schemas is critical in minimizing data collection and ensuring compliance with data privacy regulations. The process involves structuring databases to store only essential data fields directly relevant to the intended application. For example, you can optimize loyalty databases by storing only a membership ID and points balance instead of comprehensive customer profiles that may include sensitive information such as addresses, phone numbers, or purchase histories. This approach significantly reduces the risk of data breaches and limits exposure of personally identifiable information (PII):

- **Benefits:** Streamlined schemas enhance data security and improve database performance by reducing query complexity and storage requirements. Simplified schemas enable faster data retrieval, crucial for real-time applications like recommendation engines or transaction monitoring.
- **Implementation Strategies:** Begin by thoroughly analyzing existing database structures to identify redundant or non-essential fields. Tools like Erwin Data Modeler or DbSchema

can assist in visualizing and optimizing database schemas. Collaborate with cross-functional teams, including data scientists and compliance officers, to ensure that schema adjustments meet both technical and regulatory requirements.

- **Best Practices:** Incorporate role-based access controls (RBAC) to restrict access to sensitive fields within the schema. Regularly audit schema designs to ensure they align with evolving business objectives and regulatory mandates.

- **Implementation Example:** Leveraging platforms like Snowflake enables flexible schema adjustments with minimal downtime. Snowflake's architecture supports dynamic data masking, ensuring that only authorized users can view sensitive information. Additionally, its scalability allows organizations to adapt their schemas as data requirements change without disrupting ongoing operations.

- **Schema Optimization Strategies:** Schema optimization enhances database performance and security by eliminating redundancy and structuring data for efficient queries. Here is an SQL-based example using Snowflake:

```sql
-- Create optimized schema
CREATE SCHEMA IF NOT EXISTS production_data;

-- Define table with minimal necessary fields
CREATE TABLE production_data.transactions (
    transaction_id INT,
    user_id INT,
    amount DECIMAL(10, 2),
    transaction_date DATE
);

-- Add masking policy to secure sensitive fields
CREATE MASKING POLICY mask_user_id AS (val INT) RETURNS STRING ->
    CASE WHEN CURRENT_ROLE() != 'ADMIN_ROLE' THEN '******' ELSE TO_CHAR(val) END;

-- Apply masking policy
ALTER TABLE production_data.transactions MODIFY COLUMN user_id SET MASKING POLICY mask_user_id;
```

Figure 51: This schema optimizes storage while ensuring sensitive data remains protected through dynamic masking policies.

Data Collection Controls

Employ advanced controls to limit the scope of data collected during both manual inputs and automated processes.

- Add dynamic input forms and API request validations to ensure fields collect only required information.
- Use real-time data ingestion platforms like Apache Kafka to implement topic configurations that filter out non-essential data streams during collection.

Regular Audits and Monitoring

Periodically review data collection practices to confirm alignment with organizational policies and legal requirements. Tools like Collibra (see Collibra 2023) or Alation can automate compliance monitoring, generating actionable insights into gaps or inefficiencies in data handling processes.

Tip: Engage third-party auditors to validate compliance and introduce fresh perspectives.

Financial Impact

- **Positive:** Streamlining data collection significantly lowers operational expenses, particularly in cloud storage costs. For instance, a mid-sized organization saving $0.02 per gigabyte could save $200,000 annually by eliminating 10TB of redundant data.
- **Negative:** Failing to minimize data collection exposes organizations to significant financial risks. Non-compliance penalties, such as Uber's $148 million fine in 2018 for over-collecting and inadequately securing user data, highlight the need for stringent data governance.

Use Case

A health-tech startup developed an AI-powered diabetes prediction tool. Using Talend Data Integration, the team designed a pipeline that collected only age, BMI, and glucose levels from patient records, consciously avoiding names, addresses, or insurance details. This strategic approach ensured compliance with HIPAA regulations, avoiding fines that could amount to $50,000 per violation while maintaining data quality for accurate predictions. Moreover, this minimalistic approach reduced storage demands, optimizing operational efficiency and enhancing patient trust.

Formula for Measuring Data Reduction

$$\text{Data Reduction Rate (\%)} = \left(\frac{\text{Original Volume} - \text{Reduced Volume}}{\text{Original Volume}} \right) \times 100$$

Example:

- Original Data: 1TB

- Reduced Data: 700GB

$$\text{Data Reduction Rate} = \left(\frac{1000 - 700}{1000} \right) \times 100 = 30\%$$

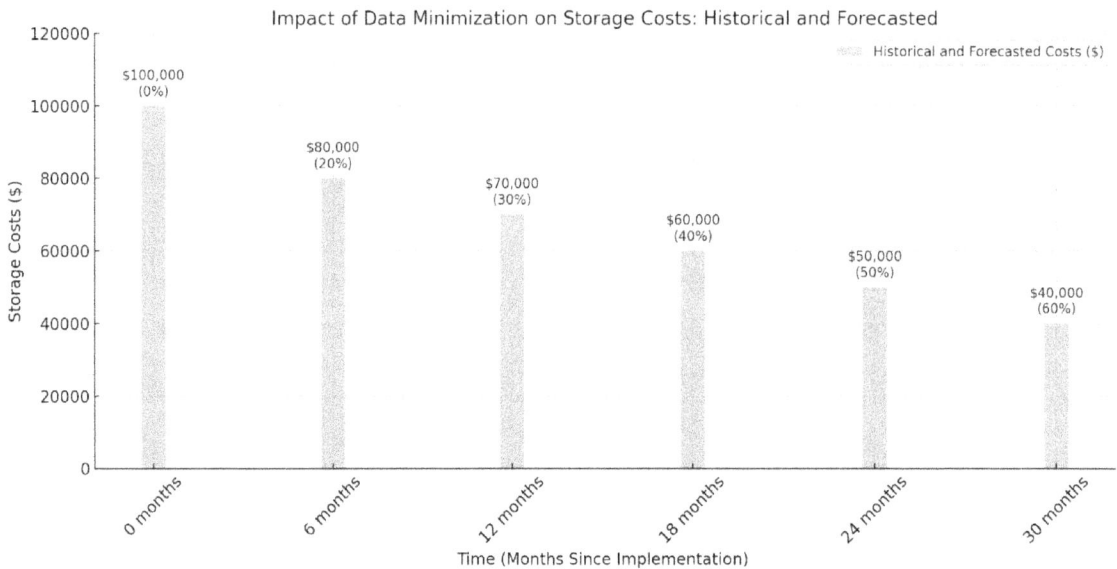

Figure 52: Impact of Data Minimization on Storage Costs.

Figure 52 demonstrates how reducing redundant data through tools like Privacera or Collibra leads to significant cost savings. Historical and forecasted storage costs with percentage reductions are presented. Future costs are projected based on a consistent reduction trend.

Figure 53 illustrates diminishing returns of repeated optimization, emphasizing the importance of the first iterations in achieving maximum gains.

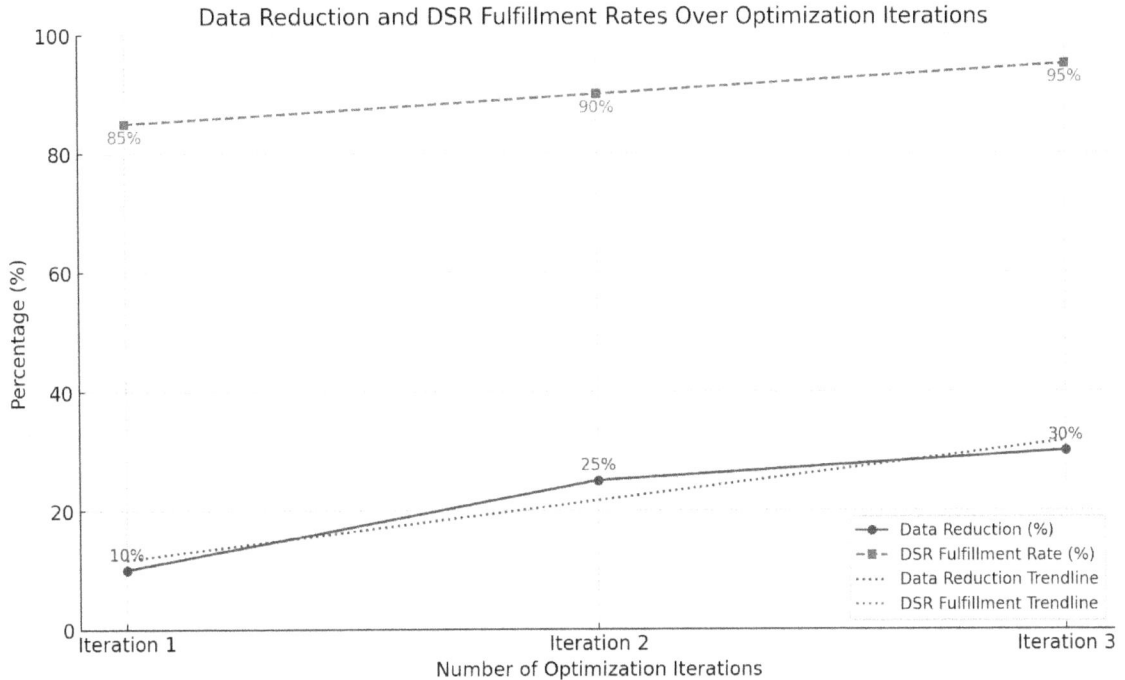

Figure 53: Data Reduction and DSR Fulfilment Rate over Optimization Operations.

Consent Management

Definition: Consent management involves obtaining and managing explicit user consent for collecting, processing, and storing their data. This ensures transparency, accountability, and compliance with global privacy regulations such as GDPR, CCPA, and LGPD.

Why Consent Management Matters

Consent management is essential for building trust between organizations and users. It empowers individuals with control over their personal data while ensuring companies adhere to legal frameworks. Without effective consent mechanisms, businesses risk significant penalties and loss of consumer confidence.

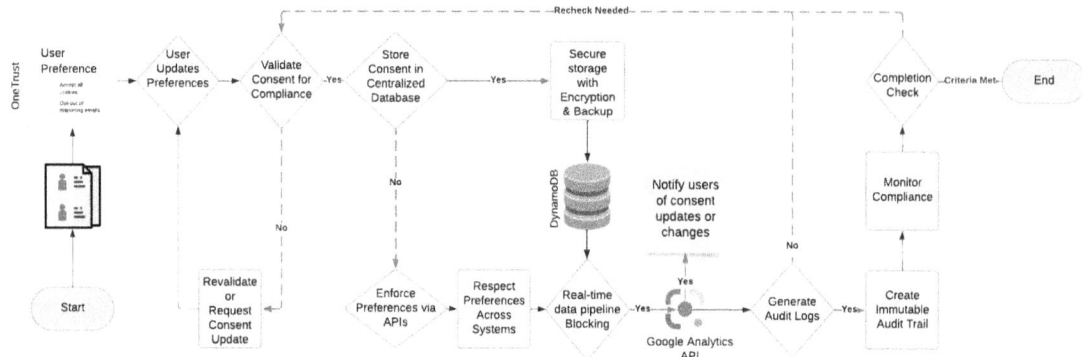

Figure 54: Consent Management System.[32]

Figure 54 contains the key components of a consent management system:

Dynamic Consent Interfaces

- Develop user-friendly interfaces to present consent options clearly and concisely.
- Use tools like CookiePro or OneTrust to deploy customizable cookie banners and consent forms, enabling users to choose granular options (e.g., allowing analytics data collection but disallowing marketing).
- Incorporate localization features to ensure compliance with region-specific laws, such as GDPR in the EU or CCPA in California.

Consent Storage

- Centralize consent logs using scalable and secure storage solutions like Amazon DynamoDB or MongoDB. These platforms support encryption to safeguard sensitive consent data.
- Record essential metadata, including timestamps, user geolocation, device details, and specific data use cases.
- Implement backup and recovery mechanisms to ensure consent logs are never lost or tampered with.

---

[32] https://docs.osano.com/hc/en-us/articles/22469396958356-Consent-Manager-Data-Flow.

Enforcement Mechanisms

- Integrate consent validation APIs into data pipelines to enforce user preferences in real time. For instance, block marketing access in the CRM system if a user opts out of promotional communications.
- Automate policy checks to align data usage with recorded consent.
- Example: If users withdraw consent for analytics, ensure systems like Google Analytics or data warehouses exclude their data immediately.

Audit Trails

- Maintain comprehensive logs to document all user interactions with consent mechanisms, including changes in preferences and timestamps.
- Use tools like Datadog or Splunk to monitor consent operations in real time and detect anomalies.
- Generate automated compliance reports to streamline audit readiness.

Consent Validation API

- Consent validation APIs are crucial in enforcing user preferences during data processing. Below is an example implementation:

```python
from flask import Flask, request, jsonify # type: ignore

app = Flask(__name__)

# Mock database for user consent
user_consent = {
    "user_1": {"analytics": True, "marketing": False},
    "user_2": {"analytics": True, "marketing": True}
}

@app.route('/validate_consent', methods=['POST'])
def validate_consent():
    data = request.json
    user_id = data.get("user_id")
    consent_type = data.get("consent_type")

    if user_consent.get(user_id, {}).get(consent_type, False):
        return jsonify({"status": "approved"}), 200
    return jsonify({"status": "denied"}), 403

if __name__ == '__main__':
    app.run(debug=True)
```

Figure 55: This API validates user consent dynamically, enabling organizations to align real-time data processing with individual preferences.

Financial Impact

- **Positive:** Robust consent management builds trust and fosters customer loyalty. A Cisco study found that organizations prioritizing data privacy experienced 20% shorter sales cycles due to enhanced user confidence.

- **Negative:** Poor consent practices can lead to substantial fines. For example, in 2018, Google was fined €50 million by French regulators for failing to provide adequate opt-out mechanisms for personalized advertising.

- **Use Case:** A global e-commerce platform deployed OneTrust to dynamically manage user consent across 50 countries. By tailoring cookie banners and privacy options to meet regional regulations (e.g., GDPR in Europe, LGPD in Brazil), the platform avoided penalties of up to 4% of global revenue. The solution also enhanced user trust, increased customer retention, and improved brand reputation.

The following table illustrates penalties for non-compliance with privacy and security regulations.

Table 7: Penalties for Non-Compliance with Major Data Privacy and Security Regulations Worldwide

Regulation	Penalty for Non-Compliance
GDPR	€20M or 4% of global revenue, whichever is higher.
CCPA	$7,500 per intentional violation and $2,500 per unintentional violation.
HIPAA	$1.5M annually for repeated offenses; $50,000 per violation.
SOX (Sarbanes-Oxley)	Up to $5M in fines and 20 years imprisonment for false reporting.
FERPA	Loss of federal funding for non-compliance in student data privacy.
FCRA	Up to $1,000 per violation and potential punitive damages.
PIPEDA (Canada)	Up to $100,000 CAD per violation.
LGPD (Brazil)	Up to 2% of a company's revenue in Brazil, capped at R$50M.

Figure 56 illustrates the number of valid consent, pending consent, and missing consent records as a function of time.

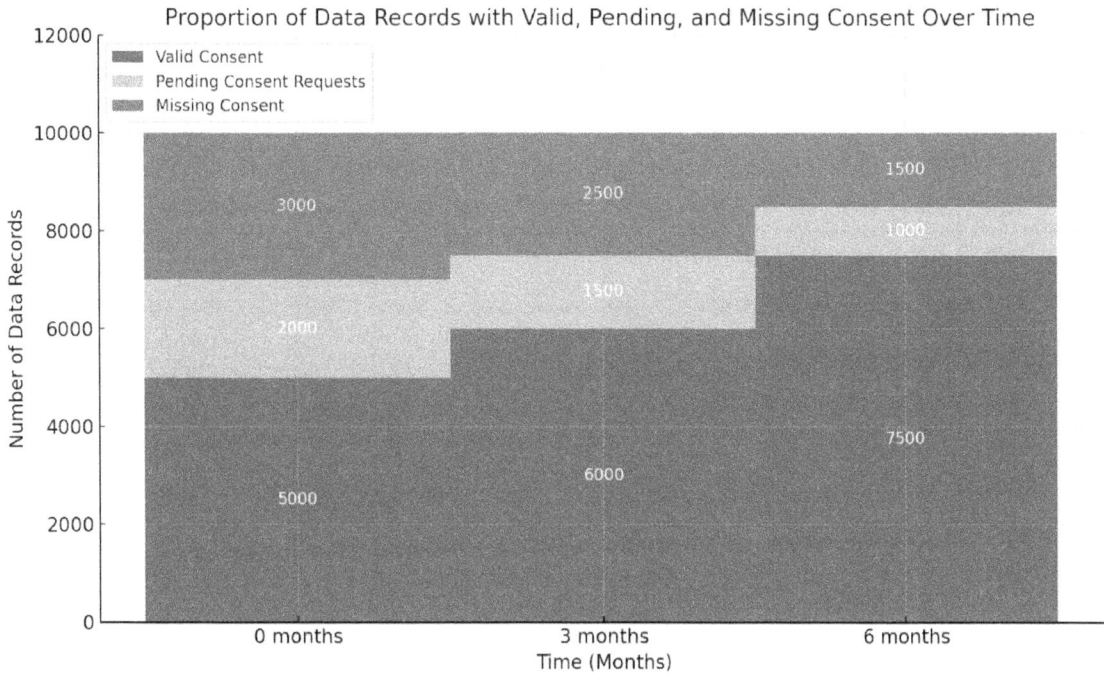

Figure 56: Data Consent Trends.[33]

Figure 56 visualizes the proportions of data records with valid, pending, and missing consent over time. The number of valid consent records rises significantly with time.

Data Anonymization

Definition: Data anonymization refers to the process of transforming data so that individual identities cannot be determined. This includes both direct identifiers (e.g., names, IDs) and indirect identifiers (e.g., location, behavioral patterns). Effective anonymization ensures compliance with privacy laws such as GDPR and CCPA while preserving data utility for analytics and AI.

How to Implement Data Anonymization

Techniques:

---

[33] https://my.onetrust.com/s/article/UUID-0d3aee4d-4c5f-c05f-8472-cb3a451e45b2.

- **Tokenization:** Sensitive values, such as credit card numbers or Social Security Numbers, are replaced with irreversible tokens using tools like TokenEx or Protegrity. These tokens maintain the format and structure of the original data for compatibility.
- **K-Anonymity:** Data is grouped into clusters where each individual is indistinguishable from at least k others. Tools like ARX Data Anonymization automate this process, ensuring no single record is unique.
- **Differential Privacy:** Statistical noise is added to datasets, making it impossible to reverse-engineer individual records. Google's TensorFlow Privacy provides prebuilt frameworks for implementing differential privacy, ensuring individual contributions remain confidential.
- **Pseudonymization:** Direct identifiers are replaced with pseudonyms, which can be re-associated only through secure mapping keys held separately. This is often used for research purposes.
- **Data Masking:** Sensitive data elements are replaced or obscured using patterns (e.g., masking all but the last four digits of a phone number).

Validation:

- Regularly evaluate the dataset for re-identification risks by simulating potential attacks. Adversarial testing methods can help identify vulnerabilities.
- Utilize tools like Data Privacy Lab's re-identification software to assess and mitigate risks.

Integration:

- Embed anonymization techniques into Extract, Transform, and Load (ETL) pipelines. Platforms such as Informatica, Apache NiFi, or Talend facilitate seamless integration of anonymization processes.

Ensure anonymization is applied consistently across all data systems, including backups and archival databases.

Financial Impact

Positive: Anonymized data enables organizations to innovate, conduct advanced analytics, and deploy ML models without violating compliance standards. For instance, a McKinsey report highlights a 30% productivity boost in AI projects leveraging anonymized or synthetic data. Reduces storage and compliance costs by eliminating the need for strict protection of anonymized datasets.

Negative: Failing to anonymize sensitive data can result in severe financial penalties and reputational damage. For example, Amazon was fined €746 million in 2021 for non-compliance with GDPR due to improper handling of customer data.

```python
from airflow import DAG # type: ignore
from airflow.operators.python_operator import PythonOperator # type: ignore
from datetime import datetime

# Define ETL tasks
def extract():
    print("Extracting data from source...")
    # Extraction logic here

def transform():
    print("Transforming data...")
    # Transformation logic here

def load():
    print("Loading data into destination...")
    # Loading logic here

# Define DAG
with DAG('etl_pipeline', start_date=datetime(2023, 1, 1), schedule_interval='@daily') as dag:
    extract_task = PythonOperator(task_id='extract', python_callable=extract)
    transform_task = PythonOperator(task_id='transform', python_callable=transform)
    load_task = PythonOperator(task_id='load', python_callable=load)

    extract_task >> transform_task >> load_task
```

Figure 57: Python ETL Script in an Airflow Pipeline

Use Case

A fintech startup leveraged Delphix to anonymize transaction data before feeding it into ML models for fraud detection. This ensured GDPR compliance by protecting sensitive customer details while preserving dataset utility. As a result, the company avoided regulatory penalties and gained a competitive edge by maintaining consumer trust. Moreover, anonymized datasets allowed the team to iterate quickly on fraud detection algorithms, enhancing accuracy and operational efficiency.

Right to be Forgotten

The "Right to be Forgotten" is a fundamental principle enshrined in privacy laws such as GDPR, giving individuals the power to request the deletion of their personal data from systems. This right ensures that organizations cannot retain data indefinitely and must comply with user requests to erase information, balancing individual privacy rights with organizational responsibilities. Figure 58 illustrates a workflow to implement the right to be forgotten:

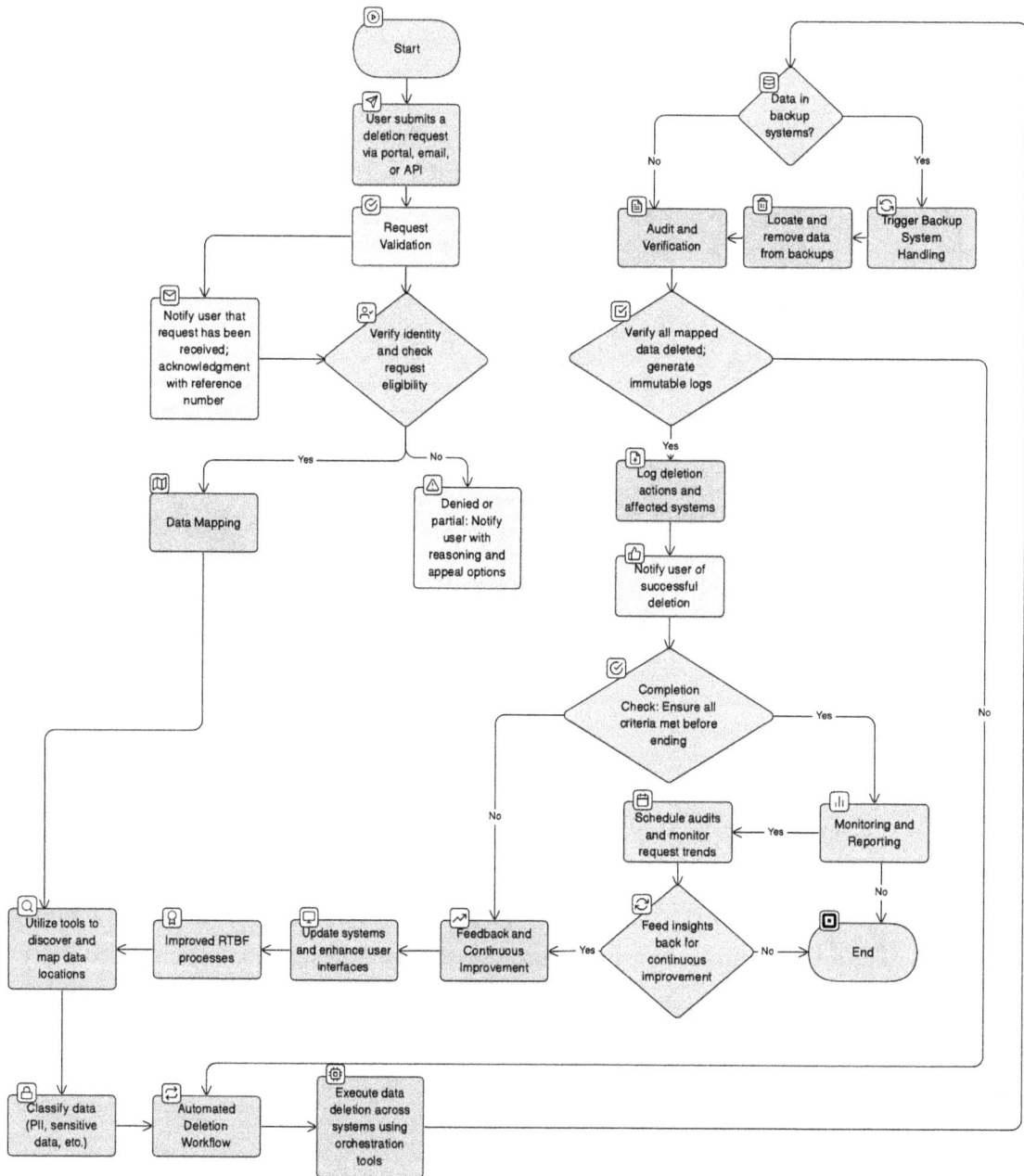

Figure 58: Right to Be Forgotten Process: Data Deletion Workflow.

Tracking and Mapping

- Identify and map all instances of user data across organizational systems, including active databases, archives, and backups.
- Employ advanced tools like BigID or Collibra to classify and locate sensitive data, creating a comprehensive data inventory.
- Maintain up-to-date documentation of data flows and storage locations to ensure complete and efficient data retrieval and deletion.

Automated Deletion Workflows

- Design and deploy automated workflows to execute data deletion requests seamlessly across interconnected systems. To build these workflows, use orchestration tools like Apache Airflow, enabling systematic removal from databases, CRM platforms, marketing tools, and file systems.
- Example: A Python script integrated with APIs triggers automated deletions across multiple platforms, ensuring the removal of user data from all applicable systems without manual intervention.
- Incorporate logging mechanisms within these workflows to provide traceability and audit readiness.

```python
import requests # type: ignore
import logging

# Configure logging
logging.basicConfig(level=logging.INFO)

# API endpoints for data deletion
API_ENDPOINTS = {
    'database': "https://api.company.com/delete_db_record",
    'backup': "https://api.company.com/delete_backup",
    'crm': "https://api.company.com/delete_crm"
}

# Function to handle deletion requests
def delete_user_data(user_id):
    success = True
    for system, endpoint in API_ENDPOINTS.items():
        response = requests.post(endpoint, json={"user_id": user_id})
        if response.status_code == 200:
            logging.info(f"Successfully deleted data from {system}.")
        else:
            success = False
            logging.error(f"Failed to delete data from {system}: {response.text}")
    return success

# Example usage
user_id = "user_12345"
if delete_user_data(user_id):
    logging.info("All user data deleted successfully.")
else:
    logging.error("Some deletions failed. Please check logs.")
```

Figure 59: This script integrates APIs from databases, backup systems, and CRM tools to ensure a seamless and comprehensive data deletion process.

Audit and Verification Mechanisms

- Implement robust verification processes to confirm that requested data has been completely removed from all systems. Employ technologies like AWS CloudTrail to generate immutable logs that verify compliance with deletion mandates.
- Conduct periodic audits to validate the effectiveness of workflows and identify potential gaps in compliance.
- Include re-validation steps for archival and backup systems to ensure that deleted data does not inadvertently re-enter active systems during restoration processes.

Financial Impact

Positive:

- Implementing efficient deletion processes builds user trust, reduces liability, and enhances brand reputation. Organizations with streamlined workflows report up to 25% lower compliance costs due to reduced manual effort and risk exposure.
- Strengthened consumer relationships lead to increased loyalty, with privacy-conscious users favoring companies that prioritize their rights.

Negative:

- Non-compliance can result in severe financial and reputational consequences. For instance, in 2020, Twitter faced a €450,000 fine under GDPR for failing to delete user data promptly, highlighting the importance of robust compliance mechanisms.

Use Case

A global social networking platform implemented an API-driven workflow to ensure user data is deleted within 30 days of receiving a request. This system integrates real-time tracking of deletion status, automated notifications for users upon completion, and regular audits to ensure GDPR compliance. By adopting this approach, the platform avoided penalties that could reach up to 4% of its annual global turnover while reinforcing user trust and operational efficiency. Additionally, the company's commitment to privacy significantly improved its public perception and customer retention.

Tool	Overview	Use Case	Outcome	Limitations
Privacera	Automates data governance and privacy enforcement across hybrid cloud environments.	A multinational retailer masked PII in its global data lake.	Avoided €20M GDPR fines.	Limited support for smaller organizations.
BigID	Discovers and classifies sensitive data across structured and unstructured datasets.	A financial firm identified PII in legacy CRMs before cloud migration.	Secure migration of 500TB of data.	High costs for scaling in multi-cloud setups.
OneTrust	Tracks user consent and processes DSARs dynamically.	An e-commerce platform tailored cookie preferences across 30 countries.	Built user trust and ensured compliance.	Primarily focuses on privacy, lacks ETL features.
Delphix	Creates secure, anonymized datasets for testing and analysis.	A pharmaceutical company masked patient trial data.	Protected privacy while enabling research.	Not suited for large-scale operational datasets.
Informatica	Provides scalable ETL and anonymization solutions.	A logistics firm automated compliance pipelines for redundant data processing.	Reduced operational overhead.	Requires extensive setup for full automation.
Collibra	Centralizes governance workflows, including data cataloging and lineage tracking.	A global enterprise streamlined GDPR audits across departments.	Improved audit readiness and reduced compliance costs by 30%.	Complex configuration for cross-functional use.
Talend	Offers ETL capabilities with integrated anonymization features.	A healthcare provider anonymized patient data for research sharing.	Enabled compliant data sharing while safeguarding PII.	Limited ML integration.
Varonis	Provides real-time data classification and security insights.	A tech firm secured sensitive intellectual property during cloud migration.	Prevented unauthorized access, reducing insider threat risks.	High dependency on pre-defined templates.
Protegrity	Implements tokenization and encryption for data security.	A payment processing company ensured secure transactions across borders.	Maintained PCI DSS compliance while enabling global operations.	Focused on tokenization, lacks broader capabilities.
AWS Macie	Uses ML to detect sensitive data and potential risks.	An e-commerce firm discovered unprotected S3 buckets containing PII.	Avoided potential data breach, bolstering customer confidence.	Limited functionality outside AWS environments.

Table 8: Tools and Platforms for Data Privacy and Governance.

Ethical Frameworks and Best Practices

Just having good data is not enough to ensure ethical AI systems. We also need robust governance frameworks to guide the responsible use of this data. Governance ensures that ethical principles are consistently applied throughout the AI lifecycle, aligning technical capabilities with societal values and legal requirements. Even well-curated data can be misused without good governance or lead to unintended consequences.

Ethical Framework	Focus Areas	Aligned Governance Practices	Examples/Implementation
EU AI Act	- Risk-based classification of AI systems - Mandatory transparency for high-risk AI - Human oversight for decision-making - Strict penalties for non-compliance	- Conduct risk assessments for AI applications before deployment - Implement explainability in high-risk AI systems (e.g., autonomous vehicles, healthcare diagnostics) - Enforce strict compliance workflows with monitoring and reporting tools	- Financial firms auditing automated credit-scoring systems for compliance with "high-risk" criteria - Autonomous vehicle companies testing decision-making under EU Act requirements
OECD Principles on AI	- Inclusive and sustainable growth - Human-centered values - Transparency and explainability - Accountability and robustness	- Conduct fairness and bias audits using tools like IBM AI Fairness 360 - Maintain traceable data lineage and decision records for accountability - Regularly monitor and validate AI system robustness against evolving requirements	- Educational platforms developing AI tutoring systems validated through fairness audits - ML-based recruitment tools reconfigured for inclusivity
UNESCO AI Ethics Recommendation	- Bias prevention in AI models - Privacy protections - Promotion of cultural diversity - Ethical use of AI for societal benefit	- Embed cultural diversity datasets for training AI systems - Implement anonymization techniques (e.g., k-anonymity, differential privacy) for sensitive data - Require stakeholder consultation during AI design stages	- Healthcare AI models tailored to diverse population data for equitable outcomes - Facial recognition systems audited to ensure non-discrimination
GDPR (General Data Protection Regulation)	- Data protection and privacy rights - User consent management - Right to be forgotten - Strict penalties for violations	- Deploy automated consent validation APIs using platforms like OneTrust - Implement the Right to Be Forgotten with workflows that delete user data across systems - Enforce strict data minimization policies with ETL pipeline controls	- Retail companies implementing dynamic cookie banners for GDPR compliance - E-commerce platforms using API-driven deletion workflows for customer data
CCPA (California Consumer Privacy Act)	- Transparency in data handling - Opt-out rights for data sales	- Create user-friendly dashboards for opt-out requests and data disclosures - Conduct regular audits for compliance with CCPA's transparency	- U.S.-based digital advertising firms providing users with ad opt-out mechanisms - Media platforms implementing

Ethical Framework	Focus Areas	Aligned Governance Practices	Examples/Implementation
	- Secure data processing - Consumer rights for information access	and security standards - Use dynamic consent interfaces to validate data handling preferences	secure APIs for consumer data access
IEEE Global Initiative on AI Ethics	- Accountability in AI design - Well-being and human safety - Inclusivity and ethical impact assessments - Establishing measurable ethical benchmarks	- Conduct regular ethical impact assessments for AI systems - Implement accountability logs using traceability tools like Collibra - Design AI decision-making aligned with the well-being and safety of users (e.g., human-in-the-loop oversight)	- AI-driven recommendation engines configured to avoid harm (e.g., misinformation) - Smart city systems implementing safety-first AI monitoring features
Singapore Model AI Governance Framework	- Transparency in AI operations - Risk assessment for AI use cases - Clear accountability for AI outcomes	- Implement AI explainability tools (e.g., SHAP, LIME) for transparent decisions - Conduct risk profiling for AI systems used in public-facing applications - Assign clear ownership of AI outcomes within cross-functional teams	- Public transport AI systems audited for explainable routing decisions - Government portals implementing transparent chatbots

Table 9: Ethical Frameworks and Best Practices.

Governance in High-Stakes Scenarios

Governance becomes critically important in high-stakes scenarios where the consequences of AI decisions directly impact human lives and societal structures. These contexts demand carefully tailored governance strategies to mitigate risks, ensure fairness, and uphold ethical standards. Below, we explore specific examples that highlight the complexities and approaches to effective governance.

Healthcare

The healthcare sector represents one of the most consequential arenas for AI governance. AI models designed for cancer detection and diagnostics have the transformative potential to improve patient outcomes significantly. However, without robust governance, these systems risk exacerbating existing disparities and introducing critical errors. Ensuring diverse and representative datasets is a cornerstone of responsible AI implementation, as these datasets mitigate biases that could otherwise lead to misdiagnoses, particularly for underrepresented populations. Complementing this, human oversight ensures that the outputs generated by AI systems undergo thorough validation before they influence clinical decisions. This dual-layered approach enhances patient safety and compliance with stringent regulations such as HIPAA. A notable achievement in this domain is a documented 25% reduction in diagnostic errors when governance frameworks are rigorously applied, showcasing the profound impact of responsible oversight.

Law Enforcement

The deployment of AI in law enforcement, including facial recognition and predictive policing, has garnered significant attention due to the ethical dilemmas it presents. While these tools promise enhanced security, their potential for misuse necessitates robust governance frameworks. Integrated with rigorous human oversight, bias detection tools such as Fairlearn form the backbone of ethical AI practices in this sector. Transparency in decision-making processes and active community engagement further build public trust, ensuring accountability. In a case where governance was effectively applied, bias in facial recognition systems was mitigated, leading to a notable reduction in wrongful arrests and avoiding subsequent legal challenges. These outcomes highlight the necessity of ethical alignment in law enforcement applications.

Finance

Financial institutions operate in a heavily regulated environment where AI systems are critical in fraud detection, credit scoring, and regulatory compliance. The sensitivity of personal financial data demands that organizations adopt stringent governance measures to ensure fairness and accountability. Regular audits and automated compliance reporting systems help prevent discriminatory practices and maintain operational integrity. For example, HSBC's implementation of AI-driven governance strategies resulted in $500K in annual savings through audit cost reductions, demonstrating the tangible benefits of robust oversight. Financial institutions can uphold ethical standards while improving efficiency by automating fraud detection mechanisms and aligning with regulations such as GDPR, AML, and KYC.

Transportation

The transportation industry, particularly the domain of autonomous vehicles, relies on rigorous governance to ensure public safety. Autonomous systems must navigate complex environments and make real-time decisions that directly affect human lives. Simulation-based testing, leveraging diverse datasets, forms the foundation of safety validation processes. Real-time monitoring systems and periodic regulatory audits ensure compliance with established safety standards. Governance frameworks also prioritize ethical decision-making protocols to address scenarios involving unavoidable harm, thereby enhancing public trust in autonomous transportation. These measures collectively fortify the reliability and societal acceptance of AI-powered transportation solutions.

Education

AI-driven personalized learning platforms hold immense potential to bridge educational gaps and enhance learning experiences. However, governance is essential to prevent these systems from perpetuating systemic biases or excluding marginalized groups. Privacy safeguards and bias mitigation strategies are critical in this sector, ensuring that sensitive student data is handled responsibly. Governance frameworks advocate for inclusive design principles, ensuring that AI systems adapt to diverse learning needs. Regular audits and feedback loops further refine these systems, resulting in enhanced accessibility and reduced disparities in education. By embedding governance into the fabric of educational AI, stakeholders can create equitable learning opportunities for all students.

Retail

The retail industry grapples with the dual challenge of personalizing customer experiences while adhering to data protection regulations like GDPR and CCPA. Governance strategies focus on real-time consent tracking, dynamic fraud prevention systems, and data minimization practices to strike this delicate balance. Companies can ensure compliance while optimizing customer engagement by leveraging technologies such as dynamic consent management and automated fraud detection. Amazon's implementation of such strategies resulted in $19M in annual savings, underscoring the financial and operational benefits of robust governance.

Technology

The technology sector, at the forefront of AI innovation, faces the intricate challenge of navigating global privacy laws and addressing algorithmic biases. Governance frameworks prioritize regular fairness audits, real-time monitoring, and adherence to international standards such as GDPR. Tools for bias detection and transparent reporting mechanisms ensure that AI systems operate within ethical boundaries. The successful deployment of governance frameworks in the technology sector has mitigated reputational risks and avoided financial penalties, such as €50M GDPR fines, demonstrating the critical role of ethical oversight. Organizations can balance innovation with ethical responsibility by applying tailored governance strategies across these high-stakes scenarios, ensuring that AI systems remain equitable, transparent, and aligned with societal values.

Metric	Target	Description
Data Privacy Incidents	Minimize annually.	Number of breaches or violations.
Fairness in AI Models	95%+ fairness.	Percentage reduction in model bias.
DSR Response Time	<30 days (GDPR).	Time taken to address user data requests.
Audit Pass Rate	100% compliance rate.	Percentage of audits passed without findings.
Explainability in AI Models	90%+ explainable models.	Percentage of models with explainability integrated.
User Trust and Engagement	Increase trust by 15% year-over-year.	Metrics reflecting user confidence in AI systems.
Model Drift Monitoring	100% drifts resolved within 7 days.	Time taken to detect and mitigate performance drifts in models.
Incident Response Time	95% incidents resolved within 72 hours.	Average time to resolve ethical/compliance incidents.
Data Retention Compliance	100% compliance with retention policies.	Ensures proper archival or deletion of datasets.
Data Lineage Completeness	100% critical datasets documented.	Tracks completeness of data provenance.
Representation in Training Data	95%+ datasets meet diversity criteria.	Ensures inclusivity in AI training datasets.
Bias Resolution Efficiency	90%+ bias issues resolved within 30 days.	Speed of bias detection and resolution.
Policy Adherence Rate	100% adherence to governance policies.	Tracks policy implementation and enforcement.
Regulatory Fines Avoidance	Zero fines.	Monitors penalties avoided through governance practices.

Table 10: Metrics to Measure Governance Effectiveness.

Role of Cross-Functional Teams in Governance

Effective governance in AI requires a cohesive effort from diverse cross-functional teams, each contributing their expertise to ensure that AI systems operate ethically, fairly, and in compliance with legal and societal expectations. The involvement of key stakeholders, equipped with collaborative tools, is pivotal to achieving comprehensive and efficient governance frameworks.

Key Stakeholders and Their Roles

Data Analysts

Data analysts bridge the gap between raw data and actionable insights, ensuring that the information fed into AI systems is meaningful, relevant, and interpretable. Their primary responsibility lies in exploring and visualizing datasets, identifying trends, outliers, and inconsistencies that may impact AI system performance. They often collaborate with data scientists to pre-clean datasets, enabling smoother model training and deployment. Furthermore, data analysts play a pivotal role in post-deployment monitoring, analyzing output trends to identify potential biases or inaccuracies in AI predictions. Leveraging tools like Tableau, Power BI, or Python libraries such as Pandas and Matplotlib ensure that decision-makers are equipped with clear, evidence-based insights.

Example Contribution: In a customer segmentation project, data analysts might discover that specific demographic groups are underrepresented in the dataset. They would flag this imbalance and work with data scientists to augment the dataset or adjust model weights, ensuring fair treatment across all customer groups.

Data Stewards

Data stewards serve as the custodians of organizational data, ensuring its quality, security, and compliance with governance policies. Their responsibilities encompass establishing data standards, maintaining comprehensive data dictionaries, and overseeing data access controls to prevent misuse. They ensure that sensitive information, such as Personally Identifiable Information (PII), is properly classified and protected. Data stewards also play a vital role in aligning data management practices with regulatory requirements like GDPR or HIPAA, collaborating closely with legal teams and governance committees. Tools such as Collibra, Alation, and Informatica are often utilized to automate data cataloging and lineage tracking, streamlining governance processes.

Example Contribution: During a GDPR compliance audit, data stewards could map data flows across the organization, ensuring that all instances of PII are properly documented, encrypted, and accessible only to authorized personnel. Their diligence minimizes the risk of non-compliance and associated penalties.

Data Scientists

Data scientists ensure that AI systems are built on high-quality, unbiased data and produce outputs that align with fairness and ethical standards. Their role involves preprocessing and analyzing data, selecting appropriate ML models, and addressing potential biases in training datasets. Data scientists also play a critical role in developing algorithms that meet transparency and explainability requirements, ensuring that non-technical stakeholders can understand and interpret AI decisions. For instance, they might utilize fairness tools such as IBM AI Fairness 360 or Fairlearn to detect and mitigate bias in predictive models.

Example Contribution: A team of data scientists working on a loan approval system might identify that historical data used to train the model contains racial or gender biases. They would then adjust the dataset or model to eliminate these biases, ensuring equitable outcomes for all applicants.

Legal Teams

Legal professionals ensure that the organization complies with the myriad of regulations governing AI deployment, such as GDPR, HIPAA, and CCPA. They interpret these laws to develop policies for data collection, processing, storage, and deletion while addressing user consent and privacy concerns. Legal teams also assist in creating frameworks for responding to regulatory audits, handling data breaches, and managing user requests like the "Right to Be Forgotten." Their expertise ensures that governance policies are technically sound and legally defensible.

Example Contribution: Legal teams might work with data scientists to ensure that AI systems used in healthcare comply with HIPAA by anonymizing patient data during model training and maintaining detailed audit trails for accountability.

Governance Committees

Governance committees act as the central authority overseeing the ethical practices of AI systems across the organization. These committees often consist of representatives from multiple departments, including executives, data scientists, legal experts, and risk managers. Their primary role is to define and enforce governance policies, monitor compliance, and ensure accountability. They also facilitate regular audits and create escalation pathways for resolving ethical concerns.

Example Contribution: A governance committee might establish a quarterly review process to audit AI systems for compliance with ethical standards, flagging models that deviate from fairness metrics or transparency guidelines for immediate remediation.

IT Teams

IT teams ensure that the infrastructure supporting AI systems is robust, scalable, and secure. They play a critical role in integrating AI models into production environments, maintaining data pipelines, and implementing real-time monitoring systems to detect and resolve technical issues. Additionally, IT teams collaborate with data stewards and scientists to ensure data integrity during extraction, transformation, and loading (ETL) processes. Their expertise is crucial in enforcing cybersecurity measures like data encryption, intrusion detection, and access controls.

Example Contribution: An IT team might implement automated workflows to enforce data deletion requests under GDPR, ensuring user data is erased across all interconnected systems, including backups.

Business Executives

Business executives provide strategic direction for AI initiatives, aligning them with the organization's overarching goals and values. They prioritize use cases, allocate resources, and ensure that governance frameworks are adequately funded and supported. Executives also serve as advocates for ethical AI practices, fostering a culture of accountability and transparency within the organization. Their involvement is critical in building trust among stakeholders, including customers, regulators, and investors.

Example Contribution: An executive might champion the adoption of an AI governance framework, securing buy-in from department heads and ensuring that metrics like fairness, transparency, and compliance are integrated into the organization's Key Performance Indicators (KPIs).

Collaboration Tools for Cross-Functional Teams

Organizations rely on advanced collaboration tools to streamline workflows and enhance stakeholder coordination. These tools facilitate the tracking, reporting, and resolution of governance-related concerns in a structured and efficient manner:

- **Collibra**: Collibra is a centralized platform for data governance workflows, enabling teams to manage data lineage, identify data assets, and ensure compliance with regulations. It allows governance committees to create a unified repository of governance policies, track their implementation across departments, and generate detailed reports for internal and external audits. *Example Use Case*: Using Collibra, legal teams can monitor whether data collected for an AI project adheres to GDPR guidelines. In contrast, data scientists can leverage the tool to track data lineage and ensure that all datasets are appropriately anonymized.

- **Jira**: Jira is a versatile tool that facilitates collaboration by tracking and resolving ethical concerns, compliance issues, and technical bugs. It enables teams to create detailed workflows for addressing governance tasks, assigning responsibilities, and monitoring progress in real time. Jira's integration capabilities allow it to work seamlessly with other governance tools, ensuring a holistic approach to issue resolution. *Example Use Case*: Governance committees can use Jira to create a ticketing system for flagging and addressing ethical concerns, such as bias in an AI model. The tool assigns tasks to relevant stakeholders—data scientists for technical fixes and legal teams for compliance checks—ensuring that all issues are resolved efficiently.

ETHICAL DATA MANAGEMENT AND GOVERNANCE FOR AI • 221

By leveraging the unique expertise of data scientists, legal teams, and governance committees, organizations can establish a robust governance framework that ensures AI systems are ethical, fair, and compliant. Collaborative tools like Collibra and Jira play a critical role in facilitating communication and coordination among these teams, enabling seamless execution of governance policies. Together, these components form the backbone of responsible AI governance, safeguarding both organizational interests and societal values.

Case Studies: Real-World Applications of Ethical AI Governance

Data management plays a pivotal role in the success stories of these case studies. It underpins every solution, from ensuring privacy and security to enabling compliance with evolving regulations. Companies leveraged robust data management strategies to address challenges like consent violations, cross-border compliance, and algorithmic bias. Effective practices—such as implementing differential privacy, encryption protocols, and dynamic consent tools—not only resolved immediate issues but also reinforced trust, improved efficiency, and ensured fairness. This table highlights how organizations have turned data governance into a strategic advantage, making it a cornerstone for ethical AI deployment.

Company	Challenge	Solution	Impact
Apple	Balancing analytics with user privacy.	Differential Privacy.	Enhanced reputation, avoided GDPR fines.
Privacera	Ensuring cross-border GDPR compliance.	Automated masking workflows.	$500K annual savings.
Google	GDPR fine for inadequate consent.	OneTrust for consent tracking.	Compliance achieved, regained trust.
A Social Platform	GDPR violations for delayed deletions.	Automated 30-day workflows.	Avoided penalties, improved efficiency.
Microsoft	Bias in hiring algorithms.	Implemented fairness audits.	Avoided reputational damage, improved diversity metrics.
Netflix	Privacy risks in recommendation algorithms.	Differential privacy techniques.	Enhanced user trust, avoided data breach penalties.
Uber	User data breach and GDPR fines.	Improved encryption protocols.	Achieved compliance, reduced security risks.
Spotify	Consent violations in personalized ads.	Dynamic consent management tools.	Avoided fines, enhanced customer loyalty.

Table 11: Real-World Applications of Ethical AI Governance.

Summary

Ethical Data Management and Governance are critical for ensuring AI systems are trustworthy, fair, and transparent. By leveraging advanced tools for privacy, compliance, bias detection, and transparency, organizations can responsibly navigate the complexities of AI. Building robust frameworks for data stewardship and governance fosters trust and mitigates risks, ensuring AI innovations align with societal values.

The next chapter will explore **How Data Moves in AI-Powered Organizations.** From data ingestion and processing to real-time streaming and model updates, we'll examine the intricate workflows that power AI-driven enterprises.

References

Stanford University, "Human-Centered Artificial Intelligence Report on AI Ethics and Risks," 2023. [Online]. Available: https://hai.stanford.edu.

IBM Institute for Business Value, "The Business of AI Ethics and Governance," 2023. [Online]. Available: https://www.ibm.com/thought-leadership/institute-business-value/.

Collibra, "Data Governance and Compliance Management," 2023. [Online]. Available: https://www.collibra.com/data-governance.

## CHAPTER 10

How Data Moves in AI-Powered Organizations

In AI-driven organizations, the seamless flow of data is critical to enable advanced analytics, ML models, and real-time decision-making. This chapter delves into how organizations leverage Extract, Transform, Load (ETL) pipelines, real-time streaming technologies, and modern data integration platforms to facilitate data movement from collection points to AI models. We also explore the role of API-based integration in ensuring smooth data workflows.

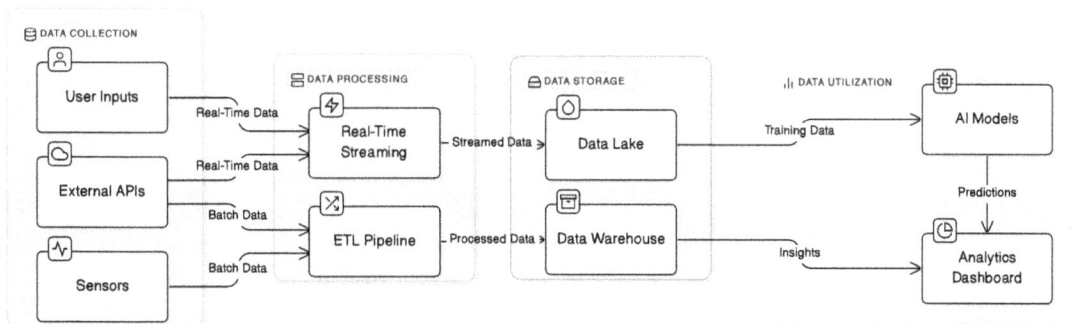

Figure 60: Data flow in AI-Powered Organizations.

Figure 60 visually represents how data moves within a sophisticated AI-focused organization.

Historical Evolution of Data Movement Technologies

From Manual Data Integration to Automated Pipelines

Data movement has evolved significantly over the years, transitioning from manual, script-based processes to automated pipelines powered by ETL tools. Early methods relied on custom scripts and manual interventions, which were error-prone and inefficient. The emergence of automated ETL tools revolutionized this process, allowing for scalability, repeatability, and reduced human error.

Emergence of Real-Time Data Streaming

The shift from batch processing to real-time streaming marked a paradigm shift in data movement. Technologies like Apache Kafka (see Kafka 2023) and Amazon Kinesis enabled organizations to handle continuous data streams, catering to applications requiring instant insights, such as fraud detection and IoT monitoring.

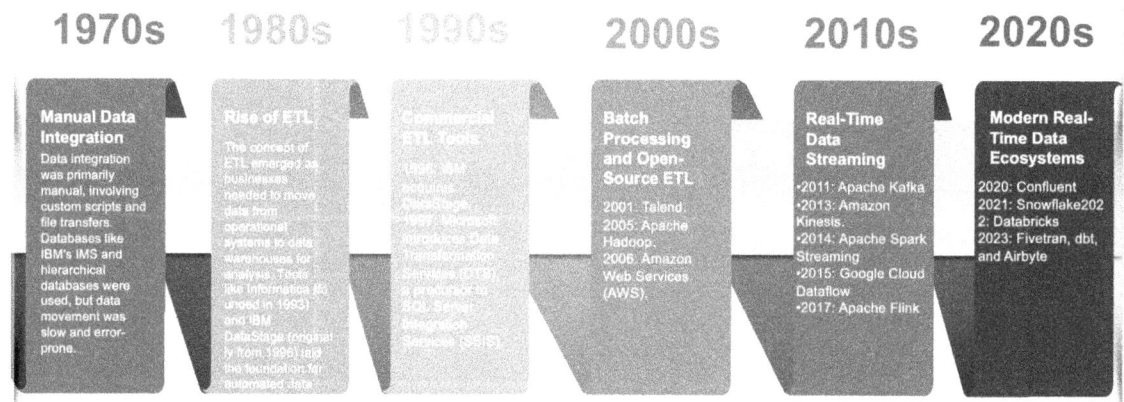

Figure 61: Timeline of Data Movement Evolution.

Figure 61 provides a data movement evolution summary over the following timeline:

1970s: Manual Data Integration

In the 1970s, data integration was a labor-intensive process, relying heavily on custom scripts and manual file transfers. Databases like IBM's IMS (Information Management System) and hierarchical databases were the primary tools for storing and managing data. However, data movement was slow, error-prone, and required significant human intervention. This era laid the groundwork for the need for more automated and efficient data integration methods.

1980s: Rise of ETL (Extract, Transform, Load)

The 1980s marked the emergence of the ETL (Extract, Transform, Load) concept as businesses began to recognize the value of moving data from operational systems to centralized data warehouses for analysis. This shift was driven by the growing complexity of data and the need for more structured and reliable data integration processes. Tools like **Informatica** (founded in 1993) and **IBM DataStage** (originally developed in 1996) became pioneers in automating data integration, setting the stage for the modern ETL landscape.

1990s: Commercial ETL Tools

The 1990s saw the rise of data warehousing as a critical component of business intelligence, leading to the development of commercial ETL tools. These tools were designed to handle the increasing volume and complexity of data, enabling organizations to streamline their data integration processes. Key milestones during this period include:

- **1996**: IBM acquired **DataStage**, solidifying its position as a leading ETL tool.
- **1997**: Microsoft introduced **Data Transformation Services (DTS)**, a precursor to **SQL Server Integration Services (SSIS)**, which became a widely used tool for data integration.

2000s: Batch Processing and Open-Source ETL

The 2000s brought significant advancements in data processing, particularly with the rise of distributed computing and open-source technologies. This era was characterized by the need to process large datasets efficiently, leading to the development of batch-processing frameworks and open-source ETL tools. Key developments include:

- **2001**: **Talend** was founded, offering open-source data integration tools that democratized access to ETL capabilities.
- **2005**: **Apache Hadoop** was introduced, revolutionizing the way large datasets were processed by enabling distributed batch processing across clusters of computers.
- **2006**: **Amazon Web Services (AWS)** launched, marking the beginning of the cloud computing era and transforming how data was stored, processed, and moved.

2010s: Real-Time Data Streaming

The 2010s witnessed a paradigm shift from batch processing to real-time data streaming, driven by the need for faster insights and decision-making. This era saw the emergence of powerful streaming platforms that enabled organizations to process and analyze data in real time. Milestones include:

- **2011**: **Apache Kafka** was open-sourced by LinkedIn, becoming a cornerstone for real-time data streaming and event-driven architectures.
- **2013**: **Amazon Kinesis** was launched, providing a fully managed service for real-time data streaming on AWS.
- **2014**: **Apache Spark Streaming** was introduced, enabling real-time processing of data streams with high throughput and low latency.
- **2015**: **Google Cloud Dataflow** was launched, offering a unified model for both stream and batch processing (see Google 2023).
- **2017**: **Apache Flink** gained popularity for its advanced real-time stream processing capabilities, further solidifying the importance of real-time data ecosystems.

2020s: Modern Real-Time Data Ecosystems

The 2020s have been defined by the maturation of real-time data ecosystems and the integration of AI-driven tools into data pipelines. Organizations now demand seamless, real-time data integration and analytics to stay competitive in a data-driven world. Key developments include:

- **2020**: **Confluent**, founded by the creators of Kafka, went public, highlighting the growing importance of real-time data platforms in modern enterprises.
- **2021**: **Snowflake** introduced **Snowpipe Streaming**, enabling real-time data ingestion and further enhancing its cloud data platform.
- **2022**: **Databricks** launched **Delta Live Tables**, simplifying the creation and management of real-time data pipelines.
- **2023**: AI-driven data integration tools like **Fivetran**, **dbt**, and **Airbyte** have gained widespread adoption, enabling organizations to automate and optimize their data workflows with minimal manual intervention.

Year	Tool/Technology	Significance
1970s	Manual Scripts	Early data integration methods
1996	IBM DataStage	Commercial ETL tool
2001	Talend	Open-source ETL tool
2005	Apache Hadoop	Distributed batch processing
2011	Apache Kafka	Real-time data streaming
2013	Amazon Kinesis	Managed real-time streaming on AWS
2014	Apache Spark Streaming	Real-time stream processing
2020	Confluent	Enterprise-grade Kafka platform
2023	AI-driven tools (e.g., Fivetran, dbt)	Modern real-time data integration and transformation

Table 12: Summary of Key Tools and Years.

ETL and Real-Time Data Streaming Technologies

The Role of ETL in Data Preparation

ETL pipelines are pivotal in data preparation and movement architecture, serving as the backbone for integrating disparate data sources into AI systems, as illustrated in Figure 62. However, implementing these pipelines presents several challenges that organizations must address. One of the primary difficulties lies in handling diverse data formats—structured, semi-structured, and unstructured—which require robust connectors and sophisticated transformation logic to ensure compatibility. Additionally, ensuring data quality is a persistent concern, as raw data often contains errors, duplicates, or inconsistencies that must be resolved through meticulous cleaning and validation processes. Scalability is also challenging, as ETL systems must accommodate growing data volumes without compromising performance.

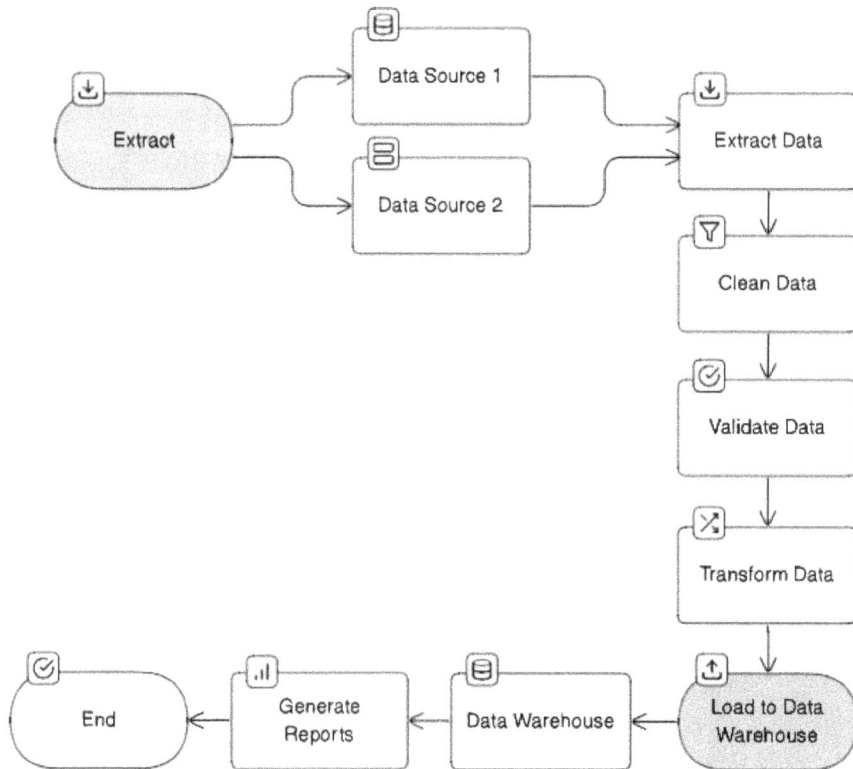

Figure 62: ETL Process Flow.

Furthermore, organizations face the complexity of maintaining data security and compliance with regulations such as GDPR and CCPA while data moves across systems. Overcoming these obstacles requires leveraging advanced tools like Apache Spark for distributed processing, schema mapping to harmonize data formats, and automation platforms to streamline repetitive tasks, ensuring that ETL pipelines remain reliable, efficient, and aligned with organizational goals. These pipelines carry out three interrelated and indispensable steps, forming a continuous flow of data:

- **Extract**: This phase focuses on the acquisition of data from a diverse array of sources, which include structured datasets like relational databases, semi-structured formats such as JSON or XML files, and unstructured inputs like log files, IoT sensor outputs, and social media feeds. The extract phase often involves sophisticated connectors and adapters tailored to interact with various data formats and protocols, ensuring comprehensive data capture.

- **Transform**: Once data is collected, it undergoes an intricate process of transformation to ensure it meets the required standards of quality, consistency, and usability. This includes cleaning to remove errors or duplicates, normalization to standardize formats, enrichment to add contextual information, and applying business rules to align data with organizational needs. Advanced techniques such as schema mapping, deduplication, and anomaly detection are often employed, leveraging tools like Apache Spark or Talend for enhanced processing.

- **Load**: The final step involves depositing the transformed data into target repositories, which may range from traditional data warehouses to modern data lakes or specialized feature stores designed for ML workflows. This phase ensures the data is accessible, structured, and optimized for downstream analytics or AI model training, often integrating with cloud platforms such as Snowflake, Amazon Redshift, or Databricks for scalability and performance.

Real-Time Data Streaming Technologies

While ETL pipelines cater to batch processing, real-time streaming technologies address the need for instantaneous data flow, which is crucial for AI systems requiring up-to-the-minute updates. Figure 63 provides a visual representation of the following components:

- **Apache Kafka**: This distributed event streaming platform is widely used for high-throughput, fault-tolerant data streaming. Kafka's architecture is built on the concept of publish-subscribe messaging, allowing multiple producers to publish data streams and multiple consumers to process these streams concurrently. Organizations use Kafka for scenarios like clickstream analysis, real-time anomaly detection, and log aggregation. Its partitioning and replication mechanisms ensure scalability and fault tolerance, making it a critical choice for high-velocity data pipelines.

- **Apache Flink**: A high-performance framework for stateful stream processing, Flink excels in real-time, low-latency applications such as fraud detection, IoT monitoring, and dynamic pricing. Its event-driven architecture supports exactly-once processing semantics and stateful computations. Flink seamlessly integrates with message brokers like Kafka and cloud storage systems, offering flexibility and precision in managing complex data flows. It is particularly valuable for applications where latency and consistency are paramount.

- **Amazon Kinesis**: This managed service enables real-time data collection and processing, providing out-of-the-box scalability and integration with the AWS ecosystem. Kinesis Streams allow organizations to build event-driven architectures, enabling real-time operational analytics, video processing, and ML inferences. Its shard-based scaling mechanism makes it adaptable to fluctuating data volumes, while its serverless nature minimizes infrastructure management overhead.

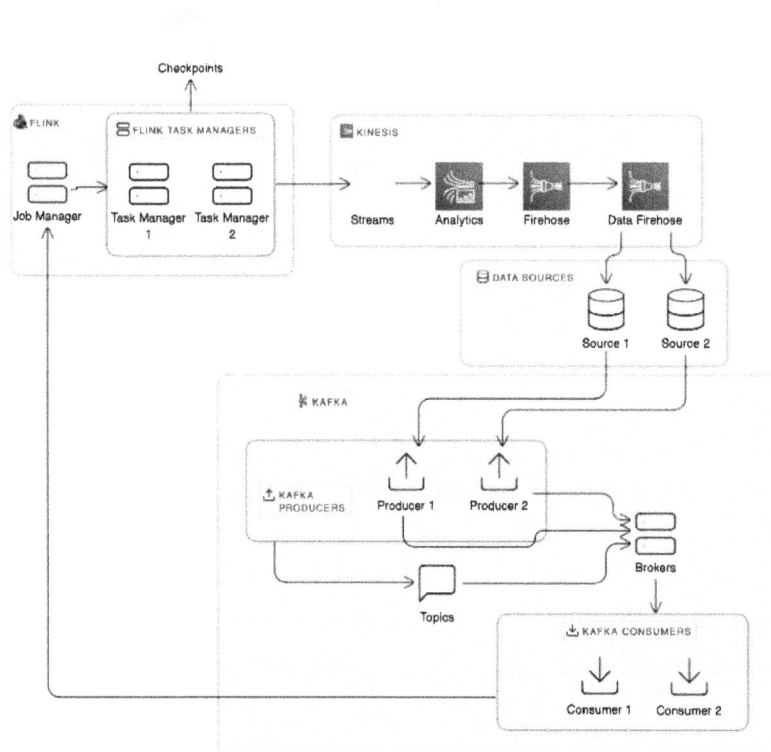

Figure 63: Apache Kafka, Flink and Amazon Kinesis Architecture.[34] [35] [36]

---

[34] https://aws.amazon.com/kinesis/.

[35] https://kafka.apache.org/documentation/.

[36] https://flink.apache.org/.

Real-time streaming technologies are indispensable in driving critical AI use cases by providing instantaneous data flow, analysis, and action. These technologies enable organizations to derive actionable insights and implement decisions at unprecedented speeds, directly impacting operational efficiency and customer satisfaction:

- **Fraud Detection Systems**: Real-time streaming technologies continuously monitor transactional data streams to identify anomalies that might indicate fraudulent activities. These systems utilize advanced ML models to detect subtle patterns, such as unusual spending behaviors or unauthorized access attempts. Organizations can mitigate financial losses and enhance customer trust by flagging suspicious activities within milliseconds.

- **Recommendation Engines**: Dynamic recommendation systems leverage real-time data streams to instantly update user preferences and interactions. These engines deliver hyper-personalized content, product suggestions, or services by analyzing clickstream data, purchase history, and contextual information. This ensures an engaging user experience, boosting retention rates and driving revenue.

- **Predictive Maintenance**: Leveraging IoT sensor data, real-time streaming frameworks facilitate the early identification of potential equipment failures. Predictive maintenance systems trigger alerts before breakdowns occur by continuously monitoring parameters such as temperature, vibration, or pressure. This approach reduces downtime, extends equipment life, and optimizes operational costs, proving invaluable across industries like manufacturing, energy, and logistics.

Organizations increasingly deploy hybrid pipelines that combine ETL and streaming technologies to bridge batch and real-time processing. Tools like Apache NiFi and Delta Lake enable organizations to manage both batch and streaming data within unified pipelines, as demonstrated in Figure 64. This approach ensures that the right data is available at the right time, supporting a wide array of AI and analytics workloads.

Unified Data Pipelines

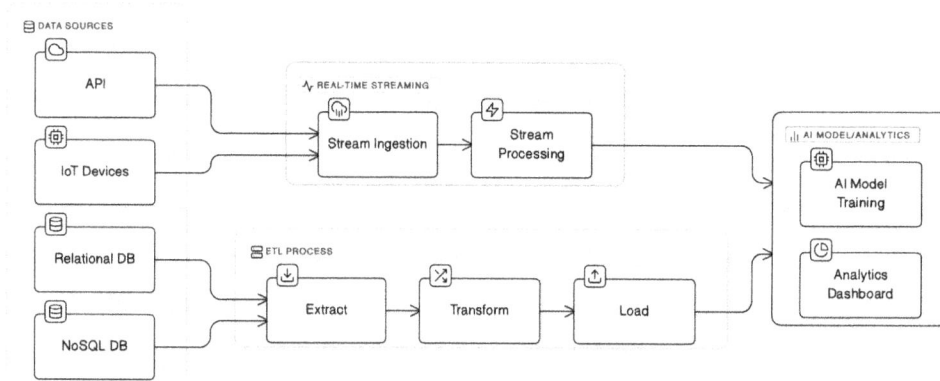

Figure 64: Hybrid Data Pipeline.

Aspect	ETL (Batch Processing)	Real-Time Streaming Technologies
Definition	ETL processes data in batches, typically at scheduled intervals (e.g., hourly, daily).	Real-time streaming processes data as it is generated, enabling immediate insights.
Use Cases	- Data warehousing and reporting	- Real-time analytics and monitoring
	- Historical data analysis	- Fraud detection and prevention
	- Business intelligence (BI) dashboards	- IoT data processing
	- Migrating data between systems	- Real-time recommendations (e.g., e-commerce)
	- Legacy system integration	- Log and event processing
Latency	High latency (minutes to hours or days)	Low latency (milliseconds to seconds)
	Data is processed in batches, leading to delays.	Data is processed in real time as it arrives.
Scalability	- Scalable for large volumes of historical data	- Highly scalable for high-velocity data streams
	- Requires significant infrastructure for large-scale batch jobs.	- Designed to handle millions of events per second.
Complexity	- Easier to implement for structured data	- More complex due to real-time processing needs
	- Requires less infrastructure for low-frequency updates.	- Requires robust infrastructure for continuous data ingestion.
Tools/Technologies	- **Traditional ETL Tools**: Informatica, Talend, IBM DataStage, SSIS	- **Streaming Tools**: Apache Kafka, Amazon Kinesis, Apache Flink, Apache Spark Streaming
	- **Cloud ETL Tools**: AWS Glue, Google Dataflow (batch mode)	- **Cloud Streaming Tools**: Google Dataflow (streaming mode), Confluent, Azure Stream Analytics
Data Freshness	Data is stale until the next batch is processed.	Data is always fresh and up-to-date.
Cost	- Lower operational costs for infrequent updates	- Higher operational costs due to continuous processing and infrastructure requirements.
Best For	- Scenarios where real-time data is not critical	- Scenarios requiring immediate insights and actions
	- Historical analysis and reporting	- Real-time decision-making and event-driven architectures

Table 13: Comparison table for ETL (Extract, Transform, Load) versus Real-Time Streaming Technologies.

Industry-Specific Data Movement Use Cases

- **Healthcare**: The healthcare industry leverages edge computing for real-time remote patient monitoring. Wearable devices and IoT-enabled sensors collect critical health data such as heart rate, oxygen levels, and blood pressure, which are processed locally on edge nodes to ensure rapid detection of anomalies. Healthcare providers can promptly respond to emergencies by minimizing latency, enhancing patient outcomes, and reducing reliance on centralized systems.

- **Finance**: Financial institutions utilize real-time transaction processing systems to detect fraud and manage risk. Data pipelines handle high-velocity streams of transactional data from global payment networks, identifying suspicious patterns such as abnormal transaction frequencies or geolocation inconsistencies. ML models integrated into these pipelines provide instant alerts, enabling proactive fraud prevention and ensuring compliance with regulatory standards.

- **Retail**: The retail sector relies on dynamic recommendation engines powered by streaming analytics. Retailers deliver personalized product recommendations by analyzing real-time customer interactions, such as clickstreams, purchase histories, and social media activity. This enhances customer engagement, increases sales conversions, and strengthens brand loyalty through hyper-personalized shopping experiences.

- **Manufacturing**: Smart factories employ real-time analytics to optimize production processes and equipment maintenance. IoT sensors embedded in machinery monitor parameters like temperature, vibration, and wear, providing continuous data streams for predictive maintenance. Advanced analytics platforms process this data in real time, minimizing equipment downtime, improving operational efficiency, and extending asset lifespans.

The Role of Metadata in Data Movement

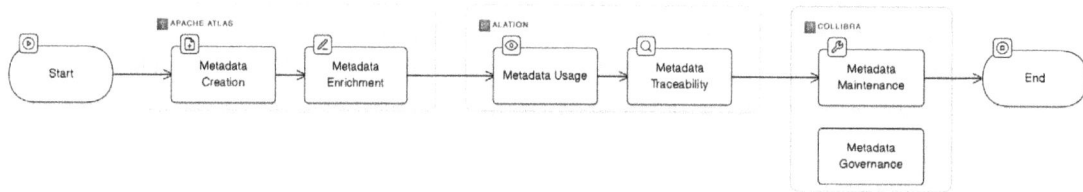

Figure 65: Metadata Lifecycle.[37]

Metadata Management

Metadata is an essential component in modern data systems, serving as a roadmap that ensures data traceability, consistency, and contextual understanding across pipelines. It acts as a bridge between raw data and actionable insights, allowing organizations to comprehend the origin, transformation, and utilization of their data assets. Proper metadata handling enables organizations to document the lineage of data, maintain compliance with regulations, and enhance collaboration between teams by ensuring a unified understanding of data processes. Effective metadata management reduces the risk of errors, accelerates troubleshooting, and strengthens the trustworthiness of AI and analytics workflows.

Metadata is also vital for enriching data with additional context. For example, in a customer recommendation system, metadata can describe the source and structure of user interaction data, detailing when and how it was collected, which algorithms processed it, and where it resides. This detailed contextual information allows AI systems to optimize their operations, ensuring accurate and relevant outputs.

---

[37] https://www.dama.org/cpages/home.

Tools for Metadata Handling

A variety of tools have been developed to streamline metadata management and ensure that organizations can track and leverage metadata effectively. Platforms like **Apache Atlas** and **Alation** are widely used to manage metadata across large-scale data ecosystems:

- **Apache Atlas**: Designed for Hadoop ecosystems, Atlas provides robust capabilities for metadata classification, lineage tracking, and data discovery. It enables organizations to map data flows across their infrastructure, offering detailed lineage visualizations that make tracing issues or evaluating data transformations easier.

- **Alation**: A leader in metadata-driven data governance, Alation integrates with diverse data sources to create a centralized metadata catalog. Its intuitive interface and AI-driven suggestions allow users to explore, annotate, and manage metadata, facilitating team collaboration.

Other tools like **Collibra** and **Informatica EDC** (Enterprise Data Catalog) extend metadata management by integrating with data governance and compliance frameworks. These platforms automate metadata collection and synchronization across disparate systems, ensuring consistency and reducing manual effort. By leveraging these tools, organizations can maintain a clear and actionable understanding of their data assets, enhance operational efficiency, and achieve greater transparency in data movement.

Data Movement in Multi-Cloud and Hybrid Environments

As organizations adopt multi-cloud and hybrid strategies, data movement becomes increasingly complex. Challenges such as latency, compliance, and governance issues arise when data spans multiple cloud providers or combines with on-premises systems. Ensuring seamless interoperability between different environments often requires overcoming proprietary formats, data sovereignty restrictions, and diverse security protocols.

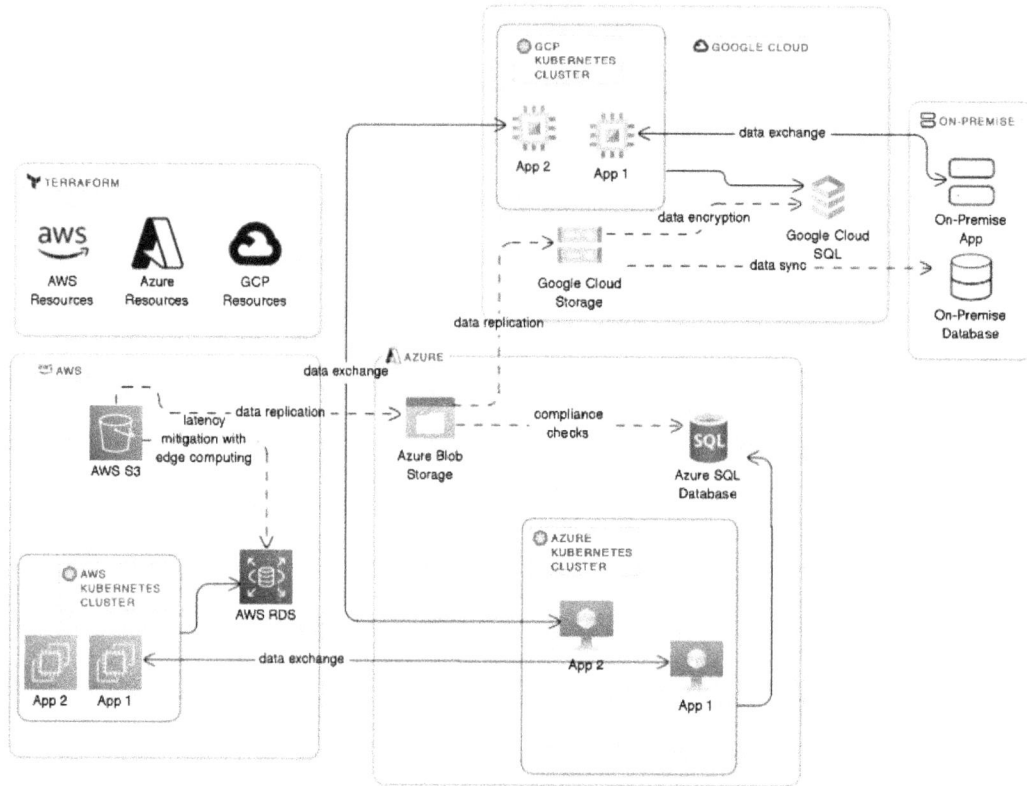

Figure 66: Data Movement in Multi-Cloud and Hybrid Environment.[38] [39] [40]

Tools for Multi-Cloud Orchestration

Tools like **Kubernetes** and **Terraform** play critical roles in facilitating seamless data movement across multi-cloud and hybrid environments:

- **Kubernetes**: By containerizing applications and workloads, Kubernetes ensures that data processes remain portable across different environments. Its orchestration capabilities

---

[38] https://aws.amazon.com/hybrid-multicloud/.

[39] https://azure.microsoft.com/en-us/products#hybrid-multicloud.

[40] https://cloud.google.com/.

enable organizations to scale applications while maintaining consistent configurations across clouds.

- **Terraform**: This infrastructure-as-code tool automates the provisioning and management of cloud resources. Terraform's ability to define infrastructure in a declarative format simplifies multi-cloud deployments and ensures reproducibility.

By combining these tools, organizations can achieve greater flexibility and control over their multi-cloud data workflows, ensuring efficient movement and minimizing operational disruptions.

Data Governance and Compliance in Data Movement

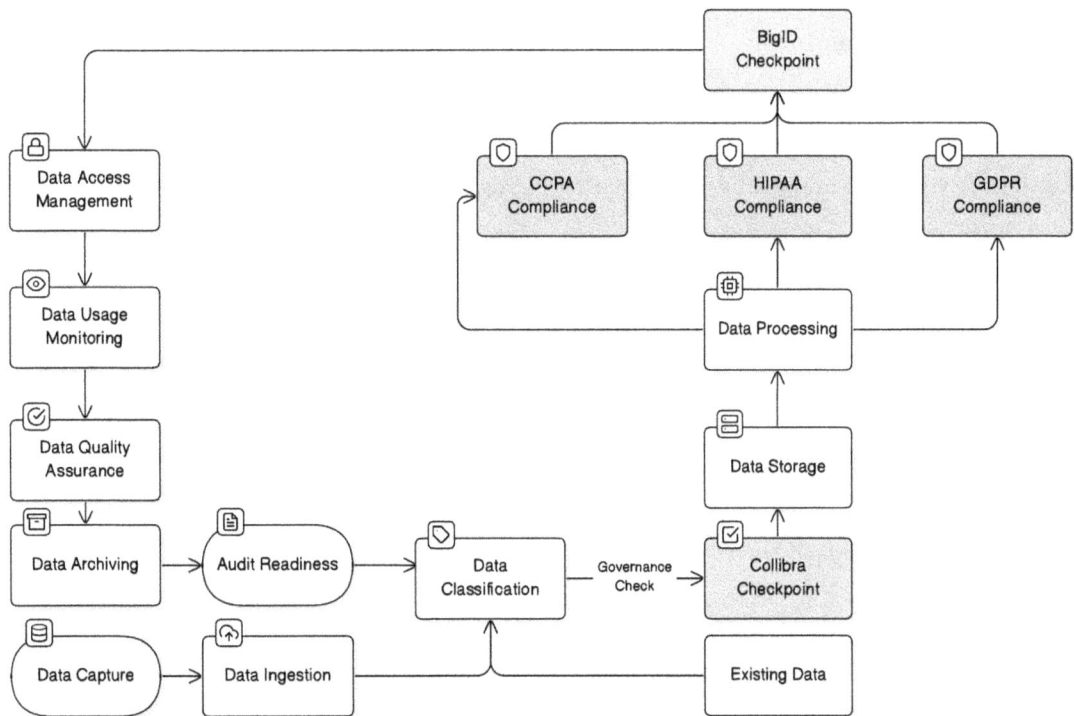

Figure 67: Data Governance and Compliance in Data Movement.[41] [42]

---

[41] https://datagovernance.com/.

[42] https://gdpr.eu/.

Adhering to Privacy Regulations

With stringent regulations like **GDPR**, **HIPAA**, and **CCPA**, organizations must prioritize data privacy and compliance. Ensuring that data movement adheres to these regulations involves implementing strict access controls, encryption, and detailed audit trails. For instance, GDPR mandates that organizations document every data processing activity, while HIPAA requires secure handling of sensitive health information.

Role of Data Observability

Platforms like **Collibra** and **BigID** are instrumental in monitoring compliance and ensuring ethical AI practices. These tools provide:

- **Real-Time Monitoring**: Automated scans to detect sensitive or non-compliant data across pipelines.
- **Audit Readiness**: Comprehensive logs and reports that facilitate regulatory audits.
- **Policy Enforcement**: Integration with governance frameworks to ensure data handling adheres to organizational policies.

Organizations can proactively address compliance risks and maintain ethical standards in their AI and analytics systems by integrating observability platforms into their data workflows.

Advanced Techniques in Real-Time Data Processing

Windowed Operations and Aggregations

Frameworks like **Apache Flink** enable temporal queries through windowed operations. These techniques allow organizations to compute metrics over sliding, tumbling, or session windows, making it possible to derive insights from continuous data streams.

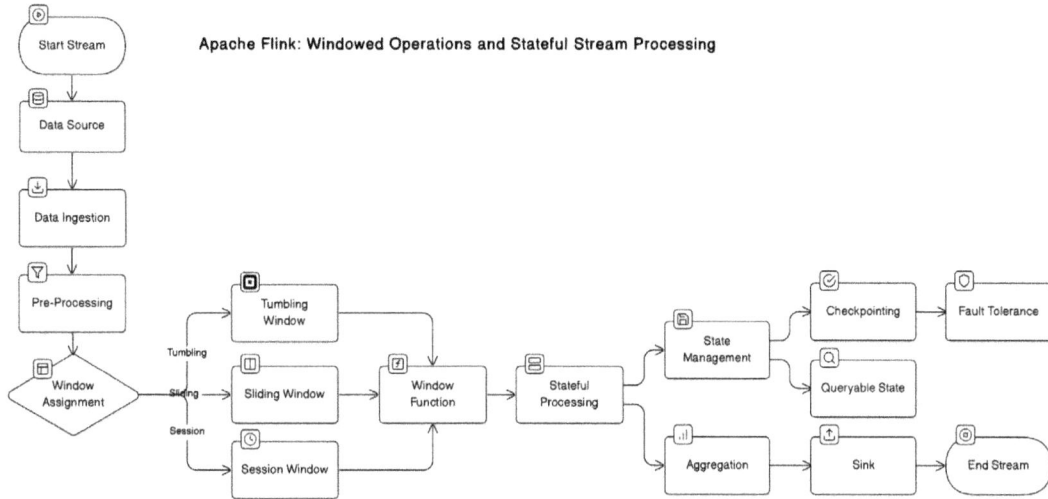

Figure 68: Windowed Operation and Stateful Streaming Process.[43]

Stateful Stream Processing

Stateful processing ensures that real-time systems retain contextual information between events. This is crucial for applications like fraud detection, where historical patterns must be analyzed alongside incoming transactions.

Event Sourcing

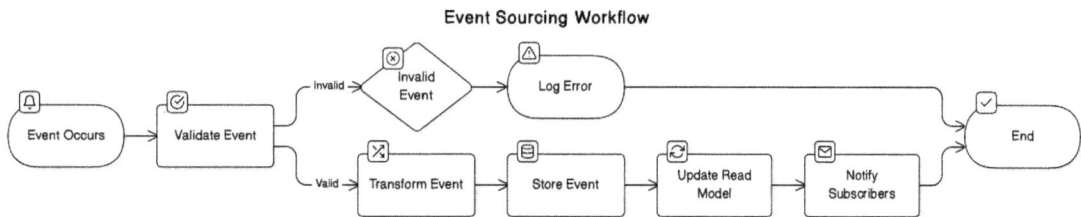

Figure 69: Event Sourcing Process.[44]

---

[43] https://www.oreilly.com/library/view/streaming-systems/9781491983874/.

[44] https://www.oreilly.com/library/view/streaming-systems/9781491983874/.

Event sourcing complements streaming technologies by persisting all changes as immutable events (see Amazon 2023). This approach enhances fault tolerance and provides a complete audit trail for data transformations, ensuring accuracy and transparency in decision-making.

Emerging Technologies and Trends

Decentralized Data Pipelines

Decentralized data pipelines powered by blockchain technology offer a groundbreaking approach to data integrity and security. These systems ensure tamper-proof records by creating immutable, distributed ledgers that store every transaction or transformation in the data pipeline. This level of transparency and reliability is particularly advantageous for sensitive workflows in finance, healthcare, and supply chain management industries. By decentralizing data movement, organizations can reduce the risk of single points of failure and enhance collaboration across multiple stakeholders.

Quantum Data Movement

Quantum computing represents a transformative advancement for data movement, especially for applications involving massive datasets or complex computations. Quantum systems can process and transfer data exponentially faster than classical systems by leveraging quantum principles such as superposition and entanglement. Potential use cases include accelerating ML model training, optimizing large-scale simulations, and solving combinatorial optimization problems. Although still in its nascent stages, quantum data movement promises to redefine performance benchmarks for AI-driven operations.

Self-Healing Data Pipelines

Self-healing data pipelines leverage AI and ML to autonomously detect, diagnose, and correct errors in real-time. These intelligent systems monitor pipeline performance continuously, identifying anomalies and implementing corrective actions without manual intervention. For example, a self-healing pipeline can reroute data flows around failed nodes, clean corrupted records, or re-execute failed jobs with updated parameters. This capability significantly reduces downtime, enhances data reliability, and minimizes operational disruptions, making it an essential feature for organizations with mission-critical data workflows.

Comparison of Data Movement Frameworks

Key Feature Matrix

There are tradeoffs with data movement frameworks. Table 14 provides a feature and cost comparison:

Framework	Latency	Scalability	Cost	Notable Use Cases
Kafka	Low	High	Moderate	Clickstream analysis
Kinesis	Low	High	High	Real-time analytics
Flink	Very Low	High	Moderate	Fraud detection

Table 14: Optimization Strategy Selection Decision Flow.[45]

Decision-Making Framework

Organizations should evaluate tools based on specific requirements, such as latency tolerance, data volume, and budget constraints. A decision matrix can guide this selection process, ensuring the chosen framework aligns with business objectives.

---

[45] https://lintool.github.io/MapReduceAlgorithms/.

Performance Optimization Strategies

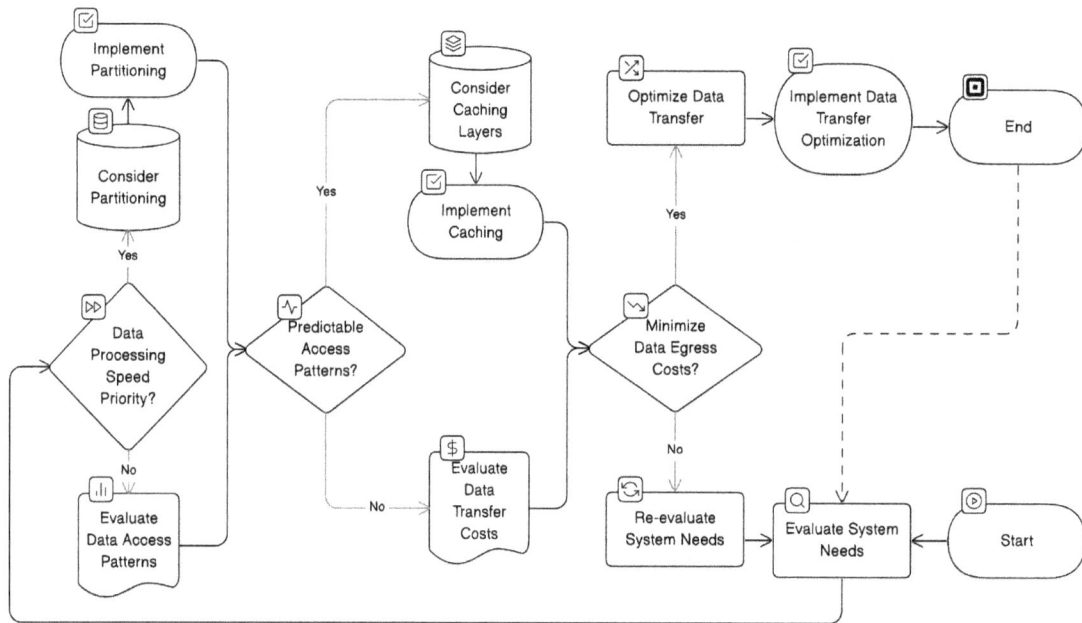

Figure 70: Optimization Strategy Selection Decision Flow.

- **Data Partitioning**: Partitioning data across nodes improves parallel processing and reduces bottlenecks in distributed systems. Strategies such as range-based partitioning, which divides data into sequential ranges, or hash-based partitioning, which distributes data evenly across nodes, ensure efficient resource utilization. Proper partitioning reduces query latency and enhances overall system performance, particularly in distributed environments.

- **Caching Layers**: Tools like Redis and Memcached significantly enhance system performance by caching frequently accessed data. These caching layers minimize the load on primary databases, reduce query latency, and ensure faster access to critical data. By serving repeated requests from memory rather than re-querying the database, caching also optimizes resource consumption and boosts application responsiveness.

- **Minimizing Data Egress Costs**: Cloud providers often impose charges for transferring data out of their systems, making egress costs a critical consideration for performance optimization. Techniques like edge processing, where data is processed closer to its source, reduce the volume of data sent to central systems. Additionally, compressing data before transfer can significantly lower egress expenses, ensuring cost-effective and efficient data movement.

Best Practices for Building Resilient Data Pipelines

Building resilient data pipelines requires a comprehensive strategy that ensures reliability, scalability, and efficiency in the face of ever-growing data demands. Effective practices empower organizations to handle real-time processing, large-scale analytics, and unforeseen disruptions without compromising data integrity or system performance:

- **Monitoring and Alerting**: A resilient pipeline is proactive, not reactive. Leveraging tools like Prometheus and Grafana allows teams to gain real-time insights into pipeline health. These platforms provide actionable metrics and visual dashboards, enabling organizations to detect and resolve issues before they escalate.

- **Error Handling and Retries**: Data pipelines often face transient failures due to network instability or system overloads. Implementing robust retry mechanisms ensures that such temporary glitches do not disrupt workflows. Error logging and automated alerts facilitate quick troubleshooting, minimizing downtime and ensuring data continuity.

- **Scalability Considerations**: In an era of exponential data growth, scalability is non-negotiable. Elastic scaling capabilities, enabled by cloud-native tools and platforms like Kubernetes, allow pipelines to seamlessly adjust to varying data loads. This ensures consistent performance during peak periods and optimizes resource usage during lulls.

- **Data Partitioning**: Efficient data distribution across nodes reduces bottlenecks and enhances parallel processing. Partitioning strategies—whether range-based, hash-based, or custom—enable better workload management and faster data processing.

- **End-to-End Automation**: Automation in data validation, transformation, and integration reduces manual intervention, minimizing human error. Workflow automation platforms like Apache Airflow or Prefect streamline complex pipeline orchestration, ensuring seamless data flow across systems.

- **Comprehensive Testing**: Resilient pipelines are tested rigorously before deployment. This includes unit tests for individual components, integration tests for system-wide functionality, and load tests to simulate peak conditions. Continuous testing as part of CI/CD pipelines ensures ongoing robustness.

- **Security and Compliance**: Data security is paramount. Pipelines must incorporate encryption for data at rest and in transit alongside role-based access controls. We achieve compliance with regulations like GDPR and CCPA through detailed audit trails, data masking, and policy enforcement.

By embracing these best practices, organizations can build pipelines that not only withstand operational challenges, but also drive innovation, efficiency, and confidence in data-driven decision-making.

Challenges in Data Movement

Despite advancements, organizations face several challenges in data movement:

- **Data Quality and Latency**: For example, a global retail company struggled with integrating data from its diverse regional stores due to inconsistencies in data formats and frequent delays in processing updates. By implementing Apache Kafka for real-time streaming and leveraging tools like Apache Flink to clean and normalize data on-the-fly, the company reduced latency issues and improved data accuracy across all systems. Similarly, a financial institution overcame data quality challenges by adopting Talend Data Fabric to automate ETL workflows, ensuring that data ingested from various customer channels met strict compliance and accuracy standards.

Summary

Efficient data movement is the backbone of AI-powered organizations. Businesses can ensure seamless data workflows by leveraging a mix of ETL, real-time streaming technologies, and API-based integration platforms. ETL pipelines excel at batch processing, offering robust mechanisms for extracting, transforming, and loading structured and semi-structured data into centralized repositories like data warehouses or lakes. On the other hand, real-time streaming technologies enable instantaneous processing of data streams, catering to use cases that demand low latency, such as fraud detection or IoT monitoring. API-based integration platforms provide the flexibility to bridge legacy systems and modern AI tools, ensuring compatibility and streamlined data exchange across diverse ecosystems.

Together, these technologies complement each other by addressing distinct but interconnected aspects of data movement, ensuring efficiency, scalability, and adaptability in AI-powered organizations. As organizations adopt cutting-edge tools and techniques, the future promises even greater scalability, flexibility, and intelligence in managing AI-driven data ecosystems.

In the next chapter, **Chapter 11: Making AI Operational**, we will explore how organizations can monitor, visualize, and integrate AI insights into business operations. We will explore real-time dashboards for AI model monitoring, visual business intelligence tools, and AI workflow integration with business applications. Additionally, we will discuss how technologies like APIs, RPA, and real-time data visualization help businesses translate AI-driven insights into actionable decisions. By operationalizing AI effectively, organizations can bridge the gap between advanced analytics and business execution, ensuring that AI models deliver real-world value through seamless automation and workflow integration.

References

Apache Software Foundation, "Apache Kafka Documentation for Streaming AI Data Pipelines," 2023. [Online]. Available: https://kafka.apache.org/documentation/.

Amazon Web Services, "AWS Lambda and Event-Driven Architectures," 2023. [Online]. Available: https://aws.amazon.com/lambda/.

Google Cloud, "Google Cloud Dataflow for Real-Time AI Processing," 2023. [Online]. Available: https://cloud.google.com/dataflow/docs/.

## CHAPTER 11

Making AI Operational

Throughout this book, we have explored the various foundational and advanced concepts surrounding AI, including data collection, storage, processing, governance, and security. Previous chapters have highlighted the importance of high-quality data, ethical AI deployment, and the role of master data management in ensuring AI-driven systems function reliably. However, for AI to provide real-world value, it must go beyond theoretical models and research-based implementation—it needs to seamlessly integrate into business workflows and decision-making processes.

This chapter focuses on operationalizing AI and bridging the gap between AI development and real-world execution. We will examine key technologies and strategies that facilitate AI deployment, including real-time monitoring dashboards, visual business intelligence tools, and AI-driven automation frameworks. The discussion will unfold in a structured manner, beginning with the significance of real-time monitoring, then exploring visual analytics tools that enhance interpretability, and concluding with methods for embedding AI insights into business operations through automation and workflow integration.

By the end of this chapter, you will have a comprehensive understanding of how AI models can be monitored, interpreted, and effectively operationalized to drive business outcomes. This chapter is a crucial step in the AI journey, ensuring that AI-generated insights are accurate, actionable, and seamlessly woven into enterprise systems.

Monitoring AI Models with Real-Time Dashboards

Monitoring AI models with real-time dashboards is essential for ensuring their optimal performance and accuracy. By providing continuous insights into the model's behavior, potential issues can be identified and addressed swiftly, minimizing risks and improving overall effectiveness. The following flow demonstrates an AI modeling flow ecosystem:

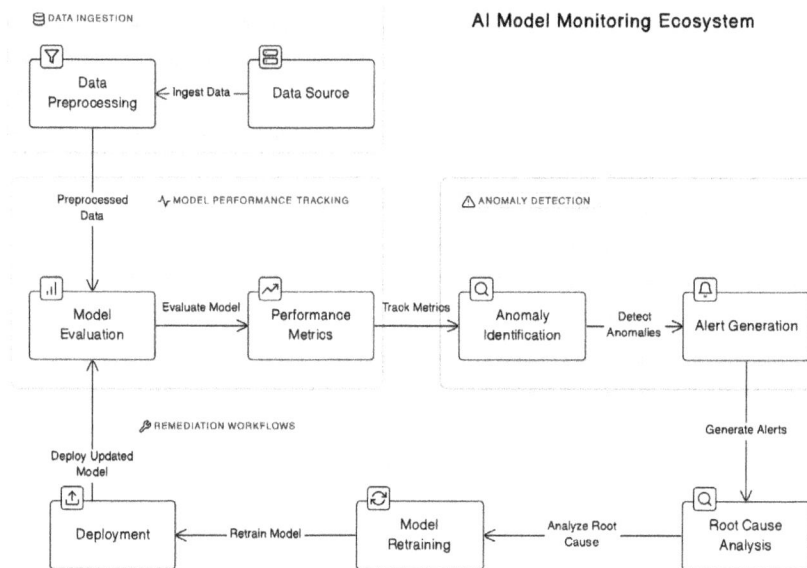

Figure 71: Optimization Strategy Selection Decision Flow.[46][47]

As AI models become increasingly integral to business operations, the need for real-time monitoring and reporting has never been more critical. Organizations today rely on AI-driven insights to optimize decision-making, enhance customer experiences, and improve operational efficiencies. However, without a robust monitoring framework, AI models can quickly degrade in accuracy, develop biases, or become inefficient due to shifting data patterns. Real-time monitoring is essential for maintaining AI reliability, fairness, and effectiveness.

---

[46] https://mlflow.org/.

[47] https://www.kubeflow.org/.

Real-time dashboards provide a dynamic and transparent window into the behavior of AI models, enabling businesses to track key performance indicators (KPIs), detect anomalies, and make data-driven adjustments in real time. These dashboards are not just static visual tools; they are interactive platforms powered by **ML observability technologies, automated alerting systems, and streaming analytics engines** that work together to ensure AI models remain optimal under various conditions.

The modern AI monitoring ecosystem relies on cutting-edge technologies to enable continuous data ingestion, automated data processing, and visualization techniques that facilitate seamless model oversight. By integrating these technologies, businesses can track AI models at multiple levels, from feature engineering to final predictions, ensuring that all aspects of AI decision-making align with intended objectives. This is especially important in regulated industries, where AI models must comply with **governance frameworks, ethical AI principles, and security protocols** to avoid potential risks and liabilities.

As AI adoption continues to expand across various industries, the role of real-time monitoring and AI observability will only grow in importance. Organizations implementing robust AI monitoring strategies can proactively detect issues, mitigate model drift, and sustain AI-driven competitive advantages. Real-time dashboards empower businesses to maximize the value of their AI investments and drive meaningful, data-informed decisions by ensuring transparency, accountability, and accuracy in AI outputs.

Key Features of Real-Time Dashboards for AI Monitoring

- **Performance Metrics Tracking:** Dashboards display critical metrics such as accuracy, precision, recall, and F1 scores, allowing teams to assess model performance in real time. These metrics are crucial in understanding whether AI models continue to perform as expected, especially in dynamic environments where input data distributions may shift.
- **Anomaly Detection:** Real-time alerts can be configured to notify teams of unexpected model behavior, such as drift in data distributions or sudden drops in performance. These systems rely on advanced statistical and ML techniques to detect even subtle deviations that may impact AI model accuracy and reliability.

- **Explainability and Transparency:** Dashboards can provide insights into model decision-making processes, helping to build trust and ensure compliance with regulatory requirements. Features such as SHAP (Shapley Additive Explanations) and LIME (Local Interpretable Model-agnostic Explanations) can be integrated to make model predictions more interpretable.

- **Scalability:** Modern dashboard technologies are designed to handle large volumes of data, making them suitable for monitoring complex AI systems deployed at scale. Whether an organization manages a single AI model or thousands of models in production, real-time dashboards ensure seamless tracking across diverse business applications.

- **Automated Remediation:** Advanced dashboards go beyond monitoring by enabling automated corrective actions. For instance, if an AI model drifts beyond an acceptable threshold, an automated retraining process can be triggered to recalibrate the model with updated data.

- **Multi-Model and Cross-Platform Support:** In large enterprises, AI models are deployed across various cloud platforms, on-premises environments, and edge computing devices. A robust AI monitoring dashboard should support multi-model management and provide a unified view of performance across different deployment environments.

- **User-Centric Customization:** Dashboards should allow stakeholders, including data scientists, engineers, compliance teams, and executives, to customize their views and access role-specific insights. For instance, executives may require high-level performance summaries, while engineers need detailed logs of model execution and feature importance.

- **Compliance and Governance Tracking:** With growing regulations such as GDPR, CCPA, and AI-specific frameworks, AI dashboards should incorporate compliance monitoring tools. This includes logging and reporting mechanisms that track AI decision-making processes, ensuring auditability and regulatory alignment.

- **Integration with DevOps and MLOps Pipelines:** AI monitoring is most effective when integrated into Continuous Deployment (CD) and Continuous Integration (CI) pipelines. Dashboards should connect seamlessly with MLOps tools like MLflow, Kubeflow, and SageMaker, ensuring real-time updates and proactive monitoring (see MLflow 2023).

- **Cross-Departmental Collaboration:** AI dashboards should facilitate communication between technical and non-technical teams. Features such as annotation tools, report sharing, and embedded discussion boards allow stakeholders to collaborate on AI-related findings and improvement strategies.

By leveraging real-time dashboards, organizations can proactively manage their AI models, ensuring that they remain accurate, reliable, and aligned with business objectives. Implementing a well-rounded monitoring framework enhances operational efficiency, strengthens trust in AI decision-making, and enables enterprises to unlock the full potential of their AI investments.

As organizations scale their AI models, continuous monitoring becomes essential to ensure performance, accuracy, and compliance. AI models can drift, degrade, or become biased over time, necessitating real-time oversight. Monitoring dashboards helps organizations track AI outputs, model health, and operational efficiency, enabling quick responses to anomalies before they negatively impact business operations. The following flowchart demonstrates real-time AI modeling:

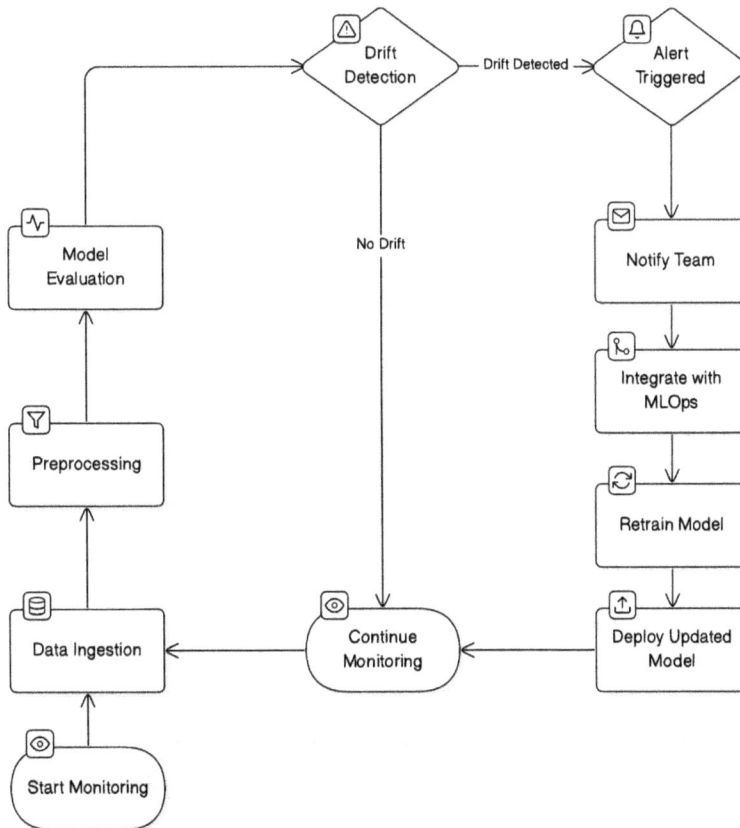

Figure 72: Realtime AI Monitoring Decision Flow.

Key Technologies for AI Model Monitoring

Key technologies for AI model monitoring encompass a range of advanced tools and techniques that enable effective tracking and maintenance of model performance. These technologies ensure that AI models remain accurate, efficient, and aligned with their intended purposes by continuously providing valuable insights and timely interventions. For example:

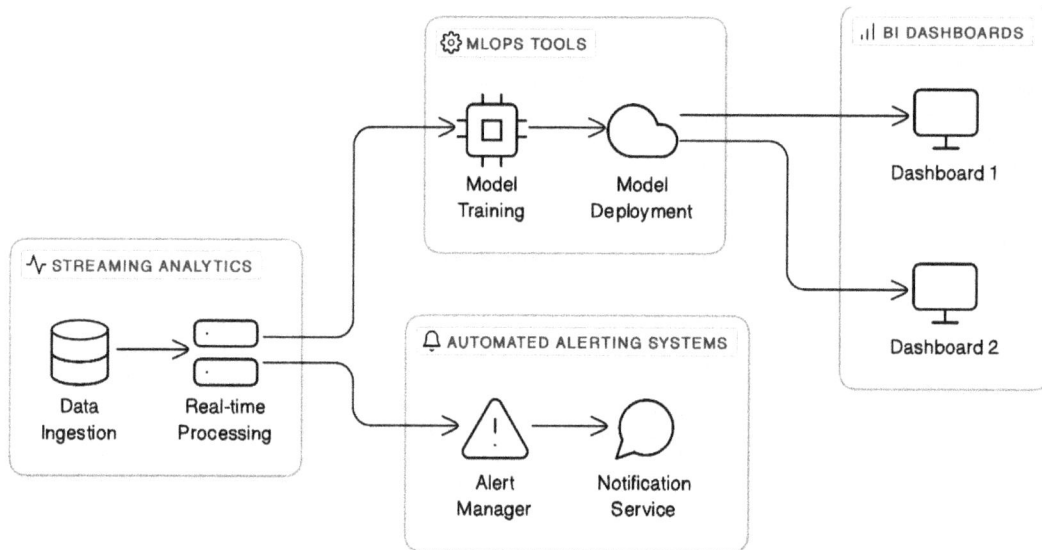

Figure 73: AI Observability Pipeline (see Amazon Web Services 2023).

This pipeline shows the importance of:

1. **Business Intelligence (BI) Dashboards**: Platforms like Tableau, Power BI, and Looker provide organizations with real-time visualization of AI model performance, enabling businesses to analyze complex data and derive insights instantly. These tools integrate with AI systems, offering user-friendly interfaces for tracking key metrics such as accuracy, recall, and precision.

2. **MLOps Pipelines**: Tools like MLflow, TensorBoard, and Databricks facilitate continuous model training and deployment. They integrate with monitoring dashboards to track AI model health, detect data drift, and ensure models remain up-to-date and aligned with business objectives.

3. **Streaming Analytics**: Technologies like Apache Kafka, Apache Flink, and AWS Kinesis enable real-time ingestion and processing of AI model predictions. These tools allow businesses to analyze live data streams, providing an always-current view of AI performance and flagging inconsistencies in predictions as they occur.

4. **Automated Alerting Systems**: AI monitoring platforms implement threshold-based alerts that notify teams when models deviate from expected performance parameters. These alerting systems can be configured to detect issues such as model drift, latency spikes, and data anomalies, ensuring swift intervention to mitigate potential risks.

Best Practices for AI Model Dashboards

Best practices for AI model dashboards focus on creating intuitive, informative, and user-friendly interfaces that enable effective monitoring and management of AI models. By implementing these practices, users can ensure timely detection of issues, clear visualization of key metrics, and enhanced decision-making capabilities. For example:

- **Monitor Drift and Bias:** Implement real-time checks to detect shifts in data patterns and model predictions. Continuously assessed AI models for changes in input data distributions and algorithmic biases that may develop over time.

- **Track Key Performance Indicators (KPIs):** Establish clear metrics such as precision, recall, latency, and error rates. Measure AI performance against defined benchmarks to ensure models maintain optimal accuracy and efficiency.

- **Integrate with Log Management:** Use tools like Splunk and ELK Stack to track logs and trace errors in AI workflows. Logging frameworks provide essential visibility into model execution, enabling teams to effectively diagnose issues and optimize performance.

- **Enable Role-Based Access:** Ensure that only authorized personnel can modify monitoring parameters, maintaining data security and compliance. AI model governance should incorporate user access controls to prevent unauthorized changes and ensure accountability.

- **Leverage Automated Retraining:** AI models should be retrained automatically when significant deviations in performance are detected. Monitoring dashboards should integrate with ML pipelines that trigger model retraining based on predefined performance degradation thresholds.

- **Enhance Model Explainability:** Implement interpretability frameworks such as SHAP (Shapley Additive Explanations) and LIME (Local Interpretable Model-Agnostic Explanations) to provide transparency into model decision-making. Explainability tools help businesses understand AI recommendations, fostering trust and regulatory compliance.

- **Ensure Cross-Departmental Collaboration:** AI dashboards should facilitate interaction between technical teams, business stakeholders, and compliance officers. Features like report-sharing, annotations, and collaborative issue tracking ensure alignment in AI monitoring and decision-making.

- **Optimize for Scalability:** AI monitoring infrastructures should be capable of scaling across multiple models, deployment environments, and business units. Cloud-based AI monitoring solutions ensure flexibility in managing diverse AI applications while maintaining centralized governance.

By implementing these best practices, organizations can enhance their AI monitoring frameworks, ensuring that models remain robust, fair, and aligned with business needs. AI operationalization is not just about deploying models—it requires ongoing vigilance, transparency, and adaptability to maintain the effectiveness of AI-driven decisions.

The Role of Visual Business Intelligence in AI Strategies

Visual Business Intelligence (BI) tools play a pivotal role in bridging the gap between AI-generated insights and actionable business decisions. These tools transform complex data into intuitive visual representations, making it easier for decision-makers to interpret and act on AI-driven insights. In the context of AI strategies, visual BI tools serve as a critical interface between data scientists and business stakeholders, enabling seamless communication and collaboration.

AI to BI Insights Flow

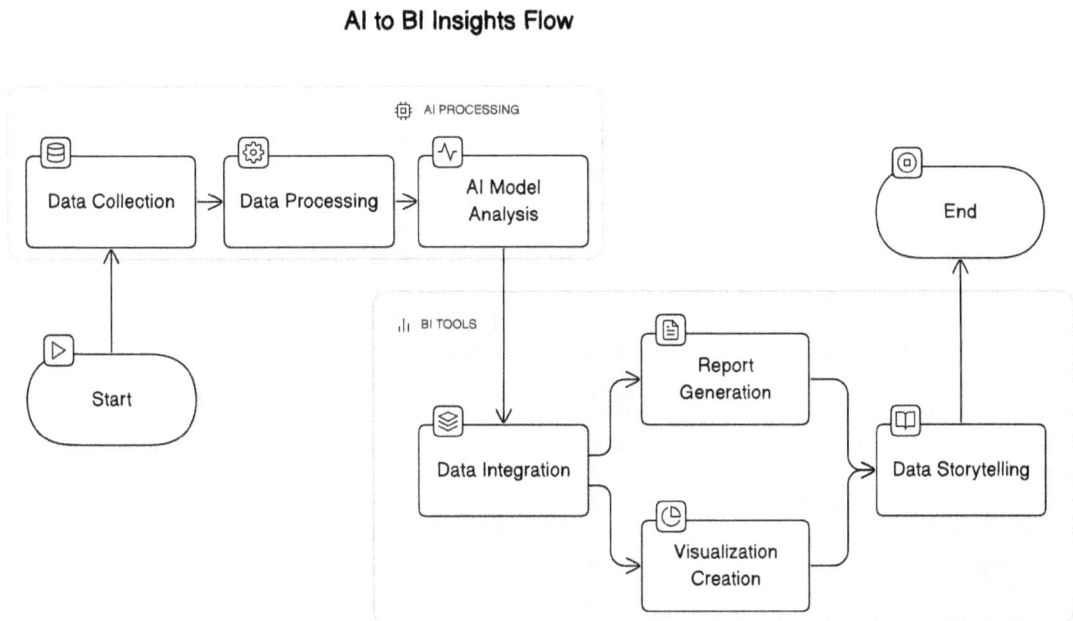

Figure 74: Conceptual Framework.

The key benefits of visual BI in AI strategies include:

- **Enhanced Interpretability:** Visualizations such as charts, graphs, and heatmaps make it easier for non-technical stakeholders to understand AI outputs and their implications. By simplifying complex AI-driven insights, BI tools help organizations make more informed decisions. These visual tools ensure that AI-generated predictions and recommendations are transparent, reducing ambiguity and increasing stakeholder trust in AI-powered processes.

- **Interactive Exploration:** BI tools allow users to drill down into data, filter results, and explore different scenarios, empowering them to make informed decisions based on AI insights. This interactive element enables dynamic decision-making based on evolving business conditions. Users can customize their dashboards to focus on key performance indicators (KPIs) that matter most to their roles, improving productivity and decision accuracy.

- **Real-Time Insights:** Integration with real-time data streams ensures that visualizations are always up-to-date, enabling timely decision-making. This capability is particularly valuable in fast-moving industries where immediate responses to AI-generated insights can provide competitive advantages. Organizations can set up alerts and automated triggers to act upon real-time changes in key data metrics, ensuring a proactive rather than reactive approach to decision-making.

- **Cross-Functional Collaboration:** Visual BI tools facilitate collaboration across departments, ensuring that AI insights are shared and acted upon by all relevant stakeholders. These tools enhance alignment between technical and business teams by providing a unified view of data, fostering a more AI-driven culture. Integrated communication features like annotation tools and shared workspaces help teams work together more effectively on data-driven projects.

- **Operational Efficiency:** By streamlining data analysis and reporting, BI tools save time and resources. Instead of manually compiling data and creating reports, AI-driven BI tools automate the process, allowing business leaders to focus on interpreting results and making strategic decisions.

- **Scalability:** BI tools can handle large volumes of data from multiple sources. Whether managing a small dataset for departmental decision-making or analyzing enterprise-wide AI models, modern BI platforms ensure smooth scalability without performance degradation.

- **Customization and Personalization:** BI dashboards can be tailored to different user needs. Executives may require high-level summaries with key takeaways, while data scientists and analysts may need granular views of AI performance and model accuracy metrics. Personalization ensures that every stakeholder receives relevant insights for their specific role.

- **Regulatory Compliance and Auditability:** With increasing AI regulations such as GDPR and CCPA, organizations must ensure transparency in their AI models. BI tools provide comprehensive audit trails, tracking how data is used and ensuring compliance with industry regulations. Organizations can generate automated compliance reports, reducing legal risks and enhancing accountability.

- **Integration with Other Enterprise Systems:** BI tools integrate with a wide range of enterprise applications, from ERP and CRM systems to cloud data warehouses and AI platforms. This seamless integration enables organizations to leverage AI insights across multiple business functions, from marketing and sales to operations and finance.

- **Advanced AI-Powered Features:** Some BI tools incorporate AI-powered Natural Language Processing (NLP) capabilities, allowing users to query data in conversational formats. AI-driven anomaly detection, pattern recognition, and auto-generated insights can further empower business users to act quickly on key findings.

By incorporating visual BI into their AI strategies, organizations can democratize access to AI insights, driving data-informed decisions across the enterprise. The ability to analyze, visualize, and act on AI-generated insights in real time enhances operational agility, improves business outcomes, and strengthens the overall AI governance framework.

How BI Enhances AI Decision-Making

Visual Business Intelligence (BI) tools transform AI-generated data into comprehensible insights. They bridge the gap between complex algorithms and business users, enabling data-driven decisions through interactive dashboards and reports. By offering real-time data visualization, businesses can monitor AI performance and adapt strategies proactively.

The key features of AI-driven BI includes:

- **Automated Reporting:** AI-powered BI tools can automatically generate reports and visual summaries, reducing the manual effort required to compile insights. These reports are dynamically updated, ensuring decision-makers can access the latest AI-driven insights.

- **Data Storytelling:** Platforms like Power BI, Qlik Sense, and Google Data Studio offer storytelling capabilities by presenting AI-driven insights in a visually intuitive manner. These features enable business leaders to craft compelling narratives based on data, making strategic communication more effective.

- **Predictive and Prescriptive Analytics:** BI tools integrate with AI models to forecast trends and suggest optimal business strategies. Predictive analytics anticipates future trends based on historical data, while prescriptive analytics recommends actionable steps to achieve desired outcomes.

- **Custom AI-Generated Visualizations:** AI-enhanced dashboards automatically highlight critical insights, reducing manual interpretation errors. Business leaders can leverage these visualizations to quickly identify trends, risks, and opportunities in their data.

- **Natural Language Querying:** Advanced BI tools allow users to interact with AI-driven insights using conversational AI, simplifying the process of extracting meaningful information from large datasets. This feature enables business users to ask questions in natural language and receive instant, AI-powered responses.

- **AI-Powered Anomaly Detection:** BI tools equipped with ML algorithms can automatically detect anomalies in data, helping businesses identify risks and irregularities in real time.

- **Automated Data Cleansing and Preparation:** AI-driven BI platforms can preprocess data by identifying missing values, detecting duplicates, and normalizing inconsistencies, ensuring high-quality data inputs for analytics.

- **Multi-Device Accessibility:** BI dashboards are now optimized for mobile and tablet devices, allowing decision-makers to access critical AI insights anytime, anywhere.

Use cases of AI-powered BI dashboards include:

Fraud Detection

- **Situation:** Financial institutions must constantly monitor vast amounts of transactional data to detect fraudulent activities. Traditional fraud detection methods often result in delayed responses and high false-positive rates.
- **Task:** The goal is to implement an AI-powered BI dashboard that enables real-time analysis of financial transactions to identify and prevent fraud before it occurs.
- **Action:** Banks leverage AI-enhanced BI tools to continuously scan transaction patterns, flagging anomalies and suspicious behaviors. These dashboards integrate ML algorithms trained to detect fraud indicators, such as unusual spending behavior, account takeovers, and duplicate transactions.
- **Result:** Financial institutions can proactively prevent fraudulent activities, reducing financial losses and improving customer trust. Automated fraud detection reduces false alarms while ensuring compliance with regulatory requirements.

Customer Retention

- **Situation:** E-commerce platforms experience high customer churn rates, impacting revenue and growth. Identifying at-risk customers and implementing targeted retention strategies is a challenge.
- **Task:** Implement AI-powered BI dashboards that analyze customer interactions, purchase behaviors, and engagement trends to predict churn and recommend personalized retention efforts.
- **Action:** AI-driven BI tools segment customers based on purchasing history, browsing behavior, and customer support interactions. Predictive analytics models assess churn probability, while dashboards suggest retention strategies, such as personalized discounts, loyalty programs, and engagement campaigns.

- **Result:** Businesses experience increased customer retention rates, improved customer satisfaction, and enhanced marketing ROI by focusing on high-risk customers with tailored interventions.

Healthcare Analytics

- **Situation:** Healthcare providers need to track patient health metrics and predict potential disease risks to deliver better care and optimize resource allocation.
- **Task:** Use AI-powered BI dashboards to analyze patient data, detect early signs of illness, and recommend personalized treatment plans.
- **Action:** AI models process historical and real-time patient data from wearable devices, electronic health records (EHRs), and clinical reports. Dashboards visualize patient risk scores, treatment effectiveness, and predictive disease models, enabling healthcare professionals to make informed decisions.
- **Result:** Improved patient outcomes through early intervention, optimized hospital resource utilization, and more efficient care planning for high-risk patients.

Supply Chain Optimization

- **Situation:** Companies struggle with supply chain inefficiencies, leading to stock shortages, delivery delays, and increased operational costs.
- **Task:** Leverage AI-driven BI dashboards to monitor inventory levels, forecast demand, and optimize logistics in real time.
- **Action:** AI-powered BI tools integrate real-time data from warehouses, transportation networks, and sales trends. ML models predict demand fluctuations, suggest optimal stock levels, and flag potential supply chain disruptions.
- **Result:** Reduced inventory holding costs, improved order fulfillment rates, and enhanced supply chain resilience, ensuring smooth business operations.

Marketing and Sales Analytics

- **Situation:** Businesses need to maximize the effectiveness of marketing campaigns and sales strategies by understanding customer behavior and market trends.

- **Task:** Implement AI-enhanced BI dashboards that provide real-time insights into marketing performance, customer preferences, and sales conversions.
- **Action:** AI-driven analytics platforms analyze social media interactions, campaign engagement, and purchase history. Dashboards display key performance indicators (KPIs), such as conversion rates, ad spend efficiency, and personalized product recommendations.
- **Result:** Increased return on marketing investments (ROI), enhanced customer engagement, and data-driven decision-making for future campaigns.

Workforce Analytics

- **Situation:** Organizations need to track employee performance, identify skills gaps, and optimize workforce planning.
- **Task:** AI-driven BI dashboards provide real-time workforce insights, helping HR teams make data-informed decisions.
- **Action:** AI-powered BI tools analyze employee performance metrics, training progress, and engagement levels. Predictive analytics models forecast attrition risks and recommend employee development plans.
- **Result:** Enhanced workforce productivity, reduced turnover rates, and data-driven talent management strategies that improve employee satisfaction and business efficiency.

Manufacturing Process Optimization

- **Situation:** Manufacturing companies need to minimize equipment downtime and reduce inefficiencies in production processes.
- **Task:** Implement AI-powered BI dashboards to monitor equipment health, predict maintenance needs, and optimize production efficiency.
- **Action:** AI-driven BI tools analyze sensor data from machinery, detecting wear and tear, predicting breakdowns, and recommending maintenance schedules. Dashboards display real-time production performance and suggest process improvements.
- **Result:** Reduced maintenance costs, minimized production downtime, and improved manufacturing efficiency through predictive maintenance and process automation.

Financial Forecasting

- **Situation:** Businesses need accurate financial insights to manage budgets, assess risks, and make strategic investments.
- **Task:** Utilize AI-powered BI dashboards to analyze financial performance, market trends, and risk factors in real time.
- **Action:** AI-driven BI tools process historical financial data, stock market trends, and economic indicators to generate predictive financial models. Dashboards provide actionable insights into cash flow management, investment strategies, and revenue forecasts.
- **Result:** Better financial decision-making, improved investment planning, and increased profitability by leveraging AI-driven financial forecasting models.

Real-Time Data Visualization for AI Model Monitoring

Integrating Business Intelligence (BI) with AI workflows is essential for creating actionable insights through live data visualization. Real-time data visualization tools enable organizations to monitor AI models continuously, providing a dynamic view of model performance and outputs. This integration allows data scientists and business users to interact with AI-generated data, uncovering trends, patterns, and anomalies that might otherwise go unnoticed.

The key aspects of real-time data visualization for AI model monitoring include:

- **Live Data Feeds:** Visualization tools are connected to live data streams, ensuring the displayed information is always current and relevant. These feeds collect real-time AI outputs, sensor data, and application metrics, allowing immediate visibility into AI model performance. This is especially critical in finance, healthcare, and cybersecurity sectors, where real-time insights can drive instant corrective actions.
- **Customizable Dashboards:** Users can tailor dashboards to display the metrics and visualizations that are most important to their specific needs, enhancing the utility of the tool. These dashboards offer drag-and-drop customization, filtering capabilities, and

modular components that cater to different stakeholders, from data scientists to executives, ensuring the right level of detail for each user.

- **Predictive Analytics:** Some visualization tools incorporate predictive analytics, allowing users to forecast future trends based on current data. By applying AI-driven forecasting models, businesses can proactively address potential issues, such as predicting equipment failures, identifying financial risks, or optimizing resource allocations before problems arise.

- **Integration with AI Platforms:** Visualization tools are often integrated with AI platforms, enabling seamless data flow and real-time updates. These integrations ensure that AI-generated insights are instantly reflected in dashboards, reducing latency in decision-making and allowing businesses to adapt quickly to changing data patterns.

- **Drill-Down Capabilities:** Advanced BI tools allow users to drill down into data layers, providing granular insights into AI model behavior. Users can analyze data at different levels, from high-level trends to specific transaction details, helping to diagnose issues and fine-tune AI models for better performance.

- **Anomaly Detection and Alerts:** Real-time dashboards can include automated anomaly detection mechanisms that highlight deviations in AI model predictions, triggering alerts when performance drops below predefined thresholds. This helps in early issue identification and immediate intervention.

- **Interactive Data Exploration:** Modern BI tools incorporate interactive visualization elements, such as heat maps, scatter plots, and geographic maps, to provide deeper insights into AI-driven data. These elements allow users to explore and manipulate datasets dynamically.

- **Collaboration and Reporting:** AI-powered visualization platforms enable teams to collaborate by sharing insights, generating automated reports, and embedding dashboards into enterprise applications. This ensures that decision-makers across different departments have synchronized access to the latest AI-driven insights.

- **Data Security and Compliance:** As real-time AI monitoring often deals with sensitive information, visualization tools implement stringent security measures, such as role-based access control, data encryption, and compliance tracking for regulations like GDPR and HIPAA.

By leveraging real-time data visualization, organizations can enhance their ability to monitor AI models, ensuring that they remain effective, adaptive, and aligned with business goals. These enhancements lead to more efficient AI governance, improved transparency, and data-driven decision-making across industries.

Feature	Traditional Monitoring	AI-Enhanced Monitoring
Speed of Detection	Lagging detection, often minutes to hours delay	Instant detection, sub-second response time
Accuracy of Insights	Rule-based, prone to false positives and negatives	ML-driven insights, high accuracy
Scalability	Limited scalability, high resource dependency	Highly scalable, cloud and edge computing support
Anomaly Detection	Basic threshold-based anomaly detection	Advanced ML-driven anomaly detection, fewer false positives
Predictive Capabilities	Historical trend analysis, minimal predictive analytics	Predictive analytics to foresee trends and risks
Automation and Adaptability	Manual tuning required for adjustments	Self-learning models adapt automatically
Integration with Business Processes	Requires human intervention for decision-making	Seamless API integrations for automated decisions
Explainability and Transparency	Limited, often black-box methodologies	Explainable AI methods improve trust and compliance
Real-Time Data Processing	Batch processing, periodic updates	Continuous, real-time streaming data processing

Table 15: Comparison Chart.

Integrating BI with AI Workflows

Real-time data visualization enables decision-makers to act swiftly on AI-generated insights. Businesses integrate AI models with visualization tools to ensure transparency, interpretability, and accountability in automated decision-making. By combining the analytical power of AI with the clarity of BI tools, organizations can extract deeper insights, reduce risks, and optimize performance across multiple business functions.

The technologies for live data visualization include:

- **Apache Superset:** An open-source BI platform that supports real-time AI model visualization. It provides interactive dashboards, customizable SQL queries, and multi-source data integration, making it a flexible solution for AI-driven analytics.

- **Grafana:** A powerful monitoring tool that visualizes AI model performance metrics in real time. It integrates seamlessly with databases, cloud services, and event-driven systems, allowing businesses to track AI-generated insights with live graphs and alerts.

- **D3.js:** A JavaScript library that enables developers to create custom AI-driven visualizations. Unlike predefined dashboard solutions, D3.js offers extensive flexibility, allowing for developing highly specialized and interactive data presentations.

- **Streamlit:** A lightweight framework designed for AI model deployment with built-in visualization capabilities. Streamlit simplifies the process of creating web applications that showcase AI model results, making it ideal for data scientists who need to share insights interactively.

- **Power BI:** A widely used BI tool from Microsoft that enables real-time AI data visualization. It integrates with ML models and cloud data sources, allowing businesses to generate dynamic reports and AI-driven insights (see Microsoft 2023).

- **Tableau:** A leading BI and visualization tool that connects with AI models to provide deep analytics. Its advanced visualization capabilities, combined with AI-driven insights, make it a preferred choice for enterprise decision-making.

- **Looker:** A Google Cloud-based analytics and BI platform that integrates seamlessly with AI and ML models. It provides advanced data exploration, allowing users to gain deep insights into AI-driven predictions and trends.

- **Kibana:** A real-time analytics and visualization platform used in conjunction with Elasticsearch. It is widely used for AI-driven log analysis, anomaly detection, and AI model performance monitoring.

- **Redash:** A cloud-native BI tool that integrates with databases and AI models to provide interactive dashboards, real-time queries, and AI-driven visualizations.

- **Qlik Sense:** A self-service data analytics platform that leverages AI to provide automated insights, trend detection, and interactive data visualization.

Technology	Description	Best Use Case	Real-Time Data Support	Customizability	Ease of Use	Integration with AI Models	Scalability	Deployment Type	Cost
Apache Superset	An open-source business intelligence (BI) tool for interactive dashboards and data visualization.	Enterprise-level BI dashboards with SQL-based querying.	Yes, supports live data connections.	High, open-source and customizable.	Moderate, requires SQL knowledge.	Yes, integrates with AI/ML models through SQL and APIs.	High, supports large datasets.	Self-hosted, cloud-based.	Free, open-source.
Grafana	A monitoring and observability platform primarily used for real-time metrics visualization.	IT infrastructure and real-time system monitoring.	Yes, optimized for real-time metrics.	Medium, flexible with plugins.	Easy for IT users, but setup requires some learning.	Limited, mostly used for system monitoring.	High, optimized for handling large-scale metrics.	Self-hosted, cloud-based.	Free (open-source) and enterprise paid version available.
D3.js	A JavaScript library for creating highly customizable and interactive data visualizations.	Custom visualizations for web applications and data-driven storytelling.	Yes, but requires additional backend setup.	Very High, fully customizable visualizations.	Difficult, requires programming expertise.	Yes, but requires custom development.	Medium, depends on implementation.	Embedded within web applications.	Free, open-source.
Tableau	A widely used commercial BI tool for enterprise-grade data visualization and analytics.	Comprehensive business intelligence and corporate reporting.	Yes, supports live and extract-based data connections.	Medium, predefined templates but some customization available.	Very easy, drag-and-drop interface.	Yes, integrates with AI platforms and cloud services.	High, used for enterprise-scale deployments.	Cloud-based, on-premises, or hybrid.	Commercial, subscription-based pricing.

Table 16: Technology Comparison Table.

The benefits of real-time AI visualization include:

- **Faster Response to Anomalies:** AI-driven visual alerts facilitate rapid decision-making. By integrating BI tools with AI monitoring systems, businesses can immediately detect and act upon deviations in model performance, preventing costly errors and failures.

- **Improved Model Interpretability:** Businesses can track AI-driven recommendations and understand their impact. Clear visual representations of AI outputs enable stakeholders to assess decision rationales, making AI more explainable and trustworthy.

- **Enhanced Collaboration:** Live dashboards enable cross-functional teams to analyze AI model performance together. By providing a centralized visualization hub, BI tools foster collaboration among data scientists, engineers, executives, and operational teams, ensuring that AI insights drive informed business strategies.

- **Scalability and Flexibility:** BI and AI integrations are scalable across various business functions, industries, and data complexities. Organizations can seamlessly expand their AI-driven BI solutions to accommodate growing data needs, ensuring continuous insights and adaptive decision-making.

- **Data-Driven Decision-Making:** By combining AI-powered analytics with BI-driven visualizations, organizations can transition from reactive to proactive decision-making. This enables businesses to anticipate trends, mitigate risks, and seize opportunities based on real-time, data-backed insights.

By effectively integrating BI with AI workflows, businesses can create a dynamic decision-making ecosystem that maximizes the value of AI-generated insights. This ensures that AI-driven recommendations are not only accurate but also accessible, interpretable, and actionable across all levels of an organization.

Real-Time Data Delivery to Business Applications

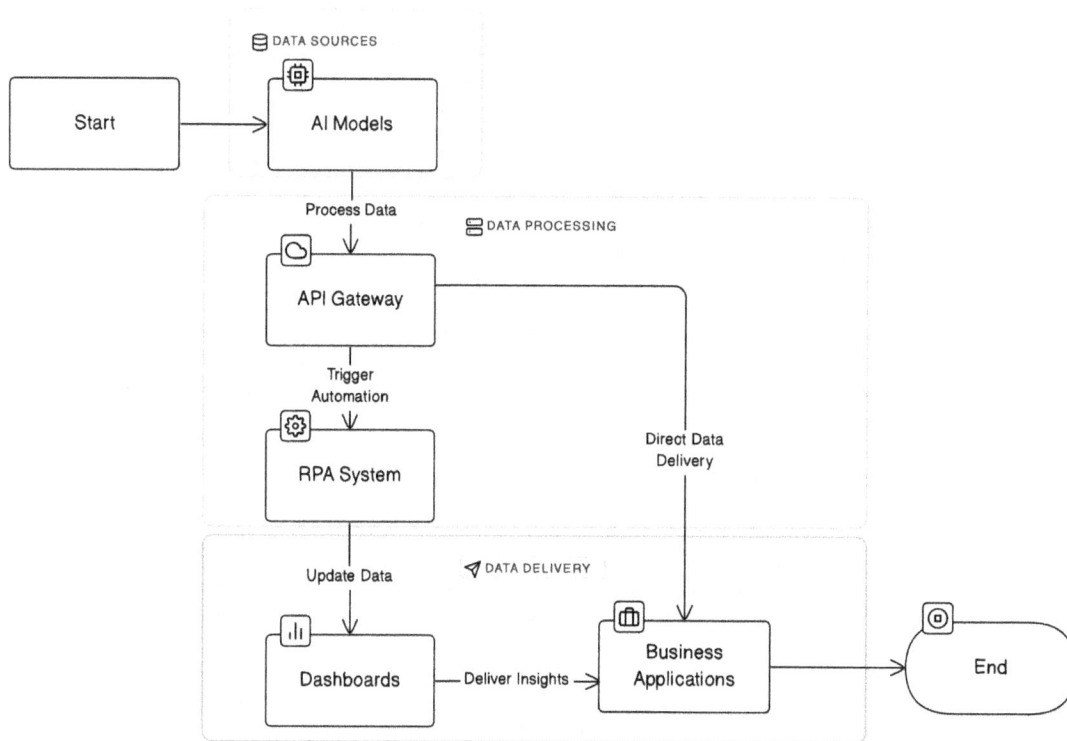

Figure 75: Realtime Data Delivery to Business Applications.

Importance of Real-Time Data Delivery

Operationalizing AI insights requires the seamless delivery of data to business applications where it can be acted upon. AI-driven insights remain siloed without effective real-time data delivery mechanisms and fail to contribute to strategic or operational decision-making. Technologies such as **APIs (Application Programming Interfaces), Robotic Process Automation (RPA), and real-time dashboards** play a crucial role in ensuring that AI-generated insights are efficiently transferred to the systems and tools used by business users.

The key technologies for real-time data delivery include:

APIs (Application Programming Interfaces)

- **Data Integration:** APIs enable seamless communication between AI models and business applications, allowing real-time data exchange across different platforms.
- **Scalability:** APIs support enterprise-wide AI implementations by connecting multiple systems such as Customer Relationship Management (CRM), Enterprise Resource Planning (ERP), and Marketing Automation platforms.
- **Automation and Efficiency:** APIs eliminate the need for manual data entry by automating data exchange processes, ensuring that AI insights are instantly available to decision-makers.
- **Security and Governance:** With API management solutions like **Apigee, AWS API Gateway, and Kong**, businesses can enforce access controls, monitor API usage, and ensure compliance with data privacy regulations.
- **Use Case Example:** A financial institution uses an API to integrate an AI-powered fraud detection model with its online banking application, instantly flagging suspicious transactions in real time.

Robotic Process Automation (RPA)

- **Automated Workflows:** RPA bots extract AI-generated insights and input them into business applications, eliminating repetitive tasks.
- **Data Transformation:** RPA tools can preprocess AI outputs, converting them into formats compatible with enterprise applications.
- **Cross-Platform Compatibility:** RPA solutions like **UiPath, Automation Anywhere, and Blue Prism** integrate with both AI models and legacy systems, ensuring seamless data delivery.
- **Error Reduction:** RPA minimizes human errors in data transfer processes, ensuring the accuracy and reliability of AI-driven insights.
- **Use Case Example:** An e-commerce company employs RPA to automatically update product demand forecasts generated by AI into its inventory management system, preventing stock shortages.

Real-Time Dashboards

- **Visual Decision-Making:** Dashboards provide executives and analysts with real-time AI insights, allowing quick and informed decision-making.

- **Multi-Source Data Aggregation:** Dashboards consolidate AI outputs from various sources into a single, easy-to-read interface.

- **Actionable Alerts and Notifications:** AI-integrated dashboards can be configured to trigger alerts when certain thresholds are met, prompting immediate action.

- **Customizability:** Business users can tailor dashboards to display AI-driven KPIs and metrics specific to their operational needs.

- **Use Case Example:** A logistics company integrates AI-powered predictive analytics into its real-time dashboard, enabling fleet managers to optimize delivery routes based on live traffic and weather conditions.

Benefits of Real-Time Data Delivery

- **Instant Decision-Making:** Businesses can act on AI-generated insights immediately, improving responsiveness and operational efficiency.

- **Enhanced Productivity:** Automating data delivery processes through APIs and RPA reduces the workload on employees, allowing them to focus on high-value tasks.

- **Seamless AI Integration:** Connecting AI models directly with business applications ensures that AI-driven decisions are executed without manual intervention.

- **Greater Business Agility:** Real-time data delivery enables organizations to adapt quickly to changing market conditions, improving their competitiveness.

- **Improved Accuracy and Compliance:** Automated, real-time data flow ensures that business decisions are based on the most accurate and up-to-date AI-generated insights, reducing the risks associated with outdated information.

By effectively integrating real-time data delivery mechanisms, businesses can ensure that AI-generated insights are instantly available, actionable, and impactful across various departments. Whether through APIs, RPA, or real-time dashboards, delivering AI insights to business applications in real time is a crucial component of AI operationalization. It enables businesses to move beyond static reports and dashboards, transforming AI insights into actionable, real-time business strategies.

Technologies Enabling AI Operationalization

For AI to drive business value, its insights must be seamlessly delivered to enterprise applications where decisions are made. This ensures that actionable intelligence is leveraged in real time for strategic and operational purposes. This integration is facilitated by a variety of advanced technologies listed below that ensure data flows efficiently, insights are accessible across multiple business units, and automated processes translate raw intelligence into impactful decision-making.

The process begins with seamless data ingestion from AI models, ensuring that insights are captured from vast data sources such as IoT devices, customer interactions, market trends, and real-time monitoring systems. The transformation layer then processes, structures, and optimizes this data, applying ML models to detect patterns, predict trends, and generate intelligent recommendations. Finally, the data is delivered through well-integrated pipelines to business applications, dashboards, automation systems, and real-time analytics platforms, ensuring instant usability and maximum efficiency.

By employing robust data governance frameworks, security protocols, and API management solutions, businesses can guarantee that AI-driven insights are accurate and comply with regulatory requirements and organizational standards. Furthermore, organizations leveraging AI operationalization techniques benefit from enhanced agility, reduced latency in decision-making, and improved efficiency, leading to increased competitiveness and innovation in their respective industries.

The key technologies for AI operationalization include:

- **APIs (Application Programming Interfaces):** RESTful and GraphQL APIs enable AI insights to be embedded in CRM, ERP, and marketing tools, allowing seamless data exchange between AI models and business applications. These APIs facilitate real-time interaction between AI-driven analytics and business workflows, ensuring that insights are actionable and can drive immediate business impact. Advanced API management solutions like Apigee and AWS API Gateway help manage access, security, and scalability.

- **Robotic Process Automation (RPA):** Bots automate AI-driven workflows, streamlining business processes and reducing the need for manual intervention. RPA platforms like UiPath, Automation Anywhere, and Blue Prism integrate AI-powered decision-making into routine operations, automating data processing, customer interactions, and compliance monitoring. By leveraging AI-driven RPA, organizations can scale operations efficiently and minimize human error in decision-critical tasks.

- **Event-Driven Architectures:** Tools like Apache Kafka, AWS Lambda, and Google Cloud Pub/Sub ensure real-time AI predictions reach relevant applications, enabling low-latency decision-making. These architectures allow AI models to process streaming data and trigger automated responses based on insights, making them critical for industries such as finance (fraud detection), retail (personalized promotions), and IoT (predictive maintenance).

- **Message Queues:** Technologies like RabbitMQ and ActiveMQ manage asynchronous AI data delivery, ensuring efficient processing across distributed systems. These queues decouple message producers and consumers, optimizing data flow and ensuring that AI-driven recommendations and alerts are processed reliably, even under high-load conditions.

- **Data Streaming Platforms:** Apache Flink, Spark Streaming, and Amazon Kinesis enable continuous AI-driven data processing and delivery, enhancing responsiveness and scalability. These platforms are essential for real-time AI applications, such as monitoring industrial equipment for predictive maintenance, analyzing social media trends, and adapting AI-driven chatbots to changing user behavior.

- **Edge Computing:** Platforms like Azure IoT Edge and AWS Greengrass process AI insights closer to the source, reducing latency and improving real-time decision-making in IoT applications. By running AI inference at the edge, organizations can reduce bandwidth costs, improve response times, and enable autonomous operations in industries such as autonomous vehicles, smart cities, and industrial automation.

AI Decision Workflow in Business Operations

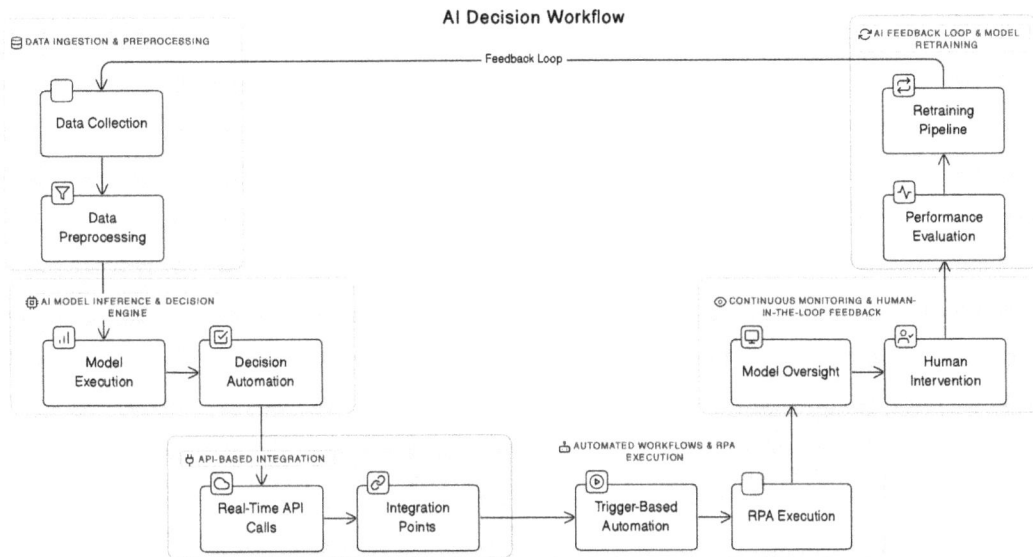

Figure 76: Realtime Data Delivery to Business Applications.

This workflow provides a step-by-step flowchart detailing how AI-driven decisions are operationalized within an enterprise setting. It includes AI model inference, decision automation, API-based integrations with business applications, and continuous learning loops for ongoing optimization.

The key steps in AI decision workflow include:

Data Ingestion and Preprocessing

- **Sources:** Data is collected from multiple sources such as enterprise databases, IoT devices, real-time customer interactions, and transactional systems.
- **Preprocessing:** AI pipelines clean, normalize, and transform raw data into structured formats suitable for AI model inference.
- **Technologies Used:** Apache Kafka (real-time ingestion), Snowflake (data storage), Spark (ETL processing).

AI Model Inference and Decision Engine

- **Model Execution:** AI models, trained on historical and real-time data, generate predictive insights.
- **Decision Automation:** AI-based decision engines classify outcomes, score risks, and recommend actions.
- **Examples:** Fraud detection models analyze transactions in real time; recommendation engines suggest products to customers.
- **Technologies Used:** TensorFlow, PyTorch, AWS SageMaker, Google Vertex AI.

API-Based Integration with Business Applications

- **Real-Time API Calls:** AI insights are delivered to business applications via APIs for immediate action.
- **Integration Points:** AI connects with CRM, ERP, marketing automation, customer service platforms, and financial systems. Examples:
  - AI-powered fraud detection integrates with online banking platforms to block suspicious transactions.
  - AI-based chatbots process user queries in real time via NLP APIs.
- **Technologies Used:** RESTful APIs, GraphQL, AWS API Gateway, Google Cloud Functions.

Automated Workflows and RPA Execution

- **Trigger-Based Automation:** AI decisions trigger Robotic Process Automation (RPA) bots to execute tasks in business workflows.
- Use Cases:
  - AI-driven customer churn models automatically trigger retention campaigns.
  - AI-powered supply chain forecasting auto-reorders stock when demand spikes.
  - AI-based document processing automates contract approvals.
- **Technologies Used:** UiPath, Automation Anywhere, Blue Prism.

Continuous Monitoring and Human-in-the-Loop Feedback

- **Model Oversight:** AI decisions are monitored through real-time BI dashboards to ensure accuracy and reliability.
- **Human Intervention:** AI-generated recommendations that exceed confidence thresholds (e.g., high-risk financial decisions) are flagged for human review.
- Use Cases:
    - AI-powered recruitment models flag hiring decisions for HR validation.
    - AI-driven risk assessments route complex cases to compliance officers.
- **Technologies Used:** Tableau, Power BI, Grafana, Looker.

AI Feedback Loop and Model Retraining

- **Performance Evaluation:** AI models continuously assess accuracy, fairness, and efficiency.
- **Retraining Pipeline:** AI pipelines retrain models based on new real-world data and human feedback to prevent drift.
- **Use Cases:**
    - AI fraud detection models update risk-scoring logic based on new fraud patterns.
    - AI sentiment analysis tools adjust language models based on emerging customer behavior.
- **Technologies Used:** MLflow, Kubeflow, Google Vertex AI Pipelines.

Example Use Cases of Real-Time AI Implementation

AI-Powered Chatbots

- **Situation:** Customer service teams face increasing pressure to handle high volumes of inquiries while maintaining quick response times, personalization, and service quality. Traditional support methods, including phone-based and email support, are labor-intensive, prone to delays, and often fail to meet customer expectations for immediate assistance.

- **Task:** Deploy an AI-powered chatbot capable of **real-time, context-aware, and personalized interactions** with customers to improve engagement, streamline customer support, and reduce operational costs.

- **Action**: AI chatbots powered by advanced Natural Language Processing (NLP) and ML models like GPT-4 and Google's Dialogflow integrate seamlessly with business applications through APIs, CRM systems, and knowledge bases. These AI chatbots analyze customer intent, conversation history, and contextual information to deliver accurate, human-like responses in real time. Chatbots also leverage sentiment analysis to adjust their tone and response strategy based on customer emotions. Additionally, they support multi-channel deployment, including integration with messaging apps (WhatsApp, Facebook Messenger), websites, mobile applications, and voice assistants.

- **Result**: Businesses experience higher customer satisfaction rates due to faster response times, enhanced personalization, and 24/7 availability. AI chatbots significantly reduce operational costs by minimizing the need for large customer support teams, while improving engagement through adaptive learning and predictive assistance. Moreover, AI-driven automation allows human agents to focus on complex inquiries, leading to a more efficient and effective customer service experience.

Automated Risk Assessment

Automated risk assessment leverages advanced algorithms and data analytics to identify and evaluate potential risks efficiently and accurately. This technology enables organizations to proactively address vulnerabilities, enhancing overall security and decision-making processes.

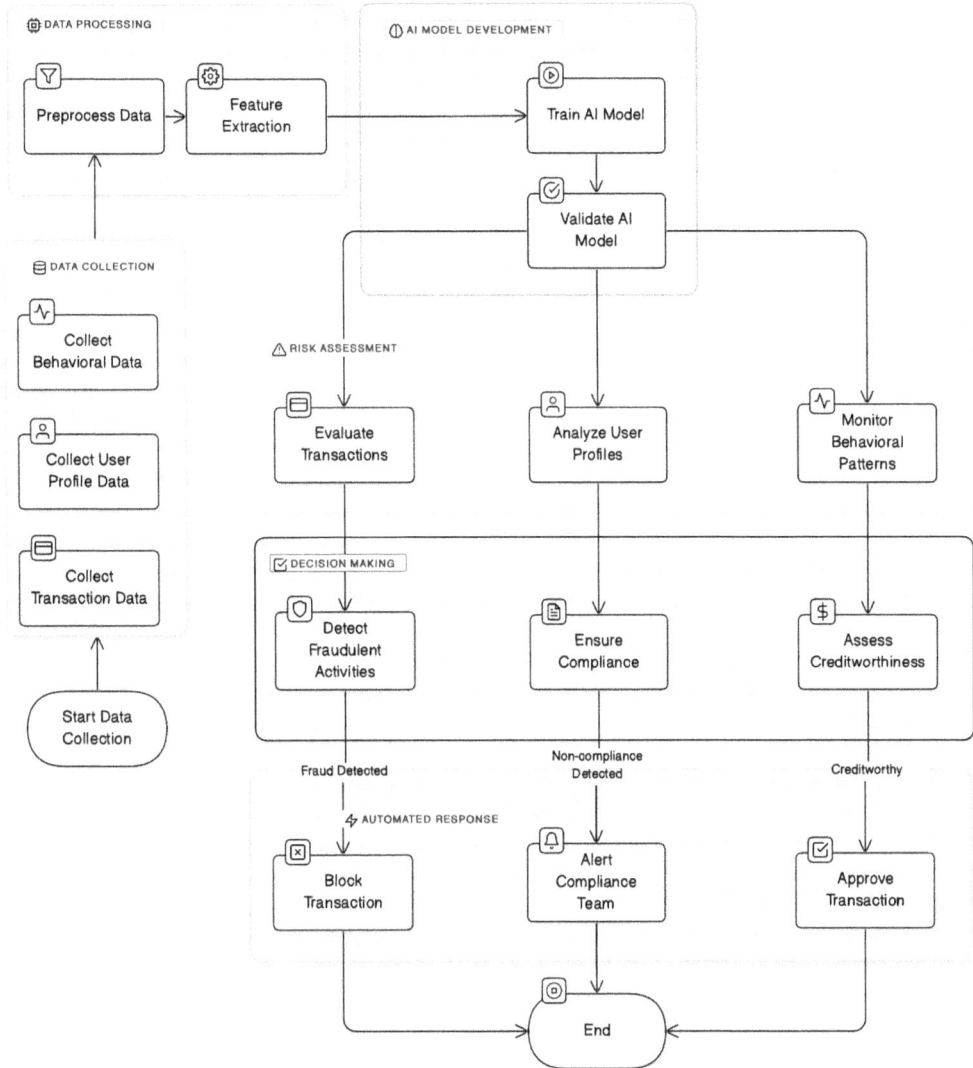

Figure 77: Realtime Data Delivery to Business Applications.

Figure 77 highlights key components of risk management, including:

- **Situation**: Financial institutions operate in an environment of increasing financial crimes, regulatory pressures, and cyber threats. They require real-time decision-making capabilities for loan approvals, fraud detection, credit risk assessments, and regulatory compliance to mitigate financial risks and ensure business continuity.

- **Task**: Develop an AI-driven risk assessment system capable of evaluating real-time transactions, user profiles, and behavioral patterns to detect fraudulent activities, ensure adherence to compliance regulations, and streamline creditworthiness assessments.

- **Action**: AI models process and analyze vast amounts of historical transaction data, user behavior anomalies, and third-party risk indicators. These models integrate with banking applications via APIs, enabling seamless fraud detection and decision-making. ML algorithms continuously learn from evolving fraud tactics and regulatory changes, while Natural Language Processing (NLP) tools scan compliance documents to flag potential risks. Additionally, graph analytics can map relationships between users and detect hidden fraud networks. The system generates real-time alerts, automated decision-making reports, and predictive risk scores for financial transactions.

- **Result**: Financial institutions achieve higher fraud detection accuracy, reducing financial losses and safeguarding customer assets. AI-powered risk assessment ensures rapid loan approvals with reduced manual intervention, enhances AML (Anti-Money Laundering) compliance monitoring, and enables real-time reporting for regulatory audits and financial crime investigations. This leads to improved operational efficiency, reduced compliance risks, and an enhanced customer trust and security framework within the financial ecosystem.

AI-Optimized Inventory Management

AI-optimized inventory management leverages AI to streamline and enhance the processes of stock tracking, demand forecasting, and supply chain optimization. By implementing AI-driven solutions, businesses can achieve greater accuracy, efficiency, and responsiveness in managing their inventory levels:

- **Situation:** Retailers, manufacturers, and logistics providers face persistent challenges in managing fluctuating consumer demand, supply chain disruptions, and changing market conditions. These fluctuations often result in excess inventory, causing increased holding costs, or stock shortages, leading to lost sales and dissatisfied customers.

- **Task:** Implement AI-powered predictive analytics to optimize inventory levels by dynamically adjusting stock according to real-time demand forecasts, supplier constraints, and logistics efficiency.

- **Action**: AI-driven inventory management systems leverage ML algorithms to analyze historical sales data, seasonal trends, macroeconomic indicators, and real-time market dynamics. These AI models continuously ingest and process live data from point-of-sale (POS) systems, warehouse management software, logistics tracking, and supplier networks, ensuring real-time synchronization of stock levels. Additionally, AI tools recommend dynamic pricing adjustments, supplier reordering strategies, and inventory allocation optimizations based on evolving consumer patterns.

- **Result:** Businesses achieve significant cost savings by reducing excess stock and minimizing markdown losses, enhancing supply chain resilience through AI-driven supplier recommendations, and increasing revenue by ensuring product availability aligns with customer demand. AI-optimized inventory management helps businesses improve operational efficiency, reduce waste, and increase profitability, ensuring a competitive edge in today's fast-paced markets.

AI-Enabled Personalized Marketing

- **Situation:** Marketing teams face challenges in engaging customers with personalized content that aligns with their preferences, behaviors, and buying intent. Traditional marketing strategies often rely on broad audience segmentation, which leads to lower engagement and ineffective targeting.

- **Task:** Implement AI-driven marketing automation tools that leverage advanced data analytics and behavioral insights to predict customer preferences, optimize engagement strategies, and deliver real-time hyper-personalized experiences.

- **Action:** AI-powered analytics platforms integrate with customer data platforms (CDPs), CRM systems, and marketing automation platforms, continuously analyzing browsing behavior, past purchases, social media interactions, and engagement history. Natural language processing (NLP) and sentiment analysis are used to understand customer intent and adjust messaging accordingly. Recommendation engines dynamically generate tailored product suggestions, email campaigns, and real-time promotions based on ML algorithms that detect patterns in customer behavior.

- **Result:** Companies like **Amazon, Netflix, and Spotify** achieve **higher conversion rates, improved brand loyalty, and increased customer retention** by delivering AI-driven, personalized experiences. AI-powered marketing automation reduces the manual workload for marketers, enhances audience segmentation, and ensures that the right content reaches the right customer at the right time. Businesses leveraging AI-driven marketing strategies also see improved **Customer Lifetime Value (CLV)** and **reduced Customer Acquisition Costs (CAC)** by optimizing marketing spend and targeting high-potential customers more effectively.

AI-Powered Predictive Maintenance

AI-powered predictive maintenance utilizes advanced ML algorithms and data analytics to predict equipment failures and maintenance needs before they occur. This proactive approach enhances operational efficiency, reduces downtime, and extends the lifespan of machinery by addressing issues early on. The following is an example of a predictive maintenance workflow:

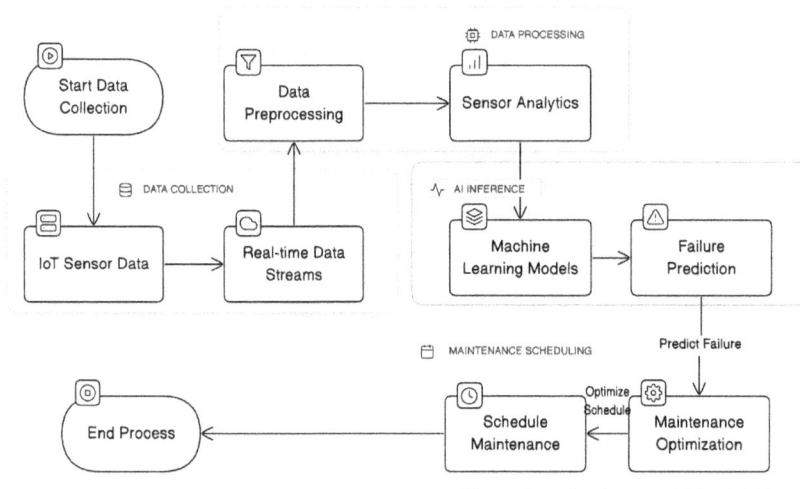

Figure 78: Predictive Maintenance Process.

- **Situation:** Manufacturing and industrial companies experience costly equipment failures and unplanned downtime due to a lack of proactive maintenance strategies. Reactive maintenance often leads to excessive repair costs, production halts, and decreased operational efficiency.

- **Task:** Implement AI-driven predictive maintenance solutions that leverage real-time data streams, sensor analytics, and ML models to anticipate failures before they occur and optimize maintenance schedules.

- **Action:** AI models continuously ingest and analyze IoT sensor data, identifying trends, usage patterns, and potential warning signs of equipment degradation. ML algorithms compare real-time performance metrics against historical data to predict failures. Insights are displayed on real-time dashboards, allowing operators to visualize performance anomalies, receive automated alerts, and schedule maintenance proactively. Additionally, AI-driven maintenance solutions can integrate with enterprise asset management (EAM) systems and industrial IoT (IIoT) platforms, ensuring seamless execution of predictive strategies.

- **Result:** Organizations achieve significant cost savings by reducing emergency repairs, minimizing downtime by performing maintenance only when needed, and extending equipment lifespan through data-driven operational insights. AI-powered predictive maintenance enhances workplace safety, prevents catastrophic failures, and ensures optimal utilization of industrial assets, making operations more resilient and cost-efficient.

AI-Augmented Cybersecurity

- **Situation:** Cyber threats are evolving at an unprecedented pace, with sophisticated attack vectors such as zero-day vulnerabilities, ransomware, insider threats, and Advanced Persistent Threats (APTs). Traditional security measures struggle to keep up with the dynamic nature of cyber risks, making real-time threat detection and response essential for protecting sensitive data and critical infrastructure.

- **Task:** Deploy AI-driven cybersecurity solutions that leverage ML and behavioral analytics to continuously monitor, detect, and respond to cyber threats in real time. The goal is to automate threat identification, enhance response efficiency, and minimize human intervention in detecting security incidents.

- **Action:** AI models analyze network traffic, access logs, endpoint activity, and cloud infrastructure using anomaly detection techniques. AI-powered threat intelligence platforms (TIPs) aggregate global cyber threat data to identify suspicious patterns. Real-time alerts are triggered, and automated responses are initiated through RPA bots or Security Orchestration, Automation, and Response (SOAR) platforms. Additionally, AI enhances behavioral biometrics for unauthorized access detection.

- **Result:** Organizations enhance proactive security, reducing attack dwell time, preventing breaches, and ensuring compliance with GDPR, CCPA, and HIPAA regulations. AI-driven automation enables security teams to focus on complex threat investigations, improving resilience against cyber threats.

By leveraging these interconnected technologies, organizations can ensure AI insights are operationalized effectively, providing decision-makers with timely, relevant, and actionable information to drive business success. A well-integrated AI operationalization framework enhances scalability, maintains data integrity, and delivers consistent, automated, and intelligent decision-making across the enterprise.

Real-Time Data Visualization for AI Model Monitoring

Integrating Business Intelligence (BI) with AI workflows is essential for creating actionable insights through live data visualization. Real-time data visualization tools enable organizations to monitor AI models continuously, providing a dynamic view of model performance and outputs. This integration allows data scientists and business users alike to interact with AI-generated data, uncovering trends, patterns, and anomalies that might otherwise go unnoticed.

Live data feeds are key aspects of real-time data visualization for AI model monitoring. Visualization tools are connected to live data streams, ensuring that the displayed information is always current and relevant. These feeds collect real-time AI outputs, IoT sensor data, log files, application performance metrics, and user-generated content. These tools provide instant visibility into AI model performance and business operations by continuously ingesting and processing data in motion.

Industries like finance, healthcare, cybersecurity, manufacturing, and e-commerce rely heavily on live data feeds for mission-critical operations. In financial trading, for instance, AI-driven trading platforms analyze live market data to execute high-frequency trades in microseconds. In healthcare, real-time AI monitoring of patient vitals enable early warning systems for critical conditions. Similarly, in cybersecurity, AI-powered threat detection systems scan incoming network traffic for anomalies, potential breaches, and insider threats, triggering alerts and automated responses to mitigate risks.

By leveraging event-driven architectures, stream processing frameworks such as Apache Kafka, Apache Flink, and AWS Kinesis, and low-latency data processing models, businesses can ensure that AI-generated insights remain timely, actionable, and responsive to evolving data landscapes. Real-time data feeds enable enterprises to shift from reactive to proactive decision-making, ultimately improving efficiency, scalability, and resilience in dynamic business environments.

- **Customizable Dashboards:** Users can tailor dashboards to display the metrics and visualizations that are most important to their specific needs, enhancing the utility of the tool. These dashboards offer drag-and-drop customization, real-time filtering, and dynamic data visualization that cater to a diverse range of stakeholders, from data scientists, analysts, and IT teams to executives and decision-makers.

Advanced dashboards feature role-based access control, allowing different users to see data relevant to their responsibilities. Additionally, AI-powered recommendation engines embedded within dashboards provide contextual insights, highlight anomalies, and suggest next-best actions.

Modern dashboards support multi-device accessibility, ensuring seamless access from desktops, tablets, and mobile devices. With Natural Language Processing (NLP) integration, users can interact with dashboards using voice commands or plain-text queries, making data retrieval more intuitive and efficient. Modular components, predictive analytics overlays, and real-time alerting systems make customizable dashboards a crucial element in AI-driven business intelligence.

- **Predictive Analytics:** Some visualization tools incorporate predictive analytics, allowing users to accurately forecast future trends based on current data. By leveraging ML algorithms, deep learning models, and statistical forecasting techniques, businesses can anticipate market fluctuations, customer behaviors, and operational challenges before they manifest.

Advanced predictive analytics platforms process historical data, real-time inputs, and external economic indicators to generate precise forecasts. These insights enable organizations to proactively optimize supply chain logistics, financial investments, workforce management, and customer engagement strategies.

For example, predictive maintenance powered by AI helps manufacturers prevent costly downtime by detecting early signs of equipment failure, ensuring that maintenance is performed before breakdowns occur. In financial services, AI-driven risk assessment models analyze transaction history, fraud patterns, and credit scores to make real-time lending and investment decisions.

Additionally, integrating predictive analytics with Natural Language Processing (NLP) enables organizations to analyze social sentiment, news trends, and consumer behavior shifts, helping businesses stay ahead of industry changes. The ability to forecast trends with AI-driven analytics allows enterprises to transition from reactive decision-making to proactive and strategic planning, enhancing resilience, efficiency, and overall performance.

- **Integration with AI Platforms:** Visualization tools are often deeply integrated with AI platforms, enabling real-time data synchronization, enhanced model interpretability, and seamless automation. These integrations ensure that AI-generated insights are instantly reflected in dashboards, reducing latency in decision-making and allowing businesses to adapt proactively to changing data patterns.

By embedding AI visualization tools into enterprise platforms such as AWS SageMaker, Google Vertex AI, Microsoft Azure AI, and IBM Watson, organizations can automate model performance monitoring, improve interpretability through explainable AI (XAI), and create adaptive AI ecosystems. These integrations also facilitate bi-directional data exchange, where visualization tools not only display AI insights, but also feed human-generated inputs back into AI models for continuous learning.

Additionally, AI-powered low-code and no-code integration frameworks allow businesses to rapidly deploy AI-enhanced dashboards without extensive technical expertise. This democratization of AI enables non-technical stakeholders to leverage advanced insights for data-driven decision-making. By leveraging AI APIs, ML pipelines, and intelligent automation workflows, organizations create end-to-end AI operationalization, ensuring that insights remain timely, actionable, and contextually relevant.

- **Drill-Down Capabilities:** Advanced BI tools allow users to drill down into data layers, providing granular insights into AI model behavior and decision-making processes. Users can analyze data at multiple levels, from high-level performance metrics and trends down to individual transaction records and specific algorithmic decision paths. This multi-layered approach enhances the ability to diagnose issues, optimize AI model performance, and improve data-driven strategies. Users can explore historical trends, real-time updates, and predictive insights within the same dashboard by incorporating interactive drill-down features. For example, a financial analyst reviewing a risk model's performance could start with an overview of fraud detection rates, drill down into specific flagged transactions, and finally examine the exact variables and confidence scores contributing to the model's decision. Modern BI tools also support cross-filtering and drill-through functionalities, allowing users to move seamlessly across datasets while maintaining contextual insights. This ensures that organizations can trace AI-driven decisions back to their underlying data sources, improving transparency, accountability, and regulatory compliance. Enhanced drill-down capabilities empower businesses to make faster, more informed decisions while ensuring that AI models remain interpretable, explainable, and continuously optimized.

- **Anomaly Detection and Alerts:** Real-time dashboards incorporate advanced anomaly detection mechanisms that continuously analyze AI model predictions, identifying deviations from expected patterns. These mechanisms leverage ML algorithms, statistical models, and real-time monitoring frameworks to detect anomalies across multiple data streams.

Using unsupervised learning techniques, such as autoencoders, clustering algorithms, and isolation forests, AI-driven anomaly detection can flag subtle shifts in data distributions, uncovering potential risks before they escalate. In highly dynamic environments like finance, cybersecurity, and healthcare, AI-based anomaly detection ensures proactive issue resolution and enhances system reliability.

When deviations occur, automated real-time alerts and notifications are triggered through email, SMS, push notifications, and workflow integrations, ensuring that incident response teams and business stakeholders are promptly informed. These alerts can be prioritized based on severity, enabling organizations to respond efficiently to critical issues while minimizing false positives. Additionally, explainable AI (XAI) techniques enhance transparency in anomaly detection by providing detailed justifications for flagged incidents, allowing decision-makers to understand the root cause and impact of anomalies. By integrating with incident management platforms and automated remediation systems, businesses can reduce downtime, prevent data breaches, and optimize AI model performance in real time.

- **Interactive Data Exploration**: Modern BI tools incorporate advanced interactive visualization elements, such as heat maps, scatter plots, dynamic bar charts, drill-through graphs, time-series plots, and geographic maps, to provide deeper insights into AI-driven data. These elements allow users to explore, manipulate, and customize datasets dynamically, uncovering hidden trends, correlations, and patterns that might not be immediately evident in static reports.

Interactive exploration capabilities include zooming, filtering, slicing, and real-time updates, enabling users to dive deeper into multi-dimensional data and make informed decisions based on dynamic, evolving insights. For instance, in financial analytics, users can adjust variables to visualize market fluctuations, while in supply chain optimization, stakeholders can simulate different scenarios to predict delivery bottlenecks. Additionally, AI-enhanced visual analytics can proactively suggest relevant data points, anomalies, or insights based on user interactions, enabling predictive exploration of datasets. These advanced capabilities make interactive data exploration a powerful tool for data-driven decision-making, storytelling, and scenario analysis, ensuring that businesses leverage AI insights with maximum clarity, usability, and impact.

- Collaboration and Reporting: AI-powered visualization platforms enable teams to collaborate effectively by sharing real-time insights, co-authoring reports, and integrating dashboards into enterprise applications. These tools facilitate seamless data exchange among teams, ensuring that decision-makers across different departments maintain synchronized access to the latest AI-driven insights.

Modern AI-driven reporting platforms support role-based access control, allowing customized data visibility for different stakeholders such as executives, analysts, and operational managers. Additionally, collaborative analytics environments enable multiple users to annotate dashboards, leave contextual comments, and discuss insights directly within visualization platforms, fostering data-driven decision-making.

Automated AI-driven reporting systems generate customized reports with narrative explanations, leveraging Natural Language Generation (NLG) to provide easy-to-understand insights for non-technical users. These reports can be automatically scheduled and distributed through email, Slack, Microsoft Teams, and enterprise portals, ensuring that key insights reach the right audience at the right time. Furthermore, AI-powered platforms integrate with business intelligence workflows, providing real-time alerts and notifications when critical KPIs change or anomalies are detected. These integrations streamline operations, improve cross-functional communication, and enhance organizational efficiency, making AI insights truly actionable across the enterprise.

- **Data Security and Compliance:** As real-time AI monitoring often deals with sensitive and highly regulated information, visualization tools implement multi-layered security protocols to protect data integrity, confidentiality, and accessibility. These measures include role-based access control (RBAC) to restrict data access based on user privileges, end-to-end encryption to secure data in transit and at rest, and real-time compliance tracking to ensure adherence to stringent regulations such as GDPR, HIPAA, CCPA, and SOC 2.

Advanced AI-driven security mechanisms incorporate behavioral anomaly detection, zero-trust architecture, and automated audit logs to identify and mitigate security threats before they escalate. Organizations also leverage federated learning and differential privacy techniques to minimize data exposure while still enabling AI models to learn from distributed data sources. By integrating AI-powered security analytics with SIEM (Security Information and Event Management) platforms, businesses can proactively monitor access logs, detect suspicious activity, and enforce security policies in real time. Additionally, automated policy enforcement ensures that organizations remain compliant with evolving legal and ethical AI governance frameworks, reducing regulatory risk while safeguarding sensitive enterprise and customer data. By leveraging real-time data visualization, organizations can enhance their ability to monitor AI models, ensuring that they remain effective, adaptive, and aligned with business goals. These enhancements lead to more efficient AI governance, improved transparency, and data-driven decision-making across industries.

Case Study: AI in Financial Services

Situation

A multinational bank faced increasing challenges in managing credit risk assessments, ensuring regulatory compliance, and optimizing loan approval processes. Traditional underwriting methods were manual, time-consuming, and prone to inconsistencies, leading to delays in loan approvals and a high risk of fraud. Additionally, the bank struggled to detect fraudulent transactions in real-time, resulting in financial losses and regulatory scrutiny.

Task

The bank sought to implement an AI-powered credit risk model that could analyze historical and real-time financial data to automate risk assessments, reduce fraud, and accelerate loan processing. The objective was to enhance decision-making efficiency, reduce manual intervention, and ensure compliance with financial regulations.

Action

- **AI-Powered Risk Scoring:** The bank integrated ML models into its loan approval workflows, assessing customer creditworthiness using behavioral patterns, spending history, and transaction risk indicators.

- **Fraud Detection Models:** AI-driven anomaly detection systems were deployed to analyze real-time transaction data, identifying suspicious patterns and flagging potentially fraudulent activities.
- **Seamless API Integration:** AI risk assessment models were embedded into the bank's CRM and digital banking platform through APIs, enabling real-time risk analysis and instant decision-making.
- **Regulatory Compliance Automation:** AI models were programmed to continuously monitor transactions for compliance with anti-money laundering (AML) and Know Your Customer (KYC) regulations, generating automated compliance reports for auditors.

Result

- **60% Reduction in Manual Underwriting Efforts:** AI automation streamlined risk assessments, accelerating the loan approval process from days to minutes.
- **Enhanced Fraud Prevention:** AI-powered real-time fraud detection led to a 30% reduction in fraudulent transactions, safeguarding customer assets.
- **Higher Customer Satisfaction:** Instant risk assessments provided faster loan eligibility notifications, improving user experience and customer trust.
- **Improved Regulatory Adherence:** AI-driven compliance monitoring ensured adherence to global banking regulations, reducing the risk of financial penalties and enhancing transparency.
- **Operational Efficiency:** By automating credit scoring and fraud detection, the bank optimized resource allocation, allowing human agents to focus on high-value financial tasks.

Conclusion

By operationalizing AI in financial decision-making, the bank enhanced risk assessment accuracy, accelerated loan approvals, reduced fraud, and ensured regulatory compliance. The integration of AI-driven decision automation transformed the bank's approach to financial risk management, improving efficiency, security, and customer trust.

Summary

Making AI operational involves more than just model deployment—it requires real-time monitoring, visualization, integration, and automation. Businesses can translate AI-driven insights into tangible business outcomes by leveraging dashboards, BI tools, real-time data delivery, and workflow automation. Organizations must focus on seamless AI integration as AI adoption accelerates to maximize efficiency, agility, and competitive advantage. Looking ahead to the final chapter, we will explore **Avoiding Common Pitfalls and The Future of AI**. This will cover key strategies for addressing AI model failures, ensuring ethical AI practices, and exploring the latest advancements in AI data technologies. Additionally, we will examine how AI-generated data shapes the future of data systems and infrastructures. Organizations can build more resilient, responsible, and forward-looking AI ecosystems by understanding these elements. Making AI operational involves more than just model deployment—it requires real-time monitoring, visualization, integration, and automation. Businesses can translate AI-driven insights into tangible business outcomes by leveraging dashboards, BI tools, real-time data delivery, and workflow automation. Organizations must focus on seamless AI integration as AI adoption accelerates to maximize efficiency, agility, and competitive advantage.

References

MLflow, "MLOps Framework and Model Monitoring," 2023. [Online]. Available: https://mlflow.org/.

Microsoft, "Power BI Documentation and Business Intelligence Dashboards," 2023. [Online]. Available: https://powerbi.microsoft.com/.

Amazon Web Services, "AWS SageMaker Model Monitor for AI Observability," 2023. [Online]. Available: https://aws.amazon.com/sagemaker/model-monitor/.

## CHAPTER 12

Avoiding Common Pitfalls and the Future of AI

As AI adoption accelerates across industries, ensuring robust and ethical AI deployment has become more critical than ever. This chapter serves as a guide to identifying and mitigating common pitfalls in AI systems, from model failures to data quality issues and bias detection. Additionally, we explore emerging trends in AI data technologies, the rise of AI-generated synthetic data, and the future of AI infrastructure. By understanding these challenges and advancements, organizations can develop AI-driven strategies that are scalable, transparent, and aligned with ethical best practices. This chapter ties together the key concepts discussed throughout the book and prepares readers for the next frontier in AI innovation.

Technological Solutions for Addressing AI Model Failures

While AI models have revolutionized industries, their deployment is fraught with challenges such as biased outputs, data drift, poor generalization, and adversarial vulnerabilities. These pitfalls often stem from underlying data issues, inadequate monitoring mechanisms, and limited interpretability in decision-making processes.

Ensuring AI models are resilient against security threats is paramount. AI systems face a wide range of adversarial challenges, including malicious attacks designed to manipulate model outputs, unauthorized access attempts, and data breaches. Addressing these concerns requires a multi-layered approach integrating robust security mechanisms throughout the AI development lifecycle.

- **Adversarial Attacks and Defenses**: AI models can be susceptible to adversarial attacks, where subtle perturbations to input data can deceive the system into making incorrect predictions. Defenses against such attacks include:

  o **Adversarial Training** – Enhancing model robustness by incorporating adversarial examples into the training dataset to make AI models resistant to manipulated inputs.

  o **Input Validation and Data Sanitization** – Implementing strict validation techniques to filter out maliciously altered inputs before they reach the model.

  o **Defensive Distillation** – Utilizing knowledge distillation techniques to train AI models in a way that reduces sensitivity to adversarial noise.

  o **Robust Feature Extraction** – Ensuring AI models focus on core, meaningful patterns in the data rather than minor, attackable variations.

Figure 79 displays a flow of adversarial attacks and remediation:

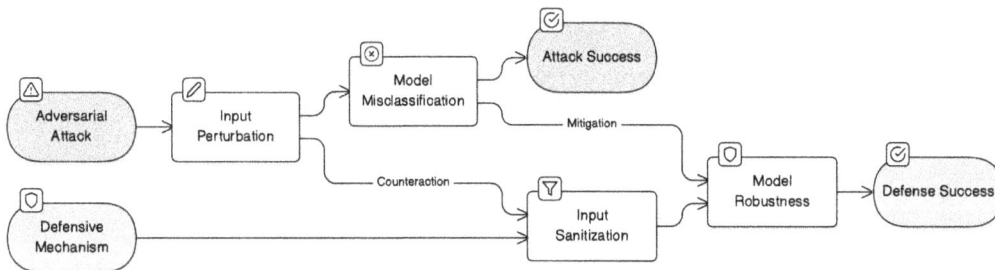

Figure 79: Adversarial Attacks vs Defenses.

Figure 79 demonstrates how adversarial attacks manipulate AI models and what defensive mechanisms counteract these threats. Deployment and AI architectures can also bolster model robustness and security:

- **Secure AI Deployment Strategies**: Ensuring that AI models are securely deployed is critical for maintaining operational integrity. Effective deployment strategies include:

- o **Encryption and Secure Data Transmission** – Encrypting data both in transit and at rest using strong cryptographic techniques to prevent unauthorized access.
- o **Access Control and Role-Based Security** – Implementing multi-level authentication and authorization to restrict access to AI models and training data.
- o **Audit Logs and Continuous Monitoring** – Maintaining detailed logs of model predictions, training processes, and access attempts to detect suspicious activities.
- o **AI Model Versioning and Rollback Mechanisms** – Storing multiple versions of AI models allows for quick rollbacks if a security breach is detected or an update introduces vulnerabilities.

- **Zero Trust AI Architectures**: As AI systems increasingly operate in decentralized and cloud-based environments, implementing a Zero Trust framework becomes essential. This approach assumes that threats exist both inside and outside the network and enforces strict verification measures at all access points:

  - o **Principle of Least Privilege (PoLP)** – Limiting AI model access only to users and applications that explicitly require it.
  - o **Continuous Verification and Dynamic Trust Assessment** – AI systems should constantly authenticate users and devices before granting access.
  - o **Micro-Segmentation** – Dividing AI workflows into isolated segments to prevent lateral movement in case of a security breach.
  - o **Behavioral Anomaly Detection** – Using AI-driven security tools to monitor for deviations in access patterns and trigger real-time alerts if suspicious behavior is detected.

Figure 80 represents a multi-layered security framework with an adversarial defense mechanism, zero-trust security architecture, and role-based access control.

By implementing these strategies, organizations can significantly enhance AI model robustness, ensuring that their AI-driven applications remain secure, trustworthy, and resistant to evolving cybersecurity threats.

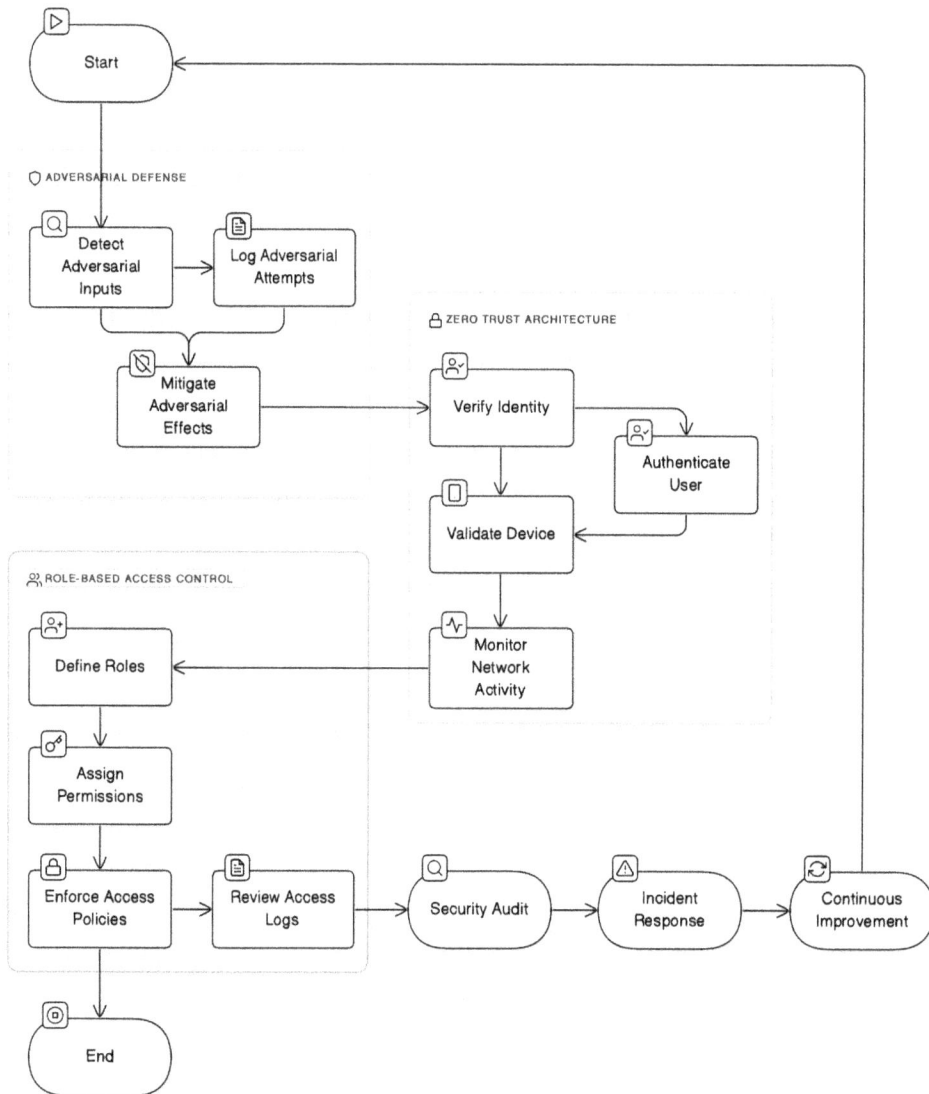

Figure 80: A Layered AI Security Model.

Human-Centered AI and Explainable AI in Practice

Integrating AI into decision-making processes presents tremendous opportunities and significant ethical concerns. AI systems have the potential to drive efficiency, accuracy, and scalability in industries such as healthcare, finance, law enforcement, and autonomous systems. However, without careful oversight, AI can reinforce biases, lead to opaque decision-making, and create unintended consequences that negatively impact individuals and communities. Human-centered AI ensures that technology serves as a tool to enhance human capabilities rather than replace them. This approach prioritizes fairness, transparency, accountability, and human oversight in AI-driven decisions.

AI-Assisted Decision-Making: A Symbiotic Approach

AI-assisted decision-making is the integration of AI-driven insights with human expertise to ensure well-rounded, ethical, and high-quality outcomes. In this model, AI does not replace human judgment but rather supports it by:

- **Providing Data-Driven Insights**: AI algorithms process vast amounts of structured and unstructured data, detecting patterns that would be difficult for humans to identify.

- **Enhancing Efficiency**: AI-driven automation reduces manual workload, allowing humans to focus on higher-order reasoning and decision-making.

- **Reducing Cognitive Load**: AI tools assist in complex decision-making scenarios by presenting summarized, contextual insights, helping humans avoid decision fatigue.

- **Acting as a Safety Net**: AI can flag inconsistencies, errors, or risky behaviors, ensuring that humans remain vigilant in critical decision-making roles.

Key Strategies for Effective AI-Human Collaboration

- **Human-in-the-Loop (HITL) Systems**: These systems ensure that humans actively participate in decision-making by reviewing AI-generated recommendations before finalizing decisions. Examples include AI-assisted medical diagnoses and financial fraud detection.

- **Human-on-the-Loop (HOTL) Systems**: Here, humans monitor AI decision-making and intervene only when anomalies or risks arise, as seen in algorithmic trading and autonomous vehicle systems.

- **Human-out-of-the-Loop (HOOTL) Systems**: In low-risk, automated environments (such as AI-driven chatbots handling routine customer service queries), minimal human intervention is needed. However, transparency remains crucial.

The AI decision-making continuum appears in Figure 81.

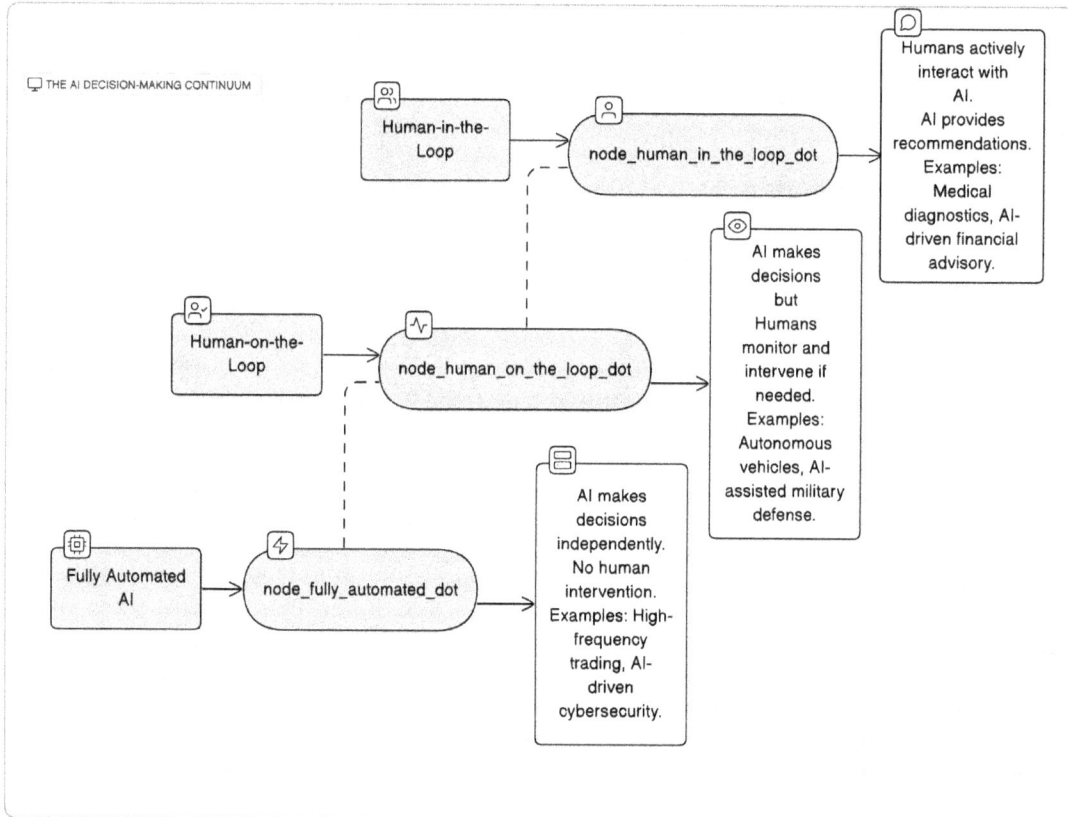

Figure 81: A Layered AI Security Model.

A real-world example of AI-assisted decision-making is in healthcare diagnostics, where AI analyzes medical scans to detect abnormalities, but a physician confirms the final diagnosis. Similarly, AI-driven risk assessment tools in criminal justice assist judges in evaluating parole decisions, but human judges retain the final authority.

Regulatory Compliance for AI Transparency: Governance and Ethical AI Practices

Some AI methods can be non-transparent, meaning it is difficult to understand how the model derives its results from the given data inputs. In certain industries, this is needed and, at times, legally required.

To ensure transparency and interpretability in AI-driven decisions, various explainability techniques provide insights into how models function. The table below compares **SHAP, LIME, Model Cards, and AI Dashboards** across five key evaluation metrics.

Technique	Best For	Strengths	Limitations
SHAP (Shapley Additive Explanations)	Feature importance analysis and global interpretability	✓ Provides both local and global explanations ✓ Based on game theory, ensuring mathematically sound results ✓ High accuracy in ranking feature importance	✗ Computationally expensive, especially for deep learning models ✗ Requires technical expertise for interpretation
LIME (Local Interpretable Model-Agnostic Explanations)	Explaining individual predictions	✓ Highly interpretable and intuitive for non-experts ✓ Works with any ML model (model-agnostic) ✓ Faster and less computationally intensive than SHAP	✗ Inconsistent due to random sampling ✗ Lacks global interpretability – only explains single predictions
Model Cards	AI governance, compliance and ethical documentation	✓ Provides structured documentation for AI models ✓ Helps with regulatory compliance (e.g., GDPR, EU AI Act) ✓ Ensures transparency for audit and risk management	✗ Does not provide real-time explanations ✗ More useful for documentation rather than active model interpretability
AI Dashboards	Monitoring AI decisions in real-time	✓ User-friendly visual interface for tracking AI behavior ✓ Helps identify bias, fairness, and accuracy trends ✓ Ideal for decision-makers and business analysts	✗ Requires significant customization for specific AI models ✗ Interpretability quality depends on dashboard configuration and setup

Table 17: Comparison of SHAP, LIME, Model Cards, and AI Dashboards.

Key takeaways from the table:

- SHAP is the best for detailed feature importance analysis but requires high computational power.
- LIME is great for explaining individual AI predictions but lacks global model insights.
- Model Cards are essential for AI governance and compliance, making them useful in regulated industries.
- AI Dashboards provide real-time interpretability but require customization for advanced analytics.

Figure 82 compares these contrasts to four explanatory techniques.

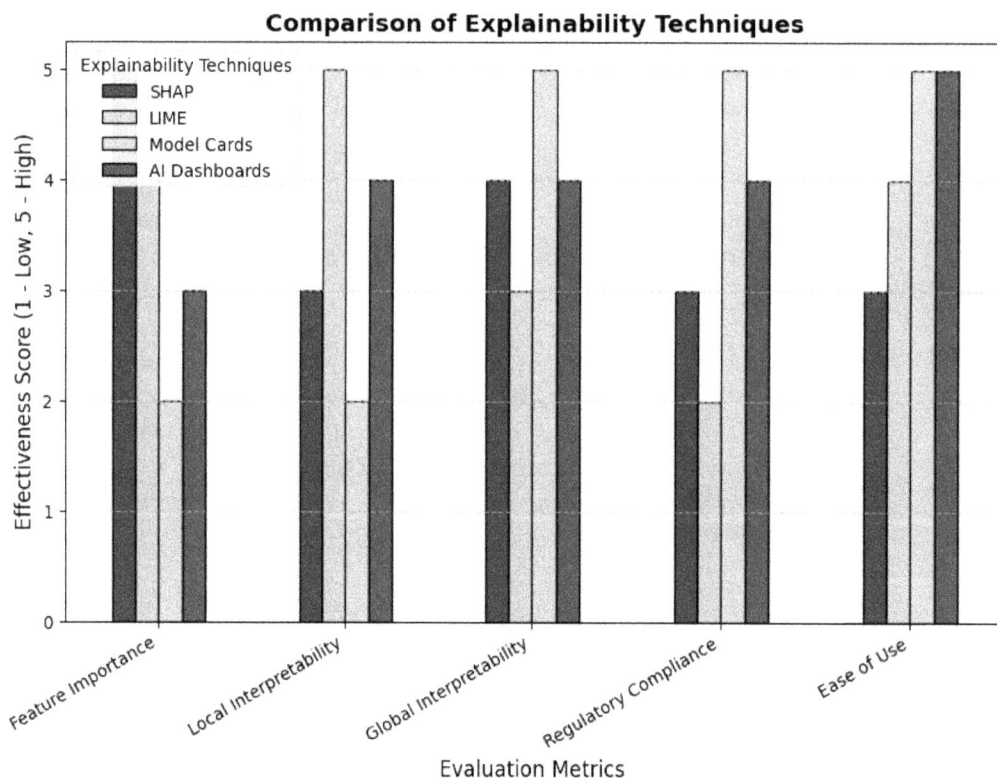

Figure 82: Explainability techniques in AI.[48] [49]

---

[48] https://shap.readthedocs.io/en/latest/.

[49] https://github.com/marcotcr/lime.

Choosing the Right Explainability Technique

Requirement	Recommended Technique
Understand which features influence AI decisions	SHAP
Explain a single prediction in an interpretable way	LIME
Ensure AI governance and regulatory compliance	Model Cards
Track AI performance and fairness dynamically	AI Dashboards

Conclusion: A hybrid approach combining SHAP, LIME, Model Cards, and AI Dashboards is ideal for achieving comprehensive AI transparency and accountability.

As AI adoption grows, regulatory bodies worldwide establish guidelines to ensure transparency, accountability, and fairness in AI systems. Regulatory compliance is essential for building trust, minimizing harm, and preventing discriminatory outcomes. Key global frameworks include:

- **EU AI Act**: One of the most comprehensive AI regulatory frameworks, categorizing AI applications into risk levels and enforcing strict requirements for high-risk AI systems.

- **NIST AI Risk Management Framework**: Developed by the U.S. National Institute of Standards and Technology, this framework provides guidance on managing AI risks and ensuring system resilience.

- **OECD AI Principles**: A set of international guidelines promoting AI innovation while ensuring it aligns with human rights, democracy, and laws.

- **ISO/IEC AI Standards**: Emerging global AI standards designed to establish best practices for AI development, deployment, and governance.

Core Elements of AI Transparency Compliance

- **Explainability and Interpretability**: Organizations must ensure that AI-driven decisions can be understood and explained to users, regulators, and stakeholders.

- **Bias Detection and Mitigation**: AI systems must be rigorously tested to prevent discrimination based on race, gender, socioeconomic status, or other protected attributes.

- **Data Governance and Privacy**: Ensuring AI models comply with data protection laws such as GDPR and CCPA, safeguarding user information from misuse.

- **Impact Assessments and Audits**: Regular external audits and impact assessments help identify risks and ensure AI operates within ethical and regulatory boundaries.
- **Redress Mechanisms**: Organizations must establish procedures for individuals affected by AI decisions to challenge or appeal outcomes.

For example, financial institutions implementing AI-driven loan approvals must ensure their models do not disproportionately deny loans to marginalized communities. By conducting fairness audits, regulators can ensure AI-driven financial services remain ethical and equitable.

Ethical AI Development Frameworks: Principles for Responsible AI

To ensure AI aligns with human values, organizations must adopt structured frameworks that integrate ethical considerations at every stage of AI development. Ethical AI frameworks emphasize:

- **Fairness**: AI must provide equitable outcomes and avoid reinforcing social biases.
- **Transparency**: The decision-making logic behind AI models must be accessible and interpretable.
- **Accountability**: Developers, organizations, and AI system operators must be responsible for AI's impact.
- **Safety and Security**: AI must function reliably in all conditions and remain resistant to adversarial manipulation.
- **Privacy Protection**: AI systems must handle sensitive data with the highest level of security and ethical responsibility.

Key Ethical AI Frameworks

- **Google's AI Principles**: Google emphasizes AI systems that are socially beneficial, unbiased, accountable, and privacy-focused.
- **Microsoft's Responsible AI Guidelines**: Microsoft integrates transparency, inclusivity, and fairness into AI development and deployment.

- **IBM's AI Ethics Framework**: IBM prioritizes trust and transparency, ensuring AI decisions remain explainable and ethical.
- **The Asilomar AI Principles**: A globally recognized set of ethical guidelines promoting safe and beneficial AI development.

Best Practices for Ethical AI Implementation

- **Diverse and Inclusive Development Teams**: Ensuring AI development teams include members from diverse backgrounds to minimize cultural and societal biases.
- **Ethics Review Boards**: Establishing internal or external committees to review AI projects before deployment.
- **Algorithmic Impact Assessments (AIAs)**: Evaluating the societal, ethical, and regulatory impact of AI before and after deployment.
- **Continuous Monitoring and Adaptation**: Ethical AI is not a one-time initiative; organizations must continuously refine models based on real-world outcomes.

Real-World Application of Ethical AI Frameworks

In facial recognition technology, ethical AI frameworks minimize bias against certain demographic groups. Microsoft and IBM have implemented fairness-driven enhancements to their facial recognition algorithms to mitigate racial and gender biases after concerns about disproportionate inaccuracies in certain groups were raised.

Similarly, AI-driven recruitment platforms must ensure their models do not favor candidates based on race, gender, or age. By integrating fairness-aware ML techniques, companies can ensure hiring decisions remain unbiased and inclusive.

By implementing human-centered AI strategies, regulatory compliance measures, and ethical AI frameworks, organizations can build AI systems that are not only innovative and effective but also responsible and fair. This approach ensures AI serves humanity in a way that respects fundamental rights, safeguards against unintended harm, and maintains public trust in technological advancements. To ensure ethical and trustworthy AI, organizations should adopt:

- **AI-Assisted Decision-Making**: Balancing automation with human oversight to prevent AI from making high-risk decisions without review.
- **Regulatory Compliance for AI Transparency**: Compliance with global AI governance frameworks such as the **EU AI Act**, **NIST AI Risk Management Framework**, and **OECD AI Principles** is essential.
- **Ethical AI Development Frameworks**: Adopting AI design principles that incorporate fairness, transparency, and accountability in model development.

AI for Sustainability and Social Good

AI is playing a transformative role in sustainability and societal impact.

- **Green AI and Energy-Efficient Computing**: AI models should be optimized for efficiency, reducing their carbon footprint through techniques like model pruning and quantization. Figure 83 contrasts traditional AI vs Green AI pruning and quantization.

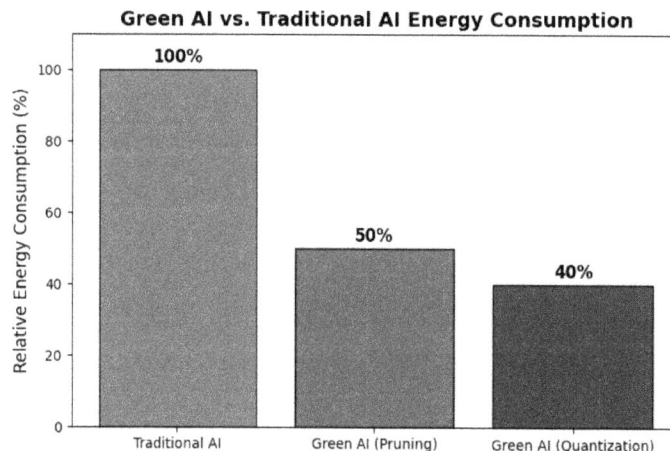

Figure 83: Green AI and Energy-Efficient Computing.[50]

---

[50] Illustration only.

- **AI for Climate Change Mitigation**: AI-driven climate modeling, disaster prediction, and real-time environmental monitoring can aid in mitigating climate risks. The striking thing is that these methods are virtually tied in their contribution.

The Role of AI in Climate Change Mitigation

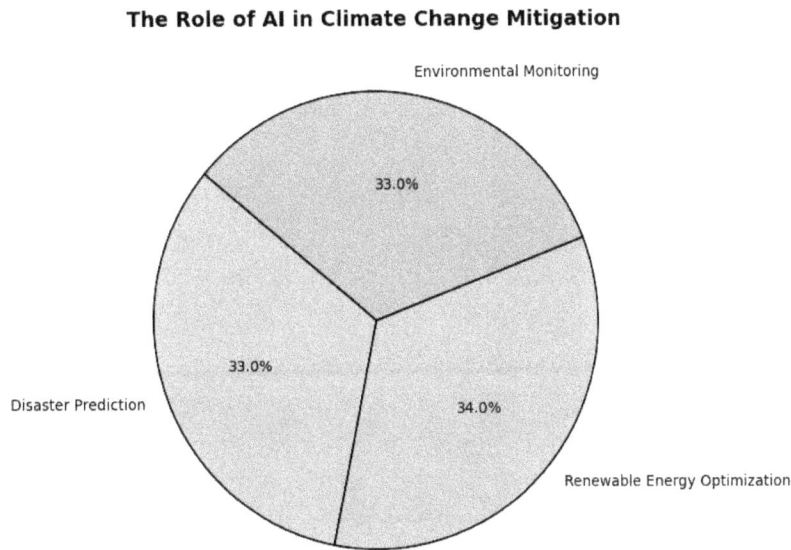

Figure 84: AI for Climate Change Mitigation.

- **AI in Public Policy and Governance**: Governments can leverage AI for urban planning, resource allocation, and improved decision-making in public administration.

Future AI Infrastructures: Towards AGI and Beyond

The next evolution of AI will be shaped by:

- **Quantum Computing in AI**: Quantum AI could revolutionize fields requiring extreme computational power, such as cryptography and materials science.

AI has traditionally relied on classical computing architectures, which process data using binary logic and deterministic computations. However, with the rise of Quantum AI, a paradigm shift is occurring where AI leverages quantum computing principles to solve problems that classical systems struggle with. The visualization above provides a workflow comparison between Quantum AI and Classical AI, detailing their respective data processing, computation, and model optimization approaches.

Key Characteristics of Classical AI

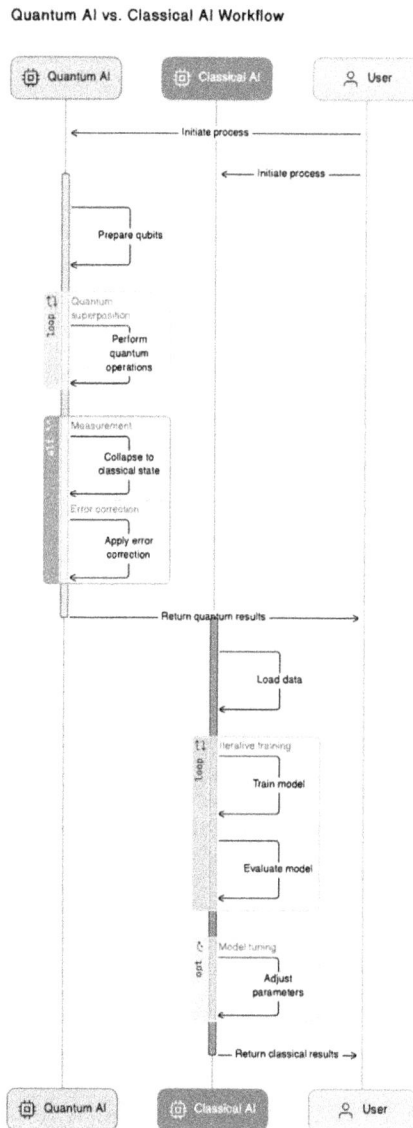

Figure 85: Quantum AI vs Classical AI.

- **Deterministic Processing**: Follows predefined rules and sequential computations.
- **Scalability Limitations**: Requires extensive computing resources for complex AI models.
- **Time-Consuming Optimization**: Hyperparameter tuning and retraining loops can be computationally expensive.

Key Characteristics of Quantum AI

- **Parallel Computation**: Performs multiple calculations simultaneously, making it superior for optimization problems.
- **Error-Prone States**: Quantum coherence is fragile; error correction is critical.
- **Exponential Speed-up**: Certain AI models (e.g., optimization, quantum neural networks) are significantly faster than classical approaches.

While **Quantum AI** presents groundbreaking potential, its current development is still in its early stages. The future of AI may combine classical and quantum architectures, where quantum computing handles complex, high-dimensional problems, while classical AI executes deterministic decision-making.

- **Self-Learning AI Systems**: AI models capable of continuous learning and adaptation without human intervention will redefine automation.
- **Neurosymbolic AI**: Hybrid approaches combining deep learning with symbolic reasoning to enhance AI's logical and inference capabilities (see OpenAI 2023).

Neurosymbolic AI combines the strengths of deep learning, which excels at processing unstructured data like images and text, with symbolic reasoning, which is great at handling structured logic and knowledge representation, as illustrated in Figure 86.

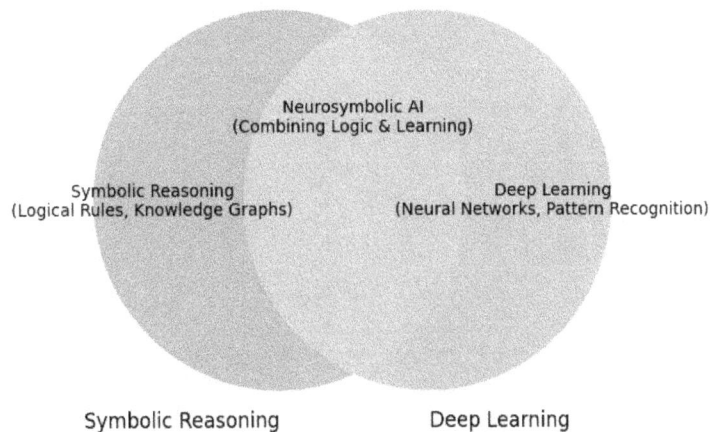

Neurosymbolic AI
(Combining Logic & Learning)

Symbolic Reasoning
(Logical Rules, Knowledge Graphs)

Deep Learning
(Neural Networks, Pattern Recognition)

Symbolic Reasoning   Deep Learning

Figure 86: Neurosymbolic AI: Integrating Symbolic Reasoning and Deep Learning.[51]

---

[51] Illustration Only.

AI-Augmented Workforce and The Future of Work

AI is transforming the way we work, necessitating:

- **AI in Workplace Automation and Augmentation**: AI will assist, rather than replace, human workers by automating repetitive tasks and enhancing decision-making.
- **Upskilling and AI Education**: Organizations must invest in AI literacy programs to prepare the workforce for AI-driven transformations.
- **AI and The Gig Economy**: AI-driven marketplaces and job platforms will redefine freelancing and remote work.

Figure 87 illustrates a roadmap for AI literacy.

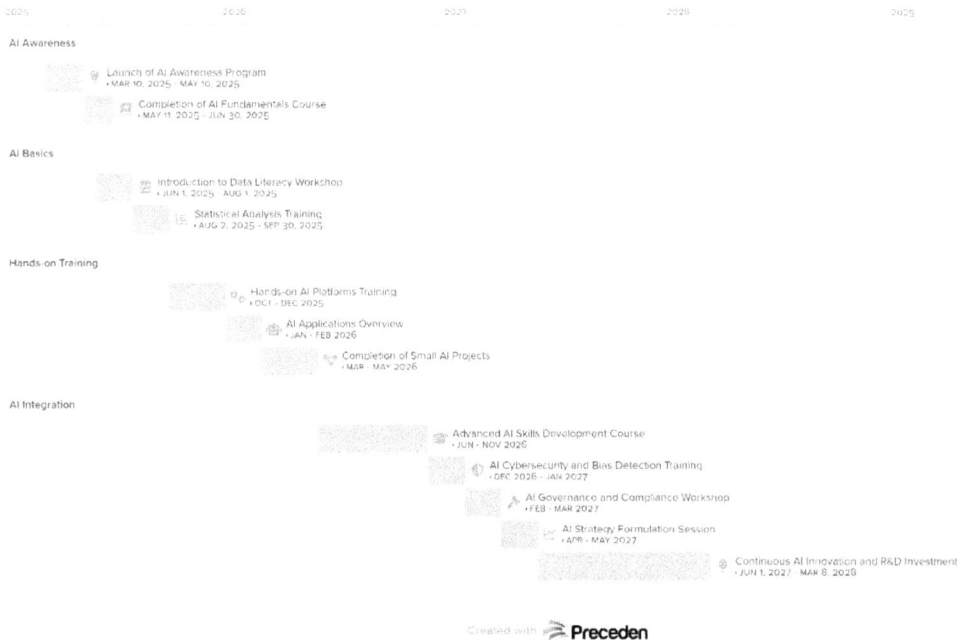

Figure 87: AI Literacy Roadmap.

There are six critical practice and knowledge areas for AI literacy in Figure 87. These are AI awareness, data and AI basics, hands-on AI practice, advanced AI skills, AI integration, and AI innovation. Simply stated:

- AI Awareness is educating employees about AI and its impact

- Data and AI Basics is developing data fluency and foundational AI skills.
- Hands-on AI is practical AI training with real-world applications.
- Advanced AI Skills is upskilling in ML, NLP, and automation.
- AI Integration is integrating AI into business processes.
- AI Innovation is driving AI-powered innovation and leadership.

Figure 88 illustrates that AI-driven marketplaces and job platforms will redefine freelancing and remote work.

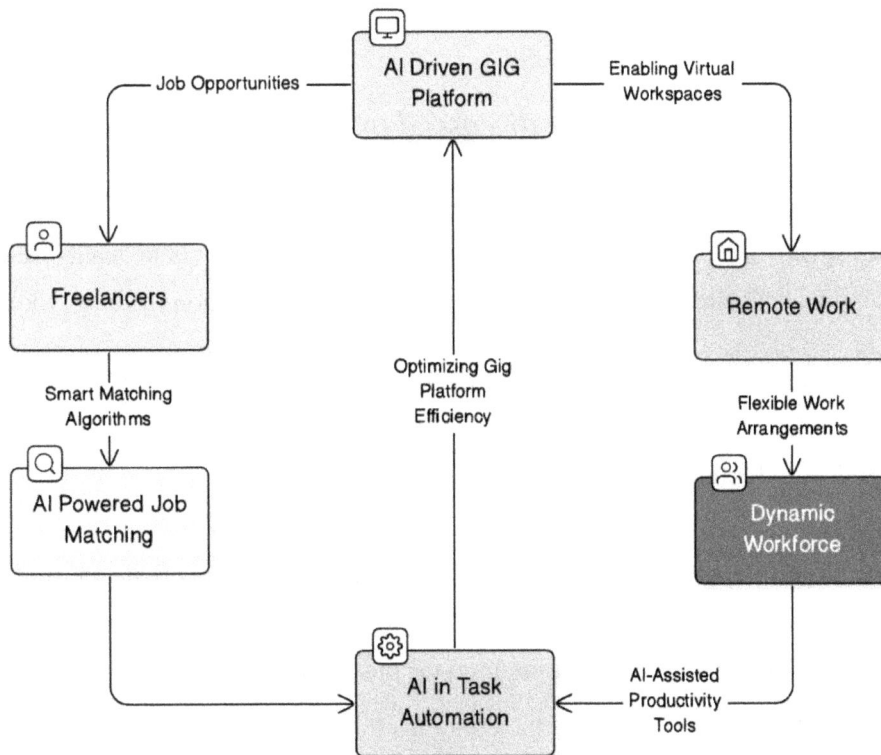

Figure 88: AI and the Gig Economy.

The Ethics of AI Self-Improvement and Decision Autonomy

As AI systems gain more autonomy, ethical considerations become critical:

- **AI and Moral Decision-Making**: AI must be programmed to align with human ethical standards in applications such as healthcare, justice, and governance.

- **Autonomous AI Systems in Warfare and Defense**: International regulations are needed to prevent the misuse of autonomous AI in military applications.
- **AI Alignment Problem**: Ensuring AI remains aligned with human values and does not develop unintended objectives.

Ensuring Data Integrity and Ethical Use of AI

Data Quality Tools (Previously discussed in Chapter 8: MDM and Data Quality for AI)

Ensuring high-quality data is the first step in addressing AI failures. Poor data quality leads to biased predictions, model hallucinations, and unreliable outcomes. Organizations leverage tools such as:

- **Informatica Data Quality**: Automates data validation, cleansing, and enrichment to reduce inconsistencies.
- **Talend Data Preparation**: Enhances dataset standardization and integrity before AI training.
- **Great Expectations**: Facilitates proactive data quality monitoring through validation rules and expectations.
- **Apache Griffin**: An open-source solution for measuring and maintaining data quality metrics across AI pipelines.

These tools improve AI performance by eliminating redundancies, ensuring data completeness, and preventing biases in model outputs.

Monitoring and Observability Technologies

AI observability is essential to maintaining optimal performance, ensuring transparency, and preventing unexpected model failures. As AI systems evolve and interact with dynamic data environments, tracking decision-making processes, detecting shifts in data distribution, and maintaining reliability at scale becomes critical.

Comprehensive AI observability solutions integrate real-time monitoring, explainability frameworks, and automated anomaly detection to address the following key concerns:

- **Model Drift Detection**: AI models degrade in performance when real-world data distributions evolve. Continuous input-output monitoring is necessary to recalibrate models and establish automated retraining mechanisms.
- **Concept Drift Analysis**: Identifying shifts in the relationships between input features and model outputs can be influenced by external factors, such as market fluctuations, consumer behavior changes, or environmental conditions.
- **Data Drift Monitoring**: Detecting variations in the statistical properties of input features that could impact model predictions. Unusual spikes or gradual shifts in data distribution indicate the need for adjustments.
- **Performance Benchmarking and Trigger-Based Retraining**: Establish baseline performance thresholds and set automated triggers for model retraining when significant deviations are detected.
- **Active Learning and Human-in-the-Loop Mechanisms**: Integrating human oversight into AI workflows, where flagged instances of drift trigger expert review before updates are deployed to production systems.

Leading organizations rely on sophisticated tools such as Evidently AI, DataRobot MLOps, and AWS SageMaker Model Monitor to automate drift detection and corrective actions. These systems continuously assess data integrity, alert teams to anomalies, and facilitate a seamless process for adapting models to evolving datasets, ensuring sustained AI performance and reliability in dynamic operational environments.

Addressing AI Bias and Overfitting

Bias Detection Platforms (*Previously discussed in Chapter 9: Ethical Data Management and Governance for AI*)

AI models often reflect biases embedded in training data, leading to unfair or skewed decisions. Bias detection and mitigation tools help ensure fairness and transparency in AI-driven decisions. Organizations implement:

- **Fairlearn**: A powerful fairness assessment toolkit that provides disparity metrics and bias mitigation techniques tailored to various AI applications (see Fairlearn 2023).
- **Aequitas**: A bias evaluation framework that offers comprehensive equity analysis, highlighting systemic imbalances in ML predictions.
- **IBM AI Fairness 360**: A leading suite of tools designed to identify and rectify AI biases, offering explainability features and fairness-enhancing model adjustments.

To establish fairness, organizations must adopt:

- **Preemptive Bias Detection**: Utilizing statistical methods, disparity analysis, and fairness-aware ML techniques to assess whether AI models disproportionately favor or disadvantage specific demographic groups.
- **Ethical Benchmarking and Compliance Standards**: Aligning AI development with frameworks such as the EU AI Act, IEEE Ethically Aligned Design, and sector-specific regulations like the Fair Credit Reporting Act (FCRA) to promote responsible AI governance.
- **Adversarial Testing and Sensitivity Analysis**: Deploying simulated edge cases to stress-test AI models under diverse real-world conditions, revealing vulnerabilities that may contribute to biased outputs.
- **Diversity in Training Data**: Ensuring representation across gender, ethnicity, socio-economic status, and geographic location to mitigate biased data distribution, thereby fostering inclusive AI development.
- **Continuous Feedback and Human-in-the-Loop Mechanisms**: Establishing mechanisms for human oversight in AI workflows where flagged instances of bias trigger expert review before deployment.

By integrating bias detection platforms within AI lifecycle management, organizations can proactively address ethical challenges, foster trust with stakeholders, and demonstrate accountability in AI-powered decision-making frameworks.

Overfitting occurs when AI models become excessively specialized in their training data, leading to a significant decline in their ability to generalize to unseen examples. This phenomenon results in models that excel in training data but fail to provide accurate predictions in real-world scenarios. Overfitting is particularly problematic in applications where AI models must make decisions in dynamic environments, such as healthcare diagnostics, financial forecasting, and autonomous systems.

To counteract overfitting and maintain AI performance, organizations employ several advanced techniques:

- **Cross-Validation and Regularization**: Techniques like k-fold cross-validation, L1/L2 regularization, dropout for neural networks, and early stopping help prevent overfitting.
- **Synthetic Data Augmentation**: Expanding training datasets using generative adversarial networks (GANs), variational autoencoders (VAEs), and traditional augmentation techniques to enhance model generalization.
- **Federated Learning**: Decentralizing AI training to preserve data privacy while allowing continuous learning across distributed environments.

Privacy-Preserving AI

AI systems processing sensitive data must integrate robust privacy measures:

- **Differential Privacy**: Injecting statistical noise into datasets to prevent user identification.
- **Homomorphic Encryption**: Enabling AI computations on encrypted data without exposing sensitive information.
- **Federated Learning with Secure Aggregation**: Ensuring models train on decentralized data while preserving confidentiality.

Transparency and Explainability

To enhance interpretability and trust, organizations leverage:

- **SHAP (Shapley Additive Explanations) and LIME (Local Interpretable Model-Agnostic Explanations)**: Techniques that provide insights into model decision-making processes.

- **Model Cards and Explainable AI Dashboards**: Documenting model capabilities, limitations, and decision rationales to ensure transparency.

Emerging Trends in AI Data Technologies

Real-Time Data Processing and Edge AI

As organizations strive for faster insights and decision-making, real-time AI data processing and edge computing have become essential components of modern AI ecosystems. The ability to process data instantly, closer to its source, transforms industries by reducing latency, increasing efficiency, and enabling seamless automation.

- **Apache Flink and Apache Kafka**: These powerful data streaming technologies enable real-time ingestion and processing of data. They support AI applications that require instantaneous decision-making, such as fraud detection, recommendation engines, and real-time monitoring of industrial systems.

- **Edge AI Platforms (NVIDIA Jetson, AWS Greengrass, Google Coral)**: Traditional cloud-based AI models often suffer from high latency due to reliance on centralized computing. Edge AI moves computation closer to the data source, enabling real-time analytics without the need for continuous cloud connectivity. This is particularly useful in applications like autonomous vehicles, IoT devices, smart surveillance, and industrial automation.

- **Federated Learning and Decentralized AI Processing**: Edge AI leverages federated learning techniques to train models across multiple decentralized devices while preserving data privacy. This allows industries such as healthcare, finance, and telecommunications to build more accurate AI models without transferring sensitive data to a centralized location.

- **5G and AI Integration**: The combination of AI with 5G technology enhances the ability to process and transmit large volumes of real-time data with minimal latency, facilitating breakthroughs in autonomous transportation, smart cities, and augmented reality.

These concepts are illustrated in Figure 89.

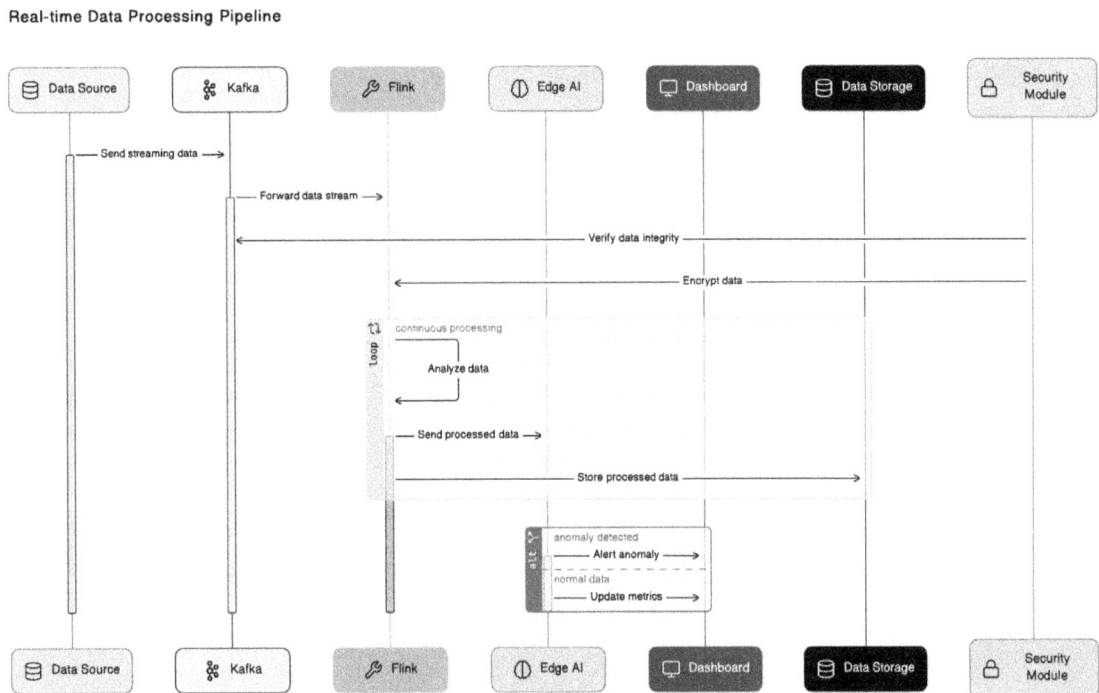

Figure 89: Real-Time Data Processing and Edge AI Pipeline.

Self-Healing AI Pipelines

As AI models become more integral to enterprise workflows, the need for robust, automated maintenance mechanisms has given rise to self-healing AI pipelines. These pipelines proactively detect anomalies, optimize performance, and autonomously correct errors without human intervention:

- **AI-Driven Root Cause Analysis**: Traditional troubleshooting of AI systems is labor-intensive and time-consuming. Self-healing pipelines use ML techniques to analyze failures, trace their origins, and suggest optimal corrective actions, significantly reducing downtime and operational risks.

- **Automated Model Retraining**: One of the most critical challenges in AI deployment is model drift, where changing data patterns degrade performance over time. Self-healing AI pipelines monitor these shifts in real time and initiate automated retraining to ensure models remain accurate and relevant.

- **Anomaly Detection with Reinforcement Learning**: Self-healing AI employs reinforcement learning techniques to dynamically adjust monitoring parameters and improve anomaly detection systems. This ensures that AI models are continuously optimized to detect fraud, cybersecurity threats, and operational inefficiencies.

- **Predictive Maintenance with AI**: In industrial settings, self-healing AI pipelines can predict failures in manufacturing equipment, supply chain logistics, and IT systems. By leveraging historical data and real-time sensor readings, AI models can proactively address issues before they impact business operations.

- **AutoML and Hyperparameter Tuning**: Self-healing AI systems integrate AutoML (Automated Machine Learning) capabilities to optimize hyperparameters and fine-tune models dynamically, reducing reliance on data scientists for continuous model improvement.

A Self-Healing AI Pipeline is illustrated in the following figure:

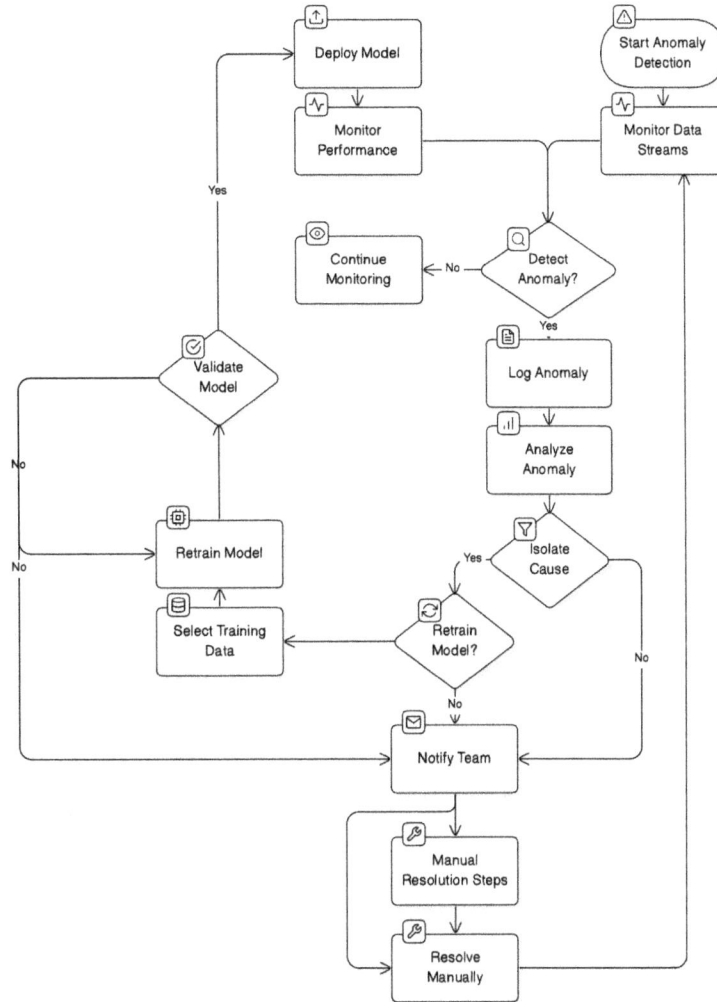

Figure 90: AI System Anomaly Detection and Resolution.

AI-Generated Synthetic Data for Model Training

As organizations face growing concerns around data privacy, bias, and limited training data, synthetic data generation has emerged as a powerful tool for AI development. Synthetic data, generated by AI itself, enables organizations to build more diverse, unbiased, and privacy-preserving datasets.

- **GANs (Generative Adversarial Networks) and VAEs (Variational Autoencoders):** These advanced deep learning techniques generate high-quality synthetic data that closely mimics real-world distributions, making them invaluable for AI model training.[52]

Feature	Generative Adversarial Networks (GANs)	Variational Autoencoders (VAEs)
Core Mechanism	Uses a generator and a discriminator in a competitive framework (adversarial training).	Uses probabilistic encoding to learn data distributions and generate synthetic outputs.
How It Works	The generator tries to create realistic data, while the discriminator distinguishes real versus fake samples.	The encoder compresses data into a latent space, and the decoder reconstructs it by sampling from a probability distribution.
Training Process	Trained through a min-max optimization problem, improving both generator and discriminator iteratively.	Optimized using variational inference by minimizing reconstruction loss and KL divergence.
Output Quality	Produces high-quality, realistic synthetic images and text but can suffer from mode collapse.	Generates smooth, diverse outputs, but results are often less sharp than GANs.
Use Cases	Image generation (DeepFake, StyleGAN), text-to-image synthesis, artistic content creation.	Data augmentation, anomaly detection, denoising images, generating interpolated data samples.
Pros	- Produces high-resolution, sharp, and realistic data. - Effective for image synthesis and creativity-based tasks.	- Provides structured latent space representation, useful for controlled sampling. - Ensures smooth transitions between generated data points.
Cons	- Difficult to train due to adversarial instability. - Susceptible to mode collapse, where the model generates repetitive outputs.	- Generates blurrier images compared to GANs. - Requires assumptions on data distributions, which may limit realism.
Best For	Creative AI applications, ultra-realistic synthetic data, deepfake creation, and generative art.	Data augmentation, unsupervised learning, anomaly detection, and structured feature extraction.

- **Bias Reduction in AI Training:** AI-generated synthetic data helps mitigate bias by ensuring diverse representation across various demographic groups, reducing the risk of discriminatory model outputs as presented in Figure 91.

---

[52] The table comparing GANs and VAEs is based on established concepts in synthetic data generation and is used in applications like DeepFake and anomaly detection.

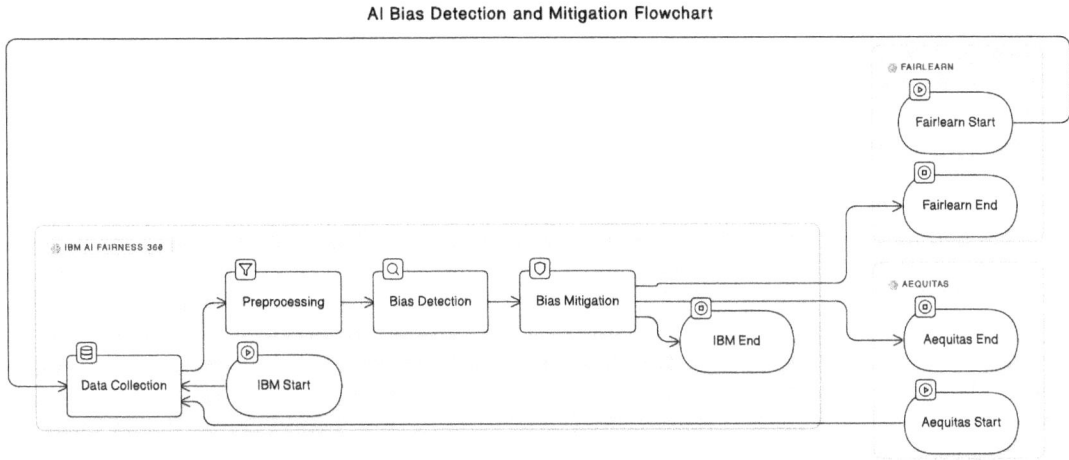

Figure 91: Real-Time Data Processing and Edge AI Pipeline.

- **Privacy-Preserving AI with Synthetic Data**: Industries handling sensitive information, such as finance and healthcare, use synthetic data to train AI models without exposing real user data, ensuring compliance with regulations like GDPR and HIPAA.

- **Scalability and Cost Efficiency**: Collecting and annotating real-world training data is expensive and time-consuming. Synthetic data generation significantly lowers these costs by providing AI models with scalable, high-quality training datasets.

Automated AI Governance and Compliance

With increasing regulatory scrutiny over AI systems, organizations must implement automated governance frameworks to ensure compliance with ethical guidelines, industry regulations, and data protection laws:

- **AI Ethics and Compliance Monitoring**: AI-powered governance tools continuously audit models for fairness, accountability, and transparency. These tools help organizations comply with frameworks such as the EU AI Act, NIST AI Risk Management Framework, and IEEE AI Ethics Standards.

- **Data Lineage and Provenance Tracking**: Understanding where and how AI models acquire their data is essential for maintaining transparency. Automated governance platforms track data lineage, ensuring that datasets used in AI models meet compliance and security requirements.

- **Explainability and Auditable AI Models**: As AI-driven decisions impact critical areas such as finance, healthcare, and legal systems, automated governance tools ensure model explainability through feature importance analysis, algorithmic audits, and compliance checks.

- **Policy-Based AI Access Controls**: To prevent unauthorized manipulation of AI models, organizations are implementing granular access control policies that dictate who can modify, deploy, or interact with AI models.

- **Responsible AI Development Pipelines**: Automated AI governance frameworks integrate responsible AI practices into every stage of development, from data collection to deployment, ensuring models align with ethical AI principles.

The Future of AI Infrastructure: Quantum AI and Beyond

As AI continues to evolve, emerging computing paradigms are set to redefine its capabilities. Quantum computing, in particular, holds the potential to revolutionize AI model training and problem-solving abilities beyond classical computing constraints.

Quantum Machine Learning (QML)

Quantum Machine Learning represents the cutting edge of computational advancement, merging the principles of quantum computing with AI to push the boundaries of problem-solving beyond what classical computers can achieve. Unlike traditional binary computing, which operates on bits represented as 0 or 1, quantum computing utilizes qubits, which can exist simultaneously in multiple states due to superposition. This allows quantum systems to process vast amounts of data in parallel, dramatically increasing computational power and efficiency (see IBM Research 2023).

Quantum computers excel in handling complex probability distributions, making them ideal for high-dimensional ML tasks such as molecular simulations, financial modeling, and climate forecasting. Key advancements in QML include:

- **Quantum Speedup in AI Training**: Quantum-enhanced optimization algorithms, such as quantum gradient descent, accelerate the training of deep learning models by minimizing computational overhead and enabling faster convergence of large datasets.

- **Quantum Neural Networks (QNNs)**: Unlike traditional neural networks, QNNs leverage quantum entanglement and parallelism to model highly intricate relationships between data points, allowing for more accurate AI predictions in fields like personalized medicine and quantum chemistry.

- **Quantum Support Vector Machines (QSVMs)**: QSVMs significantly enhance classification problems by utilizing quantum feature mapping, enabling AI to distinguish complex patterns in datasets that classical models struggle to separate.

- **Variational Quantum Algorithms**: These hybrid quantum-classical methods improve AI's ability to solve optimization problems, making them particularly useful in logistics, cybersecurity, and AI ethics.

The impact of QML is expected to revolutionize various industries. In drug discovery, for instance, quantum-powered AI can simulate molecular interactions at an unprecedented level of accuracy, significantly reducing the time required to develop new medications. In financial modeling, QML can rapidly analyze market volatility and optimize portfolios with quantum-inspired reinforcement learning techniques. In cryptography, quantum computing is both a challenge and a solution, as it has the potential to break classical encryption methods while also enabling the development of quantum-resistant cryptographic protocols.

Despite its promise, QML faces challenges, such as the need for fault-tolerant quantum processors, quantum error correction mechanisms, and scalable quantum hardware. Researchers are actively working on mitigating these limitations, ensuring that quantum computing will fully integrate into real-world AI applications as it matures, unlocking possibilities beyond human imagination. By embracing QML, organizations will gain access to an entirely new frontier of AI capabilities, transforming industries and redefining the limits of computational problem-solving.

Neuromorphic Computing and Brain-Inspired AI

Neuromorphic computing represents a paradigm shift in AI, seeking to replicate the complex structure and function of the human brain to create more efficient, intelligent, and adaptive AI systems. Unlike conventional computing architectures, which rely on von Neumann principles that separate memory and processing, neuromorphic computing integrates both artificial neurons and synapses, mimicking the parallel and highly interconnected nature of biological brains.

These AI systems utilize specialized neuromorphic hardware such as IBM's TrueNorth, Intel's Loihi, and SpiNNaker to enable faster computation, lower power consumption, and more dynamic learning capabilities. By drawing inspiration from neuroscience, these architectures foster self-learning AI that continuously adapts based on experience, reducing dependency on extensive pre-training and retraining phases.

Key Advancements in Neuromorphic Computing:

- **Spiking Neural Networks (SNNs)**: Unlike traditional artificial neural networks that process information in fixed time steps, SNNs use event-driven processing, where neurons fire spikes only when a threshold is met. This biologically inspired mechanism enhances efficiency and reduces power consumption.

- **Adaptive Learning Models**: Neuromorphic AI systems continuously learn from their environments, enabling them to process new information dynamically without requiring complete retraining. This ability mirrors how human cognition improves with experience.

- **Ultra-Low Power AI**: Conventional AI models require massive computational resources, but neuromorphic chips consume orders of magnitude less power, making them ideal for edge AI applications in IoT devices, robotics, and mobile systems.

- **Massive Parallelism**: Neuromorphic chips process information in a massively parallel manner, similar to the human brain, allowing for highly efficient computation of complex tasks such as sensory processing, pattern recognition, and autonomous decision-making.

Applications of Neuromorphic AI:

- **Autonomous Robotics**: Neuromorphic AI enables robots to perceive, reason, and act with human-like adaptability. These systems facilitate the real-time processing of sensory data, enabling more efficient and naturalistic human-robot interactions.

- **Real-Time Edge AI**: Neuromorphic chips are ideally suited for real-time AI applications on edge devices, including smart sensors, security systems, and medical implants, where ultra-low latency and power efficiency are critical.

- **Next-Generation AI Assistants**: Future AI personal assistants will leverage neuromorphic computing to anticipate user needs, adapt to evolving contexts, and communicate more naturally with humans.

- **Brain-Machine Interfaces (BMIs)**: Neuromorphic AI plays a crucial role in developing BMIs that facilitate direct communication between the brain and external devices, revolutionizing treatments for neurological disorders such as paralysis and epilepsy.

- **Cognitive Computing and Lifelong Learning AI**: By enabling AI models to learn and adapt continuously without catastrophic forgetting, neuromorphic computing paves the way for truly intelligent systems that evolve alongside human users.

While neuromorphic computing remains in its early stages, rapid advancements in neuroscience, material science, and AI are bringing this vision closer to reality. The future of AI will likely be driven by biologically inspired systems capable of reasoning, learning, and interacting in ways that closely resemble human intelligence. As research progresses, neuromorphic computing will not only enhance AI's efficiency, but also bridge the gap between artificial and biological intelligence, revolutionizing fields ranging from healthcare to space exploration.

Decentralized AI and Blockchain Integration

As AI continues to evolve and integrate into various industries, the need for trust, security, and transparency in AI-driven decision-making has become paramount. Fusing AI with blockchain technology offers a revolutionary approach to decentralized AI, ensuring that models operate in a tamper-proof, auditable, and distributed manner, reducing the risks associated with centralization. An example flowchart using blockchain is illustrated in Figure 92.

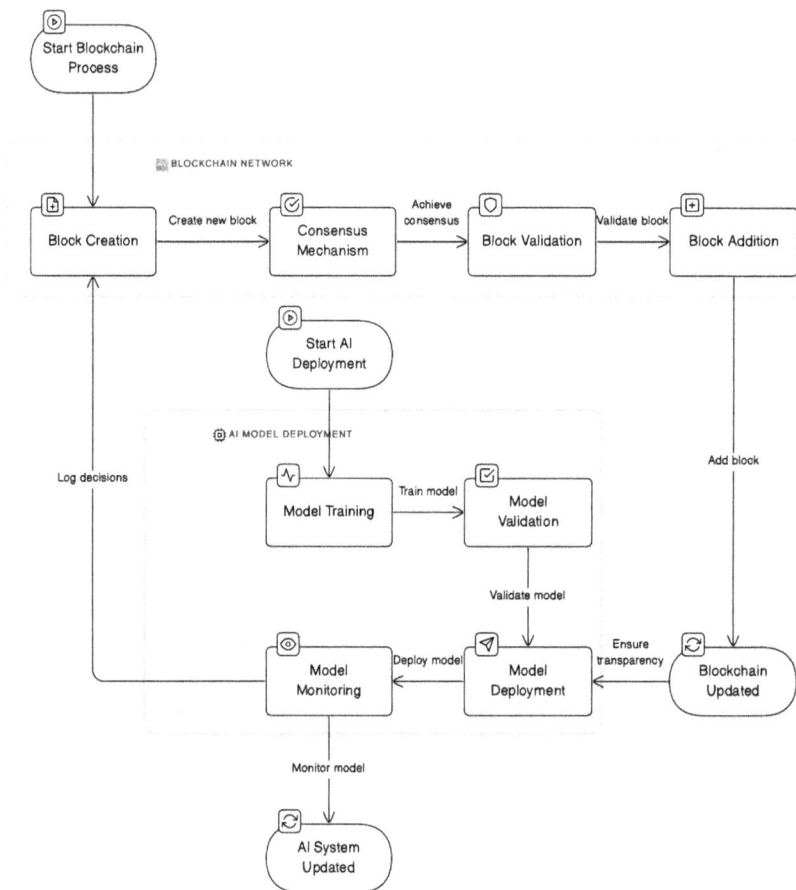

Figure 92: Blockchain for Transparent AI Decision Making and Secure Model Deployment.

Blockchain technology, best known for its application in cryptocurrencies, provides decentralized, immutable, and transparent record-keeping. When applied to AI, blockchain ensures that AI models, training data, and decision-making processes are resistant to tampering, unauthorized modifications, and biased alterations.

Key attributes of blockchain that enhance AI security include:

- Immutability: AI model versions, decisions, and data transactions recorded on a blockchain cannot be altered retrospectively, ensuring auditability and traceability.

- Decentralization: Unlike traditional AI models stored and controlled by centralized entities, decentralized AI allows multiple stakeholders to share governance, reducing the risk of monopolistic control over AI algorithms.

- Smart Contracts for AI Execution: AI models can be embedded into smart contracts on blockchain networks, enabling automated, self-executing AI decision-making that is both transparent and resistant to external manipulation.

- Data Provenance and Integrity: By recording all AI model inputs and outputs on an immutable ledger, blockchain ensures that AI systems remain accountable and explainable, mitigating concerns over biased or unethical AI decisions.

Integrating AI with blockchain technology leads to several groundbreaking advancements, revolutionizing how AI models are deployed, validated, and governed.

- **Federated Learning on Blockchain**: Traditionally, AI training requires aggregating large datasets into centralized storage, leading to security and privacy risks. **Federated learning** combined with blockchain allows multiple parties to collaboratively train AI models **without sharing raw data**, ensuring privacy compliance (GDPR, HIPAA) and maintaining **data ownership.**

- **AI Marketplaces on Blockchain**: Decentralized AI marketplaces, such as **SingularityNET**, allow AI developers and businesses to **monetize AI models** by offering them as **secure, on-chain services**. Users can access and interact with AI models in a **trustless environment**, paying for services using blockchain-based tokens.

- **Decentralized Identity Verification for AI Models**: By leveraging blockchain-based identity verification, AI models can have a **unique cryptographic signature**, ensuring that only authenticated, verified AI models can be used in real-world applications. This prevents **model spoofing, adversarial attacks, and deepfake misuse.**

- **Autonomous AI Agents and DAOs (Decentralized Autonomous Organizations)**: AI-driven **autonomous agents** can operate on **blockchain-powered DAOs**, executing complex tasks **without centralized oversight**. These AI-driven DAOs enable **self-governing, community-driven AI decision-making**, reducing bias and ensuring democratic governance of AI models.

- **AI-Enhanced Smart Contracts**: Traditional smart contracts operate on predefined rules, but integrating **AI-powered decision-making** into smart contracts allows for **dynamic, adaptive smart contracts** that can react intelligently to external data inputs, making blockchain **more versatile and powerful.** An example of AI models and blockchain smarts contracts interaction is illustrated in Figure 93.

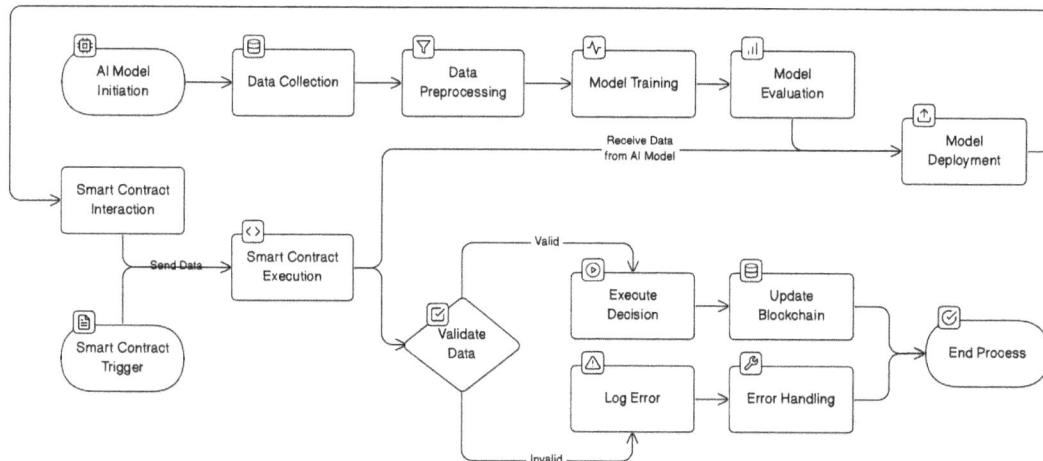

Figure 93: AI Models and Blockchain Smart Contracts Interaction.

The applications of decentralized AI and blockchain integration include:

- **Healthcare and Medical AI**: Securely sharing anonymized patient data across decentralized networks to train AI-driven predictive diagnostics and personalized **medicine models** while preserving patient confidentiality.

- **AI-Powered Fraud Detection**: Financial institutions leverage AI-blockchain integration to detect fraud in real-time transaction monitoring, ensuring audit trails for compliance and anti-money laundering (AML) regulations.
- **Supply Chain Transparency**: AI combined with blockchain enables **end**-to-end traceability of supply chains, ensuring authenticity of goods, optimizing logistics operations, and reducing counterfeiting.
- **Decentralized Finance (DeFi) and AI Trading Algorithms**: AI-driven predictive models for algorithmic trading and automated risk assessments are recorded on blockchain networks, ensuring transparency in financial AI decision-making.
- **AI-Powered Smart Cities**: By decentralizing AI governance, blockchain-enabled smart cities optimize traffic systems, waste management, and energy distribution securely and transparently.

Challenges and Future Prospects

While the integration of AI with blockchain presents significant advantages, challenges remain:

- **Scalability Issues**: Blockchain networks, particularly those based on Proof-of-Work (PoW) consensus, suffer from high computational costs and limited transaction throughput, making real-time AI execution challenging.
- **Data Storage Limitations**: AI models require vast amounts of data, whereas blockchains, due to their immutable nature, are **inefficient at handling large-scale data storage. Hybrid solutions, such as off-chain storage with on-chain verification, are** being explored.
- **Regulatory Compliance**: As decentralized AI models become widely used, regulators face difficulties in ensuring AI systems adhere to global laws and ethical guidelines.
- **Energy Consumption Concerns**: Training deep learning models and running blockchain nodes require extensive energy resources, necessitating the development of energy-efficient consensus mechanisms such as Proof-of-Stake (PoS) and federated consensus algorithms.

Despite these challenges, the future of Decentralized AI and Blockchain Integration is incredibly promising. The convergence of AI and blockchain is paving the way for a new era of secure, auditable, and bias-resistant AI models, ensuring that AI technology remains ethical, trustworthy, and accessible to all stakeholders. As research in scalable blockchain architectures and energy-efficient AI progresses, decentralized AI is set to become a foundational pillar of next-generation intelligent systems.

Bio-Inspired AI Models

The next frontier of AI seeks to transcend traditional computational paradigms by embracing the intricate mechanisms found in biological intelligence. Future AI research is increasingly focused on cognitive neuroscience, evolutionary computation, and bio-mimetic systems to create AI architectures that exhibit higher-level reasoning, adaptability, and contextual awareness. Unlike conventional AI models that rely on vast amounts of training data and rigidly programmed algorithms, bio-inspired AI aims to mimic the problem-solving efficiency, learning capabilities, and perceptual acuity of biological organisms, enabling AI systems to interact more naturally with humans and the environment.

Core Principles of Bio-Inspired AI:

- **Neurocognitive Computing**: Taking direct inspiration from the human brain, neurocognitive computing models attempt to replicate neural architectures and synaptic plasticity. For example, Spiking Neural Networks (SNNs) process information in an event-driven manner similar to biological neurons, allowing for energy-efficient computation and more natural learning processes.
- **Evolutionary Computation**: This technique involves AI models that evolve over time, simulating natural selection and genetic algorithms. These systems iteratively optimize themselves by simulating mutations, selection, and adaptation, resulting in AI that refines itself through exposure to new information.
- **Hierarchical Reinforcement Learning**: Inspired by how humans and animals learn from experience, hierarchical reinforcement learning systems break down complex tasks into sub-goals, much like how humans approach problem-solving incrementally. These models

use rewards and penalties to adjust behaviors dynamically, resulting in more flexible and autonomous decision-making AI.

- **Cognitive Architectures**: Bio-inspired AI incorporates elements of cognitive science to enhance perception, reasoning, memory retention, and self-improvement. Cognitive architectures, such as SOAR, ACT-R, and OpenCog, aim to replicate the human thought process, enabling AI to store knowledge, reason through problems, and generate innovative solutions in ways that resemble human intelligence.

Applications of Bio-Inspired AI

- **Human-Robot Collaboration and Adaptive Robotics**: Bio-inspired AI is revolutionizing robotics, creating machines that perceive and respond dynamically to environmental changes. Unlike pre-programmed industrial robots, adaptive robots powered by bio-mimetic AI can autonomously navigate unpredictable settings, making them invaluable in search-and-rescue missions, space exploration, and assistive robotics for healthcare.

- **Sensory AI for Environmental Perception**: By incorporating bio-mimetic principles from insects and animals, AI systems are being designed to process multimodal sensory information. AI-powered vision systems inspired by insect compound eyes allow for panoramic field-of-view perception, while echolocation-based AI models, modeled after bats, enable precise object detection in low-light conditions.

- **Neuromorphic Hardware for Ultra-Efficient AI**: Traditional AI models rely on energy-intensive GPUs, but neuromorphic computing—a bio-inspired approach—uses specialized hardware that mimics the efficiency of biological brains. Neuromorphic processors like Intel's Loihi and IBM's TrueNorth process information through synapse-like connections, enabling faster learning and low-power AI solutions.

- **AI-Augmented Decision Making in Healthcare**: Cognitive AI models, inspired by the human brain's ability to diagnose conditions and adapt treatments dynamically, are now being applied in precision medicine, mental health analysis, and medical imaging. AI systems modeled after biological neural networks are capable of detecting diseases earlier and recommending personalized treatment strategies.

- **Autonomous Evolutionary AI Systems**: Inspired by natural evolution, AI models that self-optimize through survival-of-the-fittest computations are deployed in automated design, cybersecurity defense, and self-assembling nanotechnology. These AI systems undergo constant refinement, improving their ability to function under dynamic conditions without human intervention.

The Future of Bio-Inspired AI

Bio-inspired AI stands at the confluence of multiple scientific disciplines, bridging the gap between computational intelligence, neuroscience, evolutionary biology, and cognitive psychology. By leveraging nature's most efficient problem-solving techniques, these models will usher in an era of AI that is adaptive, autonomous, and capable of human-like reasoning. As bio-inspired AI continues to evolve, it holds the potential to unlock unprecedented levels of artificial general intelligence (AGI), revolutionizing how machines interact, think, and learn.

Summary

As AI technology advances, organizations must remain vigilant in adopting emerging trends that enhance real-time data processing, self-healing AI pipelines, and synthetic data generation. Automated AI governance frameworks and quantum computing innovations will further shape the next era of AI. By embracing these advancements, organizations can ensure that AI remains ethical, scalable, and resilient, unlocking transformative potential across industries for years to come.

References

Fairlearn, "Fairness in Machine Learning and AI Bias Mitigation," 2023. [Online]. Available: https://fairlearn.org/.

IBM Research, "Quantum AI and Computing Innovations," 2023. [Online]. Available: https://research.ibm.com/quantum/.

OpenAI, "Self-Learning AI and Neural-Symbolic AI Reports," 2023. [Online]. Available: https://openai.com/research.

Index

www.ingramcontent.com/pod-product-compliance
Lightning Source LLC
Chambersburg PA
CBHW051750200326

41597CB00025B/4501